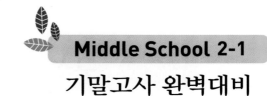

Middle School 2-1

기말고사 완벽대비

적중 100

영어 기출 문제집

중**2**

천재 | 정사열

Best Collection

구성과 특징

교과서의 주요 학습 내용을 중심으로 학습 영역별 특성에 맞춰 단계별로 다양한 학습 기회를 제공하여 단원별 학습능력 평가는 물론 중간 및 기말고사 시험 등에 완벽하게 대비할 수 있도록 내용을 구성

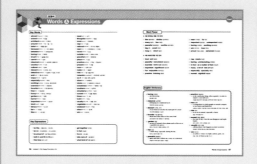

Words & Expressions

Step1 Key Words 단원별 핵심 단어 설명 및 풀이
　　　　Key Expression 단원별 핵심 숙어 및 관용어 설명
　　　　Word Power 반대 또는 비슷한 뜻 단어 배우기
　　　　English Dictionary 영어로 배우는 영어 단어

Step2 실력평가 단원별 수시평가 대비 주관식, 객관식 문제풀이

Step3 서술형 대비 학업성취도 및 수행능력평가 대비 서술형 문제풀이

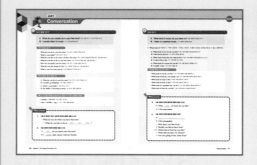

Conversation

Step1 핵심 의사소통 의사소통에 필요한 주요 표현 방법 요약
　　　　핵심 Check 기본적인 표현 방법 및 활용능력 확인

Step2 대화문 익히기 상황에 따른 대화문 활용 및 연습

Step3 기본평가 시험대비 기초 학습 능력 평가

Step4 실력평가 단원별 수시평가 대비 주관식, 객관식 문제풀이

Step5 서술형 대비 학업성취도 및 수행능력평가 대비 서술형 문제풀이

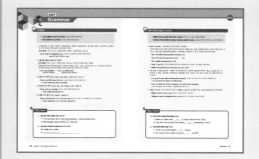

Grammar

Step1 주요 문법 단원별 주요 문법 사항과 예문을 알기 쉽게 설명

　　　　핵심 Check 기본 문법사항에 대한 이해 여부 확인

Step2 기본평가 시험대비 기초 학습 능력 평가

Step3 실력평가 단원별 수시평가 대비 주관식, 객관식 문제풀이

Step4 서술형 대비 학업성취도 및 수행능력평가 대비 서술형 문제풀이

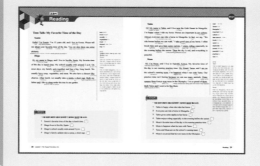

Reading

Step1 구문 분석 단원별로 제시된 문장에 대한 구문별 분석과 내용 설명
　　　　확인문제 문장에 대한 기본적인 이해와 인지능력 확인

Step2 확인학습A 빈칸 채우기를 통한 문장 완성 능력 확인

Step3 확인학습B 제시된 우리말을 영어로 완성하여 작문 능력 키우기

Step4 실력평가 단원별 수시평가 대비 주관식, 객관식 문제풀이

Step5 서술형 대비 학업성취도 및 수행능력평가 대비 서술형 문제풀이
　　　　교과서 구석구석 교과서에 나오는 기타 문장까지 완벽 학습

Composition

 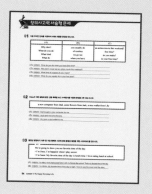  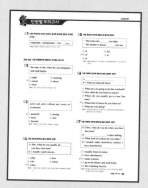

|영역별 핵심문제|

단어 및 어휘, 대화문, 문법, 독해 등 각 영역별 기출문제의 출제 유형을 분석하여 실전에 대비하고 연습할 수 있도록 문제를 배열

|서술형 실전 및 창의사고력 문제|

학교 시험에서 점차 늘어나는 서술형 시험에 집중 대비하고 고득점을 취득하는데 만전을 기하기 위한 학습 코너

|단원별 예상문제|

기출문제를 분석한 후 새로운 시험 출제 경향을 더하여 새롭게 출제될 수 있는 문제를 포함하여 시험에 완벽하게 대비할 수 있도록 준비

|단원별 모의고사|

영역별, 단계별 학습을 모두 마친 후 실전 연습을 위한 모의고사

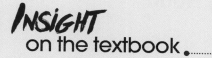
on the textbook

교과서 파헤치기

- 단어Test1~2 영어 단어 우리말 쓰기와 우리말을 영어 단어로 쓰기
- 대화문Test1~2 대화문 빈칸 완성 및 전체 대화문 쓰기
- 본문Test1~5 빈칸 완성, 우리말 쓰기, 문장 배열연습, 영어 작문하기 복습 등 단계별 반복 학습을 통해 교과서 지문에 대한 완벽한 습득
- 구석구석지문Test1~2 지문 빈칸 완성 및 전문 영어로 쓰기

Contents

Be Active, Be Safe!

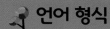 **의사소통 기능**

- 경험 묻고 답하기
  A: Have you ever heard of beach safety rules?
  B: Yes, I have.

- 금지하기
  You shouldn't swim too far.

언어 형식

- 현재완료
  I **have visited** a selfie museum before.

- 접속사 though
  Though the boys are not really riding horses, it looks like they are.

Words & Expressions

Key Words

- **active** [ǽktiv] 형 활동적인, 활발한
- **actually** [ǽktʃuəli] 부 실제로, 정말로
- **advice** [ædváis] 명 조언(= tip), 충고
- **alone** [əlóun] 부 혼자
- **back** [bæk] 명 등 부 뒤로, 다시
- **balance** [bǽləns] 명 균형, 평형
- **beach** [biːtʃ] 명 해변, 바닷가
- **before** [bifɔ́ːr] 전 ~하기 전에 부 전에, 앞에
- **behind** [biháind] 전 ~ 뒤에 부 뒤에
- **bite** [bait] 동 (이빨로) 물다, 베어 물다
- **careful** [kéərfəl] 형 조심하는, 주의 깊은(↔ careless)
- **chat** [tʃæt] 명 담소, 이야기 동 담소하다, 채팅하다
- **climb** [klaim] 동 오르다, 올라가다
- **climber** [kláimər] 명 등반가
- **close** [klouz] 형 가까운, 친한
- **clothes** [klouz] 명 옷, 의복
- **create** [kriéit] 동 창조하다, 만들다
- **dangerous** [déindʒərəs] 형 위험한(↔ safe)
- **direction** [dirékʃən] 명 방향, (주로 복수로) 지시
- **during** [djúəriŋ] 전 ~ 동안[내내], (~하는) 중에
- **else** [els] 부 또[그 밖의] 다른, 다른
- **even** [íːvən] 부 ~도[조차], 심지어
- **exist** [igzíst] 동 ~에 있다, 존재하다
- **far** [faːr] 형 먼(↔ near) 부 멀리
- **festival** [féstəvəl] 명 축제
- **figure** [fígjər] 명 인물, 모습
- **following** [fálouiŋ] 형 다음에 나오는, 그 다음의
- **fun** [fʌn] 명 재미 형 재미있는
- **grass** [græs] 명 풀, 잔디
- **harmony** [háːrməni] 명 조화, 화합
- **helmet** [hélmit] 명 헬멧
- **information** [infərméiʃən] 명 정보
- **join** [dʒɔin] 동 함께하다, 가입하다
- **kind** [kaind] 명 종류
- **later** [léitər] 부 나중에, 후에
- **loose** [luːs] 형 헐거워진, 풀린, 헐렁한(↔ tight)
- **mirror** [mírə] 명 거울
- **museum** [mjuːzíːəm] 명 박물관, 미술관
- **painter** [péintər] 명 화가, 칠장이
- **past** [pæst] 명 과거, 지난날
- **place** [pleis] 명 곳, 장소
- **pose** [pouz] 명 포즈[자세] 동 포즈[자세]를 취하다
- **practice** [prǽktis] 동 연습하다
- **princess** [prínsis] 명 공주(↔ prince)
- **probably** [prábəbli] 부 아마
- **push** [puʃ] 동 밀다(↔ pull)
- **real** [ríːəl] 형 진짜의, 현실적인
- **remember** [rimémbər] 동 기억하다(↔ forget)
- **ride** [raid] 동 타다
- **rock** [rɑk] 명 바위, 암석
- **rule** [ruːl] 명 규칙
- **safe** [seif] 형 안전한
- **safety** [séifti] 명 안전, 안전성
- **scenery** [síːnəri] 명 경치, 풍경
- **search** [səːrtʃ] 동 찾다, 수색하다
- **selfie** [sélfiː] 명 셀피(스마트폰으로 찍은 자신의 사진)
- **sign** [sain] 명 표지판, 간판
- **skill** [skil] 명 기술, 기량
- **someday** [sʌ́mdei] 부 언젠가, 훗날
- **special** [spéʃəl] 형 특별한, 특수한(↔ general)
- **street** [striːt] 명 길, 거리, 도로
- **teenage** [tineidʒ] 형 십대의
- **touch** [tʌtʃ] 동 만지다, 건드리다
- **trick** [trik] 명 비결, 요령, 속임수
- **without** [wiðáut] 전 ~ 없이, ~하지 않고
- **yet** [jet] 부 아직

Key Expressions

- **be good for** ~에 좋다
- **for example** 예를 들면, 예를 들어
- **for the first time** 처음으로
- **go up** 오르다
- **hang up** 전화를 끊다
- **hear of** ~에 대해 듣다
- **in front of** ~ 앞에
- **keep ~ in mind** ~을 명심하다, ~을 잊지 않다
- **look at** ~을 보다
- **lots of** 수많은
- **make noise** 떠들다, 소란 피우다
- **over there** 저쪽에, 저기에서

Word Power

※ 명사에 형용사 어미 -ful 이 붙으면 형용사가 되는 단어들이 있다. 이때 철자가 변하는 것도 있으므로 주의해야 한다.

- □ **care**(주의) – **careful**(주의 깊은)
- □ **help**(도움) – **helpful**(도움이 되는)
- □ **color**(색) – **colorful**(다채로운)

- □ **sorrow**(슬픔) – **sorrowful**(슬픈)
- □ **beauty**(아름다움) – **beautiful**(아름다운)
- □ **harm**(해) – **harmful**(해로운)

English Dictionary

□ **active** 활동적인, 활발한
→ moving around a lot or doing a lot of things
많이 움직이거나 많은 일을 하는

□ **advice** 조언, 충고
→ what you think someone should do in a particular situation
당신이 생각하기에 누군가가 특정한 상황에서 해야 하는 것

□ **beach** 해변, 바닷가
→ an area of sand or stones beside the sea
바다 옆의 모래나 돌이 있는 지역

□ **careful** 조심하는, 주의 깊은
→ giving serious attention to what you are doing, in order to avoid harm, damage, or mistakes
해나 손상 또는 실수를 피하기 위해 당신이 하고 있는 일에 심각한 주의를 기울이는

□ **chat** 담소[이야기]하다
→ to talk to each other in an informal and friendly way
비형식적이고 친근한 태도로 서로 이야기하다

□ **climb** 오르다, 올라가다
→ to move towards the top of something such as a tree, mountain, or ladder
나무, 산, 사다리 같은 것의 꼭대기 쪽으로 움직이다

□ **clothes** 옷, 의복
→ the things that people wear, such as shirts, coats, trousers, and dresses
셔츠, 코트, 바지, 드레스와 같은 사람들이 입는 옷들

□ **dangerous** 위험한
→ able or likely to hurt or harm you
당신을 다치게 하거나 해를 끼칠 수 있는

□ **helmet** 헬멧
→ a hat made of a strong material which you wear to protect your head
당신의 머리를 보호하기 위해 당신이 착용하는 튼튼한 재료로 만들어진 모자

□ **mirror** 거울
→ a flat piece of glass which reflects light, so that when you look at it you can see yourself reflected in it
빛을 반사하는 납작한 유리조각으로, 그것을 볼 때 당신은 그 안에 반사된 자신을 볼 수 있다

□ **painter** 화가
→ an artist who paints pictures
그림을 그리는 화가

□ **past** 과거
→ the time before the present, and the things that have happened
현재 이전의 시간과 현재까지 일어난 일들

□ **princess** 공주
→ a female member of a royal family, usually the daughter of a king or queen
왕가의 여성 일원으로 왕이나 왕비의 딸

□ **push** 밀다
→ to use force to make something move away from you or away from its previous position
어떤 것을 당신에게서 멀어지게 하거나 이전의 위치에서 멀어지게 하기 위해 힘을 사용하다

□ **ride** 타다
→ sit on a horse or bike and control its movements
말이나 자전거에 앉아 그 움직임을 통제하다

□ **rock** 바위, 암석
→ the hard substance which the Earth is made of
지구가 구성되어 있는 단단한 물질

□ **street** 길, 도로
→ a road in a city, town, or village, usually with houses along it
대개 그것을 따라 집들이 있는, 도시나 읍 또는 마을의 도로

□ **teenage** 십대의
→ aged between thirteen and nineteen years old
열세 살에서 열아홉 살 사이의 나이인

01 다음 중 나머지 넷을 대표할 수 있는 단어는?

① coats ② shirts
③ trousers ④ dresses
⑤ clothes

02 (중요) 다음 빈칸에 알맞은 말이 바르게 짝지어진 것은?

> • We met _____ the first time five years ago.
> • What are you looking _____?

① of – at ② for – at
③ on – for ④ at – for
⑤ to – over

03 다음 영영풀이에 해당하는 단어로 알맞은 것은?

> a road in a city, town, or village, usually with houses along it

① yard ② ground
③ stadium ④ street
⑤ garden

04 서답형 다음 짝지어진 두 단어의 관계가 같도록 빈칸에 알맞은 말을 쓰시오.

> remember : forget = careful : _____

05 다음 우리말에 맞게 빈칸에 알맞은 것은?

> 저기에 주유소가 있네요.
> ➡ There's a gas station _____ there.

① up ② on
③ over ④ from
⑤ along

06 서답형 다음 영영풀이에 해당하는 단어를 쓰시오.

> aged between thirteen and nineteen years old

➡ _____

07 서답형 다음 우리말에 맞게 빈칸에 알맞은 말을 쓰시오.

> 교실 안에서 소란 피우지 말아요.
> ➡ Don't _____ noise in the classroom.

08 (중요) 다음 빈칸에 공통으로 알맞은 것은?

> • He took some coins out _____ his pocket.
> • We had lots _____ fun at the party.

① in ② of
③ up ④ about
⑤ at

01 다음 짝지어진 두 단어의 관계가 같도록 빈칸에 알맞은 말을 쓰시오.

(1) care : careful = color : _____

(2) actor : actress = prince : _____

(3) dangerous : _____ = strong : weak

02 다음 우리말에 맞게 빈칸에 알맞은 말을 쓰시오.

(1) 예를 들면, 인도에서는 어떤 동전은 사각형이다.
 ➡ In India, _____ _____, some coins have square sides.

(2) 우리는 Sarah의 파티에서 아주 재미있게 보냈다.
 ➡ We _____ a lot of _____ at Sarah's party.

(3) 너의 앨범을 보아도 좋으니?
 ➡ May I _____ _____ your album?

03 다음 빈칸에 들어갈 알맞은 말을 〈보기〉에서 골라 쓰시오.

┌─ 보기 ─┐
even someday during following

(1) My grandfather died _____ the war.

(2) _____ a child can understand it.

(3) Answer the _____ questions.

(4) I hope you will visit here _____.

04 다음 괄호 안의 단어를 문맥에 맞게 고쳐 쓰시오.

(1) It's not _____ raining now. (actual)

(2) Follow your doctor's _____. (advise)

(3) The traffic here is very _____ for children. (danger)

05 다음 빈칸에 알맞은 말을 〈보기〉에서 골라 쓰시오.

┌─ 보기 ─┐
keep in mind look for
hear of good at

(1) Nancy is _____ dancing.

(2) I was surprised to _____ his failure.

(3) You had better _____ your dog at the park.

(4) Please _____ what I said.

06 다음 영영풀이에 해당하는 단어를 주어진 철자로 시작하여 쓰시오.

(1) r_____ : to sit on a horse or bike and control its movements

(2) c_____ : to move towards the top of something such as a tree, mountain, or ladder

(3) p_____ : the time before the present, and the things that have happened

Conquest **Conversation**

교과서

① 경험 묻고 답하기

> **A** Have you heard of beach safety rules? 넌 해변 안전 규칙에 대해 들어본 적 있니?
> **B** Yes, I have. 응, 있어.

■ **경험 묻기**
'~해 본 적이 있나요?'라고 과거부터 현재까지의 상대방의 경험을 물을 때는 「Have you (ever)+과거분사 ~?」 형태인 현재완료 의문문으로 물을 수 있다.

경험에 대한 물음에 대답하기

- 경험이 있으면 Yes, I have. / Yes, I have+과거분사. 등으로 한다.
- 경험이 없으면 No, I haven't. / No, I have never+과거분사. / Not yet. 등으로 한다.

- A: Have you ever seen a bear? 너는 곰을 본 적이 있니?
  B: Yes, I have. / No, I haven't. 응, 본 적이 있어. / 아니, 본 적이 없어.

cf. '~에 가본 적 있니?'라고 묻는 표현은 Have you ever gone to ~?가 아니라 Have you ever been to ~?임에 주의한다.

- have been to: ~에 가본 적이 있다(경험) / ~에 다녀 왔다(완료)
- have gone to: ~에 가버렸다(결과)

■ 경험을 나타낼 때는 다음과 같은 부사(구)를 함께 쓰는 경우가 많다. ever(지금까지), never(~한 적 없는), before(이전에), once(한 번), twice(두 번), 「숫자+times(~번, ~차례)」, many times(여러 번), often(자주)

- She has made fried rice many times. 그녀는 볶음밥을 여러 번 만든 적이 있다.

핵심 Check

1. **다음 우리말과 일치하도록 빈칸에 알맞은 말을 쓰시오.**

   (1) **A:** _____ you ever _____ *Les Miserables*? (너 '레미제라블' 읽어 봤니?)

      B: Yes, I _____. (응, 있어.)

   (2) **A:** _____ you _____ of Rock Boys? (너는 Rock Boys에 대해 들어 봤니?)

      B: No, I _____. (아니, 나는 못 들어 봤어.)

② 금지하기

> **A** May I swim in this lake? 이 호수에서 수영해도 돼요?
>
> **B** Okay, Mike, but you shouldn't swim too far. 그래, Mike야, 하지만 너무 멀리까지 수영하면 안 된다.

■ You should not ~은 '~하면 안 돼.'라는 뜻으로 어떤 일을 하지 말아야 함을 이야기할 때 사용하는 금지의 표현이다.

- A: Tony, you should not run when you cross the street. Tony, 길을 건널 때 뛰면 안 돼.
  B: Okay, I see. 응, 알겠어.

■ You should ~는 '~해야 한다.'라는 뜻으로 상대방에게 제안이나 충고를 할 때 사용한다.

- You should have breakfast every day. 너는 매일 아침식사를 해야 한다.

금지를 나타내는 표현

- You should not take pictures at the museum. 박물관에서는 사진을 찍으면 안 돼.
  = You must not take pictures at the museum.
  = Don't[Do not] take pictures at the museum.
  = You can't take pictures at the museum.
  = You'd better not take pictures at the museum.
  = You're not supposed[allowed/permitted] to take pictures at the museum.

핵심 Check

2. 다음 우리말과 일치하도록 빈칸에 알맞은 말을 쓰시오.

(1) **A:** Excuse me. You _____ _____ your cell phone here.

(실례합니다. 이곳에서 휴대 전화를 사용하시면 안 됩니다.)

B: Oh, I'm _____. (오, 죄송합니다.)

(2) **G:** Wait. _____ jump into the water yet. (잠깐만. 아직 물속으로 뛰어들지 마.)

B: Why _____? (왜 안 돼?)

G: You _____ swim without a life jacket. (구명조끼 없이 수영하면 안 돼.)

(3) **A:** I _____ I've got a _____. (나 감기에 걸린 것 같아.)

B: You'd _____ _____ _____ cold water. (너는 차가운 물을 마시지 않는 게 좋겠어.)

A. Start Off - Listen & Talk B

B: ❶Have you heard of bird watching?

M: Sure. I tried it when I was a child.

B: That's nice. ❷Actually, I'm doing it for the first time this Saturday.

M: Are you? You should bring warm clothes and something to eat.

B: Okay. What else should I keep in mind?

M: ❸You shouldn't make any noise when you watch the birds.

B: I'll keep that in mind. Thanks, Dad.

B: 새 관찰에 대해 들어보셨어요?
M: 물론이지. 어렸을 때 해 봤어.
B: 그거 멋지네요. 사실, 전 이번 주 토요일에 처음으로 그것을 할 거예요.
M: 그래? 넌 따뜻한 옷과 먹을 것을 가져가야 해.
B: 알았어요. 그 밖에 또 무엇을 명심해야 하나요?
M: 너는 새들을 관찰할 때 아무 소리도 내지 말아야 해.
B: 그것을 명심할게요. 고마워요, 아빠.

❶ Have you heard of ~?: ~에 대해 들어본 적이 있나요?(경험을 묻는 표현)
❷ I'm doing ~: 현재진행형이 미래의 일을 나타내는 경우 / it=bird watching
❸ You shouldn't ~: 너는 ~해서는 안 된다(금지를 나타내는 표현)

Check(√) True or False

(1) The boy's father tried bird watching when he was a child.　　T ☐ F ☐

(2) The boy may make some noise when he watches the birds.　　T ☐ F ☐

B. Step Up - Real-life Scene

Video Chat with Minjun from Jeju

A: Hello, Somin! It's me! Can you see me?

B: Oh, hi, Minjun! What's up?

A: ❶This is so cool, isn't it? We can video chat on the phone! Have you heard of Jeju *Olle*?

B: Yes, I have. I really want to go there someday.

A: ❷Guess what? I'm on it now. Actually, I'm going to go up Seongsan Ilchulbong now.

B: That's great!

A: ❸Don't hang up. Enjoy the beautiful scenery with me.

B: Be careful! ❹You shouldn't use your cell phone while you're walking.

A: Oh, right. Thank you. I'll send you photos later.

제주에서 걸려 온 민준과의 화상 채팅
A: 여보세요, 소민아! 나야! 나를 볼 수 있니?
B: 오, 안녕, 민준아! 무슨 일이니?
A: 이거 정말 멋지지 않니? 전화로 화상 채팅도 할 수 있어! 너 제주 올레에 대해 들어 본 적이 있니?
B: 응, 있어. 나는 언젠가 꼭 가 보고 싶어.
A: 그거 알아? 나 지금 올레에 있어. 사실은, 지금 성산 일출봉에 올라가려고 해.
B: 멋지다!
A: 끊지 마. 나와 함께 아름다운 경치를 즐겨.
B: 조심해! 걸을 때는 휴대폰을 사용해서는 안 돼.
A: 아, 맞다. 고마워. 나중에 사진 보여 줄게.

❶ This is so cool, isn't it?: 부가의문문에서 This는 it으로 받는다.
❷ Guess what?: 있잖아., 그거 알아?(어떤 것에 대해 말을 꺼낼 때 쓰는 관용적인 표현)
❸ hang up: 전화를 끊다
❹ while: ~하는 동안

Check(√) True or False

(3) Minjun is going to go up Seongsan Ilchulbong.　　T ☐ F ☐

(4) Somin wants to enjoy the beautiful scenery with Minjun.　　T ☐ F ☐

Get Ready -2

1. G: Look at that boy. He's great.
   B: ❶He's riding an MTB. Do you know about it?
   G: No. What is it?
   B: ❷It's a special bike for riding on a mountain.
2. G: Wait. Don't jump into the water yet.
   B: ❸Why not?
   G: You shouldn't swim without a life jacket.
3. G: Look at the beautiful flowers over there! ❹ I'd like to take a selfie in front of them.
   B You shouldn't go over there.
   G: Oh, okay.
4. B: ❺I want to watch the birds in the trees.
   G: You shouldn't go up too close to the birds.
   B: All right, thanks.

❶ MTB: mountain bike
❷ for riding a mountain: 산을 오르기 위한
❸ Why not?=Why can't I jump into the water?
❹ I'd like to: ~하고 싶다 / in front of: ~ 앞에서
❺ in the trees: 나무에 있는(the birds를 수식하는 형용사구)

 Start Off - Listen & Talk A

1. G: ❶Dad, have you ever heard of Kim Soyun, the rock climber?
   M: Yes, I've seen her on TV.
   G: ❷She's teaching rock climbing at a camp this Saturday. I want to join the camp.
   M: Okay, Miso, but you shouldn't climb up too high.
   G: ❸All right. Thanks, Dad.
2. G: Have you heard of Rock Boys?
   M: No, I haven't.
   G: ❹It's my favorite band. There's a concert this Saturday. Can I go?
   M: Okay, Minju, but you shouldn't come home too late.
   G: All right. Thanks, Dad.

❶ Kim Soyun과 the rock climber는 동격 관계이다.
❷ She's teaching=She will teach
❸ All right.: 알았어요., 좋아요.
❹ It = Rock Boys

 Start Off - Speak Up - Look and talk.

A: Have you heard of safety rules for mountain hiking?
B: Yes. But I don't know much about them.
A: ❶Let me tell you one. You shouldn't walk too fast.
B: ❷Oh, I see.

❶ Let me ~: 내가 ~할게 / one=a safety rule for mountain hiking
❷ I see.: 알겠어.

 Express Yourself A

1. G: Have you heard of Elvis Presley?
   B: No, I haven't. Who is he?
   G: He was a famous American singer and actor. ❶We can see a figure of Elvis here.
   B: ❷Sounds interesting. I want to take pictures with it.
   G: Okay. Let's go.
2. W: You shouldn't take selfies here. Van Gogh's painting is behind you.
   B: Don't worry, Mom. It's not his real painting. ❸So I can take selfies in front of it.
   W: Really? Sounds interesting. Can I take selfies here, too?
   B: ❹Why not?

❶ a figure of Elvis: Elvis의 모형
❷ Sounds interesting.: 흥미롭게 들린다.
❸ so: 그래서 / in front of: ~의 앞에
❹ Why not?: 물론 되고말고.

 Check Yourself - Listen & Speak

1. B: Wait, Jimin.
   G: Why?
   B: Look at that sign. ❶You shouldn't take a photo here.
   G: Oh, okay.
2. B: ❷This place is good for bike riding.
   G: Look, there's a sign. You shouldn't ride a bike here.

❶ You shouldn't ~.: 너는 ~ 해서는 안 된다.
❷ be good for: ~에 좋다

● 다음 우리말과 일치하도록 빈칸에 알맞은 말을 쓰시오.

Get Ready - 2

1. **G:** Look _____ that boy. He's _____.
   B: He's _____ an MTB. Do you _____ about it?
   G: No. _____ is it?
   B: It's a _____ bike for _____ on a mountain.

2. **G:** Wait. _____ jump _____ the water yet.
   B: _____ not?
   G: You _____ swim _____ a life jacket. _____ it _____.

3. **G:** _____ at the beautiful flowers _____ there! I'd _____ to _____ a selfie in _____ of them.
   B: You shouldn't go _____ there.
   G: Oh, _____.

4. **B:** I want to _____ the birds _____ the trees.
   G: You shouldn't go _____ too close to the _____.
   B: All _____, thanks.

1. **G:** 저 소년을 봐. 그는 대단하다.
   B: 그는 MTB를 타고 있어. 넌 그것에 대해 알고 있니?
   G: 아니. 그게 뭐지?
   B: 그것은 산에서 타는 특별한 자전거야.

2. **G:** 기다려. 아직 물속으로 뛰어들지 마.
   B: 왜 안 돼?
   G: 구명조끼 없이 수영하면 안 돼. 이것을 입어.

3. **G:** 저기 있는 아름다운 꽃들을 봐! 그 꽃들 앞에서 셀피를 찍고 싶어.
   B: 거기 가면 안 돼.
   G: 아, 알았어.

4. **B:** 나는 나무에 있는 새들을 보고 싶어.
   G: 새들에게 너무 가까이 가지 마.
   B: 알았어, 고마워.

Start Off - Listen & Talk A

1. **G:** Dad, have you _____ heard of Kim Soyun, the rock _____?
   M: Yes, I've _____ her _____ TV.
   G: She's teaching rock _____ at a _____ this Saturday. I want to _____ the camp.
   M: Okay, Miso, _____ you shouldn't _____ up too high.
   G: All _____. Thanks, Dad.

2. **G:** _____ you _____ of Rock Boys?
   M: No, I _____.
   G: It's my _____ band. There's a _____ this Saturday. _____ I go?
   M: Okay, Minju, but you _____ come home _____ late.
   G: All _____. Thanks, Dad.

1. **G:** 아빠, 암벽 등반가인 김소윤에 대해 들어 본 적 있으세요?
   M: 응, TV에서 봤어.
   G: 그녀가 이번 토요일에 캠프에서 암벽 등반을 가르쳐요. 저는 캠프에 참가하고 싶어요.
   M: 알았어, 미소야, 하지만 너무 높이 올라가면 안 돼.
   G: 알았어요. 고마워요, 아빠.

2. **G:** Rock Boys에 대해 들어보셨어요?
   M: 아니, 듣지 못했다.
   G: 그건 제가 제일 좋아하는 밴드에요. 이번 토요일에 콘서트가 있어요. 가도 돼요?
   M: 좋아, 민주야, 하지만 너무 늦게 집에 오면 안 돼.
   G: 알았어요. 고마워요, 아빠.

Start Off - Listen & Talk B

B: Have you _____ _____ bird watching?

M: Sure. I tried it _____ I was a child.

B: That's nice. Actually, I'm _____ it _____ the first time this Saturday.

M: Are you? You _____ _____ warm clothes and something to eat.

B: Okay. What else _____ I _____ in mind?

M: You _____ make any noise _____ you watch the birds.

B: I'll keep that _____ _____. Thanks, Dad.

Step Up - Real-life Scene

Video Chat with Minjun from Jeju

A: Hello, Somin! _____ me! Can you _____ me?

B: Oh, _____, Minjun! What's _____?

A: This is so cool, _____ it? We can video _____ on the phone! Have you _____ of Jeju *Olle*?

B: Yes, I have. I really _____ to go there someday.

A: _____ what? I'm on it now. Actually, I'm _____ to go up Seongsan Ilchulbong now.

B: That's _____!

A: Don't hang _____. Enjoy the beautiful _____ with me.

B: _____ careful! You shouldn't _____ your cell phone _____ you're walking.

A: Oh, _____. _____ you. I'll _____ you photos _____.

Express Yourself A

1. **G:** Have you _____ of Elvis Presley?

   B: No, I _____. _____ is he?

   G: He was a famous American _____ and _____. We can see a _____ of Elvis here.

   B: _____ interesting. I want to _____ pictures with it.

   G: Okay. _____ go.

2. **W:** You shouldn't _____ selfies here. Van Gogh's _____ is behind you.

   B: Don't _____, Mom. It's not his _____ painting. _____ I can take selfies in _____ of it.

   W: Really? Sounds interesting. _____ I take _____ here, too?

   B: Why _____?

B: 새 관찰에 대해 들어보셨어요?

M: 물론이지. 어렸을 때 해 봤어.

B: 그거 멋지네요. 사실, 전 이번 주 토요일에 처음으로 그것을 할 거예요.

M: 그래? 넌 따뜻한 옷과 먹을 것을 가져가야 해.

B: 알았어요. 그 밖에 또 무엇을 명심해야 하나요?

M: 너는 새들을 관찰할 때 아무 소리도 내지 말아야 해.

B: 그것을 명심할게요. 고마워요, 아빠.

제주에서 걸려온 민준과의 화상 채팅

A: 여보세요, 소민아! 나야! 나를 볼 수 있니?

B: 오, 안녕, 민준아! 무슨 일이니?

A: 이거 정말 멋지지 않니? 전화로 화상 채팅도 할 수 있어! 너 제주 올레에 대해 들어 본 적이 있니?

B: 응, 있어. 나는 언젠가 꼭 가 보고 싶어.

A: 그거 알아? 나 지금 올레에 있어. 사실은, 지금 성산 일출봉에 올라가려고 해.

B: 멋지다!

A: 끊지 마. 나와 함께 아름다운 경치를 즐겨.

B: 조심해! 걸을 때는 휴대폰을 사용해서는 안 돼.

A: 아, 맞다. 고마워. 나중에 사진 보내줄게.

1. **G:** 엘비스 프레슬리에 대해 들어 본 적 있니?

   B: 아니, 없어. 그는 누구인데?

   G: 그는 유명한 미국 가수이자 배우였어. 우리는 여기서 엘비스의 모형을 볼 수 있어.

   B: 재미있을 것 같다. 그것과 함께 사진을 찍고 싶어.

   G: 좋아. 가자.

2. **W:** 넌 여기서 셀피를 찍으면 안 돼. 반 고흐의 그림이 네 뒤에 있어.

   B: 엄마, 걱정하지 마세요. 그건 그의 진짜 그림이 아니에요. 그래서 그 앞에서 셀피를 찍을 수 있어요.

   W: 정말이지? 재미있겠다. 나도 여기서 셀피를 찍을 수 있을까?

   B: 물론이죠.

01 다음 두 문장의 의미가 같은 뜻이 되도록 빈칸에 알맞은 말을 쓰시오.

> You shouldn't swim too far.
>
> = You had _____ _____ swim too far.

02 다음 대화의 밑줄 친 우리말에 해당하는 것은?

> A: Jina, I'm going to Vietnam with my family this winter.
> B: Wow. That sounds like fun.
> A: <u>너 전에 그곳에 가 본 적 있니?</u>
> B: No, I haven't.

① Were you there before?
② Had you been there before?
③ Have you been there before?
④ Have you gone there before?
⑤ When did you go there before?

03 다음 대화의 빈칸에 알맞은 것은?

> A: It's going to rain. _____
> B: Okay. If it rains, I'll stay inside.

① You will go outside.　　② You shouldn't go outside.
③ You would go outside.　④ You might not go outside.
⑤ You can go outside.

stay 머물다
inside 안에

04 다음 대화의 빈칸에 알맞은 것은?

> A: Have you eaten this food?
> B: No, _____.

① I don't　　　　② I didn't
③ I haven't　　　④ I hadn't
⑤ I have eaten it

중요

01 다음 대화의 밑줄 친 부분과 바꿔 쓸 수 있는 것은?

> A: Is it okay to eat chocolate?
> B: Sure, but don't eat too much.

① you can eat too much
② you don't have to eat too much
③ you won't eat too much
④ you should eat too much
⑤ you'd better not eat too much

서답형

02 다음 대화의 빈칸에 알맞은 말을 쓰시오.

> A: _____ you _____ tried kimchi, Ann?
> B: Yes, I _____. It was very tasty.

03 다음 대화를 의미가 통하도록 알맞게 배열한 것은?

> (A) Why not?
> (B) Really? Sounds interesting. Can I take selfies here, too?
> (C) You shouldn't take selfies here. Van Gogh's painting is behind you.
> (D) Don't worry, Mom. It's not his real painting. So I can take selfies in front of it.

① (A) – (D) – (B) – (C)
② (B) – (C) – (D) – (A)
③ (C) – (D) – (B) – (A)
④ (D) – (B) – (C) – (A)
⑤ (D) – (C) – (B) – (A)

04 다음 대화의 빈칸에 가장 알맞은 것은?

> A: Have you seen the movie, *Avatar*, Sue?
> B: No, I haven't. _____
> A: Yes, it's my favorite movie.

① Do you?　② Will you?
③ Had you?　④ Have you?
⑤ What do you want to see?

중요

05 다음 대화의 빈칸에 들어갈 말로 알맞은 것은?

> A: You should not _____.
> B: Oh, I'm sorry. I won't do that again.

① walk to school
② recycle plastics
③ reuse gift boxes
④ leave computers on
⑤ take a short shower

[06~09] 다음 대화를 읽고, 물음에 답하시오.

> G: Dad, have you ever ⓐhear of Kim Soyun, the rock climber?
> M: Yes, I've seen her 　ⓑ　 TV.
> G: She's teaching rock climbing at a camp this Saturday. I want to join the camp.
> M: Okay, Miso, but you 　ⓒ　 climb up too high.
> G: All right. Thanks, Dad.

서답형

06 위 대화의 밑줄 친 ⓐ를 알맞은 형으로 고치시오.

　➡ _____

07 위 대화의 빈칸 ⓑ에 알맞은 것은?

① in   ② on   ③ by

④ with   ⑤ from

08 위 대화의 빈칸 ⓒ에 들어갈 수 <u>없는</u> 것은? (2개)

① don't   ② must not

③ need not   ④ shouldn't

⑤ had better not

09 위 대화의 내용과 일치하지 <u>않는</u> 것은?

① 미소의 아버지는 김소윤을 알고 있다.

② 김소윤은 암벽 등반가이다.

③ 김소윤은 캠프에서 이번 토요일에 암벽 등반을 강의할 것이다.

④ 미소는 캠프에 참여하기를 원한다.

⑤ 미소의 아버지는 미소가 암벽 등반하는 것을 반대했다.

[10~14] 다음 대화를 읽고, 물음에 답하시오.

> A: Hello, Somin! It's me! Can you see me?
>
> B: Oh, hi, Minjun! What's ___ⓐ___ ?
>
> A: This is so cool, ___ⓑ___ ? We can video chat on the phone! Have you heard of Jeju *Olle*?
>
> B: Yes, I have. I really want to go there someday.
>
> A: Guess what? I'm on it now. ⓒActual, I'm going to go up Seongsan Ilchulbong now.
>
> B: That's great!
>
> A: Don't hang up. Enjoy the beautiful ___ⓓ___ with me.
>
> B: Be careful! You shouldn't use your cell phone while you're walking.
>
> A: Oh, right. Thank you. I'll send you photos later.

10 위 대화의 빈칸 ⓐ에 알맞은 것은?

① on   ② to

③ at   ④ up

⑤ for

11 위 대화의 빈칸 ⓑ에 알맞은 것은?

① is this   ② does it

③ isn't this   ④ doesn't it

⑤ isn't it

서답형

12 위 대화의 밑줄 친 ⓒ를 알맞은 어형으로 고치시오.

➡ _____

서답형

13 위 대화의 빈칸 ⓓ에 다음 영영풀이에 해당하는 단어를 쓰시오.

> the land, water, or plants that you can see around you

➡ _____

14 위 대화를 읽고, 답할 수 <u>없는</u> 질문은?

① Can Somin see Minjun?

② Where is Minjun now?

③ Where does Somin want to go someday?

④ Is Minjun going to go up Seongsan Ilchulbong?

⑤ How many photos will Minjun send to Somin?

[01~02] 다음 대화의 빈칸에 알맞은 말을 쓰시오.

01

> G: Wait. Don't jump into the water yet.
> B: Why not?
> G: You _____ swim without a life jacket.

02

> G: _____ you ever slept in a tent?
> B: No, I _____.

03 다음 대화를 의미가 통하도록 알맞게 배열하시오.

> (A) It's a special bike for riding on a mountain.
> (B) Look at that boy. He's great.
> (C) He's riding an MTB. Do you know about it?
> (D) No. What is it?

➡ _____

[04~06] 다음 대화를 읽고, 물음에 답하시오.

> G: Have you heard of Rock Boys?
> M: ⓐNo, I have.
> G: ⓑIt's my favorite band. There's a concert this Saturday. Can I go?
> M: Okay, Minju, ⓒ _____ you shouldn't come home too late.
> G: All right. Thanks, Dad.

04 위 대화의 밑줄 친 ⓐ에서 어법상 어색한 것을 고치시오.

_____ ➡ _____

05 위 대화의 밑줄 친 ⓑ가 가리키는 것을 영어로 쓰시오.

➡ _____

06 위 대화의 빈칸 ⓒ에 알맞은 접속사를 쓰시오.

➡ _____

[07~08] 다음 대화를 읽고, 물음에 답하시오.

> G: Have you heard of Elvis Presley?
> B: No, I haven't. Who is he?
> G: He was a famous American singer and ⓐ _____. We can see a figure of Elvis here.
> B: Sounds interesting. I want to take pictures with ⓑit.
> G: Okay. Let's go.

07 위 대화의 빈칸 ⓐ에 다음 정의에 해당하는 단어를 쓰시오.

> someone whose job is acting in plays or films

➡ _____

08 위 대화의 밑줄 친 ⓑ가 가리키는 것을 우리말로 쓰시오.

➡ _____

Grammar

① 현재완료

> • I **have visited** a selfie museum before. 나는 전에 셀피 박물관을 방문한 적이 있다.
> • **Have** you ever **heard** of beach safety rules? 너는 해변 안전 규칙에 대해 들어본 적이 있니?

■ **현재완료의 형태**
  'have[has]+과거분사'의 형태를 취한다.
  • It **has been** such a long time. 정말 오랜만이다.
  • I **have had** many different jobs. 나는 많은 다양한 직업을 가져왔다.

cf. yesterday, two days ago, last Sunday 등과 같이 특정한 과거 시점을 나타내는 표현이 오면 현재
  완료시제로 쓰지 않고 과거시제로 써야 한다.
  • I read the book yesterday. (○) 나는 어제 그 책을 읽었다.
  • I have read the book yesterday. (✕)

■ **현재완료의 용법**
  현재완료는 경험, 계속, 완료, 결과의 용법이 있다.

분류	용법	예문
경험	과거부터 현재까지의 경험 before, ever, never, often 등과 쓰임	I **have** never **been** to Rome. (나는 로마에 가 본 적이 없다.)
계속	과거의 일이 지금까지 계속됨 'since+특정 시점', 'for+기간' 등과 쓰임	I **have known** him since I was a little child. (나는 어릴 때부터 그를 알아 왔다.)
완료	과거에 시작된 일이 이제 막 완료됨 just, already, yet 등과 쓰임	He **has** just **finished** his homework. (그는 방금 숙제를 끝냈다.)
결과	과거의 일이 현재의 결과를 가져옴 '~해서 (지금) …하다'의 의미임	They **have gone** to Madrid. (그들은 마드리드에 가고 없다.)

■ **현재완료의 부정문**
  'have[has]와 과거분사 사이에 not을 넣는다.
  • He **has not written** the letter yet. 그는 아직 그 편지를 쓰지 않았다.

■ **현재완료의 의문문**
  'Have[Has]+주어+과거분사 ~?'의 형태를 취한다.
  • **Have** you ever **seen** a lion? 너는 사자를 본 적이 있니?

핵심 Check

1. 다음 괄호 안에서 알맞은 것을 고르시오.

  (1) Ann has just (did / done) her homework.

  (2) They (have / do) not (ate / eaten) the pizza.

  (3) He (lived / has lived) in this town since he was seven.

  (4) I have known her (for / since) three years.

2 접속사 though

- **Though** there's a fire, you can be safe. 비록 화재가 나도 너는 안전할 수 있다.
- **Though** the boys are not riding horses, it looks like they are.
  비록 그 소년들은 말을 타고 있지 않지만, 말을 타고 있는 것처럼 보인다.
- **Though** it was raining, the children played outside.
  비록 비가 오고 있었지만 아이들은 밖에서 놀았다.

■ 접속사 though는 '비록 ~이지만'의 의미로 사용되며 양보의 부사절을 이끄는 접속사이다.
  - **Though** it was cold, she wasn't wearing a coat. 비록 날씨가 추웠지만, 그녀는 코트를 입고 있지 않았다.
  - **Though** I'm on a diet, I'll eat every hamburger here.
    비록 나는 다이어트를 하고 있지만, 여기에 있는 모든 햄버거를 먹겠다.

■ though 대신 although나 even though를 써도 같은 의미가 된다.
  - **Though** they are so poor, they seem happy. 그들은 아주 가난하지만, 행복해 보인다.
    = **Alhough** they are so poor, they seem happy.
    = **Even though** they are so poor, they seem happy.

  - **Though** you do not like it, you must do it. 너는 그것을 좋아하지 않아도 해야 한다.
    = **Alhough** you do not like it, you must do it.
    = **Even though** you do not like it, you must do it.

■ 종속접속사 though 대신 등위접속사 but을 써서 같은 뜻의 문장으로 바꿔 쓸 수 있다.
  - **Though** I like tennis, I'm not very good at it. 나는 테니스를 좋아하지만, 그것을 별로 잘하지 못한다.
    = I like tennis, **but** I'm not very good at it. 나는 테니스를 좋아한다. 그러나 그것을 별로 잘하지 못한다.

핵심 Check

2. 다음 괄호 안에서 알맞은 것을 고르시오.

(1) (Though / Because) they were rich, they weren't very happy.

(2) (As / Though) the man was very old, he was strong.

(3) (If / Though) I like baseball, I am not a good player.

(4) (Although / While) it was cold, Frank didn't wear a coat.

Grammar 시험대비 기본평가

01 다음 괄호 안에서 알맞은 것을 고르시오.

(1) Jane (was / has been) busy since last week.

(2) How often have you (gone / been) to the United States?

(3) He (has finished / finished) reading a book two hours ago.

(4) He (has just finished / just finishes) his homework.

(5) We (arrived / have arrived) here yesterday.

(6) When (have you reached / did you reach) here?

reach 도착하다

02 다음 문장에서 어법상 <u>어색한</u> 것을 찾아 고쳐 쓰시오.

(1) Because Jenny is so thin, she is strong.

_____ ➡ _____

(2) We lost the game since everyone played well.

_____ ➡ _____

(3) As the sun was shining, it wasn't very warm.

_____ ➡ _____

thin 마른

03 다음 괄호 안에 주어진 단어를 어법상 알맞은 형태로 바꾸어 문장을 다시 쓰시오.

(1) He (be) sick in bed since last Friday.

➡ _____

(2) How long (you know) Miss Smith?

➡ _____

(3) (you ever read) the Christmas Carol?

➡ _____

(4) My father (not read) the newspaper yet.

➡ _____.

sick 아픈
newspaper 신문

중요

01 다음 두 문장을 한 문장으로 만들 때 빈칸에 알맞은 것은?

> I moved here two years ago. I still live here.
> ➡ I _____ here for two years.

① live
② lived
③ will live
④ am living
⑤ have lived

[02~03] 다음 문장의 빈칸에 알맞은 것을 고르시오.

02

> _____ the car is old, it still runs well.

① As
② If
③ Unless
④ Because
⑤ Though

중요

03

> Ted is hungry because he _____ nothing since this morning.

① eat
② eats
③ ate
④ has eaten
⑤ had eaten

서답형

 04 다음 빈칸에 공통으로 알맞은 말을 쓰시오.

> • _____ the service was slow, the waiters were kind.
> • His speech was very good. It was a little too long, _____.

서답형

05 다음 빈칸에 공통으로 알맞은 말을 쓰시오.

> • Sorry to _____ kept you waiting. I _____ been to the station.
> • We _____ known each other since our childhood.

중요

06 다음 문장의 빈칸에 들어갈 수 없는 것은? (2개)

> _____ I met the girl once, I can't remember her name.

① Whether
② Though
③ Although
④ As though
⑤ Even though

07 다음 문장의 빈칸에 알맞지 않은 것은?

> They have been to England _____.

① once
② twice
③ before
④ never
⑤ many times

서답형

08 다음 우리말과 일치하도록 주어진 단어를 바르게 배열하시오.

> 비록 교통체증이 심했지만 우리는 제시간에 도착했다.
> (we, was, the, on, traffic, time, though, heavy, arrived).

➡ _____

_____

09 다음 괄호 안에 주어진 단어를 어법상 바르게 쓴 것은?

> I know some good restaurants here because I (live) in this town for five years.

① live
② lived
③ is living
④ have lived
⑤ had lived

10 다음 우리말과 같은 뜻이 되도록 빈칸에 알맞은 것은?

> 내일 비가 올지라도, 나는 집에 있지 않을 것이다.
> ➡ _____ it rains tomorrow, I won't stay home.

① As
② Since
③ While
④ Although
⑤ Because

서답형
11 다음 빈칸에 알맞은 말을 쓰시오.

> My mother has gone shopping. She is _____ here.

12 다음 두 문장의 뜻이 같도록 할 때 빈칸에 알맞은 것은?

> Though Mike likes dogs, his wife doesn't.
> ➡ Mike likes dogs, _____ his wife doesn't.

① and
② so
③ but
④ for
⑤ because

서답형
13 다음 두 문장의 의미가 같도록 빈칸에 알맞은 말을 쓰시오.

> We have been married for ten years.
> ➡ Ten years have passed _____ we got married.

14 다음 문장의 빈칸에 가장 알맞은 것은?

> _____, I tried not to fall asleep.

① Although I was sleepy
② Though I tried my best
③ Even though we played well
④ Although my family was poor
⑤ Even though my sister was young

15 다음 대화의 빈칸에 알맞은 것은?

> A: Have you ever heard the news?
> B: No, I _____ the news.

① heard
② have not heard
③ was not heard
④ did not hear
⑤ had not heard

서답형
16 다음 문장의 밑줄 친 부분을 어법에 맞도록 고쳐 문장을 다시 쓰시오.

> Because he played well, he lost the soccer game.

➡ _____

_____

17 다음 두 문장의 뜻이 같도록 할 때 빈칸에 알맞은 것은?

> Though the boy was sick, he went to school.
>
> ➡ _____ the boy was sick, he went to school.

① So   ② Such
③ Although   ④ Therefore
⑤ Whatever

18 다음 중 어법상 어색한 문장은?

① I have had a fever since last Friday.
② Two years have passed since I came here.
③ We have known each other for many years.
④ He has been seventy years old when he died.
⑤ It has been a long time since I saw you.

19 다음 중 문맥상 어색한 문장은?

① I waited until he came.
② He couldn't buy the camera though he had no money.
③ He has played soccer since he was a boy.
④ Although he was tired, he studied hard.
⑤ Though I was tired, I had to do my homework.

서답형

20 다음 대화의 빈칸에 알맞은 말을 쓰시오.

> A: How long has she been absent from school?
> B: She _____ _____ _____ from school since this Wednesday.

서답형

21 다음 빈칸에 공통으로 알맞은 말을 쓰시오.

> • Have you done your homework _____?
> • She hasn't come home _____.

22 다음 빈칸에 알맞은 것을 순서대로 바르게 짝지은 것은?

> • _____ they were poor, they were very happy.
> • _____ you are late, you must hurry up.

① If – Because
② Though – As
③ When – Even though
④ Unless – Since
⑤ Because – Although

23 다음 밑줄 친 부분의 쓰임이 나머지 넷과 다른 하나는?

① I have seen the movie before.
② My uncle has never lived in China before.
③ How many times have they been to England?
④ Mr. Smith has gone to Berlin on business.
⑤ Sora and Minjun have been to America once.

01 다음 우리말과 같도록 문장을 완성하시오.

(1) 그들은 이미 프로젝트를 끝마쳤다.
➡ They _____ already _____ the project.

(2) 그는 아직 런던에서 돌아오지 않았다.
➡ He _____ _____ _____ from London yet.

(3) 죄송하지만, 그녀는 회의에 가고 없습니다.
➡ I'm sorry, but she _____ _____ _____ a meeting.

02 다음 두 문장의 뜻이 같도록 빈칸에 알맞은 말을 쓰시오.

(1) Even though Kathy couldn't concentrate well, she did her homework.
➡ _____ Kathy couldn't concentrate well, she did her homework.

(2) She doesn't come, but I will finish the work.
➡ I will finish the work _____ she doesn't come.

03 다음 문장에서 어법상 어색한 것을 찾아 바르게 고쳐 쓰시오.

(1) She has gone to Bangladesh last Friday.
_____ ➡ _____

(2) My father hasn't left Seoul already.
_____ ➡ _____

04 다음 빈칸에 공통으로 알맞은 말을 쓰시오.

- _____ he is rich, he has few friends.
- I didn't buy that cap; I liked it, _____.

05 다음 문장에서 어법상 어색한 것을 찾아 바르게 고쳐 쓰시오.

(1) Jack has seen the koala last year.
_____ ➡ _____

(2) The weather is good for ten days.
_____ ➡ _____

06 다음 주어진 단어를 바르게 배열하여 문장을 완성하시오.

(1) (Italy / many / he / to / been / times / has)
➡ _____

(2) (very / days / I / busy / these / been / have)
➡ _____

(3) (have / Paris / before / I / visited / never)
➡ _____

07 다음 보기에서 알맞은 말을 골라 빈칸에 쓰시오.

> ┤ 보기 ├
>
> since / if / that / though /
> because / before

(1) Take a bath _____ you go to bed.

(2) He was so tired _____ he went to bed early.

(3) Mike has known Mary _____ he was a baby.

(4) Tim couldn't finish the project _____ he was very busy.

(5) I won't go on a picnic _____ it rains tomorrow.

(6) Ann isn't good at swimming _____ she lives near the river.

08 다음 문장에서 어법상 어색한 부분을 바르게 고쳐 문장을 다시 쓰시오.

(1) I have been to London four years ago.

➡ _____

(2) When have you seen a white lion?

➡ _____

(3) I have often played with her when I was a child.

➡ _____

(4) He has been ill in bed last month.

➡ _____

09 다음 문장에서 어법상 어색한 부분을 고치시오.

(1) Because the boy is so young, he is very wise.

_____ ➡ _____

(2) I failed the exam as I studied hard.

_____ ➡ _____

10 다음 주어진 단어를 이용하여 우리말을 영어로 옮기시오.

(1) 그는 1970년 이래로 뉴욕에서 살았다.
(live, since)

➡ _____

(2) 너는 이 이야기를 벌써 다 읽었니?
(finish, this, story, yet)

➡ _____

(3) 나는 그 영화를 한 번 본 적이 있다.
(see, once)

➡ _____

11 다음 우리말과 뜻이 같도록 빈칸에 주어진 철자로 시작하는 알맞은 말을 쓰시오.

> 비록 과일이 건강에 좋다고 해도, 그는 과일을 좋아하지 않는다.
>
> ➡ A_____ fruit is good for his health, he doesn't like it.

Reading

A Selfie Show

Have you ever heard of a "selfie"? When you take a photograph of yourself, it's a selfie. The students from Minji's photo club have searched for information about selfies for one month. Here are some of their presentations about selfies.

Selfies in the Past – Minji

Did people in the past take selfies? Though it wasn't easy at that time, the answer is yes. Look at this photo of Princess Anastasia. She used a mirror to take a picture of herself. She looks nervous. Can you guess why? Well, I think it was her first selfie. And it was probably the world's first teenage selfie ever.

Fun Places for Selfies – Yunho

You can take selfies at world-famous places like Big Ben and the Leaning Tower of Pisa. To take great pictures, just do fun poses and use camera tricks.

You can also visit special museums to take fun selfies. For example, there is a famous selfie museum in the Philippines. It has special spots to take selfies. You can touch the paintings and even step inside them. Look at the following pictures. Though the boys are not really riding horses, it looks like they are. Though the man is just holding a big brush, it looks like he is painting the Mona Lisa. Selfie museums exist in Korea, too.

---

selfie 셀피
search 찾다
presentation 프레젠테이션, 발표
past 과거
nervous 초조한
mirror 거울
probably 아마
teenage 10대의
fun 재미; 재미있는
pose 포즈, 자세
for example 예를 들면
touch 손을 대다
exist 있다, 존재하다

확인문제

● 다음 문장이 본문의 내용과 일치하면 T, 일치하지 않으면 F를 쓰시오.

1 Minji belongs to the photo club. ☐

2 People in the past didn't take selfies. ☐

3 Princess Anastasia took pictures of herself several times. ☐

4 There is a famous selfie museum in the Philippines. ☐

5 There aren't any selfie museums in Korea. ☐

I have visited one in Chuncheon before. Why don't you go there yourself?

경험을 나타내는 현재완료 / ~하지 그래요? / 주어를 강조하는 재귀대명사

Selfie Safety – Jihun

These selfies look great, but were they a good idea? I don't think so. They don't look safe. You should take special care when you take selfies in the wild or at high places like these. A monkey could bite you at any time, or you could fall. Here are some safety tips:

look+형용사: ~해 보이다 / = these selfies / = they were a good idea / ~ 해야 한다 / ~할 때 - 때를 나타내는 접속사 / 야생에서 / ~와 같은 / ~할 수 있다: 가능성 / some+복수 명사

1. Don't take selfies while you're walking.
   부정명령문 / ~하는 동안 -때를 나타내는 접속사
2. Do not pose with or near wild animals.
   = Don't: 부정명령문 / ~ 가까이에서: 전치사
3. Never take selfies in dangerous places.
   결코 ~하지 마라: 부정명령문

Selfies for a Better School Life – Soyun

I think we can use selfies to make a better school life. We can do good things at school and take selfies. Then we can post the photos on our school website. I've watered the plants and flowers at school for one month. I've also helped the teacher at the school library many times. Look at my selfies of those things. How about joining me to create a better school life?

앞에 접속사 that이 생략 / good의 비교급 / do와 함께 can에 연결됨 / = have watered: 계속을 나타내는 현재완료 / 경험을 나타내는 현재완료 / 여러 번 / How about -ing?: ~하는 게 어때?

before 전에
safety 안전
safe 안전한
special 특별한
care 관심
wild 야생; 야생의
place 장소, 곳
bite 물다
at any time 언제고
while: ~하는 동안
dangerous 위험한
post 올리다, 게재하다
plant 식물
create 창조하다, 만들어 내다

확인문제

● 다음 문장이 본문의 내용과 일치하면 T, 일치하지 않으면 F를 쓰시오.

1 There is a selfie museum in Chuncheon. ☐

2 You should take special care when you take selfies in dangerous places. ☐

3 A monkey doesn't bite you. ☐

4 Selfies can be used to make a better school life. ☐

5 Soyun has watered the plants and flowers at school for a year. ☐

● 우리말을 참고하여 빈칸에 알맞은 말을 쓰시오.

1 _____ you ever _____ of a "selfie"?

2 When you _____ a photograph of _____, it's a selfie.

3 The students from Minji's photo _____ have searched _____ information about selfies _____ one month.

4 _____ are some of their presentations _____ selfies.

5 Did _____ in the past _____ selfies?

6 _____ it wasn't easy at that time, the _____ is yes.

7 _____ at this photo of Princess Anastasia.

8 She _____ a mirror to take a picture of _____.

9 She looks _____.

10 Can you guess _____?

11 Well, I _____ it was her _____ selfie.

12 And it was _____ the world's first _____ selfie ever.

13 You can _____ selfies at world-famous places _____ Big Ben and the Leaning Tower of Pisa.

14 To _____ great pictures, just do fun poses and use camera _____.

15 You can _____ visit special museums to take _____ selfies.

16 For _____, there is a _____ selfie museum in the Philippines.

17 It has _____ spots to _____ selfies.

18 You can _____ the paintings and _____ step inside them.

19 Look at the _____ pictures.

20 _____ the boys are not really _____ horses, it looks _____ they are.

1 여러분은 "셀피"에 대해 들어 본 적이 있나요?

2 여러분 자신의 사진을 찍을 때 그것이 셀피예요.

3 민지의 사진 동아리 학생들은 한 달 동안 셀피에 대한 정보를 찾았습니다.

4 여기 셀피에 대한 그들의 발표 내용이 있습니다.

5 과거의 사람들은 셀피를 찍었나 요?

6 그 때는 셀피를 찍는 것이 쉽지는 않았지만. 답은 '그렇다'입니다.

7 아나스타샤 공주의 이 사진을 보세요.

8 그녀는 거울을 사용하여 자신의 사진을 찍었습니다.

9 그녀는 긴장되어 보입니다.

10 왜인지 추측할 수 있나요?

11 글쎄. 나는 그것이 그녀의 첫 번 째 셀피였다고 생각해요.

12 그리고 그것은 아마도 세계 최초 의 10대 소녀의 셀피였을 거예요.

13 여러분은 빅벤과 피사의 사탑과 같은 세계적으로 유명한 장소에 서 셀피를 찍을 수 있습니다.

14 멋진 사진을 찍기 위해서, 단지 재미있는 포즈를 취하고 카메라 기술을 이용하세요.

15 여러분은 또한 재미있는 셀피를 찍기 위해 특별한 박물관을 방 문할 수 있습니다.

16 예를 들어. 필리핀에는 유명한 셀피 박물관이 있습니다.

17 그곳은 셀피를 찍기 위한 특별한 장소들이 있습니다.

18 여러분은 그림들을 만질 수 있 고 심지어 그림들 안으로 들어 갈 수도 있어요.

19 다음 사진들을 보세요.

20 비록 그 소년들은 말을 타고 있 는 것이 아니지만, 말을 타고 있 는 것처럼 보입니다.

21 Though the man is _____ holding a big _____, it looks like he is _____ the Mona Lisa.

22 Selfie museums _____ in Korea, too.

23 I have _____ one in Chuncheon _____.

24 Why _____ you go there _____?

25 These selfies _____ great, _____ were they a good idea?

26 I don't think _____.

27 They don't look _____.

28 You _____ take special care _____ you take selfies in the wild or at high _____ like these.

29 A monkey _____ bite you at any _____, or you could _____.

30 Here are some _____ tips:

31 1. Don't _____ selfies _____ you're walking.

32 2. Do not _____ with or near _____ animals.

33 3. _____ take selfies in dangerous _____.

34 I think we can _____ selfies to make a _____ school life.

35 We can do good _____ at school and _____ selfies.

36 Then we can _____ the photos on our school _____.

37 I've _____ the plants and flowers at _____ for one month.

38 I've _____ helped the teacher _____ the school library many _____.

39 Look _____ my selfies of _____ things.

40 How _____ joining me to _____ a better school life?

21	비록 그 남자는 단지 커다란 붓을 잡고 있지만, 모나리자를 그리고 있는 것처럼 보입니다.
22	한국에도 셀피 박물관이 있습니다.
23	나는 전에 춘천에 있는 한 박물관을 방문한 적이 있습니다.
24	여러분도 직접 그곳에 가는 게 어때요?
25	이 셀피들은 멋져 보이지만, 그것들은 좋은 생각이었나요?
26	난 그렇게 생각하지 않아요.
27	그것들은 안전해 보이지 않습니다.
28	여러분은 야생이나 이와 같이 높은 곳에서 셀피를 찍을 때 특별한 주의를 기울여야 합니다.
29	원숭이가 언제든지 당신을 물거나 또는 당신은 떨어질 수 있습니다.
30	여기 몇 가지 안전 수칙이 있습니다.
31	1. 걸으면서 셀피를 찍지 마세요.
32	2. 야생 동물들과 함께 또는 가까이에서 포즈를 취하지 마세요.
33	3. 위험한 곳에서는 절대 셀피를 찍지 마세요.
34	나는 우리가 더 나은 학교생활을 만들기 위해 셀피를 이용할 수 있다고 생각해요.
35	우리는 학교에서 좋은 일을 할 수 있고 셀피를 찍을 수도 있습니다.
36	그리고 나서 우리는 학교 웹사이트에 사진을 올릴 수 있어요.
37	나는 한 달 동안 학교에서 식물과 꽃에 물을 주었습니다.
38	나는 또한 학교 도서관에서 선생님을 여러 번 도왔습니다.
39	그런 것들에 대한 내 셀피를 보세요.
40	저와 함께 더 나은 학교생활을 만들어 보는 건 어떨까요?

● 우리말을 참고하여 본문을 영작하시오.

1 여러분은 "셀피"에 대해 들어 본 적이 있나요? 여러분 자신의 사진을 찍을 때 그것이 셀피에요.
➡ _____

2 민지의 사진 동아리 학생들은 한 달 동안 셀피에 대한 정보를 찾았습니다.
➡ _____

3 여기 셀피에 대한 그들의 발표 내용이 있습니다.
➡ _____

4 과거의 사람들은 셀피를 찍었나요?
➡ _____

5 그 때는 셀피를 찍는 것이 쉽지는 않았지만. 답은 '그렇다'입니다.
➡ _____

6 아나스타샤 공주의 이 사진을 보세요. 그녀는 거울을 사용하여 자신의 사진을 찍었습니다.
➡ _____

7 그녀는 긴장되어 보입니다. 왜인지 추측할 수 있나요?
➡ _____

8 글쎄, 나는 그것이 그녀의 첫 번째 셀피였다고 생각해요.
➡ _____

9 그리고 그것은 아마도 세계 최초의 10대 소녀의 셀피였을 거예요.
➡ _____

10 여러분은 빅벤과 피사의 사탑과 같은 세계적으로 유명한 장소에서 셀피를 찍을 수 있습니다.
➡ _____

11 멋진 사진을 찍기 위해서, 단지 재미있는 포즈를 취하고 카메라 기술을 이용하세요.
➡ _____

12 여러분은 또한 재미있는 셀피를 찍기 위해 특별한 박물관을 방문할 수 있습니다.
➡ _____

13 예를 들어, 필리핀에는 유명한 셀피 박물관이 있습니다.
➡ _____

14 그곳은 셀피를 찍기 위한 특별한 장소들이 있습니다.
➡ _____

15 여러분은 그림들을 만질 수 있고 심지어 그림들 안으로 들어갈 수도 있어요.
➡ _____

16 다음 사진들을 보세요.
➡ _____

17 비록 그 소년들은 말을 타고 있는 것은 아니지만, 말을 타고 있는 것처럼 보입니다.
➡ _____

18 비록 그 남자는 단지 커다란 붓을 잡고 있지만, 모나리자를 그리고 있는 것처럼 보입니다.
➡ _____

19 한국에도 셀피 박물관이 있습니다. 나는 전에 춘천에 있는 한 박물관을 방문한 적이 있습니다.
➡ _____

20 여러분도 직접 그곳에 가는 게 어때요? 이 셀피들은 멋져 보이지만, 그것들은 좋은 생각이었나요?
➡ _____

21 난 그렇게 생각하지 않아요. 그것들은 안전해 보이지 않습니다.
➡ _____

22 여러분은 야생이나 이와 같이 높은 곳에서 셀피를 찍을 때 특별한 주의를 기울여야 합니다.
➡ _____

23 원숭이가 언제든지 당신을 물거나 또는 당신은 떨어질 수 있습니다.
➡ _____

24 여기 몇 가지 안전 수칙이 있습니다.
➡ _____

25 걸으면서 셀피를 찍지 마세요.
➡ _____

26 야생 동물들과 함께 또는 가까이에서 포즈를 취하지 마세요.
➡ _____

27 위험한 곳에서는 절대 셀피를 찍지 마세요.
➡ _____

28 나는 우리가 더 나은 학교생활을 만들기 위해 셀피를 이용할 수 있다고 생각해요.
➡ _____

29 우리는 학교에서 좋은 일을 할 수 있고 셀피를 찍을 수도 있습니다.
➡ _____

30 그러고 나서 우리는 학교 웹사이트에 사진을 올릴 수 있어요.
➡ _____

31 나는 한 달 동안 학교에서 식물과 꽃에 물을 주었습니다.
➡ _____

32 나는 또한 학교 도서관에서 선생님을 여러 번 도왔습니다.
➡ _____

33 그런 것들에 대한 내 셀피를 보세요.
➡ _____

34 저와 함께 더 나은 학교생활을 만들어 보는 건 어떨까요?
➡ _____

[01~04] 다음 글을 읽고, 물음에 답하시오.

> **A Selfie Show**
>
> Have you ever heard of a "selfie"? ⓐ you take a photograph of yourself, it's a selfie. The students from Minji's photo club have searched ⓑ information about selfies ⓒ one month. ⓓHere are some of their presentations about selfies.

01 위 글의 빈칸 ⓐ에 알맞은 것은?

① What　　　　② How
③ When　　　　④ Because
⑤ While

02 위 글의 빈칸 ⓑ와 ⓒ에 공통으로 알맞은 것은?

① of　　　　② to
③ with　　　④ for
⑤ along

03 위 글의 밑줄 친 ⓓ와 문형이 같은 것은?

① Mike likes music very much.
② The man is strong.
③ Birds fly in the sky.
④ The news made her glad.
⑤ Jane sent me a birthday card.

04 위 글의 뒤에 이어질 내용으로 가장 알맞은 것은?

① 셀피의 의미
② 셀피의 유래
③ 셀피를 찍는 이유
④ 민지의 사진 동아리 학생들이 찍은 여러 가지 셀피들
⑤ 민지의 사진 동아리 학생들이 모은 셀피에 대한 여러 가지 정보

[05~07] 다음 글을 읽고, 물음에 답하시오.

> **Selfies in the Past – Minji**
>
> Did people in the past take selfies? (①) Though it wasn't easy at that time, the answer is yes. (②) ⓐShe used a mirror to take a picture of her. (③) She looks nervous. (④) ⓑCan you guess why? (⑤) Well, I think it was her first selfie. And it was probably the world's first teenage selfie ever.

05 위 글의 ①~⑤ 중 다음 주어진 문장이 들어갈 알맞은 곳은?

> Look at this photo of Princess Anastasia.

①　　　②　　　③　　　④　　　⑤

서답형

06 위 글의 밑줄 친 ⓐ에서 어법상 어색한 것을 고치시오.

＿＿＿＿＿ ➡ ＿＿＿＿＿

서답형

07 위 글의 밑줄 친 ⓑ를 why의 의미가 구체적으로 드러나도록 우리말로 옮기시오.

➡ ＿＿＿＿＿＿＿＿＿＿

[08~11] 다음 글을 읽고, 물음에 답하시오.

(①) You can take selfies at world-famous places ⓐlike Big Ben and the Leaning Tower of Pisa. (②) To take great pictures, just do fun poses and use camera tricks. (③)

You can also visit special museums to take fun selfies. (④) ____ⓑ____, there is a famous selfie museum in the Philippines. (⑤)

08 위 글의 ①~⑤ 중 다음 주어진 문장이 들어갈 알맞은 곳은?

> It has special spots to take selfies.

①   ②   ③   ④   ⑤

09 위 글의 밑줄 친 ⓐ와 같은 용법으로 쓰인 것은?

① Do you like apples?
② I like to watch baseball on TV.
③ How do you like this movie?
④ I like to walk in the park on Sundays.
⑤ I want to buy a hat like yours.

10 위 글의 빈칸 ⓑ에 알맞은 것은?

① However   ② For example
③ Therefore   ④ At last
⑤ As a result

11 위 글의 주제로 가장 알맞은 것은?

① 세계적으로 유명한 장소들
② 셀피를 찍는 요령
③ 셀피를 찍기 위한 재미있는 장소
④ 세계의 유명한 박물관들
⑤ 필리핀의 관광 명소

[12~15] 다음 글을 읽고, 물음에 답하시오.

You can touch the paintings and even step inside them. Look at the following pictures. ____ⓐ____ the boys are not really riding horses, it looks like they are. ____ⓑ____ the man is just holding a big brush, it looks like he is painting the Mona Lisa. Selfie museums ⓒare in Korea, too. I have visited one in Chuncheon before. ____ⓓ____ don't you go there yourself?

12 위 글의 빈칸 ⓐ와 ⓑ에 공통으로 알맞은 것은? (2개)

① Though   ② If
③ When   ④ Although
⑤ Since

13 위 글의 밑줄 친 ⓒ와 바꿔 쓸 수 있는 것은?

① fix   ② join
③ exist   ④ stay
⑤ belong

서답형

14 위 글의 빈칸 ⓓ에 알맞은 말을 쓰시오.

➡ _____

15 위 글의 내용과 일치하지 않는 것은?

① 여러분은 그림들을 만질 수 있다.
② 소년들은 실제로 말을 타고 있다.
③ 남자는 모나리자를 그리고 있는 것처럼 보인다.
④ 셀피 박물관은 한국에도 있다.
⑤ 글쓴이는 춘천에 있는 셀피 박물관을 방문한 적이 있다.

[16~19] 다음 글을 읽고, 물음에 답하시오.

Selfie Safety - Jihun

(①) These selfies look great, ___ⓐ___ were they a good idea? (②) I don't think so. (③) ⓑYou should take special care when you take selfies in the wild or at high places like these. (④) A monkey could bite you at any time, or you could fall. (⑤) Here are some safety tips:

1. Don't take selfies ___ⓒ___ you're walking.
2. Do not pose with or near wild animals.
3. Never take selfies in dangerous places.

16 위 글의 ①~⑤ 중 다음 주어진 문장이 들어갈 알맞은 곳은?

> They don't look safe.

①   ②   ③   ④   ⑤

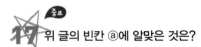

17 위 글의 빈칸 ⓐ에 알맞은 것은?

① and   ② but
③ or   ④ so
⑤ for

18 위 글의 밑줄 친 ⓑ를 우리말로 옮기시오.

➡ _____

_____

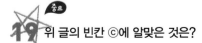

19 위 글의 빈칸 ⓒ에 알맞은 것은?

① if   ② though
③ because   ④ since
⑤ while

[20~24] 다음 글을 읽고, 물음에 답하시오.

Selfies for a Better School Life - Soyun

I think we can use selfies ⓐto make a better school life. We can do good things at school and take selfies. ⓑThen we can post the photos on our school website. I've watered the plants and flowers at school ___ⓒ___ one month. I've also helped the teacher at the school library many times. Look at my selfies of those things. ⓓHow about joining me to create a better school life?

20 위 글의 밑줄 친 ⓐ와 같은 용법으로 쓰인 것은?

① My hope is to work as a doctor in Africa.
② It's time to go to bed now.
③ My job is to report the news.
④ The boys hoped to find the hidden treasure.
⑤ Kate went to a shopping mall to buy clothes.

서답형
21 위 글의 밑줄 친 ⓑ를 우리말로 옮기시오.

➡ _____

중요
22 위 글의 빈칸 ⓒ에 알맞은 것은?

① for   ② during
③ from   ④ since
⑤ while

서답형
23 위 글의 밑줄 친 ⓓ 대신 쓸 수 있는 것을 쓰시오.

➡ _____

24 위 글의 내용으로 보아 대답할 수 <u>없는</u> 질문은?

① What can Soyun use to make a better school life?
② Does Soyun take selfies at school?
③ Where can Soyun post the photos?
④ How long has Soyun watered the plants at school?
⑤ Why did Soyun help the teacher at the school library?

[25~26] 다음 글을 읽고, 물음에 답하시오.

A Selfie Show

Have you ever heard ____ⓐ____ a "selfie"? When you take a photograph ____ⓑ____ yourself, it's a selfie. The students from Minji's photo club ⓒhave searched for information about selfies for one month. Here are some of their presentations about selfies.

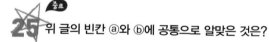

25 위 글의 빈칸 ⓐ와 ⓑ에 공통으로 알맞은 것은?

① of
② for
③ about
④ into
⑤ from

26 위 글의 밑줄 친 ⓒ와 용법이 같은 것은? (2개)

① I <u>have been</u> in this country since last month.
② Yumi <u>has seen</u> this movie many times.
③ Mike <u>has</u> just <u>cleaned</u> his room.
④ Lisa <u>has had</u> this cat for ten years.
⑤ She <u>has gone</u> out and this room is cold.

[27~30] 다음 글을 읽고, 물음에 답하시오.

Selfies in the Past - Minji

Did people in the past take selfies? ____ⓐ____ it wasn't easy at that time, the answer is yes. Look ____ⓑ____ this photo of Princess Anastasia. ⓒ그녀는 자신의 사진을 찍기 위해 거울을 사용했다. She looks nervous. Can you guess why? Well, I think it was her first selfie. And it was probably the world's first teenage selfie ever.

27 위 글의 빈칸 ⓐ에 알맞은 것은?

① If
② For
③ Though
④ When
⑤ Since

28 위 글의 빈칸 ⓑ에 알맞은 것은?

① at
② in
③ to
④ for
⑤ on

서답형

29 위 글의 밑줄 친 ⓒ를 주어진 단어를 이용하여 영어로 옮기시오.

(use, mirror, take, picture, herself)

➡ _____

30 위 글의 내용과 일치하지 <u>않는</u> 것은?

① 옛날 사람도 셀피를 찍었다.
② Anastasia 공주는 자신의 셀피를 찍었다.
③ Anastasia 공주는 종종 셀피를 찍었다.
④ Anastasia 공주는 초조해 보인다.
⑤ 민지는 Anastasia 공주가 찍은 이 셀피가 세계에서 십대의 첫 번째 셀피라고 생각한다.

[01~05] 다음 글을 읽고, 물음에 답하시오.

> **Fun Places for Selfies - Yunho**
>
> ⓐYou can take selfies at world-famous places like Big Ben and the Leaning Tower of Pisa. To take great pictures, just do fun ___ⓑ___ and use camera tricks.
>
> You can also visit special museums to take fun selfies. ___ⓒ___ example, there is a famous selfie museum in the Philippines. ⓓIt has special spots to take selfies. You can touch the paintings and even step inside them.

01 위 글의 밑줄 친 ⓐ를 우리말로 옮기시오.

➡ _____

_____

02 위 글의 빈칸 ⓑ에 다음 정의에 해당하는 단어를 쓰시오. 필요하면 어형 변화를 할 것.

> a particular way that you stand, sit, or lie, for example when you are being photographed or painted

➡ _____

03 위 글의 빈칸 ⓒ에 알맞은 전치사를 쓰시오.

➡ _____

04 위 글의 밑줄 친 ⓓ가 가리키는 것을 우리말로 쓰시오.

➡ _____

05 Where can you go to take fun selfies? Answer in English.

➡ _____

[06~09] 다음 글을 읽고, 물음에 답하시오.

> Look ___ⓐ___ the following pictures. ⓑThough the boys are not really riding horses, it looks like they are. Though the man is just holding a big brush, it looks like he is painting the Mona Lisa. Selfie museums exist in Korea, too. I have visited ⓒone in Chuncheon before. Why don't you go there ⓓyou?

06 위 글의 빈칸 ⓐ에 알맞은 전치사를 쓰시오.

➡ _____

07 위 글의 밑줄 친 ⓑ를 우리말로 옮기시오.

➡ _____

08 위 글의 밑줄 친 ⓒ가 가리키는 것을 영어로 쓰시오.

➡ _____

09 위 글의 밑줄 친 ⓓ를 알맞은 어형으로 고치시오.

➡ _____

[10~14] 다음 글을 읽고, 물음에 답하시오.

Selfie Safety - Jihun

  These selfies look great, but were they a good idea? I don't think ⓐso. ⓑThey don't look safely. You should take special care when you take selfies in the wild or at high places like these. A monkey could bite you ____ⓒ____ any time, or you could fall. Here are some safety tips:

  1. Don't take selfies while you're walking.
  2. Do not pose with or near wild animals.
  3. Never take selfies in ⓓdanger places.

10 위 글의 밑줄 친 ⓐ가 가리키는 것을 영어로 쓰시오.

  ➡ _____

11 위 글의 밑줄 친 ⓑ에서 어법상 어색한 것을 고치시오.

  _____ ➡ _____

12 위 글의 빈칸 ⓒ에 알맞은 전치사를 쓰시오.

  ➡ _____

13 위 글의 밑줄 친 ⓓ를 알맞은 어형으로 고치시오.

  ➡ _____

14 Why should you take special care when you take selfies in the wild or at high places? Answer in Korean.

  ➡ _____

[15~18] 다음 글을 읽고, 물음에 답하시오.

Selfie for a Better School Life - Soyun

  ⓐI think we can use selfies to make a better school life. We can do good things at school and take selfies. Then we can post the photos on our school website. I've ⓑwater the plants and flowers at school ____ⓒ____ one month. I've also helped the teacher at the school library many times. Look at my selfies of those things. How ____ⓓ____ joining me to create a better school life?

15 위 글의 밑줄 친 ⓐ를 우리말로 옮기시오.

  ➡ _____
  _____

16 위 글의 밑줄 친 ⓑ를 알맞은 어형으로 고치시오.

  ➡ _____

17 위 글의 빈칸 ⓒ에 알맞은 단어를 쓰시오.

  ➡ _____

18 위 글의 빈칸 ⓓ에 알맞은 단어를 쓰시오.

  ➡ _____

해석

Fun Time

A: You shouldn't push others when you go swimming.
~해서는 안 된다 = other people

B: Okay. Thank you for your advice.
thank A for B: A에 대해서 B에게 감사하다

구문해설 · push: 밀다 · advice: 충고

A: 수영하러 갈 때 다른 사람들을 밀면 안 돼.
B: 알았어. 충고 고마워.

Express Yourself - C

Have you heard of the pyramids in Egypt? Though I have never been to
= Although: 비록 ~이지만 ~에 다녀오다. ~에 가 본 적이 있다

Egypt before, I'm standing in front of a pyramid in this picture. I took it at the
현재진행형

selfie museum.

구문해설 · before: 전에 · in front of: ~ 앞에

여러분은 이집트의 피라미드에 대해 들어 본 적이 있나요? 나는 전에 이집트에 가 본 적이 없지만, 이 사진에서 나는 피라미드 앞에 서 있어요. 나는 이 사진을 셀피 박물관에서 찍었어요.

Project - Step 2

Fire Safety Rules

Have you heard of fire safety rules? Though there's a fire, you can be safe.

You shouldn't take the elevator. You should follow the teacher's directions.
should not의 축약형: 금지의 표현 = must: ~해야 한다

구문해설 · safety: 안전 · rule: 규칙, 수칙 · safe:: 안전한 · follow: 따르다 · direction: 지시

화재 안전 수칙
당신은 화재 안전 수칙에 대해 들어 본 적이 있습니까? 불이 났지만, 당신은 안전할 수 있어요. 엘리베이터를 타지 마세요. 선생님의 지시에 따라야 해요.

Link to the World

BMX Bike Riding

Riding a BMX bike is very exciting. You can try lots of skills. You can turn
동명사 주어 동명사 주어는 단수 취급 excited(X) 많은(=many = a lot of)

the bike freely and even jump with the bike. Though it's not easy, it's very
접 비록 ~이지만

exciting. You can start with standing skills. When you try standing skills,
접 ~할 때

balancing is very important. But be careful! You should wear a helmet and
명령문: 동사원형 ~

gloves. Also, you shouldn't go too fast when you're riding.
shouldn't+동사원형: ~해서는 안 된다

구문해설 · exciting: 흥미진진한, 신나는 · try: 시도하다 · freely: 자유롭게 · even: ~도[조차]
· easy: 쉬운 · skill: 기술 · balancing: 균형(잡기) · important: 중요한
· careful: 조심하는, 주의 깊은

BMX 자전거 타기
BMX 자전거를 타는 것은 매우 흥미롭다. 여러분은 많은 기술을 시도할 수 있다. 여러분은 자전거를 자유롭게 돌릴 수 있고 심지어 자전거와 함께 점프할 수도 있다. 쉽지는 않지만, 매우 흥미롭다. 여러분은 서 있는 기술과 함께 시작하면 된다. 서 있는 기술을 시도할 때, 균형을 잡는 것이 매우 중요하다. 하지만 조심해라! 헬멧과 장갑을 착용해야 한다. 또한, 자전거를 탈 때는 너무 빨리 가지 말아야 한다.

Words & Expressions

01 다음 중 짝지어진 단어의 관계가 나머지와 <u>다른</u> 것은?

① loose – tight
② advice – tip
③ kind – unkind
④ birth – death
⑤ remember – forget

02 다음 빈칸에 들어갈 말로 적절하지 <u>않은</u> 것은?

- Kate didn't receive a letter from him _____.
- He turned and looked _____.
- He found the place _____ difficulty.
- What _____ did he say?

① else
② without
③ other
④ yet
⑤ back

03 다음 빈칸에 알맞은 단어를 쓰시오.

_____ : present : future

04 다음 문장의 빈칸에 알맞은 것은?

Vegetables are good _____ health.

① in
② on
③ to
④ for
⑤ with

05 다음 영영풀이에 해당하는 단어는?

an action that is intended to deceive someone

① object
② joke
③ humor
④ plan
⑤ trick

06 다음 문장의 빈칸에 공통으로 들어갈 말을 쓰시오.

- I went to London _____ the first time.
- I like juicy fruits, _____ example, watermelons.

07 다음 우리말에 맞게 빈칸에 알맞은 말을 쓰시오.

전화 끊기 전에 나도 그녀에게 말하게 해 줘.
➡ Let me speak to her before you _____ _____.

Conversation

08 다음 대화의 빈칸에 알맞은 말을 쓰시오.

A: _____ you visited a selfie museum before?
B: Yes, I _____. It was very interesting.

09 다음 대화에서 밑줄 친 부분의 의도로 알맞은 것은?

> A: Can you take a picture of me?
> B: Sure.
> A: You'd better not use the flash here, David. The baby animals will wake up.
> B: I see.

① 질문하기   ② 요청하기
③ 금지하기   ④ 허락하기
⑤ 칭찬하기

[10~15] 다음 대화를 읽고, 물음에 답하시오.

> A: Hello, Somin! It's me! Can you see me?
> B: Oh, hi, Minjun! What's ___ⓐ___ ?
> A: ⓑThis is so cool, isn't this? We can video chat on the phone! Have you heard of Jeju *Olle*?
> B: Yes, I have. I really want to go there someday.
> A: Guess ___ⓒ___ ? I'm on it now. Actually, I'm going to go up Seongsan Ilchulbong now.
> B: That's great!
> A: Don't hang ___ⓓ___ . Enjoy the beautiful scenery with me.
> B: Be ⓔcare! You shouldn't use your cell phone ___ⓕ___ you're walking.
> A: Oh, right. Thank you. I'll send you photos later.

10 위 대화의 빈칸 ⓐ와 ⓓ에 공통으로 들어갈 것은?

① on   ② to
③ with   ④ up
⑤ for

11 위 대화의 밑줄 친 ⓑ에서 어법상 어색한 것을 고치시오.

_____ ➡ _____

12 위 대화의 빈칸 ⓒ에 알맞은 말을 쓰시오.

➡ _____

13 위 대화의 밑줄 친 ⓔ를 알맞은 어형으로 고치시오.

➡ _____

14 위 대화의 빈칸 ⓕ에 알맞은 것은?

① if   ② that
③ though   ④ because
⑤ while

15 위 대화의 내용과 일치하지 <u>않는</u> 것은?

① 소민과 민준은 화상 채팅을 하고 있다.
② 소민은 제주 올레에 관해 들은 적이 있다.
③ 민준은 지금 성산 일출봉을 오르려고 한다.
④ 소민은 민준과 아름다운 경치를 즐길 것이다.
⑤ 민준은 나중에 소민에게 사진들을 보낼 것이다.

Grammar

16 다음 문장의 빈칸에 알맞은 것은?

> I _____ never seen such a beautiful mountain.

① be   ② did
③ have   ④ was
⑤ must

17 다음 문장의 빈칸에 알맞은 것은?

> _____ I live near the sea, I'm not good at swimming.

① As   ② Since
③ Unless   ④ Though
⑤ Because

18 다음 괄호 안에 주어진 단어를 어법상 바르게 쓴 것은?

> Jack (want) this video game since last year.

① wants   ② want
③ wanted   ④ has wanted
⑤ is wanting

19 다음 우리말과 일치하도록 주어진 단어를 바르게 배열하시오.

> 날씨가 추웠지만, 공원에는 사람들이 많이 있었다.
> (was, a lot of, cold, although, were, in the park, people, there, it).

➡ _____

_____

20 다음 중 어법상 <u>어색한</u> 것은?

① He has been sick in bed for a week.
② How long have you stayed in America?
③ I have climbed that mountain last week.
④ You have already walked 100 kilometers.
⑤ I have never been to America.

21 다음 우리말을 영어로 바르게 옮긴 것은?

> 그녀는 비록 돈이 많지만, 행복하지 않다.

① Since she has plenty of money, she is not happy.
② So she has plenty of money, she is not happy.
③ Because she has plenty of money, she is not happy.
④ Although she has plenty of money, she is not happy.
⑤ Even although she has plenty of money, she is not happy.

22 다음 문장과 뜻이 가장 가까운 것은?

> Jack's father has gone to Rome.

① Jack's father is going to Rome.
② Jack's father went to Rome.
③ Jack's father went to Rome but he is here now.
④ Jack's father went to Rome and he isn't here now.
⑤ Jack's father went to Rome and he has just come back.

23 다음 〈보기〉의 밑줄 친 부분과 같은 용법으로 사용된 것은?

> ┤ 보기 ├
>
> Nancy has read the novel three times.

① I have lived here since last year.
② Ted has seen a panda before.
③ My mother has finished washing the dishes.
④ Jack has wanted to have a cat for a long time.
⑤ Mrs. Brown has lost her purse somewhere.

24 다음 중 문맥상 어색한 문장은?

① My mother often sings as she works.
② As it started to rain, we stopped playing baseball.
③ I went home early though I felt sick.
④ My camera can take good pictures though it is very old.
⑤ Though it was very warm, she didn't take off her coat.

25 다음 중 밑줄 친 부분의 쓰임이 올바르지 않은 것은?

① I've been to Madrid ten years ago.
② Kate has lived in Seoul for five years.
③ Mike has been sick in hospital since last Monday.
④ She has never seen such a beautiful lake.
⑤ How often have you been to Paris?

26 다음 두 문장의 의미가 같도록 빈칸에 알맞은 말을 쓰시오.

> Though you fall from a high tree, I will catch you.
>
> ➡ _____ _____ you fall from a high tree, I will catch you.

Reading

[27~30] 다음 글을 읽고, 물음에 답하시오.

BMX Bike Riding
 Riding a BMX bike is very ⓐexcite. You can try ⓑlots of skills. You can turn the bike freely and even jump with the bike. Though it's not easy, it's very exciting. You can start with standing skills. When you try standing skills, balancing is very important. But be careful. You should wear a helmet and gloves. Also, you shouldn't go too fast ⓒ you're riding.

27 위 글의 밑줄 친 ⓐ를 알맞은 어형으로 고치시오.

➡ _____

28 위 글의 밑줄 친 ⓑ 대신 쓸 수 있는 것은?

① much   ② little
③ enough   ④ many
⑤ several

29 위 글의 빈칸 ⓒ에 알맞은 것은?

① if   ② because
③ when   ④ although
⑤ since

30 위 글의 내용으로 보아 알 수 <u>없는</u> 것은?

① BMX 자전거 타는 것은 재미있다.

② BMX 자전거는 값이 비싸다.

③ BMX 자전거를 타려면 많은 기술이 필요하다.

④ BMX 자전거를 타고 점프할 수 있다.

⑤ BMX 자전거를 탈 때는 안전에 주의해야 한다.

[31~35] 다음 글을 읽고, 물음에 답하시오.

You can also visit special museums to take fun selfies. _____ⓐ_____ example, there is a famous selfie museum in the Philippines. ⓑIt has special spots to take selfies. You can touch the paintings and even step inside them. Look at the following pictures. Though the boys are not really riding horses, it looks like they are. ⓒThough the man is just holding a big brush, it looks like he is painting the Mona Lisa. Selfie museums exist in Korea, too. I have visited one in Chuncheon before. _____ⓓ_____ don't you go there yourself?

31 위 글의 빈칸 ⓐ에 알맞은 것은?

① To   ② In

③ As   ④ For

⑤ With

32 위 글의 밑줄 친 ⓑ가 가리키는 것을 영어로 쓰시오.

➡ _____

33 위 글의 밑줄 친 ⓒ를 우리말로 옮기시오.

➡ _____

_____

34 위 글의 빈칸 ⓓ에 알맞은 것은?

① Why   ② How

③ What   ④ When

⑤ Where

35 위 글의 내용과 일치하지 <u>않는</u> 것은?

① 재미있는 셀피를 찍기 위해 특별한 박물관을 방문할 수 있다.

② 필리핀에는 유명한 셀피 박물관이 있다.

③ 필리핀의 셀피 박물관에서는 그림에 손을 댈 수 없다.

④ 한국에도 셀피 박물관이 있다.

⑤ 글쓴이는 춘천에 있는 셀피 박물관을 다녀온 적이 있다.

[36~37] 다음 글을 읽고, 물음에 답하시오.

Have you heard of fire ⓐsafe rules? _____ⓑ_____ there's a fire, you can be safe. You shouldn't take the elevator. You should follow the teacher's directions.

36 위 글의 밑줄 친 ⓐ를 알맞은 형으로 고치시오.

➡ _____

37 위 글의 빈칸 ⓑ에 알맞지 <u>않은</u> 것은? (2개)

① Though   ② Since

③ Although   ④ As though

⑤ Even though

출제율 95%

01 다음 중 짝지어진 단어의 관계가 <u>다른</u> 것은?

① king : queen
② husband : wife
③ uncle : aunt
④ child : kid
⑤ prince : princess

출제율 90%

02 다음 빈칸에 공통으로 알맞은 것은?

- I was fond _____ sports when I was young.
- The bus stops right in front _____ our house.

① in
② of
③ from
④ with
⑤ onto

출제율 85%

03 다음 짝지어진 두 단어의 관계가 같도록 빈칸에 알맞은 말을 쓰시오.

advise : advice = arrive : _____

출제율 90%

04 다음 중 영영풀이가 <u>잘못된</u> 것은?

① alone: without any other people
② clothes: the things that people wear, such as shirts, coats, trousers, and dresses
③ painter: an artist who paints pictures
④ pull: to use force to make something move away from you or away from its previous position
⑤ mirror: a flat piece of glass which reflects light, so that when you look at it you can see yourself reflected in it

출제율 100%

05 다음 우리말에 맞게 빈칸에 알맞은 말을 쓰시오.

그는 이제 더 이상 네 친구가 아니란 걸 명심해.
➡ Keep _____ _____ that he is not your friend anymore.

출제율 85%

06 다음 대화의 밑줄 친 부분의 의도로 알맞은 것은?

B: I want to watch the birds in the trees.
G: <u>You shouldn't go up too close to the birds.</u>
B: All right, thanks.

① 요청하기
② 비난하기
③ 제안하기
④ 금지하기
⑤ 칭찬하기

출제율 90%

07 다음 대화의 빈칸에 알맞은 것은?

A: _____
B: No, I haven't, but I've heard of it many times.

① How often have you been to Haeundae?
② Did you go to Haeundae?
③ When did you go to Haeundae?
④ Have you ever been to Haeundae?
⑤ How many times did you visit Haeundae?

[08~13] 다음 대화를 읽고, 물음에 답하시오.

> B: Have you heard of bird watching?
> M: Sure. I tried ⓐit when I was a child. (①)
> B: That's nice. Actually, I'm doing it ⓑ____ the first time this Saturday. (②)
> M: Are you? You should bring warm clothes and something to eat. (③)
> B: Okay. (④)
> M: You shouldn't ⓒ____ any noise when you watch the birds. (⑤)
> B: I'll keep ⓓthat in mind. Thanks, Dad.

08 위 대화의 ①~⑤ 중 다음 주어진 문장이 들어갈 알맞은 곳은?

> What else should I keep in mind?

① ② ③ ④ ⑤

09 위 대화의 밑줄 친 ⓐ가 가리키는 것을 영어로 쓰시오.

➡ _____

10 위 대화의 빈칸 ⓑ에 알맞은 것은?

① on ② to
③ for ④ in
⑤ with

11 위 대화의 빈칸 ⓒ에 알맞은 것은?

① get ② make
③ do ④ bring
⑤ take

12 위 대화의 밑줄 친 ⓓ가 가리키는 것을 우리말로 쓰시오.

➡ _____

13 위 글의 내용과 일치하지 않는 것은?

① 소년의 아버지는 들새 관찰을 해 본 적이 있다.
② 소년은 이번 토요일에 들새 관찰을 할 예정이다.
③ 소년은 따뜻한 옷과 먹을 것을 가져가야 한다.
④ 들새 관찰을 할 때에는 조용해야 한다.
⑤ 소년의 취미는 들새 관찰이다.

14 다음 문장의 빈칸에 알맞지 않은 것은?

> Jenny has seen the movie _____.

① once ② twice
③ never ④ before
⑤ many times

15 다음 문장의 빈칸에 알맞은 것은?

> _____ Tom's family is poor, they are always happy.

① If ② As
③ Since ④ Unless
⑤ Although

16 다음 밑줄 친 단어의 올바른 형태를 쓰시오. 출제율 85%

> Jane lived in England since she was ten years old.

➡ _____

17 다음 문장에서 어법상 어색한 부분을 바르게 고쳐 문장을 다시 쓰시오. 출제율 95%

> I didn't see him since I was eleven.

➡ _____

18 다음 두 문장의 뜻이 같도록 할 때 빈칸에 알맞은 것은? 출제율 85%

> Though I looked for your pencil, I couldn't find it.
> = I looked for your pencil, _____ I couldn't find it.

① so ② but
③ and ④ for
⑤ because

19 다음 〈보기〉 문장과 뜻이 가장 가까운 것은? 출제율 85%

> ┌ 보기 ┐
> Tom has lost his watch.

① Tom lost his watch.
② Tom lost his watch and he forgot it.
③ Tom lost his watch, but he found it.
④ Tom lost his watch, and he hasn't found it yet.
⑤ Tom lost his watch, so he is going to buy a new one.

20 다음 문장 중 밑줄 친 부분이 어색한 것은? 출제율 100%

① I think that your answer is right.
② It was snowing when I got up.
③ I often sing while I'm taking a shower.
④ Although the boy was sick, he went to school.
⑤ Because Mozart's life was short, he changed music history.

21 다음 밑줄 친 부분의 쓰임이 나머지 넷과 다른 하나는? 출제율 90%

① Jenny has seen the actor before.
② My grandfather has never visited Seoul.
③ Mr. Lincoln has gone to Berlin on business.
④ How many times have they been to China?
⑤ They have been to Italy three times.

[22~25] 다음 글을 읽고, 물음에 답하시오.

> **Selfies in the Past - Minji**
> Did people in the past take selfies? Though ⓐit wasn't easy at that time, the answer is yes. (①) Look at this photo of Princess Anastasia. (②) She used a mirror ⓑto take a picture of herself. (③) She looks nervous. (④) Well, I think it was her first selfie. (⑤) And it was probably the world's first teenage selfie ever.

22 위 글의 ①~⑤ 중 다음 주어진 문장이 들어갈 알맞은 곳은? 출제율 90%

> Can you guess why?

① ② ③ ④ ⑤

23 위 글의 밑줄 친 ⓐ가 가리키는 것을 우리말로 쓰시오.

➡ _____

24 위 글의 밑줄 친 ⓑ와 용법이 같은 것은?

① We decided to visit the house.
② He has no friends to play with.
③ Do you want to go skating now?
④ I had no house to live in.
⑤ He worked hard to support his family.

25 민지는 Anastasia가 왜 긴장하고 있다고 생각하는지 우리말로 간단히 쓰시오.

➡ _____
_____

[26~31] 다음 글을 읽고, 물음에 답하시오.

ⓐRiding a BMX bike is very excited. You can try ⓑ많은 skills. You can turn the bike freely and even jump with the bike. ⓒThough it's not easy, it's very exciting. (①) You can start with standing skills. (②) ⓓ_____ you try standing skills, balancing is very important. (③) But be ⓔcare. (④) Also, you shouldn't go too fast when you're riding. (⑤)

26 위 글의 ①~⑤ 중 다음 주어진 문장이 들어갈 알맞은 곳은?

You should wear a helmet and gloves.

①   ②   ③   ④   ⑤

27 위 글의 밑줄 친 ⓐ에서 어법상 어색한 것을 고치시오.

_____ ➡ _____

28 위 글의 밑줄 친 ⓑ를 영어로 바꿔 쓸 때 알맞지 않은 것은? (2개)

① many   ② much
③ a few   ④ lots of
⑤ a lot of

29 위 글의 밑줄 친 ⓒ와 같은 뜻이 되도록 다음 문장의 빈칸에 알맞은 말을 쓰시오.

It's not easy, _____ it's very exciting.

30 위 글의 빈칸 ⓓ에 알맞은 것은?

① When   ② If
③ After   ④ Because
⑤ Though

31 위 글의 밑줄 친 ⓔ를 알맞은 어형으로 고치시오.

➡ _____

[01~03] 다음 대화를 읽고, 물음에 답하시오.

> G: Dad, have you ever heard of Kim Soyun, the rock ⓐ_____?
> M: Yes, I've ⓑsee her on TV.
> G: She's teaching rock climbing at a camp this Saturday. I want to join the camp.
> M: Okay, Miso, but you shouldn't climb up too high.
> G: All right. Thanks, Dad.

01 위 대화의 빈칸 ⓐ에 다음 정의에 해당하는 단어를 쓰시오.

> someone who climbs rocks or mountains as a sport or a hobby

➡ _____

02 위 대화의 밑줄 친 ⓑ를 알맞은 형으로 고치시오.

➡ _____

03 What will Kim Soyun do this Saturday? Answer in English.

➡ _____

04 다음 대화의 순서를 바르게 배열하시오.

> (A) Oh, okay.
> (B) Wait, Jimin.
> (C) Why?
> (D) Look at that sign. You shouldn't take a photo here.

➡ _____

05 다음 〈보기〉와 같이 현재완료 시제를 이용해 두 문장을 한 문장으로 쓰시오.

> ┤ 보기 ├
> Jane moved to Tokyo ten years ago. She still lives there.
> ➡ Jane has lived in Tokyo for ten years.

(1) Peter moved to Peking in 2010. He still lives in Peking.

➡ _____

(2) Tom went to hospital a week ago. He is still in hospital.

➡ _____

(3) My mother went shopping. She is not here.

➡ _____

06 다음 〈조건〉에 맞게 괄호 안의 단어를 이용하여 우리말을 영어로 옮기시오.

> ┤ 조건 ├
> 1. 필요시 관사를 붙이거나 단어를 추가하고 동사의 어형 변화를 할 것.
> 2. 대·소문자 및 구두점에 유의할 것.
> 3. (1), (2)는 접속사로 시작하는 부사절이 주절의 앞에 오고 (3)은 주절의 뒤에 올 것.

(1) 비록 바람이 불기는 했지만, 날씨가 별로 춥지 않았다. (though, it, windy, very, cold)

➡ _____

(2) Tim은 종종 Anne을 짜증스럽게 했지만, 그녀는 그를 좋아했다. (although, often, annoy, fond, of)

➡ _____
_____

(3) 너는 비록 그것이 마음에 들지 않는다고 해도 해야 한다. (though, must, do, it, like)

➡ _____

07 다음 문장에서 어법상 어색한 것을 찾아 바르게 고치시오.

(1) He has gone to Spain last year.

_____ ➡ _____

(2) When have you seen Kathy's little brother?

_____ ➡ _____

(3) I have often played the piano when I was a child.

_____ ➡ _____

[08~11] 다음 글을 읽고, 물음에 답하시오.

Have you ever ⓐhear of a "selfie"? ⓑWhen you take a photograph of you, it's a selfie. The students from Minji's photo club have searched ⓒ information about selfies ⓓ one month. Here are some of their presentations about selfies.

08 위 글의 밑줄 친 ⓐ를 알맞은 형으로 고치시오.

➡ _____

09 위 글의 밑줄 친 ⓑ에서 어법상 어색한 것을 고치시오.

_____ ➡ _____

10 위 글의 빈칸 ⓒ와 ⓓ에 공통으로 알맞은 전치사를 쓰시오.

➡ _____

11 What is a selfie? Answer in Korean.

➡ _____

[12~15] 다음 글을 읽고, 물음에 답하시오.

Selfies for a Better School Life - Soyun

I think we can use selfies ⓐ(making, to make) a better school life. We can do good things at school and ⓑ_____ selfies. Then we can post the photos on our school website. I've watered the ⓒ_____ and flowers at school for one month. I've also helped the teacher at the school library many times. Look at my selfies of those things. How about ⓓjoin me to create a better school life?

12 위 글의 괄호 ⓐ에서 알맞은 것을 고르시오.

➡ _____

13 위 글의 빈칸 ⓑ에 알맞은 단어를 쓰시오.

➡ _____

14 위 글의 빈칸 ⓒ에 다음 정의에 해당하는 단어를 쓰시오. 필요하면 어형 변화를 하시오.

a living thing that grows in the earth and has a stem, leaves, and roots, especially one that is smaller than a tree or bush

➡ _____

15 위 글의 밑줄 친 ⓓ를 알맞은 형으로 고치시오.

➡ _____

01 다음 주어진 말을 이용하여 현재완료형의 문장을 만드시오.

(1) I, just, send, e-mail

➡ _____

(2) Kate, just, clean, room

➡ _____

(3) Mike, already, finish, job

➡ _____

(4) you, take, medicine, yet

➡ _____

(5) Mary, sing, yet

➡ _____

(6) you, study, yet

➡ _____

(7) Tom, do, homework, yet

➡ _____

02 다음 괄호 안에 주어진 어구를 이용하여 자유롭게 문장을 만드시오. (A)는 접속사로 시작하는 부사절이 주절의 앞에 오고, (B)는 주절의 뒤에 올 것.

(1) (though)

➡ (A) _____
   (B) _____

(2) (although)

➡ (A) _____
   (B) _____

(3) (even though)

➡ (A) _____
   (B) _____

단원별 모의고사

01 다음 중 우리말 뜻이 잘못된 것은?

① go up: 오르다
② for example: 예를 들면
③ over there: 저쪽에
④ be good for: ~을 잘하다
⑤ hang up: 전화를 끊다

02 다음 영영풀이에 해당하는 단어로 알맞은 것은?

> better or more important than other people or things

① real
② special
③ popular
④ common
⑤ strange

03 다음 빈칸에 알맞은 것으로 짝지어진 것은?

> • Will you call me _____ your lunch time?
> • Ask somebody _____ to help you.

① for – else
② for – other
③ during – other
④ during – else
⑤ while – other

04 다음 짝지어진 두 단어의 관계가 같도록 빈칸에 알맞은 말을 쓰시오.

> safe : dangerous = push : _____

05 다음 빈칸에 공통으로 들어갈 말을 쓰시오.

> • We were very sorry to hear _____ your father's death.
> • There are lots _____ nice parks in San Francisco.

06 다음 대화를 의미가 통하도록 알맞게 배열한 것은?

> (A) No, I haven't. How was it?
> (B) Have you ever ridden a horse?
> (C) Yes, I have. How about you?
> (D) It was fun, but it was a little scary, too.

① (A) – (D) – (B) – (C)
② (B) – (C) – (A) – (D)
③ (C) – (D) – (B) – (A)
④ (D) – (B) – (C) – (A)
⑤ (D) – (C) – (A) – (B)

07 다음 대화의 빈칸에 알맞은 것은?

> A: Have you ever caught a big fish?
> B: _____ I wish to catch one someday.

① Yes, I have.
② No, I haven't.
③ I caught a big fish.
④ Yes, my uncle caught a big fish.
⑤ I caught it and put it back.

08 다음 대화의 밑줄 친 부분과 바꾸어 쓸 수 있는 것은?

> A: Peter, you'd better not run when you cross the street.
> B: Okay, I will.

① you may run when you cross the street
② you must run when you cross the street
③ you need to run when you cross the street
④ you have to run when you cross the street
⑤ you shouldn't run when you cross the street

[09~13] 다음 대화를 읽고, 물음에 답하시오.

> B: Have you heard ⓐ bird watching?
> M: Sure. I tried it when I was a child.
> B: That's nice. Actually, I'm doing it ⓑ the first time this Saturday.
> M: Are you? You should bring warm clothes and something ⓒto eat.
> B: Okay. ⓓ(in / else / I / keep / what / mind / should)?
> M: You shouldn't make any noise ⓔ you watch the birds.
> B: I'll keep that in mind. Thanks, Dad.

09 위 대화의 빈칸 ⓐ와 ⓑ에 알맞은 것으로 짝지어진 것은?

① of – to   ② of – at
③ of – for   ④ at – for
⑤ from – at

10 위 대화의 밑줄 친 ⓒ와 용법이 같은 것은?

① We wished to reach the North Pole.
② Kathy was very sad to hear the song.
③ Please give me something to drink.
④ Do you want to go on a picnic now?
⑤ He must study hard to pass the math exam.

11 위 대화의 괄호 ⓓ를 알맞은 어순으로 배열하시오.

➡ _____

12 위 대화의 빈칸 ⓔ에 알맞은 것은?

① when   ② if
③ before   ④ after
⑤ although

13 위 대화의 내용으로 보아 알 수 없는 것은?

① The boy's father has tried bird watching.
② The boy is fond of bird watching.
③ The boy will do bird watching this Saturday.
④ The boy should bring warm clothes.
⑤ The boy will need food when he watches the birds.

14 다음 괄호 안에 주어진 단어를 어법상 바르게 쓴 것은?

> He left home at six and (not return) yet.

① doesn't return
② wasn't returned
③ didn't return
④ hasn't returned
⑤ hadn't returned

15 다음 두 문장의 뜻이 같도록 빈칸에 알맞은 것은?

> Even though we were hungry, we didn't eat the food.
> = _____ we were hungry, we didn't eat the food.

① Since   ② Before
③ Though   ④ Therefore
⑤ Because

16 다음 중 밑줄 친 부분의 쓰임이 바르지 <u>않은</u> 것은?

① I've been to Paris five years ago.
② Jack has practiced the piano since last year.
③ Ann has been sick in bed for two weeks.
④ I have never seen such a wonderful movie.
⑤ Has your teacher ever been to Europe?

17 다음 우리말과 같은 뜻이 되도록 빈칸에 알맞은 것은?

> 비록 어제 아팠지만, 나는 학교에 갔다.
> ➡ _____ I was sick yesterday, I went to school.

① If   ② As
③ Besides   ④ Though
⑤ But

18 다음 두 문장의 뜻이 같도록 빈칸에 알맞은 말을 쓰시오.

> I _____ _____ my car key.
> = I lost my car key. I don't have the key now.

19 다음 우리말을 영작한 것으로 <u>어색한</u> 것을 <u>모두</u> 고르면?

> 네가 비록 부자일지라도 내 마음을 살 수는 없다.

① Though you're rich, you can't buy my heart.
② Since if you're rich, you can't buy my heart.
③ Although you're rich, you can't buy my heart.
④ Unless you're rich, you can't buy my heart.
⑤ Even though you're rich, you can't buy my heart.

20 다음 문장의 빈칸에 알맞은 것은?

> Frank _____ never seen such a cute cat.

① be   ② did   ③ has
④ was   ⑤ must

[21~23] 다음 글을 읽고, 물음에 답하시오.

> Have you heard ⓐ _____ the pyramids in Egypt? Though I ⓑhave never been to Egypt before, I'm standing in front ⓒ _____ a pyramid in this picture. I took it at the selfie museum.

21 위 글의 빈칸 ⓐ와 ⓒ에 공통으로 알맞은 것은?

① to   ② at   ③ of
④ on   ⑤ about

22 위 글의 밑줄 친 ⓑ와 같은 용법으로 쓰인 것은?

① I have been in Japan since last month.
② I have seen a koala before.
③ My father has already eaten breakfast.
④ He has wanted to be a painter for a long time.
⑤ My grandmother has lost her smartphone somewhere.

23 Where did the writer take the picture? Answer in English.

➡ _____

[24~27] 다음 글을 읽고, 물음에 답하시오.

Selfie Safety – Jihun

These selfies look great, but were they a good idea? ⓐI don't think so. They don't look ___ⓑ___. You should take special care when you take selfies in the wild or at high places like these. A monkey could bite you at any time, ___ⓒ___ you could fall. Here are some safety tips:

1. Don't take selfies while you're walking.
2. Do not pose with or near wild animals.
3. Never take selfies in dangerous places.

24 위 글의 밑줄 친 ⓐ를 so의 의미가 구체적으로 드러나도록 우리말로 옮기시오.

➡ _____

25 위 글의 빈칸 ⓑ에 들어갈 알맞은 것은?

① safe   ② exciting
③ easy   ④ dangerous
⑤ difficult

26 위 글의 빈칸 ⓒ에 알맞은 것은?

① so   ② then
③ or   ④ but
⑤ for

27 위 글의 내용으로 보아 알 수 없는 것은?

① 이 글은 셀피를 찍을 때의 안전 수칙이다.
② 야생에서 사진을 찍을 때는 주의해야 한다.
③ 원숭이는 사람을 잘 따른다.
④ 걸을 때는 셀피를 찍으면 안 된다.
⑤ 야생 동물 근처에서 포즈를 취하면 위험하다.

[28~30] 다음 글을 읽고, 물음에 답하시오.

Have you heard of fire safety ___ⓐ___? ___ⓑ___ there's a fire, you can be safe. You shouldn't take the elevator. You should follow the teacher's directions.

28 위 글의 빈칸 ⓐ에 다음 정의에 해당하는 단어를 쓰시오.

instructions that tell you what you are allowed to do and what you are not allowed to do

➡ _____

29 위 글의 빈칸 ⓑ에 알맞은 것은?

① If   ② When
③ As   ④ Though
⑤ Because

30 위 글의 내용과 일치하도록 다음 문장의 빈칸에 알맞은 말을 쓰시오.

When there is a _____, you shouldn't take the _____.

Lesson 4

Memories in Your Heart

🎙️ 의사소통 기능

- 기억 여부 묻기
  Do you remember Mr. Kim, our 6th grade teacher?

- 생각할 시간 요청하기
  Let me see.

🎙️ 언어 형식

- 주격 관계대명사
  Wilfrid was a little boy **who** lived next to a nursing home.

- 목적격 관계대명사의 생략
  It is something (**that**) you remember.

교과서
Words & Expressions

Key Words

- **again**[əgén] 부 다시, 한 번 더
- **ago**[əgóu] 부 전에
- **album**[ǽlbum] 명 앨범
- **alone**[əlóun] 부 혼자, 홀로
- **airplane**[ɛ́ərplein] 명 비행기
- **aunt**[ænt] 명 숙모, 이모, 아주머니
- **board**[bɔːrd] 명 판자, 널빤지
- **bounce**[bauns] 동 ~을 튀기다
- **bring**[briŋ] 동 가져다주다, 가지고 오다
- **cartoon**[kɑːrtúːn] 명 만화
- **clean**[kliːn] 동 닦다, 청소하다
- **competition**[kɑ̀mpətíʃən] 명 대회, 시합, 경쟁
- **cook**[kuk] 동 요리하다
- **delicious**[dilíʃəs] 형 맛있는
- **each other** 서로
- **enjoy**[indʒɔ́i] 동 즐기다
- **far**[fɑːr] 부 멀리
- **favorite**[féivərit] 형 가장 좋아하는
- **February**[fébruèri] 명 2월
- **fly(–flew–flown)**[flai] 동 날다, 비행하다
- **field trip** 현장 학습
- **fresh**[freʃ] 형 갓 낳은, 신선한
- **fun**[fʌn] 형 재미있는
- **funny**[fʌ́ni] 형 우스운, 웃기는, 재미있는
- **grade**[greid] 명 학년, 성적
- **hairpin**[hɛ́ərpìn] 명 머리핀
- **hen**[hen] 명 암탉
- **hot air balloon** 열기구
- **laughter**[lǽftər] 명 웃음

- **lose(–lost–lost)**[luːz] 동 잃다
- **medal**[médl] 명 메달
- **memory**[méməri] 명 기억, 추억
- **move**[muːv] 동 옮기다, 이사[이동]하다
- **neighbor**[néibər] 명 이웃(사람)
- **next to** ~ 옆에
- **nursing home** 양로원
- **perform**[pərfɔ́ːrm] 동 공연하다
- **person**[pə́ːrsn] 명 사람
- **practice**[prǽktis] 동 연습하다
- **precious**[préʃəs] 형 귀중한
- **puppet**[pʌ́pit] 명 꼭두각시, 인형
- **remember**[rimémbər] 동 기억하다
- **round**[raund] 명 (경기의) 판, 라운드, 회
- **school nurse** 양호 선생님
- **science**[sáiəns] 명 과학
- **secret**[síːkrit] 명 비밀
- **sock**[sɑk] 명 양말
- **special**[spéʃəl] 형 특별한
- **sunlight**[sʌ́nlait] 명 햇빛
- **super**[súːpər] 부 매우 형 굉장히 좋은
- **teach**[tiːtʃ] 동 가르치다
- **tear**[tiər] 명 눈물
- **thick**[θik] 형 두꺼운
- **together**[təgéðər] 부 함께, 같이
- **traditional**[trədíʃənl] 형 전통적인, 전통의
- **visit**[vízit] 동 방문하다
- **wear(–wore–worn)**[wɛər] 동 입다, 신다, 쓰다, 착용하다
- **whisper**[hwíspər] 동 속삭이다

Key Expressions

- **cut holes** 구멍을 내다
- **get married** 결혼하다
- **go into** ~으로 들어가다
- **Guess what?** 있잖아
- **have a great time** 즐거운 시간을 보내다
- **Let's see(= Let me see)**
  어디 보자 (생각을 하거나 무엇을 기억하려고 하면서 하는 말)
- **look for** ~을 찾다
- **look like + 명사** ~처럼 보이다

- **one by one** 하나씩, 차례차례
- **remember + -ing** ~한 것을 기억하다
- **smile at** ~을 보고 미소 짓다
- **thank A for B** B 때문에 A에게 감사하다
- **thanks to** ~ 덕분에
- **the same as** ~ ~와 똑같은, 동종의, 동일한
- **throw a party** 파티를 열다
- **wait for** ~을 기다리다
- **What[How] about + -ing** ~? ~하는 게 어때?

Word Power

※ 서로 반대되는 뜻을 가진 단어

- □ **together** (같이, 함께) ↔ **apart** (따로, 떨어져)
- □ **thick** (두꺼운) ↔ **thin** (얇은, 가는)
- □ **fun** (재미있는) ↔ **boring** (지루한)
- □ **bring** (가져오다) ↔ **take** (가져가다)
- □ **hen** (암탉) ↔ **rooster, cock** (수탉)

- □ **remember** (기억하다) ↔ **forget** (잊다)
- □ **special** (특별한) ↔ **general** (일반적인)
- □ **far** (멀리; 먼) ↔ **near** (가까이; 가까운)
- □ **precious** (귀중한) ↔ **worthless** (가치 없는)
- □ **whisper** (속삭이다) ↔ **shout** (소리치다)

※ 서로 비슷한 뜻을 가진 단어

- □ **wear : put on** (입다, 쓰다, 신다, 착용하다)
- □ **next to : beside** (~ 옆에)
- □ **special : particular** (특별한)
- □ **whisper : murmur** (속삭이다)

- □ **super : extremely** (매우)
- □ **delicious : tasty** (맛있는)
- □ **alone : solely** (혼자, 홀로)
- □ **go into : enter** (들어가다)

English Dictionary

- □ **bounce** 튀기다
  → to move up or away after hitting a surface
  표면을 치고 나서 위로 또는 멀리 이동하다

- □ **favorite** 가장 좋아하는
  → best liked or most enjoyed
  가장 좋아하거나 가장 즐겨 하는

- □ **hole** 구멍
  → an empty space in an object, usually with an opening to the object's surface
  물체의 빈 공간, 대개 물체의 표면에 있는 틈[구멍]

- □ **laughter** 웃음
  → the act or sound of laughing
  웃는 행동 또는 소리

- □ **memory** 기억
  → someone's ability to remember things, places, experiences, etc.
  물건, 장소, 경험 등을 기억하는 사람의 능력

- □ **neighbor** 이웃
  → someone who lives near you
  당신 근처에 사는 사람

- □ **perform** 공연하다
  → to do something to entertain people by acting a play or playing a piece of music
  연기를 하거나 음악을 연주함으로써 사람을 즐겁게 하는 일을 하다

- □ **precious** 귀중한
  → of great value because of being rare, expensive, or important
  희귀하거나 비싸거나 중요하기 때문에 매우 소중한

- □ **puppet** 인형, 꼭두각시
  → a toy in the shape of a person or animal that you can move with strings or by putting your hand inside
  끈으로 또는 안에 손을 넣음으로써 움직일 수 있는 사람 또는 동물 모양의 장난감

- □ **secret** 비밀
  → something that is kept hidden or that is known about by only a few people
  숨겨져 있거나 극소수의 사람들에 의해 알려져 있는 것

- □ **special** 특별한
  → not ordinary or usual
  평범하거나 일반적이지 않은

- □ **tear** 눈물
  → a drop of salty liquid that flows from the eye
  눈에서 흐르는 짠 액체 방울

- □ **whisper** 속삭이다
  → to speak very quietly
  매우 조용히 말하다

서답형

01 다음 짝지어진 두 단어의 관계가 같도록 빈칸에 알맞은 단어를 쓰시오.

> thick : thin – general : _____

서답형

02 다음 글의 빈칸에 주어진 영영 풀이에 맞는 알맞은 형태의 단어를 쓰시오.

> • Wilfrid told her all his _____.
> something that is kept hidden or that is known about by only a few people

➡ _____

03 다음 중, 밑줄 친 단어의 우리말 뜻이 잘못된 것은?

① We watched TV together last weekend.
　　　　　　　　　　　　　같이, 함께
② Mr. Hunter was cleaning his medal.
　　　　　　　　　닦고 있었다.
③ She has lost her memory.
　　　　　　　　기억
④ His sock puppet always brought laughter
　to his parents.　　　　　　　웃다
⑤ The two girls smiled at each other.
　　　　　　　　　　　서로

[04~05] 다음 영영풀이에 해당하는 단어를 고르시오.

04
> a drop of salty liquid that flows from the eye

① hole　　　　　② tear
③ puppet　　　　④ egg
⑤ water

05
> of great value because of being rare, expensive or important

① fresh　　　　　② favorite
③ thick　　　　　④ special
⑤ precious

서답형

06 다음 우리말에 맞게 주어진 철자로 시작하는 단어를 쓰시오.

> 우리는 매우 열심히 연습했어.
> We practiced s_____ hard.

➡ _____

07 다음 빈칸에 들어갈 말로 알맞은 것은?

> She _____ the football to him.

① whispered　　　② remembered
③ bounced　　　　④ started
⑤ practiced

08 다음 빈칸에 들어갈 단어가 알맞게 짝지어진 것은?

> • His football was as _____ as gold to him.
> • Ms. Cooper got her memory back thanks _____ the little boy.

① fun – of　　　　② productive – as
③ fresh – to　　　④ precious – to
⑤ special – for

01 다음 빈칸에 들어갈 말을 〈보기〉에서 찾아 쓰시오. (필요하면 변형하여 쓰시오.)

> ┤ 보기 ├
>
> laugh   one by one   lose   jump

(1) Wilfrid went to Ms. Cooper and gave her the things _____.

(2) His sock puppet always brought _____ to his parents.

(3) She is a poor old lady because she's _____ her memory.

02 다음 우리말과 같은 표현이 되도록 문장의 빈칸을 채우시오.

(1) 그녀는 자신의 과거를 기억해 내기 시작했다.
➡ She started to _____ her _____.

(2) 그는 암탉이 품고 있던 따뜻한 달걀을 꺼냈다.
➡ He took a warm egg from _____ a _____.

(3) 우리는 열기구를 탔어. 그것은 코끼리처럼 생겼어.
➡ We rode a _____ _____ balloon. It _____ _____ an elephant.

03 다음 문장의 밑줄 친 단어의 반의어를 쓰시오.

(1) Don't forget to <u>bring</u> your books with you.

(2) I never <u>forget</u> your face.
➡ (1) _____ (2) _____

04 다음 문장에 들어갈 알맞은 단어를 〈보기〉의 영영 풀이를 보고 쓰시오.

> ┤ 보기 ├
>
> (1) to speak very quietly
> (2) someone who lives near you
> (3) to move up or away after hitting a surface
> (4) not ordinary or usual

(1) She _____ed to him, "Long ago, I found a small blue egg."

(2) He wanted to know more, so he went to his _____.

(3) The ball _____d twice before he could reach it.

(4) She's a very _____ student.

05 다음 그림에 해당하는 단어를 주어진 철자로 시작하여 쓰시오.

(1)

➡ c_____ a hole

(2)

➡ g_____

(3)

➡ t_____ a party

(4)

➡ s_____ _____

Conversation

1 기억 여부 묻기

Do you remember Mr. Kim, our 6th grade teacher?
우리 6학년 때 선생님이셨던 김 선생님 기억하니?

- Do you remember ~?는 '~를 기억하니?'라는 뜻으로, 특정한 사람이나 사물, 사건에 대한 기억 여부를 묻는 표현이다.

- remember 앞에 '여전히'라는 의미의 still을 넣어 Do you still remember ~?라고 묻기도 한다.

기억 여부를 묻는 표현들

- Don't you remember it? 너는 그것이 기억나지 않니?
- Can[Can't] you remember it? 너는 그것을 기억할 수 있니[없니]?
- Have you forgotten it? 너는 그것을 잊어버렸니?

핵심 Check

1. 다음 대화의 빈칸에 알맞은 말을 쓰시오.

   A: Minji, _____

   B: Sure. I met her last year.

   ① long time no see.
   ② do you remember my aunt?
   ③ how have you been doing?
   ④ what does that mean?
   ⑤ would you like to meet my aunt?

2. 다음 대화의 밑줄 친 부분의 의도로 알맞은 것은?

   A: We had a good time last month. <u>Do you remember that, Sujin?</u>

   B: Sure, Jieun.

   ① 기억 묻기   ② 강조하기
   ③ 허락 구하기   ④ 안부 묻기
   ⑤ 설명하기

② 생각할 시간 요청하기

Let me see. 어디 보자.

- 상대방에게 생각할 시간을 요청할 때는 'Let me think.(생각 좀 해 볼게.)', 'Let me see.(어디 보자.)', 'Just a moment, please.(잠깐만요.)', 'Can[May] I think about it for a moment[while]?'(잠시 생각해 봐도 될까요?) 등으로 말할 수 있다.
  또한 '아직 생각 중이에요.'라는 뜻의 'I'm still thinking.'이라는 말을 덧붙이기도 한다. 앞에 'well', 'hmm'과 같이 주저할 때 쓰는 표현을 붙여 더 자연스럽게 말할 수도 있다.
  생각할 시간 요청을 수락할 때는 'OK.' 혹은 'Sure.'와 같은 표현을 쓰거나 'Take your time.(천천히 하세요.)'과 같은 말을 덧붙이기도 한다.

  - A: What do you see in this picture? 이 사진에서 무엇이 보이니?
    B: Let me see. 생각 좀 해 볼게.
      = Let's see.
      = Let me think.
      = Let me think about it.

- let은 동사원형을 목적격보어로 취하는 점에 유의한다.
  - Let me think about it. (○)
  - Let me thinking about it. (×)
  - Let me to think about it. (×)

핵심 Check

3. 다음 대화의 밑줄 친 부분과 바꾸어 쓸 수 <u>없는</u> 것은?

   A: May I take your order?

   B: <u>Let me see.</u>... What's today's special?

   A: Tomato spaghetti with green salad.

   ① Let me think.
   ② Just a moment.
   ③ Take your time.
   ④ Can I think about it for a while?
   ⑤ May I think about it for a moment?

4. 다음 우리말에 맞도록 괄호 안에서 알맞은 것을 고르시오.

   • 그에 대해 생각해 볼게.

   ➡ Let me (think / to think) about him.

Conversation 교과서 대화문 익히기

Get Ready

(1) G: How are you, Ms. Hwang? We watched TV together last weekend. ❶Do you remember that?

W: Sure, Jieun. I ❷had a great time with you.

(2) M: Hi, Minjun. So, you learned to ❸cut holes in the board last time. ❹Let's practice again now.

B: Okay. Let's see. Is this right?

M: Yes. You remember everything.

(3) G: Hello, Mr. Yang. ❺This is Minji. Do you remember me?

M: Sure, Minji. ❻Thank you for calling.

(1) G: 황 여사님, 안녕하세요? 우리 지난 주말에 함께 TV 를 봤어요. 기억하세요?

W: 물론이지, 지은아. 너랑 즐거운 시간을 보냈지.

(2) M: 안녕, 민준아. 자, 지난번에 판자에 구멍 뚫는 걸 배웠지. 지금 다시 연습해보자.

B: 네. 어디 보자. 이렇게 하는 게 맞나요?

M: 그래, 모두 기억하고 있구나.

(3) G: 안녕하세요, 양 선생님. 저 민지예요. 저 기억하세요?

M: 물론이지, 민지야. 전화 줘서 고맙다.

❶ '그것을 기억하니?'라는 의미로 상대방의 기억을 묻는 표현이다.
❷ have a great time: 즐거운 시간을 보내다.
❸ cut holes는 '구멍을 뚫다'는 의미다.
❹ 'Let's + 동사원형'은 '~하자' '~하는 게 어때?'라는 의미로 상대방에게 권유할 때 사용하는 표현이다.
❺ This is ~.는 전화 통화를 할 때 '저는 ~입니다.'라는 표현이다.
❻ 'Thank you for+ing/명사' 형태로 '~해 주어서 고마워'라는 표현이다.

Check(√) True or False

(1) Ms. Hwang remembers watching TV with Jieun last weekend. T ☐ F ☐

(2) Minjun learned to cut holes in the board. T ☐ F ☐

Start Off Listen & Talk A-1

G: Do you remember Mr. Kim, our 6th grade teacher?

B: Of course. He wore ❶super thick glasses.

G: ❷Guess what? He moved to a new school in February this year.

B: I didn't know that. ❸Let's visit him together.

G: Okay. Good idea.

G: 6학년 때 선생님이셨던 김 선생님 기억나니?

B: 물론이지. 그분은 엄청나게 두꺼운 안경을 쓰고 계셨는데.

G: 있지. 그분이 올해 2월에 새 학교로 옮기셨대.

B: 몰랐어. 함께 찾아뵙자.

G: 응. 좋은 생각이야.

❶ super는 부사로 '매우'란 의미로 사용된다.
❷ 'Guess what?'은 대화를 시작할 때나 대화의 화제를 바꿀 때 사용하는 표현으로 '있잖아'라는 뜻이다.
❸ 'Let's+동사원형'은 '~하자', '~하는 게 어때?'라는 의미로 상대방에게 권유할 때 사용하는 표현이다.

Check(√) True or False

(3) Mr. Kim wore very thick glasses. T ☐ F ☐

(4) The boy knows that Mr. Kim moved to a new school. T ☐ F ☐

Start Off Listen & Talk A-2

B: ❶Do you remember Ms. Lee?

G: Ms. Lee? Who is she?

B: She was our 4th grade English teacher.

G: Now I remember. She taught a lot of pop songs in her class.

B: ❷She was a good dancer, too.

❶ '~을 기억하니?'라는 의미로 상대방의 기억을 묻는 표현이다.
❷ She danced well, too.와 같은 의미다.

Start Off Listen & Talk B

B: Do you remember ❶Ms. Kang, the school nurse?

G: Sure. She was nice to everyone.

B: ❷Guess what? She's getting married next month.

G: Wow! ❸What shall we do for her?

B: ❹Let me see. ❺What about making a special album?

G: That's a good idea.

❶ Ms. Kang, the school nurse의 콤마는 동격을 나타낸다.
❷ 'Guess what?'은 대화를 시작할 때나 대화의 화제를 바꿀 때 사용하는 표현으로 '있잖아'라는 뜻이다.
❸ 'What shall we do~?'는 '우리 무엇을 할까?'라는 제안의 표현이다.
❹ 상대방에게 생각할 시간을 요청할 때 사용하는 표현이다.
❺ 'What about -ing?'는 '~하는 게 어때?'라고 제안하는 표현이다.

Speak Up Look and talk.

A: ❶Do you remember the field trip last year?

B: Of course. We played fun games.

A: I have some funny pictures from ❷it on my phone.

B: That's great!

❶ '~을 기억하니?'라는 의미로 상대방의 기억을 묻는 표현이다.
❷ it은 the field trip을 가리키는 대명사이다.

Speak Up Mission

A: Do you remember my birthday?

B: ❶Let me see. ❷It's June 3. Right?

A: That's right. / That's not right. It's June 13.

❶ 상대방에게 생각할 시간을 요청할 때 사용하는 표현이다.
❷ it은 날짜를 나타내는 비인칭 주어다.

Real-life Scene

G: Do you remember Ms. Park, the old lady ❶who lives alone?

B: Of course. We ❷threw her a birthday party last year.

G: And she cooked *japchae* for us. She put some chicken in it.

B: Right. It was delicious. And we played card games together. Do you remember ❸that?

G: Yes. She won all the rounds. She's really good at games.

B: When are we going to see her next, Mina?

G: ❹Let me see. Next Saturday.

B: Let's take some pictures with her this time.

G: Great idea, Junsu.

❶ who는 주격 관계대명사로 선행사 lady를 수식하는 형용사절을 이끈다.
❷ '파티를 열다'는 의미로 throw 또는 give, have, hold 등의 동사를 사용할 수 있다.
❸ that은 앞 문장의 'we played card games together'를 가리키는 지시대명사다.
❹ 상대방에게 생각할 시간을 요청할 때 사용하는 표현이다.

Express Yourself

1. G: Do you remember the hot air balloon? We rode ❶it in Turkey.

   M: Of course. ❷It looked like an elephant.

2. G: Do you remember the rock?

   M: Is it ❸the one in Taiwan?

   G: Right.

   M: I remember it. It looked like a queen's head.

❶ it은 the hot air balloon을 가리키는 인칭대명사다.
❷ look like + 명사: ~처럼 보이다
❷ the one은 the rock을 가리키는 부정대명사다.

Learning Diary Check Yourself

B: Do you remember the singing competition last year?

G: Of course. We practiced ❶super hard.

B: I have some funny pictures from ❷it on my phone.

G: That's great!

❶ super는 부사로 '매우'의 의미로 사용된다.
❷ it은 the singing competition을 가리킨다.

● 다음 우리말과 일치하도록 빈칸에 알맞은 말을 쓰시오.

Get Ready

1. **G:** _____ are you, Ms. Hwang? We watched TV together last
   weekend. Do you _____ that?

   W: Sure, Jieun. I _____ _____ _____ _____ with you.

2. **M:** Hi, Minjun. So, you learned to_____ holes in the board last
   time. Let's _____ again now.

   B: Okay. _____ _____. Is this right?

   M: Yes. You remember everything.

3. **G:** Hello, Mr. Yang. _____ _____ Minji. Do you remember me?

   M: Sure, Minji. Thank you _____ _____.

Start Off Listen & Talk A

1. **G:** Do you remember Mr. Kim, our 6th grade teacher?

   B: Of course. He _____ _____ thick glasses.

   G: _____ _____? He _____ to a new school in February this
   year.

   B: I didn't know that. _____ visit him together.

   G: Okay. Good idea.

2. **B:** Do you _____ Ms. Lee?

   G: Ms. Lee? _____ is she?

   B: She was our 4th _____ English teacher.

   G: Now I _____. She _____ a lot of pop songs in her class.

   B: She was a _____ dancer, too.

Start Off Listen & Talk B

B: Do you remember Ms. Kang, the _____ _____?

G: Sure. She was nice to everyone.

B: _____ _____? She's _____ _____ next month.

G: Wow! What _____ _____ do for her?

B: _____ _____ _____. What about _____ a special album?

G: That's a good idea.

1. **G:** 황 여사님, 안녕하세요? 우리 지난 주말에 함께 TV를 봤어요. 기억하세요?
   W: 물론이지, 지은아. 너랑 즐거운 시간을 보냈지.

2. **M:** 안녕, 민준아. 자, 지난번에 판자에 구멍 뚫는 걸 배웠지. 지금 다시 연습해 보자.
   B: 네. 어디 보자. 이렇게 하는 게 맞나요?
   M: 그래, 모두 기억하고 있구나.

3. **G:** 안녕하세요, 양 선생님. 저 민지예요. 저 기억하세요.
   M: 물론이지, 민지야. 전화 줘서 고맙다.

1. **G:** 6학년 때 선생님이셨던 김 선생님 기억나니?
   B: 물론이지. 그분은 엄청나게 두꺼운 안경을 쓰고 계셨는데.
   G: 있지. 그분이 올해 2월에 새 학교로 옮기셨대.
   B: 몰랐어. 함께 찾아뵙자.
   G: 응. 좋은 생각이야.

2. **B:** 너 이 선생님 기억나니?
   G: 이 선생님? 누구신데?
   B: 4학년 때 영어 선생님이셨어.
   G: 이제 기억난다. 그분은 수업시간에 팝송을 많이 가르쳐 주셨지.
   B: 춤도 잘 추셨어.

B: 학교 보건 선생님이셨던 강 선생님 기억하니?
G: 물론이지. 그분은 우리 모두에게 친절하셨잖아.
B: 있지. 그분이 다음 달에 결혼하신대.
G: 와. 그분에게 우리 뭘 해드릴까?
B: 어디 보자. 특별한 앨범을 만들어 드리는 게 어떨까?
G: 좋은 생각이야.

해석

Speak Up Look and talk.

A: Do you remember the _____ _____ last year?

B: Of course. We _____ fun games.

A: I have some _____ pictures from it _____ my phone.

B: That's great!

A: 작년에 간 체험학습 기억하니?
B: 물론이지. 우리 신나는 게임을 했잖아.
A: 내 휴대 전화에 그때 찍은 재미있는 사진이 좀 있어.
B: 멋지다!

Speak Up Mission

A: Do you remember my birthday?

B: _____ _____ _____. It's June 3. Right?

A: That's right. / That's not right. It's June 13.

A: 내 생일 기억하니?
B: 어디 보자. 6월 3일이지. 그렇지?
A: 맞아. / 아니야. 6월 13일이야.

Real-life Scene

G: Do you remember Ms. Park, the old lady _____ lives _____?

B: Of course. We _____ her a birthday party last year.

G: And she cooked *japchae* _____ us. She _____ some chicken _____ it.

B: Right. It was delicious. And we _____ card games _____. Do you remember that?

G: Yes. She _____ all the _____. She's really _____ at games.

B: When _____ we _____ _____ see her next, Mina?

G: _____ _____ _____. Next Saturday.

B: _____ _____ some pictures with her this time.

G: Great idea, Junsu.

G: 혼자 사시는 할머니, 박 여사님 기억하니?
B: 물론이지. 작년에 우리가 생신 잔치를 해 드렸잖아.
G: 그리고 그분이 우리를 위해 잡채 요리를 해주셨지. 안에 닭고기를 넣으셨어.
B: 맞아. 맛있었어. 그러고 나서 함께 카드 게임도 했는데. 그거 기억나?
G: 응. 그분이 모든 판을 다 이기셨지. 게임을 정말 잘하셔.
B: 미나야. 다음에 언제 그분을 뵈러 갈 거야?
G: 어디 보자. 다음 주 토요일.
B: 이번에는 그분과 같이 사진을 몇 장 찍자.
G: 좋은 생각이다, 준수야.

Express Yourself

1. **G:** Do you remember the hot air balloon? We _____ it in Turkey.

   M: Of course. It _____ _____ an elephant.

2. **G:** Do you remember the rock?

   M: Is it the _____ in Taiwan?

   G: Right.

   M: I remember it. It _____ _____ a queen's head.

1. G: 그 열기구 기억나? 터키에서 탔었지.
   M: 물론이지. 그것은 코끼리처럼 생겼었지.
2. G: 그 바위 기억나?
   M: 대만에 있는 거지?
   G: 맞아.
   M: 기억나지. 그것은 여왕의 머리처럼 생겼었지.

Learning Diary Check Yourself

B: Do you remember the _____ _____ last year?

G: Of course. We practiced _____ hard.

B: I have some _____ pictures from it on my phone.

G: That's great!

B: 작년에 한 노래 경연 대회 기억하니?
G: 물론이지. 우리 엄청나게 연습했잖아.
B: 내 휴대 전화에 그때 찍은 재미있는 사진이 좀 있어.
G: 멋지다!

01 다음 우리말에 맞도록 빈칸에 들어갈 알맞은 말을 쓰시오.

> G: Hello, Mr. Yang. This is Minji. Do you remember me?
> M: Sure, Minji. 전화 줘서 고맙다.

➡ Thank you _____ _____.

02 다음 대화의 빈칸에 들어갈 말로 알맞지 <u>않은</u> 것은?

> M: Hi, Minjun. So, you learned to cut holes in the board last time. Let's practice again now.
> B: Okay. _____. Is this right?

① Let me see   ② Just a moment
③ Take your time   ④ Let me think
⑤ Let's see

03 다음 대화의 빈칸에 들어갈 말로 가장 적절한 것은?

> B: Do you remember Ms. Lee?
> G: Ms. Lee? Who is she?
> B: She was our 4th grade English teacher.
> G: _____ She taught a lot of pop songs in her class.
> B: She was a good dancer, too.

① I don't know her.   ② Now I remember.
③ Do I know her?   ④ No. She is a math teacher.
⑤ What do you say?

04 다음 대화의 밑줄 친 우리말에 맞게 주어진 어구를 알맞은 순서로 배열하시오.

> A: <u>작년에 간 체험학습 기억하니?</u>
> B: Of course. We played fun games.

(remember, the, last year, do, field trip, you, ?)

➡ _____

[01~02] 다음 대화를 읽고 물음에 답하시오.

> B: Do you remember Ms. Kang, the school nurse?
>
> G: Sure. She was nice to everyone.
>
> B: _____(A)_____ She's getting married next month.
>
> G: Wow! What shall we do for her?
>
> B: Let me see. (B)특별한 앨범을 만들어 드리는 게 어떨까?
>
> G: That's a good idea.

01 위 대화의 빈칸 (A)에 들어갈 말로 알맞은 것은?

① Do you think so?

⑤ That sounds great.

③ Guess what?

④ I don't think so.

② Do you know when she is getting married?

서답형

02 위 대화의 밑줄 친 (B)의 우리말에 맞게 주어진 말로 문장을 시작하여 쓰시오.

➡ What about _____?

[03~04] 다음 대화를 읽고 물음에 답하시오.

> Jenny: Do you remember Mr. Kim, our 6th grade teacher?
>
> Ben: Of course. He wore ⓐsuper thick glasses.
>
> Jenny: Guess what? He moved to a new school in February this year.
>
> Ben: I didn't know that. Let's visit him together.
>
> Jenny: Okay. Good idea.

03 위 대화의 밑줄 친 ⓐsuper의 뜻과 같은 것은?

① We had a super time in Italy.

② She was super when I was having problems.

③ Shakespeare is a super old English poet, playwright, and actor.

④ What a super idea!

⑤ You got the job? That's super!

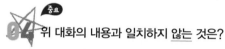

04 위 대화의 내용과 일치하지 않는 것은?

① Mr. Kim was Jenny's teacher.

② Ben remembers Mr. Kim, too.

③ Mr. Kim wore glasses.

④ Mr. Kim moved to another school.

⑤ Ben can't visit Mr. Kim with Jenny.

[05~06] 다음 대화를 읽고 물음에 답하시오.

> G: Do you _____(A)_____ the rock?
>
> M: Is it the one in Taiwan?
>
> G: Right.
>
> M: I _____(B)_____ it. It _____(C)_____ a queen's head.

05 위 대화의 빈칸 (A)와 (B)에 공통으로 들어갈 말로 알맞은 것은?

① remember   ② think

③ win   ④ play

⑤ practice

서답형

06 위 대화의 빈칸 (C)에 들어갈 말을 주어진 단어를 이용하여 과거형으로 쓰시오.

> look

➡ _____

[07~09] 다음 대화를 읽고 물음에 답하시오.

> G: Do you remember Ms. Park, the old lady ___(A)___ lives alone?
> B: (①) Of course. We ___(B)___ her a birthday party last year.
> G: And she cooked *japchae* ___(C)___ us. She put some chicken in it. (②)
> B: Right. It was delicious. And we played card games together. (③) Do you remember that?
> G: Yes. She won all the rounds. She's really good at games. (④)
> B: When are we going to see her next, Mina?
> G: (⑤) Next Saturday.
> B: Let's take some pictures with her this time.
> G: Great idea, Junsu.

07 위 대화의 빈칸 (A)에 들어갈 말로 알맞은 것은?

① what   ② who
③ whose   ④ which
⑤ whom

중요
08 위 대화의 빈칸 (B)와 (C)에 들어갈 말로 알맞은 것은?

① gave – of   ② held – on
③ threw – for   ④ have – for
⑤ had – off

09 위 대화의 (①)~(⑤)에서 다음 주어진 문장이 들어갈 위치로 알맞은 것은?

Let me see.

①   ②   ③   ④   ⑤

중요
10 다음 중 짝지어진 대화가 어색한 것을 고르시오.

① A: Do you remember Anne?
   B: Of course. She had red hair.
② A: What do you remember about her?
   B: Let me see. Ah, she loved flowers.
③ A: Do you remember my birthday?
   B: That's not right. It's July 26.
④ A: Why is she a poor old lady?
   B: Because she's lost her memory.
⑤ A: Do you know the girl who is singing?
   B: Sure. That is Mira.

[11~12] 다음 대화를 읽고 물음에 답하시오.

> (1)
> G: How are you, Ms. Hwang? We watched TV together last weekend. Do you ___(A)___ that?
> W: Sure, Jieun. I had a great time with you.
> (2)
> G: Hello, Mr. Yang. This is Minji. Do you ___(B)___ me?
> M: Sure, Minji. Thank you for ___(C)___.

서답형
11 위 대화의 빈칸 (A)와 (B)에 공통으로 들어갈 단어에 대한 영어 설명을 읽고 알맞은 단어를 쓰시오.

to be able to bring back a piece of information into your mind, or to keep a piece of information in your memory

➡ _____

서답형
12 위 대화의 빈칸 (C)에 주어진 단어를 이용하여 알맞은 형태로 쓰시오.

call

➡ _____

01 다음 대화의 밑줄 친 (A)의 우리말에 맞게 주어진 단어를 이용하여 영어로 쓰시오.

> remember, Ms. Lee

> B: (A)너 이 선생님 기억하니?
> G: Ms. Lee? Who is she?
> B: She was our 4th grade English teacher.
> G: Now I remember. She taught a lot of pop songs in her class.
> B: She was a good dancer, too.

➡ _____

[02~03] 다음 대화를 읽고 물음에 답하시오.

> G: Do you ①remember Ms. Park, the old lady who lives alone?
> B: Of course. We ②threw her a birthday party last year.
> G: And she cooked *japchae* for us. She ③put some chicken in it.
> B: Right. It was delicious. And we played card games together. Do you remember that?
> G: Yes. She won all the rounds. She's really ④bad at games.
> B: When are we going to see her next, Mina?
> G: _____(A)_____ Next Saturday.
> B: Let's ⑤take some pictures with her his time.
> G: Great idea, Junsu.

02 위 대화의 밑줄 친 ①~⑤ 중 어휘의 쓰임이 어색한 것을 찾아 바르게 고치시오.

➡ 틀린 번호: _____

➡ 고쳐 쓰기: _____ → _____

03 위 대화의 빈칸 (A)에 들어갈 표현을 주어진 영영 풀이를 참고하여 세 단어로 쓰시오.

> used when you want to think carefully about something or are trying to remember

➡ _____

[04~05] 다음 대화를 읽고 물음에 답하시오.

> B: Do you remember Ms. Kang, the school nurse?
> G: Sure. She was nice to everyone.
> B: _____(A)_____ She's getting married next month.
> G: Wow! What shall we do for her?
> B: Let me see. _____(B)_____
> G: That's a good idea.

04 위 대화의 빈칸 (A)에 들어갈 표현을 주어진 영영 풀이를 참고하여 쓰시오.

> used before telling someone something interesting or surprising

➡ _____

05 위 대화의 빈칸 (B)에 두 사람이 선생님을 위해 해줄 일을 그림을 참고해서 주어진 단어를 이용하여 쓰시오.

> what, make, a, special

➡ _____

Grammar

교과서

① 주격 관계대명사

> - Wilfrid was a little boy **who** lived next to a nursing home.
>   Wilfrid는 요양원 옆에 사는 어린 소년이었다.
>
> - I bought a book **that** has many pretty pictures. 나는 많은 예쁜 그림이 있는 책을 샀다.

■ 관계대명사는 접속사와 대명사의 역할을 한다. 관계대명사가 이끄는 절은 명사를 수식해 주는 형용사절의 한 종류로 관계대명사절이 꾸며 주는 말을 선행사라고 하고 관계대명사는 앞의 선행사와 같은 대상을 가리킨다. 관계대명사절에서 주어의 역할을 대신하는 관계대명사를 주격 관계대명사라고 하며, 그 다음에는 동사가 온다. 관계대명사 that은 who와 which 대신 사용할 수 있으며 소유격은 없다.

- Einstein was a scientist. He was born in Germany.

  = Einstein was a scientist **who[that]** was born in Germany. Einstein은 독일에서 태어난 과학자였다.

- The dog is very cute. It has a long tail.

  = The dog **which[that]** has a long tail is very cute. 긴 꼬리를 가진 그 개는 매우 귀엽다.

- I know the boy and his dog **that** are running together. 나는 함께 뛰고 있는 소년과 그의 개를 안다.

■ 주격 관계대명사는 선행사에 따라 다음과 같이 사용된다.

선행사	주격 관계대명사
사람	who/that
동물, 사물	which/that
사람 + 동물[사물]	that

■ 주격 관계대명사는 생략할 수 없으나 뒤에 분사가 오는 경우 '주격 관계대명사 + be동사'를 생략할 수 있다.

- The boy (**who is**) playing the piano on the stage is my son.
  무대에서 피아노를 연주하고 있는 소년이 내 아들이다.

핵심 Check

1. 다음 우리말에 맞게 빈칸에 알맞은 말을 쓰시오.

(1) 그는 지난달에 우리 학교에 온 영어 선생님이다.

➡ He's the English teacher ＿＿＿＿＿ came to our school last month.

(2) 나는 설거지를 할 수 있는 로봇을 가지고 싶다.

➡ I want to have a robot ＿＿＿＿＿ can do the dishes.

② 목적격 관계대명사

- It is something **that** you remember. 그것은 네가 기억하는 것이란다.
- The girl **whom** I met was Susan. 내가 만났던 소녀는 Susan이었다.

■ 관계대명사절에서 동사 또는 전치사의 목적어의 역할을 대신하는 관계대명사를 말하며 그 다음에는 '주어+동사 ~'가 온다. 목적격 관계대명사의 선행사가 사람일 경우 who(m), 사물일 경우에는 which가 쓰이며 선행사에 상관없이 that을 쓸 수도 있다.

■ 목적격 관계대명사는 선행사에 따라 다음과 같이 사용된다.

선행사	목적격 관계대명사
사람	whom[who]/that
동물, 사물	which/that
사람 + 동물[사물]	that

- Do you know that lady **whom[that]** he is talking with? 그가 함께 이야기하고 있는 저 여자를 아니?
- I like the dog **which[that]** I adopted last year. 나는 내가 작년에 입양한 개를 좋아한다.

■ 주격 관계대명사와 달리 목적격 관계대명사는 흔히 생략되지만 목적격 관계대명사 바로 앞에 전치사가 오는 경우에는 생략할 수 없다.

- The man (**who/whom/that**) Audrey loves is Jack. Audrey가 사랑하는 남자는 Jack이다.
- The man with **whom** Audrey falls in love is Jack. Audrey가 사랑에 빠진 남자는 Jack이다.

■ 관계대명사절 내에서 관계대명사가 전치사의 목적어 역할을 할 때, 전치사는 관계대명사절 끝이나 관계대명사 바로 앞에 올 수 있다. 전치사가 관계대명사 바로 앞에 올 경우 관계대명사 that은 쓸 수 없다.

- This is the house in **which** she lives. = This is the house **which** she lives in. 이것이 그녀가 사는 집이다.
- This is the house in that she lives. (×)

■ 소유격 관계대명사는 관계대명사절이 되기 전의 문장에서 소유격으로 쓰였던 대명사와 접속사의 역할을 하며 다음에는 명사가 나오고 다른 관계대명사와 달리 완전한 절이 이어진다. 소유격 관계대명사는 whose이며 선행사가 사물일 경우 whose나 of which를 쓴다.

- I saw a house **whose** roof is red. 나는 지붕이 빨간색인 집을 보았다.

핵심 Check

2. 다음 우리말에 맞게 빈칸에 알맞은 말을 쓰시오.

(1) 그는 그가 타려고 하는 기차를 놓쳤다.

➡ He missed the train _____ he wanted to take.

(2) 그는 그가 사랑하는 여자를 그리워했다.

➡ He missed the woman _____ he loved.

01 다음 빈칸에 들어갈 알맞은 것은?

> Do you know the girl _____ is singing?

① whom   ② whose   ③ what

④ which   ⑤ that

02 다음 문장에서 어법상 어색한 부분을 바르게 고쳐 쓰시오.

(1) We met a girl which wore a beautiful dress.

_____ ➡ _____

(2) Do you like that dog who is running around?

_____ ➡ _____

(3) Jiwon is reading a letter whom Mike wrote to her.

_____ ➡ _____

(4) The man with that she is talking is my math teacher.

_____ ➡ _____

03 다음 우리말에 맞게 괄호 안에 주어진 단어를 바르게 배열하시오. (필요하면 어형을 바꿀 것)

(1) Kate는 예쁜 정원이 있는 집에서 살고 싶어 한다.

(garden, have, pretty, that, a)

➡ Kate wants to live in a house _____.

(2) Brian은 그가 갖고 싶어 하는 책을 샀다.

(he, have, want, that, to)

➡ Brian bought the book _____.

04 다음 문장에서 생략할 수 있는 것을 찾아 쓰시오.

(1) She is the girl whom I met yesterday.

(2) Peter gave me a wallet which was made of leather.

➡ (1) _____ (2) _____

01 다음 빈칸에 들어갈 수 있는 말이 나머지와 <u>다른</u> 하나는?

① Do you know the lady _____ is dancing?

② I like the rabbit _____ ears are long.

③ He is the boy _____ I met at the shop yesterday.

④ I like my history teacher _____ is very kind to students.

⑤ The pictures _____ Steve took are very nice.

02 주어진 어휘를 이용하여 다음 우리말을 영어로 쓰시오.

이것이 내가 찾고 있는 책이다. (looking, for)

➡ _____

03 다음 중 어법상 바르지 <u>않은</u> 것은?

① A dictionary is a book which we use to find the meaning of words.

② Do you know the man who is clapping his hands?

③ This is the watch that I bought yesterday.

④ Marianne has a cousin which lives in San Francisco.

⑤ Jiwon is eating the cookies her dad baked for her.

04 다음 괄호 안에서 알맞은 말을 고르시오.

(1) Where is the picture (which / who) was on my desk?

(2) The doctor (who / which) works in this office is very kind.

(3) We had Korean dishes (that / who) were very delicious last night.

(4) It's the key for (that / which) I am looking.

(5) Mariel met the actor (whom / which) she always wanted to meet.

(6) This is the girl (who / whom) came to see you yesterday.

(7) There were an old man and his dog (that / which) used to take a walk together in the afternoon.

05 다음 밑줄 친 that의 성격이 나머지 넷과 <u>다른</u> 것은?

① Someone <u>that</u> I don't know gave me some flowers yesterday.

② I know the man <u>that</u> is playing baduk with his friends.

③ Do you know the girl <u>that</u> is wearing sunglasses?

④ The cap <u>that</u> Mom bought for me is very nice.

⑤ People believed <u>that</u> the earth was flat.

06 다음 빈칸에 알맞은 말이 순서대로 짝지어진 것은?

> • Do you know the girl _____ is playing the piano?
> • She ran a restaurant _____ sold Korean food.

① who – who   ② who – which
③ which – who   ④ which – that
⑤ that – who

서답형

07 다음 중 생략할 수 있는 것을 찾아 쓰시오.

(1) This is the card which I got from Miso.
(2) Do you know the man who is standing just behind a tall woman?

➡ (1) _____ (2) _____

08 다음 중 어법상 어색한 문장을 고르시오.

① Is this the novel you were talking about it yesterday?
② How do you like the cake that I cooked for you?
③ The cat which has yellow eyes belongs to Ms. Han.
④ She is the girl whom I talked to about the problem.
⑤ This is the boy who showed me the way to the library.

09 다음 빈칸에 들어갈 수 있는 것을 모두 고르면?

> Christine is a kind girl _____ everyone loves.

① who   ② whom   ③ what
④ that   ⑤ which

10 다음 두 문장을 한 문장으로 바르게 바꾸면?

> • This is a gold medal.
> • We won at the race.

① This is that a gold medal we won at the race.
② This is a gold medal which we won it at the race.
③ This is a gold medal that we won at the race.
④ This is a gold medal that won at the race.
⑤ This is a gold medal who we won at the race.

11 다음 빈칸에 들어갈 알맞은 것은?

> Who broke the vase _____?

① that I made
② which it is very expensive
③ who looks really good
④ that my dad gave it to me
⑤ that I bought it at the shop

중요

12 다음 중 어법상 옳은 문장을 고르시오.

① I hope there is a robot who can do my homework.
② The man which is writing a letter is Mick.
③ Melina likes to take pictures of friends with that she hangs around.
④ Van Gogh painted *Starry Night* who is very famous.
⑤ The girl who I met yesterday was very kind.

13 〈보기〉에서 알맞은 표현을 골라 문장을 완성하시오.

보기
- which I took a rest
- that looked like an elephant
- whom I can trust

(1) We rode a hot air balloon _____

_____.

(2) The sofa on _____ was too hard.

(3) He is the only man _____.

14 다음 밑줄 친 부분의 쓰임이 <u>어색한</u> 것은?

① This is my favorite book <u>which</u> has many beautiful pictures.
② Children <u>who</u> are too young shouldn't use it.
③ Mom bought me a chair on <u>that</u> I take a rest.
④ Alexander <u>who</u> came from Greece made friends with Sandra.
⑤ Frank Jones is the singer <u>who</u> Michelle likes most.

15 주어진 문장의 밑줄 친 부분과 동일한 역할을 하는 것을 두 개 고르시오.

Laura <u>who</u> is my best friend is kind.

① Try to make friends with someone <u>who</u> you can depend on.
② I know a girl <u>who</u> is very honest.
③ <u>Who</u> is the letter from?
④ Sam has a friend <u>who</u> lives in Jeju.
⑤ Kim likes Richard <u>who</u> Amalia loves.

16 관계대명사를 이용하여 주어진 두 문장을 한 문장으로 연결하시오.

(1) • I met a man yesterday.
 • This is the man.
➡ _____
_____

(2) • I don't know the girl.
 • She is singing.
➡ _____
_____

(3) • Julie bought a computer yesterday.
 • She likes it very much.
➡ _____
_____

(4) • He completed drawing two pictures.
 • They look very similar.
➡ _____
_____

(5) • Mary took a picture of a man and his dog.
 • They were crossing the road.
➡ _____
_____

(6) • Mike needs a friend.
 • He wants to play with the friend.
➡ _____
_____

17 우리말에 맞게 괄호 안의 어휘를 바르게 배열하시오.

Amanda는 Steve가 지난주에 그녀에게 말했던 영화를 봤다. (Steve, movie, her, week, watched, talked, that, last, the, to, about)
Amanda _____.

➡ _____
_____

01 다음 두 문장을 관계대명사를 이용하여 한 문장으로 연결하여 쓰시오.

(1) • Sejong was a great King.
　　 • He invented Hangeul.

➡ _____

　 _____

(2) • An elephant is an animal.
　　 • It has a long nose.

➡ _____

(3) • Sharon met a man.
　　 • She loved him very much.

➡ _____

　 _____

(4) • Tony bought a nice bag.
　　 • He gave it to Karen.

➡ _____

　 _____

(5) • There are Ms. Han and her cats.
　　 • They are playing together.

➡ _____

　 _____

02 다음 두 문장을 관계대명사를 써서 한 문장으로 쓰시오.

> This is the bank. Melanie works at the bank.

= (1) This is the bank _____ at.

= (2) This is the bank at _____ .

= (3) This is the bank _____ at.

= (4) This is the bank _____ .

03 다음 그림을 보고 괄호 안에 주어진 어휘를 이용하여 질문을 완성하시오.

(1) Q: Do you know the man _____

　 _____ _____ _____ _____

　 _____? (sitting, wheelchair)

　 A: Yes, I do. He is Mr. Kim.

(2) Q: Do you know the girl _____

　 _____ _____ _____?

　 (playing, cards)

　 A: Yes, I do. She is Jieun.

(3) Q: Do you know the dog _____

　 _____ _____ _____ _____

　 _____? (sleeping, on, chair)

　 A: Yes, I do. It is my pet dog.

04 다음 문장의 잘못된 부분을 바르게 고치시오.

(1) This is the book who was on the table.

_____ ➡ _____

(2) The man which is singing on the stage is the most famous entertainer.

_____ ➡ _____

(3) Abigail will meet the boy whom loves her.

_____ ➡ _____

(4) She bought a scarf which were nice and cheap.

_____ ➡ _____

(5) John wrote a letter which he sent it to his parents.

_____

05 다음 두 문장을 관계대명사를 사용하여 한 문장으로 썼을 때, 빈칸에 해당하는 문장을 쓰시오.

(1) • _____
   • It shows your brand and products.
   ➡ You can create a scene that shows your brand and products.

(2) • Jack sent some flowers to Michelle.
   • _____
   ➡ Jack sent some flowers which he bought at the shop to Michelle.

(3) • The photos show the outside of the building well.
   • _____
   ➡ The photos that I took yesterday show the outside of the building well.

(4) • I want to adopt a dog.
   • _____
   ➡ I want to adopt a dog which can be my friend.

06 아래 〈보기〉 (A)와 (B)에서 각각 서로 관계있는 문장을 선택한 후 관계대명사 who, whom, which 중 하나를 사용하여 한 문장으로 연결하시오.

┌─ 보기 A ─┐
• She has a son.
• Do you like the dog?
• This is the hospital.

┌─ 보기 B ─┐
• I was born in the hospital.
• She is very proud of him.
• It is jumping near the piano.

(1) _____
   _____
(2) _____
(3) _____
   _____

07 다음 문장에서 어법상 어색한 것을 바르게 고쳐 다시 쓰시오.

(1) There are a lot of active seniors which share their knowledge and talents.
   ➡ _____
   _____

(2) What is the title of the film whom you saw yesterday?
   ➡ _____
   _____

(3) Emma bought a dress who looked very expensive.
   ➡ _____
   _____

(4) The woman who is wearing nice glasses are talking on the phone.
   ➡ _____
   _____

(5) The computer which Mom bought it for me last week is really cool.
   ➡ _____
   _____

08 괄호 안에 주어진 어휘를 이용하여 영작하시오.

(1) Adelene은 원하는 컴퓨터를 사려고 돈을 저축한다. (save, that, 10 단어)
   ➡ _____
   _____

(2) 나는 나를 많이 도와주는 친구가 한 명 있다. (have, who, a lot, 9 단어)
   ➡ _____

(3) Sam은 2년 전에 함께 일했던 사람을 만났다. (a man, that, work with, 11 단어)
   ➡ _____
   _____

Reading

What's a Memory?

Wilfrid Gordon Parker was a little boy who lived next to a nursing
who 이하의 절은 앞의 'a little boy'를 수식하는 주격 관계대명사절이다.
home. He liked all the people who lived there. But his favorite person
*'all the people'을 주격 관계대명사절인 'who lived there'가 수식하고 있다. 흔히 선행사에
'all'이 오면 관계대명사는 'that'을 쓰는데, 선행사가 사람을 지칭할 때는 'who'를 쓰는 경향이 있다.*
was Ms. Nancy Gordon Cooper because her middle name was the
same as his. He told her all his secrets.
…와 같은, …와 동일한 '그의 것'이라는 뜻의 소유대명사 = his middle name
One day, Wilfrid's parents were talking about Ms. Cooper.

"Poor old lady," said his mother. "Why is she a poor old lady?" asked

Wilfrid. "Because she's lost her memory," said his father.
'she has lost'를 줄인말(현재완료의 결과 용법)
"What's a memory?" asked Wilfrid.
Wilfrid는 '기억력'의 의미를 이해하지 못하는 어린아이이므로 할머니가 기억이라는 셀 수 있는 물건을 잃어버렸다고 생각하여, 'a memory'
"It is something you remember," said his father. *라고 표현하였다. 즉, Wilfrid는 셀 수 있는 '기*
something과 you 사이에 목적격 관계대명사 that[which]이 생략되어 있음. *억'이라는 물건이 무엇인지 묻고 있다.*
Wilfrid wanted to know more, so he went to his neighbors.
to부정사의 명사적 용법(목적어)
Ms. Jordan was enjoying the sunlight.
과거 진행형
"What's a memory?" he asked.

"Something warm, my child," she said.
문장 앞에 'It is'가 생략되었다. 'something, anything' 등 '-thing'으로 끝나는 부정대명사는 형용사가
Ms. Mitchell was reading a cartoon. *뒤에 오는 후치 수식이 적용된다.*

"What's a memory?" he asked.

"Something that brings you laughter," she said.
문장 앞에 'It is'가 생략되었다. 'that' 이하의 절은 앞의 'something'을 꾸며 주는 관계사절로, 'that'은 주격 관계대명사로 쓰였다. 선행사
Mr. Hunter was cleaning his medal. *가 'something, everything, anything, nothing'일*
때는 관계대명사로 보통 'that'을 쓴다.
"It's something as precious as gold, young man," he said.
'as+형용사/부사의 원급+as'는 '~만큼 …한/하게'를 의미하는 비교 표현이다.

---

memory 기억, 기억력, 추억
next to …의 옆에(= beside)
nursing home 요양원, 양로원
person 사람, 개인
the same as …와 같은, 동종의, 동일한
secret 비밀
sunlight 햇볕, 햇빛
laughter 웃음, 웃음소리
medal 메달, 훈장
precious 귀중한, 값비싼
gold 금

확인문제

● 다음 문장이 본문의 내용과 일치하면 T, 일치하지 않으면 F를 쓰시오.

1 Wilfrid Gordon Parker lived next to a nursing home. ☐

2 Wilfrid didn't like all the people living in a nursing home. ☐

3 Wilfrid's father said Ms. Cooper was a poor old lady. ☐

4 Wilfrid's father said a memory is something you remember. ☐

5 Ms. Jordan was reading a cartoon. ☐

So Wilfrid went back home to look for memories for Ms. Cooper. He

'to look for'는 목적을 나타내는 to부정사의
부사적 용법으로, '…하기 위해'로 해석한다.

'memories'는 복수형으로 쓰여, '추억, 기억 내용'을 뜻하는데, 어린 소년 Wilfrid의 입장에서의 'memories'는 요양원
에 있는 어르신들이 알려 준 '특성을 가진 여러 가지 물건'이라고 생각하고, 해당 물건을 찾고 있음이 뒤에서 밝혀진다.

went into the hen house and took a fresh, warm egg from under a hen.

'from under'는 이중전치사(double prepositions)로 두 개의 전치사가 한 개의 전치사 역할을 한다.
'from behind, from among, since before, till after' 등이 이에 해당한다.

Next, he looked for his sock puppet. It always brought laughter to his

parents. Finally, he found his football in his toy box. It was as precious

동등비교

as gold to him.

Wilfrid went to Ms. Cooper and gave her the things one by one. "What

'gave' 이하는 '동사+간접목적어(…에게)+직접목적어(~을/를)'의 4형식 문형으로 쓰였으며,
3형식 문형인 'gave the things to her one by one'으로 바꿔 쓸 수 있다.

a strange, sweet child!" thought Ms. Cooper, "He's brought all these

'He's brought'는 'He has brought'가 축약된 현재완료 시제의 문장이다.
Wilfrid가 과거에 물건을 가져온 행위가 현재에까지 영향을 미치고 있음을 나타내고 있다.

wonderful things." Then she started to remember her past.

명사적 용법의 to부정사

She held the warm egg and whispered to Wilfrid, "Long ago, I found

a small blue egg in my aunt's garden." She smiled at the sock puppet

~에게 미소를 지었다

and remembered performing a puppet show for her sister. "My sister

'remember+동명사(동사 -ing)'는 과거에 한 일을 기억해 내는 것을 나타내고,
'remember+to부정사'는 앞으로 할 일을 기억하고 있다는 것을 나타낸다.

laughed a lot," said Ms. Cooper. She bounced the football to Wilfrid

많이

and remembered him. "Wilfrid? Wilfrid Gordon Parker! My friend!"

She also remembered their secrets one by one.

The two smiled at each other. Ms. Cooper got her memory back

서로에게

thanks to the little boy with the same middle name as hers.

… 덕분에 = her middle name

hen 암탉
sock 양말(보통 복수형으로 씀)
puppet 인형, 꼭두각시
football 축구공, 축구(미국에서는 미식
축구, 영국에서는 축구 또는 럭비)
one by one 하나씩
share 함께 나누다, 공유하다
whisper 속삭이다
ago … 전에 (과거시제와 함께 쓰이며, 현
재완료 시제와는 함께 쓰지 않음)
aunt 이모, 고모, (외)숙모
perform 공연하다, 연주하다, 수행하다
bounce (공이) 튀다, 튀기다

확인문제

● 다음 문장이 본문의 내용과 일치하면 T, 일치하지 않으면 F를 쓰시오.

1 Wilfrid looked for memories for Ms. Cooper. ☐

2 A warm egg brought laughter to Wilfrid's parents. ☐

3 Wilfrid's football was as precious as gold to him. ☐

4 Ms. Cooper thought Wilfrid was a very strange, unkind child. ☐

5 Ms. Cooper smiled at the sock puppet. ☐

6 Ms. Cooper's sister performed a puppet show for her. ☐

7 Ms. Cooper got her memory back thanks to Wilfrid. ☐

● 우리말을 참고하여 빈칸에 알맞은 말을 쓰시오.

1 _____ a Memory?

2 Wilfrid Gordon Parker was a little boy _____ lived _____ _____ a nursing home.

3 He liked all the people _____ _____ _____.

4 But _____ _____ _____ was Ms. Nancy Gordon Cooper because her middle name was _____ _____ _____ _____.

5 He told her _____ _____ _____.

6 One day, Wilfrid's parents _____ _____ _____ Ms. Cooper.

7 "_____ _____ _____," said his mother.

8 "_____ is she a poor old lady?" _____ Wilfrid.

9 "_____ _____ _____ her memory," said his father.

10 "_____ a memory?" asked Wilfrid.

11 "It is _____ _____ _____," said his father.

12 Wilfrid wanted _____ _____ _____, so he went to his neighbors.

13 Ms. Jordan _____ _____ the sunlight.

14 "What's a memory?" _____ _____.

15 "_____ _____, my child," she said.

16 Ms. Mitchell _____ _____ a cartoon.

17 "_____ _____ _____?" he asked.

18 "Something that _____ _____ _____," she said.

---

1 추억이란 무엇일까?

2 Wilfrid Gordon Parker는 요양원 옆에 사는 어린 소년이었다.

3 그는 그곳에 사는 모든 사람들을 좋아했다.

4 하지만 그가 가장 좋아하는 사람은 Nancy Gordon Cooper 할머니였는데, 그 이유는 그녀의 가운데 이름이 그의 것과 같았기 때문이었다.

5 그는 자기의 모든 비밀을 그녀에게 말했다.

6 어느 날, Wilfrid의 부모님은 Cooper 할머니에 관해 이야기를 하고 있었다.

7 "불쌍한 분." 그의 어머니가 말했다.

8 "왜 불쌍한 분이세요?"라고 Wilfrid가 물었다.

9 "왜냐하면 그분은 기억을 잃으셨거든." 그의 아버지가 말했다.

10 "기억이 뭐예요?" Wilfrid가 물었다.

11 "그것은 네가 기억하는 것이란다."라고 그의 아버지가 말했다.

12 Wilfrid는 더 알고 싶어서, 그의 이웃들에게 갔다.

13 Jordan 할머니는 햇볕을 즐기고 있었다.

14 "기억이 뭐예요?" 그가 물었다.

15 "따뜻한 거란다, 아가야." 그녀가 말했다.

16 Mitchell 할머니는 만화책을 읽고 있었다.

17 "기억이 뭐예요?" 그가 물었다.

18 "너에게 웃음을 가져다주는 것이란다." 그녀가 말했다.

19 Mr. Hunter was _____ _____ _____.

20 "It's something _____ _____ _____ _____, young man," he said.

21 So Wilfrid went back home _____ _____ _____ _____ for Ms. Cooper.

22 He _____ _____ the hen house and took a fresh, warm egg _____ _____ a hen.

23 _____, he _____ _____ his sock puppet.

24 It always _____ laughter _____ his parents.

25 _____, he found his football in his toy box.

26 It was _____ _____ _____ _____ to him.

27 Wilfrid went to Ms. Cooper and gave her the things _____ _____ _____.

28 "What a strange, sweet child!" thought Ms. Cooper, "He's brought _____ _____ _____ _____."

29 Then she started _____ _____ her past.

30 She _____ the warm egg and _____ _____ Wilfrid, "Long ago, I found a small blue egg in my aunt's garden."

31 She _____ _____ the sock puppet and remembered _____ a puppet show _____ her sister.

32 "My sister laughed _____ _____," said Ms. Cooper.

33 She _____ _____ _____ to Wilfrid and remembered him.

34 "Wilfrid? Wilfrid Gordon Parker! _____ _____!"

35 She also remembered their secrets _____ _____ _____.

36 The two smiled at _____ _____.

37 Ms. Cooper _____ her memory _____ thanks to the little boy _____ the same middle name _____ _____.

19 Hunter 할아버지는 자신의 메달을 닦고 있었다.

20 "그건 금처럼 소중한 거지, 어린 친구."라고 그가 말했다.

21 그래서 Wilfrid는 Cooper 할머니께 드릴 기억들을 찾으러 집으로 돌아갔다.

22 그는 닭장 안으로 들어가서 암탉이 품고 있던 신선하고 따뜻한 달걀을 꺼냈다.

23 다음으로, 그는 자신의 양말 인형을 찾았다.

24 그것은 항상 그의 부모님께 큰 웃음을 안겨 주었다.

25 마지막으로, 그는 자신의 장난감 상자 속에서 축구공을 찾아냈다.

26 그것은 그에게는 금만큼이나 소중했다.

27 Wilfrid는 Cooper 할머니께 가서 그녀에게 그 물건들을 하나씩 드렸다.

28 "이상하면서도 귀여운 아이구나! 이 멋진 물건들을 다 가져오다니 말이야."라고 Cooper 할머니는 생각했다.

29 그러다가 그녀는 자신의 과거를 기억해 내기 시작했다.

30 그녀는 따뜻한 달걀을 쥐고 Wilfrid에게, "오래 전에, 나는 나의 이모님 댁 정원에서 작고 푸른 알을 찾았단다."라고 속삭였다.

31 그녀는 양말 인형을 보며 미소를 짓다가 자기 여동생에게 인형극을 공연해 주었던 것을 기억해 냈다.

32 "내 여동생이 엄청나게 웃었지."라고 Cooper 할머니가 말했다.

33 그녀는 축구공을 바닥에 튀게해서 Wilfrid에게 던져 주다가 그를 기억해 냈다.

34 "Wilfrid? Wilfrid Gordon Parker! 내 친구!"

35 그녀는 또한 그들만의 비밀을 하나씩 기억해 냈다.

36 두 사람은 서로 바라보며 미소지었다.

37 Cooper 할머니는 가운데 이름이 자신의 것과 같은 어린 소년 덕분에 기억을 다시 찾게 되었다.

● 우리말을 참고하여 본문을 영작하시오.

1 추억이란 무엇일까?
➡ _____

2 Wilfrid Gordon Parker는 요양원 옆에 사는 어린 소년이었다.
➡ _____

3 그는 그곳에 사는 모든 사람들을 좋아했다
➡ _____

4 하지만 그가 가장 좋아하는 사람은 Nancy Gordon Cooper 할머니였는데, 그 이유는 그녀의 가운데 이름이 그의 것과 같았기 때문이었다..
➡ _____

5 그는 자기의 모든 비밀을 그녀에게 말했다.
➡ _____

6 어느 날, Wilfrid의 부모님은 Cooper 할머니에 관해 이야기를 하고 있었다.
➡ _____

7 "불쌍한 분." 그의 어머니가 말했다.
➡ _____

8 "왜 불쌍한 분이세요?"라고 Wilfrid가 물었다.
➡ _____

9 "왜냐하면 그분은 기억을 잃으셨거든." 그의 아버지가 말했다.
➡ _____

10 "기억이 뭐예요?" Wilfrid가 물었다
➡ _____

11 "그것은 네가 기억하는 것이란다."라고 그의 아버지가 말했다.
➡ _____

12 Wilfrid는 더 알고 싶어서, 그의 이웃들에게 갔다.
➡ _____

13 Jordan 할머니는 햇볕을 즐기고 있었다.
➡ _____

14 "기억이 뭐예요?" 그가 물었다.
➡ _____

15 "따뜻한 거란다, 아가야." 그녀가 말했다.
➡ _____

16 Mitchell 할머니는 만화책을 읽고 있었다.
➡ _____

17 "기억이 뭐예요?" 그가 물었다.
➡ _____

18 "너에게 웃음을 가져다주는 것이란다." 그녀가 말했다.
➡ _____

19 Hunter 할아버지는 자신의 메달을 닦고 있었다.

➡ _____

20 "그건 금처럼 소중한 거지, 어린 친구."라고 그가 말했다.

➡ _____

21 그래서 Wilfrid는 Cooper 할머니께 드릴 기억들을 찾으러 집으로 돌아갔다.

➡ _____

22 그는 닭장 안으로 들어가서 암탉이 품고 있던 신선하고 따뜻한 달걀을 꺼냈다.

➡ _____

23 다음으로, 그는 자신의 양말 인형을 찾았다.

➡ _____

24 그것은 항상 그의 부모님께 큰 웃음을 안겨 주었다.

➡ _____

25 마지막으로, 그는 자신의 장난감 상자 속에서 축구공을 찾아냈다.

➡ _____

26 그것은 그에게는 금만큼이나 소중했다.

➡ _____

27 Wilfrid는 Cooper 할머니께 가서 그녀에게 그 물건들을 하나씩 드렸다.

➡ _____

28 "이상하면서도 귀여운 아이구나! 이 멋진 물건들을 다 가져오다니 말이야."라고 Cooper 할머니는 생각했다.

➡ _____

29 그러다가 그녀는 자신의 과거를 기억해 내기 시작했다.

➡ _____

30 그녀는 따뜻한 달걀을 쥐고 Wilfrid에게, "오래 전에, 나는 나의 이모님 댁 정원에서 작고 푸른 알을 찾았단다."라고 속삭였다.

➡ _____

31 그녀는 양말 인형을 보며 미소를 짓다가 자기 여동생에게 인형극을 공연해 주었던 것을 기억해 냈다.

➡ _____

32 "내 여동생이 엄청나게 웃었지."라고 Cooper 할머니가 말했다.

➡ _____

33 그녀는 축구공을 바닥에 튀게 해서 Wilfrid에게 던져 주다가 그를 기억해 냈다.

➡ _____

34 "Wilfrid? Wilfrid Gordon Parker! 내 친구!"

➡ _____

35 그녀는 또한 그들만의 비밀을 하나씩 기억해 냈다.

➡ _____

36 두 사람은 서로 바라보며 미소 지었다.

➡ _____

37 Cooper 할머니는 가운데 이름이 자신의 것과 같은 어린 소년 덕분에 기억을 다시 찾게 되었다.

➡ _____

[01~03] 다음 글을 읽고 물음에 답하시오.

Wilfrid Gordon Parker was a little boy _____ⓐ_____ lived next to a nursing home. He liked all the people _____ⓑ_____ lived there. But his favorite person was Ms. Nancy Gordon Cooper because her middle name was the same as ⓒhis. He told her all his secrets.

01 위 글의 빈칸 ⓐ와 ⓑ에 공통으로 들어갈 알맞은 말을 모두 고르시오.

① that   ② whom   ③ what
④ who   ⑤ which

02 다음 질문에 대한 알맞은 대답을 주어진 단어로 시작하여 쓰시오. (8 단어)

> Q: Why did Wilfrid like Ms. Cooper most?
> A: Because _____.

➡ _____

03 위 글의 밑줄 친 ⓒhis가 가리키는 것을 영어로 쓰시오.

➡ _____

[04~06] 다음 글을 읽고 물음에 답하시오.

ⓐWilfrid wanted knowing more, so he went to his neighbors.
Ms. Jordan was enjoying the sunlight.
"What's a memory?" he asked.
"Something warm, my child," she said.
Ms. Mitchell was reading a cartoon.
"What's a memory?" he asked.
"ⓑ너에게 웃음을 가져다주는 것이란다," she said.
Mr. Hunter was cleaning his medal.
"It's something as precious as gold, young man," he said.

04 위 글의 밑줄 친 ⓐ에서 어법상 틀린 부분을 찾아 고치시오.

_____ ➡ _____

05 위 글의 제목으로 알맞은 것을 고르시오.

① How to Enjoy the Sunlight
② What's a Memory?
③ Memory Is Something Warm
④ Memory Brings Smile to You
⑤ What Is As Precious As Gold?

06 위 글의 밑줄 친 ⓑ의 우리말에 맞게 한 단어를 보충하여, 주어진 어휘를 바르게 배열하시오.

laughter / you / brings / something

➡ _____

[07~09] 다음 글을 읽고 물음에 답하시오.

So Wilfrid went back home ⓐto look for memories _____ⓑ_____ Ms. Cooper. He went into the hen house and took a fresh, warm egg from under a hen. Next, he looked for his sock puppet. It always brought laughter to his parents. Finally, he found his football in his toy box. It was as precious as gold _____ⓒ_____ him.

07 위 글의 밑줄 친 ⓐto look과 to부정사의 용법이 다른 것을 모두 고르시오.

① It's not easy to be a math teacher.
② He must be smart to solve it.
③ Give me a pen to write with.
④ I stopped to listen to music.
⑤ She was surprised to see him there.

08 위 글의 빈칸 ⓑ와 ⓒ에 들어갈 전치사가 바르게 짝지어진 것은?

① for – from
② at – by
③ on – to
④ for – to
⑤ on – for

09 다음 질문에 대한 알맞은 대답을 주어진 단어로 시작하여 쓰시오. (4 단어)

Q: After Wilfrid went into the hen house, where did he take a fresh, warm egg?
A: He took it _____.

➡ _____

[10~12] 다음 글을 읽고 물음에 답하시오.

Wilfrid went to Ms. Cooper and ⓐgave her the things one by one. "ⓑWhat a strange, sweet child!" thought Ms. Cooper, "ⓒHe's brought all this wonderful things." Then she started to remember her past.

10 위 글의 밑줄 친 ⓐ를 3형식으로 고칠 때 필요한 전치사를 고르시오.

① for
② by
③ of
④ on
⑤ to

11 위 글의 밑줄 친 ⓑ를 다음과 같이 바꿔 쓸 때 빈칸에 들어 갈 알맞은 말을 쓰시오.

➡ He is a _____ strange, sweet child!

12 위 글의 밑줄 친 ⓒ에서 어법상 틀린 부분을 찾아 고치시오.

_____ ➡ _____

[13~15] 다음 글을 읽고 물음에 답하시오.

Wilfrid Gordon Parker was a little boy who lived next to a nursing home. He liked all the people who lived there. But his favorite person was Ms. Nancy Gordon Cooper because her ⓐ name was the same as his. He told her all his secrets.
One day, Wilfrid's parents were talking about Ms. Cooper.
"Poor old lady," said his mother.
"Why is she a poor old lady?" asked Wilfrid.
"Because ⓑshe's lost her memory," said his father.
"ⓒWhat's a memory?" asked Wilfrid.
"It is something you remember," said his father.

13 위 글의 빈칸 ⓐ에 들어갈 알맞은 말을 쓰시오.

➡ _____

14 위 글의 밑줄 친 ⓑshe's와 ⓒWhat's가 각각 무엇의 줄임말 인지 쓰시오.

➡ ⓑ _____ ⓒ _____

15 위 글의 내용과 일치하지 않는 것은?

① Wilfrid는 요양원 옆에 살았다.
② Wilfrid는 Cooper 할머니를 가장 좋아했다.
③ Cooper 할머니는 Wilfrid에게 자신의 모든 비밀을 말했다.
④ Wilfrid의 어머니는 Cooper 할머니가 불쌍하다고 말했다.
⑤ Cooper 할머니는 기억을 잃어버렸다.

[16~18] 다음 글을 읽고 물음에 답하시오.

Wilfrid wanted to know more, so he went to his neighbors.

Ms. Jordan was ⓐenjoying the sunlight.

"What's a memory?" he asked.

"Something warm, my child," she said.

Ms. Mitchell was reading a cartoon.

"What's a memory?" he asked.

"Something that brings you laughter," she said.

Mr. Hunter was cleaning his medal.

"It's something as precious as gold, young man," he said.

16 위 글의 밑줄 친 ⓐenjoying과 문법적 쓰임이 다른 것을 모두 고르시오.

① Playing soccer is good for your health.
② I saw her crying in her room.
③ He is a walking dictionary.
④ Do you mind opening the window?
⑤ She came home running from school.

서답형

17 다음 문장에서 위 글의 내용과 다른 부분을 찾아서 고치시오.

When Wilfrid went to his neighbors, Ms. Jordan was reading a cartoon and said that a memory is something that brings you laughter.

_____ ➡ _____

중요

18 위 글의 주제로 알맞은 것을 고르시오.

① the way to find something warm
② the value of a memory
③ the meaning of a memory
④ the thing which is as precious as gold
⑤ how to get back your memory

[19~21] 다음 글을 읽고 물음에 답하시오.

She held the warm egg and whispered to Wilfrid, "Long ago, I found a small blue egg in my aunt's garden." She smiled at the sock puppet and remembered performing a puppet show for her sister. "My sister laughed a lot," said Ms. Cooper. She bounced the football to Wilfrid and remembered him. "Wilfrid? Wilfrid Gordon Parker! My friend!" She also remembered their secrets one by one.

The two smiled at each other. Ms. Cooper got her memory back ⓐ덕분에 the little boy with the same middle name as ____ⓑ____.

서답형

19 위 글의 밑줄 친 ⓐ의 우리말을 두 단어로 쓰시오.

➡ _____

서답형

20 위 글의 빈칸 ⓑ에 she를 알맞은 형태로 쓰시오.

➡ _____

21 위 글의 요지로 알맞은 것을 고르시오.

① 따뜻한 달걀은 기억력 회복에 좋다.
② Cooper 할머니는 여동생에게 인형극을 공연해 주었다.
③ Cooper 할머니의 제일 친한 친구는 Wilfrid이다.
④ Cooper 할머니는 Wilfrid와 공놀이 하는 것을 좋아했다.
⑤ Cooper 할머니는 Wilfrid 덕분에 기억을 다시 찾게 되었다.

[22~24] 다음 글을 읽고 물음에 답하시오.

So Wilfrid went back home to look for memories for Ms. Cooper. He went into the hen house and took a fresh, warm egg ⓐ암탉이 품고 있던. Next, he looked for his sock puppet. It always brought laughter to his parents. Finally, he found his football in his toy box. It was as precious as gold to him.

서답형

22 Wilfrid가 Ms. Cooper에게 주려고 찾은 물건들을 다음 (A)~(C)로 분류하여 각각 우리말로 쓰시오.

➡ (A) 따뜻한 것: _____
　(B) 웃음을 가져다주는 것: _____
　(C) 소중한 것: _____

서답형

23 위 글의 밑줄 친 ⓐ의 우리말을 네 단어로 쓰시오.

➡ _____

24 위 글을 읽고 알 수 없는 것을 고르시오.

① the reason Wilfrid went back home
② the reason Wilfrid went into the hen house
③ the thing which always brought laughter to Wilfrid's parents
④ the reason the football was as precious as gold to Wilfrid
⑤ the things which Wilfrid found for Ms. Cooper.

[25~27] 다음 글을 읽고 물음에 답하시오.

(①) Wilfrid Gordon Parker is a little boy and he is friends with the old people at the nursing home. (②) His favorite person is Ms. Nancy Gordon Cooper because she has the same middle name as Wilfrid.

(③) He asks everyone he knows about the meaning of a memory. (④) Wilfrid finds a fresh egg for warmth, a sock puppet for laughter, and his precious football. (⑤) When he gives ⓐthem to Ms. Cooper, she gets her memory back.

25 위 글의 흐름으로 보아, 주어진 문장이 들어가기에 가장 적절한 곳은?

One day, Wilfrid hears from his parents that Ms. Cooper has lost her memory.

①　　②　　③　　④　　⑤

서답형

26 위 글의 밑줄 친 ⓐthem이 가리키는 것을 본문에서 찾아 쓰시오.

➡ _____
_____

중요

27 위 글을 읽고 대답할 수 없는 질문은?

① Does Wilfrid get along well with the old people at the nursing home?
② Who is Wilfrid's favorite person in the nursing home?
③ What do Wilfrid's parents say?
④ Does Wilfrid know the meaning of a memory?
⑤ Why is the football precious to Wilfrid?

[01~03] 다음 글을 읽고 물음에 답하시오.

Wilfrid Gordon Parker was a little boy ① who lived next to a nursing home. He liked all the people ②who lived there. But his favorite person was Ms. Nancy Gordon Cooper because her middle name was the same as ③him. He told her all his secrets.

One day, Wilfrid's parents were talking about Ms. Cooper.

"Poor old lady," said his mother.

"Why is she a poor old lady?" asked Wilfrid.

"Because ④she's lost her memory," said his father.

"⑤What's a memory?" asked Wilfrid.

"ⓐIt is something you remember," said his father.

01 위 글의 밑줄 친 ①~⑤ 중 어법상 틀린 것을 찾아 고치시오.

_____ ➡ _____

02 위 글의 밑줄 친 문장 ⓐ에 생략된 단어를 넣어 문장을 다시 쓰시오.

➡ _____

03 본문의 내용과 일치하도록 다음 빈칸에 알맞은 단어를 쓰시오.

> Wilfrid liked Ms. Cooper most because she had _____ _____ _____ _____ as he did.

[04~06] 다음 글을 읽고, 물음에 답하시오.

One day, Wilfrid's parents were talking about Ms. Cooper.

"Poor old lady," said his mother.

"Why is she a poor old lady?" asked Wilfrid.

"Because ⓐshe's lost her memory," said his father.

"What's a memory?" asked Wilfrid.

"ⓑIt is something you remember," said his father.

04 다음 질문에 대한 알맞은 대답을 주어진 단어로 시작하여 쓰시오. (4 단어)

> Q: Why does Wilfrid's mother say that Ms. Cooper is a poor old lady?
>
> A: Because _____.

➡ _____

05 위 글의 밑줄 친 ⓐ를 다음과 같이 바꿔 쓸 때 빈칸에 들어갈 알맞은 말을 쓰시오.

➡ she lost her memory and she _____ it now.

06 위 글의 밑줄 친 ⓑIt이 가리키는 것을 본문에서 찾아 쓰시오.

➡ _____

[07~09] 다음 글을 읽고 물음에 답하시오.

Wilfrid wanted to know more, so he went to his neighbors.

Ms. Jordan was enjoying the sunlight.

"What's a memory?" he asked.

ⓐ"Something warm, my child," she said.

Ms. Mitchell was reading a cartoon.

"What's a memory?" he asked.

ⓑ"Something that brings you laughter," she said.

Mr. Hunter was cleaning his medal.

ⓒ"It's something as precious as gold, young man," he said.

So Wilfrid went back (A)[to home / home] to look (B)[at / for] memories for Ms. Cooper. He went into the hen house and took a fresh, warm egg from under a hen. Next, he looked for his sock puppet. It always (C)[brought / took] laughter to his parents. Finally, he found his football in his toy box. It was as precious as gold to him.

07 다음 빈칸 (a)~(d)에 알맞은 단어를 넣어, 위 글의 ⓐ~ⓒ를 듣고 Wilfrid가 한 행동과 그 이유를 완성하시오.

> ⓐ He went into the hen house and took a fresh, ____(a)____ because it was warm.
>
> ⓑ He looked for his sock puppet because it always brought his parents ____(b)____ .
>
> ⓒ He found his ____(c)____ in his toy box because it was as ____(d)____ as gold to him.

➡ (a) _____ (b) _____
   (c) _____ (d) _____

08 위 글의 괄호 (A)~(C)에서 문맥이나 어법상 알맞은 낱말을 골라 쓰시오.

➡ (A) _____ (B) _____ (C) _____

09 본문의 내용과 일치하도록 다음 빈칸에 알맞은 단어를 쓰시오.

> Wilfrid's parents always laughed when they saw _____ .

[10~12] 다음 글을 읽고, 물음에 답하시오.

She held the warm egg and ____ⓐ____ to Wilfrid, "Long ago, I found a small blue egg in my aunt's garden." She smiled at the sock puppet and ⓑ자기 여동생에게 인형극을 공연해 주었던 것을 기억해 냈다. "My sister laughed a lot," said Ms. Cooper. She bounced the football to Wilfrid and remembered him. "Wilfrid? Wilfrid Gordon Parker! My friend!" She also remembered their secrets one by one.

The two smiled at each other. Ms. Cooper got her memory back thanks to the little boy with the same middle name as hers.

10 주어진 영영풀이를 참고하여 빈칸 ⓐ에 철자 w로 시작하는 단어를 알맞은 형태로 쓰시오.

> to say something very quietly, using your breath rather than your throat, so that only one person can hear you

➡ _____

11 위 글의 밑줄 친 ⓑ의 우리말에 맞게 한 단어를 보충하여, 주어진 어휘를 알맞게 배열하시오.

> for / a puppet show / her sister / remembered

➡ _____

12 다음 문장에서 위 글의 내용과 <u>다른</u> 부분을 찾아서 고치시오.

> Ms. Cooper got her memory back thanks to the little boy who had the same first name as hers.

_____ ➡ _____

해석

Express Yourself

- On May 29, 2017, we went to India. This is a painting that we bought in the
  날짜 앞에 on   목적격 관계대명사
  market. I'll never forget the experience.

- We took pictures of Korean traditional dancers. We saw them at the town
  take a picture: 사진을 찍다   Korean traditional dancers
  festival.

- On June 7, 2017, we arrived in Laos. We met a girl who was wearing a
  날짜 앞에 on   주격 관계대명사
  beautiful dress. I'll never forget the experience.
               라오스에서 아름다운 옷을 입고 있는 소녀를 만난 것

- We saw a rock. It looked like a queen's head.
             look like+명사: ~처럼 보이다

구문해설 · bought: buy의 과거 · experience: 경험 · traditional 전통적인 · festival: 축제
· arrive in: ~에 도착하다

2017년 5월 29일에 우리는 인도에 갔다. 이것은 우리가 시장에서 산 그림이다. 나는 그 경험을 결코 잊지 못할 것이다.
우리는 한국 전통 무용수들의 사진을 찍었다. 우리는 그들을 마을 축제에서 보았다.
2017년 6월 7일에 우리는 라오스에 도착했다. 우리는 아름다운 옷을 입고 있는 한 소녀를 만났다. 나는 그 경험을 결코 잊지 못할 것이다.
우리는 바위를 보았다. 그것은 여왕의 머리처럼 생겼다.

Do It Yourself

I'd like to tell you about a student teacher I can't forget.
                                        목적격 관계대명사 who[whom. that] 생략
That person is Ms. Jeon.
지시형용사
Don't forget that you're great, Miso! Just go for it.
         명사절을 이끄는 접속사   명령문
This is the bookmark that she gave to me on the last day. When I feel stressed,
                    목적격 관계대명사   스트레스를 받는 것이므로 과거분사를 사용
I always look at this.

구문해설 · go for it: 단호히 목적을 추구하다, 한 번 해보다

나는 잊을 수 없는 교생 선생님에 대해서 너희들에게 말하고 싶다.
그분은 전 선생님이시다.
"네가 훌륭하다는 걸 잊지 마. 미소야! 목적하는 것을 해 보렴."
이건 그분이 마지막 날 내게 주신 책갈피다. 나는 스트레스를 받을 때면, 언제나 이것을 본다.

Link to the World

- There are a lot of active seniors who share their knowledge and talents.
                                  주격 관계대명사절로 선행사 active seniors를 수식한다.
- Mr. Kim in Busan is a smart farmer and teaches people about farming.
                              동사 is와 병렬 형태로 단수 동사 teaches를 사용한다.
- Ms. Lee was a science teacher in the past. Now she works in a park to teach
                                      to teach는 부사적 용법의 부정사로 '~하기 위해'의 의미를 가지고 있다.
  children about plants and birds.

- In Ms. Choi's cooking class, young people learn to make *gimchi* and Korean
                                      learn의 목적어 자리에 사용된 명사적 용법의 부정사다.
  hot pepper sauce.

구문해설 · a lot of 많은 · active 활동적인, 활발한 · senior 노인 · knowledge 지식
· talent 재능 · farming 농사 · past 과거

자신의 지식과 재능을 나누는 활동적인 어르신들이 많이 계시다.
부산의 김 선생님은 스마트 농부이신데 사람들에게 농사에 관한 것을 가르치신다.
이 선생님은 이전에 과학 선생님이셨다. 지금은 공원에서 일하시며 아이들에게 식물과 새에 관해서 가르치신다.
최 여사님의 요리 교실에서는 젊은이들이 김치와 한국의 고추장을 만드는 것을 배운다.

01 다음 주어진 두 단어의 관계가 같도록 빈칸에 알맞은 단어를 쓰시오.

together : apart = general : _____

02 다음 대화의 빈칸 ⓐ와 ⓑ에 들어갈 단어로 바르게 짝지어진 것은?

G: Do you remember Mr. Kim, our 6th grade teacher?
B: Of course. He wore ___ⓐ___ thick glasses.
G: Guess ___ⓑ___? He moved to a new school in February this year.
B: I didn't know that. Let's visit him together.
G: Okay. Good idea.

① super – how
② always – how
③ always – what
④ superly – what
⑤ super – what

03 다음 밑줄 친 부분의 뜻이 <u>잘못된</u> 것은?

① Let's <u>take some pictures</u> with her.
　　 사진을 몇 장 찍다
② <u>What else</u> do you remember about her?
　　 다른 무엇
③ Something that brings you <u>laughter</u> is memory.
　　　　　　　　　　　　　　　　　웃음
④ He went back home to <u>look for</u> memories for her.
　　　　　　　　　　　　 보다
⑤ She started to remember her <u>past</u>.
　　　　　　　　　　　　　　　 과거

04 다음 영영 풀이에 해당하는 것을 고르시오.

to do something to entertain people by acting a play or playing a piece of music

① cut
② throw
③ perform
④ laugh
⑤ remember

05 다음 문장의 빈칸에 들어갈 알맞은 단어를 쓰시오.

We sat _____ to each other.

➡ _____

06 빈칸에 들어갈 말로 알맞은 것은?

Nancy Gordon Cooper's middle name was _____ as Wilfrid Gordon Parker's.

① so
② the same
③ like
④ different
⑤ strange

07 다음 대화의 빈칸에 들어갈 말로 <u>어색한</u> 것은?

M: Hi, Minjun. So, you learned to cut holes in the board last time. Let's practice again now.
B: Okay. _____. Is this right?

① Let me think
② Let's see
③ Just a moment
④ Take your time
⑤ Let's see

08 다음 대화를 알맞은 순서로 배열한 것은?

> (A) Of course. We practiced super hard.
> (B) I have some funny pictures from it on my phone.
> (C) Do you remember the singing competition last year?
> (D) That's great!

① (A) – (B) – (C) – (D)
② (B) – (A) – (C) – (D)
③ (B) – (C) – (A) – (D)
④ (C) – (A) – (B) – (D)
⑤ (C) – (B) – (A) – (D)

[09~10] 다음 대화를 읽고 물음에 답하시오.

> (1)
> G: Do you remember the hot air balloon? We rode ⓐit in Turkey.
> M: Of course. It _____(A)_____ an elephant.
> (2)
> G: Do you remember the rock?
> M: Is it the one in Taiwan?
> G: Right.
> M: I remember ⓑit. It _____(B)_____ a queen's head.

09 대화의 흐름상 빈칸 (A)와 (B)에 공통으로 들어갈 알맞은 어구를 쓰시오.

➡ _____

10 위 대화의 밑줄 친 ⓐ와 ⓑ가 각각 가리키는 것을 찾아 쓰시오.

➡ ⓐ _____
　 ⓑ _____

[11~12] 다음 대화를 읽고 물음에 답하시오.

> G: Do you remember Ms. Park, (A)혼자 사는 할머니?
> B: Of course. We ⓐthrew her a birthday party last year.
> G: And she cooked *japchae* ⓑfor us. She put some chicken ⓒin them.
> B: Right. It was delicious. And we played card games together. Do you remember that?
> G: Yes. She won all the rounds. She's really good at games.
> B: When are we ⓓgoing to see her next, Mina?
> G: Let me see. Next Saturday.
> B: ⓔLet's take some pictures with her this time.
> G: Great idea, Junsu.

11 위 대화의 밑줄 (A)의 우리말에 맞게 주어진 단어를 알맞은 순서로 배열하시오.

> lives, the, old, who, lady, alone

➡ _____

12 위 대화의 밑줄 친 ⓐ~ⓔ 중 어법상 어색한 것은?

① ⓐ　② ⓑ　③ ⓒ　④ ⓓ　⑤ ⓔ

Grammar

13 다음 빈칸에 알맞은 말을 모두 고르시오.

> My grandfather remembers all the people _____ he met in Gyeongju National Park last year.

① who　② whose　③ whom
④ which　⑤ that

14 다음 밑줄 친 부분의 쓰임이 나머지 넷과 <u>다른</u> 것은?

① Wilfrid was a little boy <u>who</u> lived next to a nursing home.

② This is my favorite painting <u>which</u> was painted by Klimt.

③ Kim is satisfied with her cell phone <u>that</u> she bought the previous day.

④ The cute baby <u>who</u> has golden hair is sleeping on the bed.

⑤ I stayed at a hotel in Kuala Lumpur <u>which</u> had big rooms.

15 관계대명사를 이용하여 만든 다음 문장을 원래의 두 문장으로 쓰시오.

> This is the bookmark that she gave to me on the last day.

➡ _____

_____

16 두 문장을 관계대명사를 사용하여 한 문장으로 쓰시오.

(1) • Jiwon is wearing the ribbon.
  • Mira bought it for her.
  ➡ _____
  _____

(2) • Harry chats with the man.
  • Harry made friends with him on line.
  ➡ _____
  _____

(3) • Ginseng is a food.
  • It can make you stay healthy.
  ➡ _____
  _____

(4) • We saw many children.
  • They were playing soccer together.
  ➡ _____
  _____

17 다음 빈칸에 들어갈 수 있는 말이 나머지와 <u>다른</u> 하나는?

① Did you meet the girl _____ came to meet you?

② There lived a princess _____ name was Snow White.

③ Alexander sang the song _____ he liked most.

④ Nancy looked for the medal _____ she won at the race.

⑤ The girl _____ is taking a walk is my daughter.

18 다음 중 어법상 바르지 <u>않은</u> 것은?

① I want to marry someone whom trusts me.

② Take a look at the birds that are flying high in the sky.

③ Diana has two puppies which are brown and white.

④ I know a lady who has the same middle name as mine.

⑤ I know the girl whom you had lunch with at school today.

19 다음 중 어법상 옳은 것은?

① I like Christine from that I got a letter.

② A mentor is a person whom we meet for advice.

③ Dan has two dogs which has brown hair.

④ We saw a rock who looked like a queen's head.

⑤ A computer is a thing whom we do many things with.

20 다음 중 두 문장을 한 문장으로 만들 때 의미가 <u>다른</u> 하나는?

① I want to be a hiphop dancer. A hiphop dancer is loved by many people.
➡ I want to be a hiphop dancer who is loved by many people.
② I will catch the train. It leaves for San Francisco.
➡ I will catch the train that leaves for San Francisco.
③ Mom bought me a present. I liked it very much.
➡ Mom liked a present that bought for me.
④ Mariel is a You-tuber. She is Estonian.
➡ Mariel who is Estonian is a You-tuber.
⑤ Jack lives with Julia. He loves her a lot.
➡ Jack lives with Julia whom he loves a lot.

Reading

[21~23] 다음 글을 읽고 물음에 답하시오.

Wilfrid wanted ⓐto know more, so he went to ①his neighbors.
Ms. Jordan was enjoying the sunlight.
"What's a memory?" he asked.
"Something warm, ②my child," she said.
Ms. Mitchell was reading a cartoon.
"What's a memory?" ③he asked.
"Something that brings you laughter," she said.
Mr. Hunter was cleaning his medal.
"ⓑ그건 금처럼 소중한 거지, ④young man," ⑤he said.

21 위 글의 밑줄 친 ⓐto know와 to부정사의 용법이 같은 것을 모두 고르시오.

① He wished to go to Italy someday.
② She grew up to be a great pianist.
③ I tried to make the dinner in an hour.
④ Do you know the time to meet them?
⑤ I felt very sad to see the sight.

22 밑줄 친 ①~⑤ 중에서 가리키는 대상이 나머지 넷과 <u>다른</u> 것은?

①   ②   ③   ④   ⑤

23 위 글의 밑줄 친 ⓑ의 우리말에 맞게 주어진 어휘를 이용하여 6 단어로 영작하시오.

> something, precious

➡ _____

[24~26] 다음 글을 읽고 물음에 답하시오.

Wilfrid Gordon Parker was a little boy who lived next to a nursing home. He liked all the people who lived there. But ⓐhis favorite person was Ms. Nancy Gordon Cooper because her middle name was the same as ⓑhis. He told her all ⓒhis secrets.
(①) One day, Wilfrid's parents were talking about Ms. Cooper.
(②) "Poor old lady," said ⓓhis mother.
(③) "Why is she a poor old lady?" asked Wilfrid.
(④) "Because Ⓐshe's lost her memory," said his father.
(⑤) "It is something you remember," said ⓔhis father.

24 위 글의 밑줄 친 ⓐ~ⓔ 중에서 문법적 쓰임이 나머지 넷과 다른 것은?

① ⓐ   ② ⓑ   ③ ⓒ   ④ ⓓ   ⑤ ⓔ

25 위 글의 흐름으로 보아, 주어진 문장이 들어가기에 가장 적절한 곳은?

> "What's a memory?" asked Wilfrid.

①   ②   ③   ④   ⑤

26 위 글의 밑줄 친 Ⓐ와 현재완료의 용법이 같은 것을 고르시오.

① I have never seen it before.
② She has been here since last year.
③ Tom has gone to New York.
④ How long have you known him?
⑤ He has already finished the work.

[27~28] 다음 글을 읽고 물음에 답하시오.

So Wilfrid went back home to look for memories for Ms. Cooper. He went into the hen house and took a fresh, warm egg from under a hen. (A)[To begin with / Next], he looked for his sock puppet. It always brought laughter to his parents. Finally, he found his football in his toy box. ⓐIt was as precious as gold to him.

Wilfrid went to Ms. Cooper and gave her the things one by one. "(B)[How / What] a strange, sweet child!" thought Ms. Cooper, "He's brought all these wonderful things." Then she started to remember her (C)[future / past].

27 위 글의 괄호 (A)~(C)에서 문맥이나 어법상 알맞은 낱말을 골라 쓰시오.

➡ (A) _____ (B) _____ (C) _____

28 위 글의 밑줄 친 ⓐit이 가리키는 것을 본문에서 찾아 쓰시오.

➡ _____

[29~30] 다음 글을 읽고 물음에 답하시오.

She held the warm egg and whispered to Wilfrid, "Long ago, I found a small blue egg in my aunt's garden." She smiled at the sock puppet and remembered performing a puppet show for her sister. "My sister laughed a lot," said Ms. Cooper. She bounced the football to Wilfrid and remembered him. "Wilfrid? Wilfrid Gordon Parker! My friend!" She also remembered their secrets one by one.

The two smiled at each other. Ms. Cooper got her memory back thanks to the little boy with _____ⓐ_____ middle name __ⓑ__ her.

29 위 글의 빈칸 ⓐ와 ⓑ에 들어갈 알맞은 말을 고르시오.

① the usual – with
② the same – as
③ the exact – to
④ the same – for
⑤ the similar – as

30 위 글의 내용과 일치하지 않는 것은?

① 오래 전에 Cooper 할머니는 이모님 댁 정원에서 작고 푸른 알을 찾았다.
② Cooper 할머니는 작은 양말 인형을 보고 자기 여동생에게 인형극을 공연해 주었던 것을 기억해 냈다
③ Wilfrid가 축구공을 바닥에 튀게 해서 Cooper 할머니에게 던져 주었다.
④ Cooper 할머니는 Wilfrid와의 비밀들을 하나씩 기억했다.
⑤ Cooper 할머니는 Wilfrid 덕분에 기억을 되찾았다.

출제율 90%

01 다음 짝지어진 단어의 관계가 같도록 빈칸에 알맞은 말을 쓰시오.

> delicious : tasty = _____ : particular

출제율 100%

02 우리말에 맞게 빈칸에 알맞은 단어를 쓰시오.

> • 이것은 금메달이야. 우리가 경주에 참가해서 그것을 땄지.
> (A) This is a gold medal. We _____ it at the race.
> • 그는 요양원 옆에 사는 어린 소년이었다.
> (B) He was a little boy _____ lived _____ _____ a nursing home.

출제율 90%

03 다음은 활동적인 노후 생활에 관한 글이다. 알맞은 단어를 고르시오.

> • There are a lot of active seniors who (A)[share / lack] their knowledge and talents.
> • Ms. Lee was a science teacher in the past. Now she works in a park to (B) [learn / teach] children about plants and birds.
> • Mr. Kim in Busan is a smart (C) [businessman / farmer] and teaches people about farming.

	(A)	(B)	(C)
①	lack	learn	businessman
②	lack	teach	businessman
③	share	learn	farmer
④	share	teach	farmer
⑤	share	teach	businessman

출제율 95%

04 다음 영영 풀이에 해당하는 단어는?

> an empty space in an object, usually with an opening to the object's surface

① plant   ② system
③ hole   ④ space
⑤ bottle

출제율 90%

05 다음 대화의 내용과 일치하지 <u>않는</u> 것은?

> Ariel: Do you remember Ms. Park, the old lady who lives alone?
> Ben: Of course. We threw her a birthday party last year.
> Ariel: And she cooked *japchae* for us. She put some chicken in it.
> Ben: Right. It was delicious. And we played card games together. Do you remember that?
> Ariel: Yes. She won all the rounds. She's really good at games.
> Ben: When are we going to see her next, Ariel?
> Ariel: Let me see. Next Saturday.
> Ben: Let's take some pictures with her this time.
> Ariel: Great idea, Ben.

① Ariel and Ben threw a party for Ms. Park.
② Ms. Park lives alone.
③ The food that Ms. Park cooked was delicious.
④ Ariel and Ben played card games with Ms. Park.
⑤ Ben hopes to take pictures with Ariel.

[06~07] 다음 대화를 읽고 물음에 답하시오.

> B: Do you remember Ms. Kang, ⓐthe school nurse? (①)
> G: Sure. (②) She was nice ⓑto everyone.
> B: Guess what? She's ⓒgetting married next month. (③)
> G: Wow! (④)
> B: ⓓLet me to see. (⑤) What about ⓔmaking a special album?
> G: That's a good idea.

출제율 90%

06 다음 주어진 문장이 들어갈 위치로 알맞은 것은?

> What shall we do for her?

① ② ③ ④ ⑤

출제율 95%

07 위 대화의 밑줄 친 ⓐ~ⓔ 중 어법상 어색한 것은?

① ⓐ ② ⓑ ③ ⓒ ④ ⓓ ⑤ ⓔ

출제율 85%

08 다음 대화의 빈칸에 들어갈 말로 알맞은 것은?

> A: _____
> B: Of course. We played fun games.
> A: I have some funny pictures from it on my phone.
> B: That's great!

① Let me see.
② Do you remember the field trip last year?
③ Do you remember my aunt?
④ Long time no see! How have you been?
⑤ Do you still play the game?

출제율 95%

09 다음 대화의 빈칸에 들어갈 말로 알맞은 것은?

> G: Do you remember Mr. Kim, our 6th grade teacher?
> B: Of course. He wore super thick glasses.
> G: Guess what? He moved to a new school in February this year.
> B: _____ Let's visit him together.
> G: Okay. Good idea.

① I didn't know that.
② How do you know that?
③ That sounds great.
④ I'm happy to hear that.
⑤ Where is he now?

출제율 90%

10 다음 대화의 빈칸 (A)와 (B)에 들어갈 말로 알맞은 것은?

> G: Do you ___(A)___ Mr. Kim, our 6th grade teacher?
> B: Of course. He wore super thick glasses.
> G: Guess what? He moved to a new school in February this year.
> B: I didn't know that. ___(B)___ visit him together.
> G: Okay. Good idea.

① remember – Let's
② forget – Let me see
③ remember – How about
④ remember – What about
⑤ forget – Let's

출제율 90%

11 밑줄 친 who의 용법이 나머지와 다른 하나는?

① He had a son who became a teacher.
② The boy who went out was Josh.
③ I know the boy who Tim met yesterday.
④ The lady who visited Italy is Cindy.
⑤ Rick is my friend who lives in Seoul.

12 밑줄 친 부분 중 어법상 어색한 것은?

> I ①took ②some photos ③of a man and his car ④which ⑤were in the park.

📝 출제율 90%

13 빈칸에 공통으로 들어갈 단어는?

> • Charlotte is the B-boy dancer _____ appeared on TV.
> • The dress _____ Anne is wearing is pretty.

① whose   ② who   ③ that
④ which   ⑤ what

📝 출제율 95%

14 잘못된 부분을 바르게 고쳐 문장을 다시 쓰시오

(1) Jieun is the girl whose I like the best.

➡ _____

(2) These are the pictures who were taken by my brother.

➡ _____

_____

[15~17] 다음 글을 읽고 물음에 답하시오.

Wilfrid wanted to know more, so he went to his neighbors.
Ms. Jordan was enjoying the sunlight.
"What's a memory?" he asked.
"(A)[Warm something / Something warm], my child," she said.
Ms. Mitchell was reading a cartoon.
"What's a memory?" he asked.
"Something ⓐthat brings (B)[you / to you] laughter," she said.
Mr. Hunter was cleaning his medal.
"It's something (C)[as / so] precious as gold, young man," he said.

📝 출제율 90%

15 위 글의 괄호 (A)~(C)에서 어법상 알맞은 것을 골라 쓰시오.

➡ (A) _____ (B) _____
(C) _____

📝 출제율 90%

16 위 글의 밑줄 친 ⓐthat과 문법적 쓰임이 같은 것을 모두 고르시오.

① What's that over there?
② I like the bag that is on the floor.
③ He said that the story was true.
④ Can you see that dog over there?
⑤ It's the best novel that I've ever read.

📝 출제율 95%

17 위 글의 내용과 일치하지 않는 것은?

① Jordan 할머니는 햇볕을 즐기고 있었다.
② Jordan 할머니는 기억이란 따뜻한 것이라고 말했다.
③ Mitchell 할머니는 기억이란 너에게 웃음을 가져다주는 것이라고 말했다.
④ Hunter 할아버지가 그의 메달을 닦고 있었다.
⑤ Hunter 할아버지는 금이 기억보다 더 소중하다고 말했다.

[18~19] 다음 글을 읽고 물음에 답하시오.

So Wilfrid went back home to look for memories for Ms. Cooper. He went into the hen house and took a fresh, warm egg from under a hen. Next, he looked for his sock puppet. It always brought laughter to his parents. ⓐFinally, he found his football in his toy box. It was as precious as gold to him.

18 위 글의 밑줄 친 ⓐFinally와 바꿔 쓸 수 있는 고르시오.

① At first　　② In addition
③ At last　　④ Therefore
⑤ Above all

19 다음 질문에 대한 알맞은 대답을 영어로 쓰시오. (7 단어)

> **Q:** Where did Wilfrid find his football?
> **A:** _____

➡ _____

[20~22] 다음 글을 읽고 물음에 답하시오.

So Wilfrid went back home to look for memories for Ms. Cooper. He went into the hen house and took a fresh, warm egg from under a hen. Next, he looked for his sock puppet. It always brought laughter to his parents. Finally, he found his football in his toy box. It was as precious as gold to him.

Wilfrid went to Ms. Cooper and gave her the things ⓐ하나하나씩. "ⓑWhat a strange, sweet child!" thought Ms. Cooper, "He's brought ⓒ all these wonderful things." Then she started to remember her past.

20 위 글의 밑줄 친 ⓐ의 우리말을 세 단어로 쓰시오.

➡ _____

21 위 글의 밑줄 친 ⓑ를 How로 시작하여 바꿔 쓰시오.

➡ _____

22 다음 중 위 글의 밑줄 친 ⓒ에 해당하지 <u>않는</u> 것을 <u>모두</u> 고르시오.

① the hen house　　② a fresh, warm egg
③ his sock puppet　　④ his football
⑤ his toy box

[23~25] 다음 글을 읽고 물음에 답하시오.

She held the warm egg and whispered to Wilfrid, "Long ago, I found a small blue egg in my aunt's garden." She smiled _____ⓐ_____ the sock puppet and remembered performing a puppet show for her sister. (①) "My sister laughed a lot," said Ms. Cooper. (②) "Wilfrid? Wilfrid Gordon Parker! My friend!" (③) She also remembered ⓑtheir secrets one by one. (④) The two smiled _____ⓐ_____ each other. (⑤) Ms. Cooper got her memory back thanks to the little boy _____ⓒ_____ the same middle name as hers.

23 위 글의 흐름으로 보아, 주어진 문장이 들어가기에 가장 적절한 곳은?

> She bounced the football to Wilfrid and remembered him.

①　　②　　③　　④　　⑤

24 위 글의 빈칸 ⓐ와 ⓒ에 들어갈 전치사가 바르게 짝지어진 것은?

① for – with　　② in – by
③ in – for　　④ at – with
⑤ at – to

25 위 글의 밑줄 친 ⓑtheir가 가리키는 것을 영어로 쓰시오. (소유격으로 쓸 것)

➡ _____

01 다음은 노래 경연대회 추억에 관한 대화다. 대화의 흐름상 알맞은 말을 빈칸에 쓰시오.

> B: _____ last year?
>
> G: Of course. We practiced super hard.
>
> B: I have some funny pictures from it on my phone.
>
> G: That's great!

➡ _____

02 다음은 Mina와 Junsu가 작년에 갔던 봉사활동과 올해 갈 예정인 봉사활동에 관한 대화다. 대화를 읽고 아래 문장을 완성하시오.

> G: Do you remember Ms. Park, the old lady who lives alone?
>
> B: Of course. We threw her a birthday party last year.
>
> G: And she cooked *japchae* for us. She put some chicken in it.
>
> B: Right. It was delicious. And we played card games together. Do you remember that?
>
> G: Yes. She won all the rounds. She's really good at games.
>
> B: When are we going to see her next, Mina?
>
> G: Let me see. Next Saturday.
>
> B: Let's take some pictures with her this time.
>
> G: Great idea, Junsu.

> Last Year
> Mina and Junsu _____ _____ _____ for Ms. Park. And she _____ *japchae* for them. It was _____. After that, they played _____ _____ together.

> This Year
> They are going to visit Ms. Park _____ _____. They are going to _____ _____ with her.

03 다음 대화의 밑줄 친 우리말에 맞게 주어진 어휘를 이용하여 영어로 쓰시오.

> B: Do you remember Ms. Kang, the school nurse?
>
> G: Sure. She was nice to everyone.
>
> B: Guess what? (A)그분이 다음 달에 결혼하셔. (is, get)
>
> G: Wow! What shall we do for her?
>
> B: Let me see. (B)특별한 앨범을 만들어 드리는 게 어떨까? (what about, a special)
>
> G: That's a good idea.

➡ (A) _____

　 (B) _____

04 다음 두 문장을 관계대명사를 이용하여 한 문장으로 바꿔 쓰시오.

(1) • This is a picture.
　　• We bought it at the market.
　➡ _____

_____

(2) • That is the house.
　　• Tom was born in the house.
　➡ _____

_____

(3) • Marilyn is talking with a man.
　　• He is wearing a thick coat.
　➡ _____

_____

ⓐWilfrid wanted to know more, so he went to his neighbors.

Ms. Jordan was enjoying the sunlight.

"What's a memory?" he asked.

"Something warm, my child," she said.

Ms. Mitchell was reading a cartoon.

"What's a memory?" he asked.

"Something that brings you laughter," she said.

Mr. Hunter was cleaning his medal.

"It's something as precious as gold, young man," he said.

05 위 글의 밑줄 친 문장 ⓐ를 as로 시작하여 바꿔 쓰시오.

➡ _____

_____

06 다음 질문에 대한 알맞은 대답을 주어진 단어로 시작하여 쓰시오.

> Q: What did Wilfrid's neighbors say about memory?

➡ • Ms. Jordan: It's _____.

• Ms. Mitchell: It's _____

_____.

• Mr. Hunter: It's _____

_____.

07 위 글의 내용을 다음과 같이 정리하고자 한다. 빈칸에 들어갈 알맞은 단어를 쓰시오.

> Wilfrid asked his three neighbors about the _____ of a memory because he wanted to know more about it.

She held the warm egg and whispered to Wilfrid, "Long ago, I found a small blue egg in my aunt's garden." ⓐShe smiled at the sock puppet and remembered to perform a puppet show for her sister. "My sister laughed a lot," said Ms. Cooper. She bounced the football to Wilfrid and remembered him. "Wilfrid? Wilfrid Gordon Parker! My friend!" She also remembered their secrets one by one.

ⓑThe two smiled at each other. Ms. Cooper got her memory back ⓒ자신의 것과 같은 가운데 이름을 가진 어린 소년 덕분으로.

08 위 글의 밑줄 친 ⓐ에서 어법상 틀린 부분을 찾아 고치시오.

_____ ➡ _____

09 위 글의 밑줄 친 ⓑThe two가 구체적으로 가리키는 것을 영어로 쓰시오.

➡ _____

10 위 글의 밑줄 친 ⓒ의 우리말에 맞게 주어진 어휘를 이용하여 12 단어로 영작하시오.

with, as

➡ _____

_____

창의사고력 서술형 문제

01 다음은 여행에 관한 두 사람의 기억에 관한 글이다. 〈보기〉처럼 여행지에서 한 일과 그에 관한 기억을 묻고 답하는 대화문을 완성하시오.

> ── 보기 ──
>
> **A:** We won a gold medal in London. Do you remember that?
>
> **B:** Sure. / Of course. We won it at the race.

> 〈여행지〉
>
> London - This is a gold medal. / Turkey – We rode a hot air balloon.
> Taiwan – We saw a rock. / Korea – We took pictures of Korean traditional dancers.
>
> 〈기억〉
>
> We won it at the race. / It looked like an elephant.
> It looked like a queen's head. / We saw them at the town festival.

(1) _____

_____

(2) _____

_____

(3) _____

_____

02 관계대명사를 이용하여 자신이 하고 싶은 일을 설명하는 문장을 쓰시오.

> (1) I want to do something _____.
> (2) I want to do something _____.
> (3) I want to do something _____.
> (4) I want to do something _____.
> (5) I want to do something _____.

03 어린 시절의 추억에 관한 이야기를 바탕으로 추억이 담긴 미니북에 쓸 내용을 완성하시오.

> I'd like to tell you about a student teacher I can't forget. That person is Ms. Jeon.

> Don't forget (A)_____ you're great, Miso! Just go for it.
>
> This is the bookmark (B)_____ she gave to me on the last day. When I feel (C)_____,
> I always look (D)_____ this.

단원별 모의고사

01 다음 단어에 대한 영어 설명이 <u>어색한</u> 것은?

① alone: without other people
② hen: an adult female chicken
③ super: a main meal eaten in the evening
④ favorite: best liked or most enjoyed
⑤ puppet: a toy in the shape of a person or animal that you can move with strings or by putting your hand inside

02 다음 짝지어진 단어의 관계가 같도록 빈칸에 알맞은 말을 쓰시오.

answer : reply = go into : _____

03 다음 영영풀이에 해당하는 단어를 고르시오.

the name some people have between their first name and their last name

① middle name   ② surname
③ family name   ④ nickname
⑤ given name

04 다음 대화의 밑줄 친 ⓐ가 가리키는 대상을 찾아 영어로 쓰시오.

A: Do you remember the field trip last year?
B: Of course. We played fun games.
A: I have some funny pictures from ⓐit on my phone.
B: That's great!

➡ _____

05 빈칸 (A)와 (B)에 들어갈 알맞은 단어는?

She smiled ____(A)____ the sock puppet and remembered ____(B)____ a puppet show for her sister.

      (A)   (B)
① on – to show
② at – showing
③ on – performing
④ for – to perform
⑤ at – performing

06 다음 대화의 빈칸에 들어갈 말로 알맞은 것은?

B: Do you remember Ms. Lee?
G: Ms. Lee? Who is she?
B: She was our 4th grade English teacher.
G: _____ She taught a lot of pop songs in her class.
B: She was a good dancer, too.

① Do I know her?
② You're right. I forgot.
③ Now I remember.
④ I don't think she was my English teacher.
⑤ Sorry, I can't remember her.

07 다음 대화의 빈칸에 들어갈 말을 주어진 단어를 이용하여 두 단어의 영어로 쓰시오.

A: Do you remember my birthday?
B: _____ (let) It's June 3. Right?
A: That's not right. It's June 13.

➡ _____

[08~09] 다음 대화를 읽고 물음에 답하시오.

G: Do you remember Ms. Park, the old lady who lives alone? (①)

B: Of course. We threw her a birthday party last year.

G: And she cooked *japchae* for us. She put some chicken in it. (②)

B: Right. It was delicious. And we played card games together. (③)

G: Yes. She won all the rounds. She's really good at games. (④)

B: When are we going to see her next, Mina?

G: Let me see. (⑤) Next Saturday.

B: Let's take some pictures with her this time.

G: Great idea, Junsu.

08 다음 주어진 문장이 들어갈 위치로 알맞은 것은?

> Do you remember that?

① ② ③ ④ ⑤

09 위 대화의 내용과 일치하는 것은?

① Mina visited her grandmother with Junsu.

② The old lady cooked chicken soup.

③ Mina as well as Ms. Park is good at games.

④ Mina and Junsu are going to visit Ms. Park.

⑤ Mina took many pictures with Ms. Park last year.

10 다음 두 사람의 대화가 어색한 것은?

① A: Do you remember the singing competition last year?
B: Of course. We practiced super hard.

② A: Do you remember my birthday?
B: Let me see.

③ A: Do you remember the field trip last year?
B: Of course. I can't remember that.

④ A: Guess what? She's getting married next month.
B: Wow! What shall we do for her?

⑤ A: Hello, Mr. Yang. This is Minji. Do you remember me?
B: Sure, Minji. Thank you for calling.

11 다음 대화를 읽고 답할 수 없는 질문은?

> B: Do you remember Ms. Kang, the school nurse?
>
> G: Sure. She was nice to everyone.
>
> B: Guess what? She's getting married next month.
>
> G: Wow! What shall we do for her?
>
> B: Let me see. What about making a special album?
>
> G: That's a good idea.

① What is Ms. Kang?

② How was Ms. Kang to the students?

③ When is Ms. Kang going to get married?

④ What will they do for Ms. Kang?

⑤ When will they make a special album?

12 대화의 빈칸 (A)와 (B)에 들어갈 말로 자연스러운 것은?

> B: Do you remember Ms. Kang, the school nurse?
> G: Sure. She was nice to everyone.
> B: _____(A)_____ She's getting married next month.
> G: Wow! What shall we do for her?
> B: _____(B)_____ What about making a special album?
> G: That's a good idea.

① Let's see. – I don't know.
② Let's visit her – I don't know.
③ Guess what? – Let me see.
④ Really? – Guess what?
⑤ Just a moment. – Do you think so?

13 다음 중 밑줄 친 that이 관계대명사로 쓰인 것을 모두 고르시오.

① The trouble is that we are short of money.
② Jacky Rose is the pop singer that Jiwon likes.
③ She warned me that I should be more careful.
④ Paul gave me a purse that was made of leather.
⑤ No one can deny the fact that you are wrong.

14 다음 빈칸에 들어갈 알맞은 말을 모두 고르시오.

> Oliver whispered to his aunt _____ was sitting next to him.

① who   ② whose   ③ whom
④ which   ⑤ that

15 다음 주어진 글의 밑줄 친 부분의 쓰임이 어색한 것은?

① Do you remember Ms. Park, the old lady who lives alone?
② Do you like the dog that is chasing the cat?
③ The police are looking for the man and his car which caused the accident.
④ Bella is the smartest girl that I have ever met.
⑤ This is the ring which I bought for her.

[16~18] 다음 글을 읽고 물음에 답하시오.

> Wilfrid wanted to know more, so he went to his neighbors.
> Ms. Jordan was enjoying the sunlight.
> "What's a memory?" he asked.
> "Something warm, my child," she said.
> Ms. Mitchell was ⓐreading a cartoon.
> "What's a memory?" he asked.
> "ⓑSomething that bring you laughter," she said.
> Mr. Hunter was cleaning his medal.
> "It's something as precious as gold, young man," he said.

16 아래 〈보기〉에서 위 글의 밑줄 친 ⓐ와 문법적 쓰임이 같은 것의 개수를 고르시오.

> ┤ 보기 ├
> ① My hobby is reading a cartoon.
> ② Were you reading a cartoon during class?
> ③ Do you enjoy reading a cartoon?
> ④ The boy reading a cartoon is my friend.
> ⑤ She is fond of reading a cartoon.

① 1개   ② 2개   ③ 3개   ④ 4개   ⑤ 5개

17 위 글의 밑줄 친 ⓑ에서 어법상 틀린 부분을 찾아 고치시오.

_____ ➡ _____

18 위 글을 읽고 대답할 수 없는 질문은?

① Why did Wilfrid go to his neighbors?
② Who said that a memory is something warm?
③ What was Ms. Mitchell doing?
④ Why did Mr. Hunter get a medal?
⑤ What did Mr. Hunter say about a memory?

[19~21] 다음 글을 읽고 물음에 답하시오.

So Wilfrid went back home to look for memories for Ms. Cooper. He went into the hen house and took a fresh, warm egg from under a hen. Next, he looked for his sock puppet. ⓐIt always brought laughter to his parents. Finally, he found his football in his toy box. It was as precious as gold to him.

Wilfrid went to Ms. Cooper and gave her the things one by one. "What a strange, sweet child!" thought Ms. Cooper, "He's brought all these wonderful things." ⓑThen she started to remember her past.

19 위 글의 밑줄 친 ⓐ를 4형식으로 고치시오.

➡ _____

20 위 글의 밑줄 친 ⓑ를 다음과 같이 바꿔 쓸 때 빈칸에 들어갈 알맞은 말을 쓰시오.

➡ Then she started _____ her past.

21 위 글의 내용과 일치하지 <u>않는</u> 것은?

① Wilfrid는 닭장 안으로 들어가서 신선하고 따뜻한 달걀을 꺼냈다.
② Wilfrid의 양말 인형은 그의 부모님께 항상 큰 웃음을 안겨 주었다.
③ Wilfrid에게 장난감 상자는 축구공만큼이나 소중했다.
④ Cooper 할머니는 Wilfrid가 이상하면서도 귀여운 아이라고 생각했다.
⑤ Cooper 할머니는 자신의 과거를 기억해 내기 시작했다.

[22~23] 다음 글을 읽고 물음에 답하시오.

She held the warm egg and whispered to Wilfrid, "Long ago, I found a small blue egg in my aunt's garden." She smiled at the sock puppet and remembered performing a puppet show for her sister. "My sister laughed a lot," said Ms. Cooper. She bounced the football to Wilfrid and remembered him. "Wilfrid? Wilfrid Gordon Parker! My friend!" She also remembered their secrets ⓐone by one.

The two smiled at each other. Ms. Cooper got her memory back thanks to the little boy with the same middle name as ⓑhers.

22 위 글의 밑줄 친 ⓐone by one과 바꿔 쓸 수 있는 말을 고르시오.

① side by side   ② one another
③ one after another   ④ time after time
⑤ more and more

23 위 글의 밑줄 친 ⓑhers가 구체적으로 가리키는 것을 영어로 쓰시오.

➡ _____

Lesson

Special

Little Red Writing Hood

교과서
Words & Expressions

Key Words

□ **basket** [bǽskit] 명 바구니

□ **blow** [blou] 동 (입으로) 불다, (바람이) 불다

□ **check** [tʃek] 동 점검하다

□ **dangerous** [déindʒərəs] 형 위험한

□ **end** [end] 명 끝, 마지막

□ **excited** [iksáitid] 형 신난

□ **famous** [féiməs] 형 유명한

□ **follow** [fálou] 동 따라가다, 뒤따르다

□ **front** [frʌnt] 명 정면, 앞

□ **hood** [hud] 명 (외투 등에 달린) 모자

□ **knock** [nɑk] 동 두드리다

□ **laugh** [læf] 동 웃다

□ **leave** [liːv] 동 떠나다

□ **lose** [luːz] 동 잃어버리다, 지다

□ **need** [niːd] 동 ~을 필요로 하다

□ **piggy** [pígi] 명 **pig**의 애칭 (*pl.* **piggies**)

□ **please** [pliːz] 동 ~을 기쁘게 하다

□ **road** [roud] 명 길, 도로

□ **safe** [seif] 형 안전한

□ **scene** [siːn] 명 장면, 광경

□ **shake** [ʃeik] 동 흔들리다

□ **stop** [stɑp] 동 (~하는 것을) 막다, 그만두게 하다

□ **together** [təgéðər] 부 함께

□ **under** [ʌ́ndər] 전 ~ 아래에

□ **writer** [ráitər] 명 작가

Key Expressions

□ **be good for** ~에 좋다

□ **blow one's nose** 코를 풀다

□ **by the way** 그런데, 그건 그렇고

□ **get + 형용사** ~해지다

□ **go away** 가 버리다, 사라지다

□ **Have you ever heard of** ~?
  ~에 대해 들어 본 적 있니?

□ **Let me see.** 어디 보자.. 글쎄.

□ **look at** ~을 보다

□ **look into** …을 들여다보다

□ **No problem.** 그럼요., 전혀 문제되지 않아요.

□ **out of** ~의 밖으로

□ **should not + 동사원형** ~해선 안 된다

□ **take a break** 휴식을 취하다

□ **take out** ~을 꺼내다

□ **talk to oneself** 혼잣말하다

□ **thank A for B** B에 대해 A에게 감사하다

□ **watch + 목적어 + 목적격보어(동사원형/-ing)**
  목적어가 ~하는 것을 보다

□ **What do you mean by that?** 그게 무슨 말이야?

Word Power

※ 서로 반대되는 뜻을 가진 단어

□ **safe**(안전한) ↔ **dangerous**(위험한)

□ **front**(정면, 앞) ↔ **back**(뒤)

□ **kind**(친절한) ↔ **unkind**(불친절한)

□ **famous**(유명한) ↔ **unknown**(알려지지 않은)

□ **end**(끝, 마지막) ↔ **beginning**, **start**(시작)

□ **together**(함께) ↔ **alone**(혼자), **separately**(따로따로)

※ 서로 비슷한 뜻을 가진 단어

□ **check**(점검하다) : **inspect**(점검[검사]하다)

□ **famous**(유명한) : **well-known**(잘 알려진)

□ **follow**(따라가다, 뒤따르다) : **go after**(~를 뒤쫓다, 따라가다)

□ **please**(~을 기쁘게 하다) : **entertain**, **delight**(즐겁게 하다)

□ **end**(끝, 마지막) : **finish**(마지막 부분, 끝)

□ **writer**(작가) : **author**(저자, 작가)

□ **need**(~을 필요로 하다) : **require**(필요로 하다)

□ **dangerous**(위험한) : **harmful**(해로운, 유해한)

English Dictionary

□ **blow** (입으로) 불다
→ to send air out from your mouth
입 밖으로 공기를 내보내다

□ **end** 끝, 마지막
→ the last part of a period of time, event, activity, or story
시간, 사건, 활동 또는 이야기의 마지막 부분

□ **famous** 유명한
→ known about by many people in many places
많은 장소에서 많은 사람들에 의해 알려진

□ **follow** 따라가다, 뒤따르다
→ to go, walk, drive, etc behind or after someone else
다른 어떤 사람의 뒤에서 또는 다른 어떤 사람을 따라서 가거나 걷거나 운전하다

□ **front** 앞, 정면
→ the part of something that faces you
당신과 마주보고 있는 어떤 것의 부분

□ **hood** (외투 등에 달린) 모자
→ a part of a coat, jacket, etc that you can pull up to cover your head
머리를 덮을 수 있게 당겨 쓸 수 있는 코트나 재킷의 부분

□ **knock** 두드리다
→ to hit a door or window with your closed hand to attract the attention of the people inside
안에 있는 사람들의 주의를 끌기 위해 주먹 쥔 손으로 문이나 창문을 치다

□ **leave** 떠나다
→ to go away from a place or a person
한 장소나 한 사람으로부터 떠나가다

□ **please** ~을 기쁘게 하다
→ to make someone happy or satisfied
누군가를 행복하거나 만족스럽게 만들다

□ **safe** 안전한
→ not likely to cause any physical injury or harm
신체적인 손상이나 피해를 유발할 것 같지 않은

□ **stop** (~하는 것을) 막다, 그만두게 하다
→ to not continue, or to make someone or something not continue
계속하지 않거나 또는 다른 사람이나 어떤 것이 계속 이어지지 않도록 만들다

□ **writer** 작가
→ someone who writes books, stories, etc especially as a job
특히 직업으로 책이나 이야기를 쓰는 사람

Little Red Writing Hood

Scene 1: In front of the three little piggies' house
(*Red comes in with a basket of cakes and cookies.*)
Red: Now I can see the three little piggies' house. I'll take a break here under the tree.
(*Wolf walks in and looks into the house.*)
Wolf: Baby piggies! They look delicious. I'll eat them for lunch.
(*Wolf blows the house hard and it is shaking.*)
Red: Oh, that bad Wolf! What can I do to stop him? Let me see. ... That's it! (*To Wolf*) Hey, you! I'll change the story!
Wolf: What do you mean by that?
Red: (*Taking out a pen and writing something*) "There lived three big strong piggies in the house."
There is 구문의 변형: ~이 살았다
Wolf: You shouldn't do that!
'should not+동사원형': '…해선 안 된다'
(*Wolf blows again, but the three big strong piggies come out of the house.*)
Three Piggies: Hey there! Why did you blow our house?
Wolf: Um ... I didn't. I just blew my nose.
Three Piggies: Don't do that again here. Go away!
Wolf: Okay. I'm so sorry.
(*The piggies go back into the house.*)
Wolf: I can't believe this happened. I'm so hungry! (*Looking at Red's basket*) What are those? 'this' 앞에 접속사 'that'이 생략. '(that) this happened'는 'believe'의 목적어
Red: These are cookies for Grandma.
Wolf: Where does she live?
Red: She lives at the end of this road.
Wolf: (*To himself*) Grandma is good for lunch, too. (*To Red*) See you later. (*Wolf leaves.*)
Red: Bye. (*Talking to herself*) Hmm .... He's going to Grandma's. I think I should change the story again. (*Taking out the pen and writing something*) Okay. If my story works, Grandma will be safe. I'll follow 'if'절에서는 현재시제로 미래를 나타내므로 'will work'가 아니라 'works'
him. (*Red leaves.*)

piggy pig의 애칭 (*pl.* piggies)

blow (입으로) 불다, (바람이) 불다

shake 흔들거리다

go away 가 버리다, 사라지다

end 끝, 마지막

talk to oneself 혼잣말하다

📎 **확인문제**

● 다음 문장이 본문의 내용과 일치하면 T, 일치하지 않으면 F를 쓰시오.

1   Red says she'll take a break under the tree. ☐

2   Wolf ate three baby piggies for lunch. ☐

3   Wolf thinks that Grandma is good for lunch, too. ☐

4   Red tells Wolf to go to Grandma's. ☐

5   Red thinks she should change the story again. ☐

Scene 2: Grandma's house

(*Wolf dances around Grandma. She looks very happy and excited.*)

Red: (*Knocking on the door*) Grandma, it's me. Are you okay?

Grandma: (*Laughing happily and opening the door*) Sure, Red. Come on in. I was watching Wolf dance for me. 과거진행형: '보고 있었다.' 'watch + 목적어 + 동사원형'

Red: Hey, Wolf. Thank you for pleasing my grandmother.

Wolf: Well, that's ....

Prince: (*Opening the door and running in*) Hey, you bad Wolf! (*Prince jumps over Wolf.*)

Red: No, no! Stop. He's not dangerous.

Grandma: Right. Look. He is dancing for us. 'you're' 앞에 접속사 'that'이 생략된 구문

Prince: Really? Wolf, I'm sorry. I'm glad you're kind to Grandma.

Wolf: Well, ... I'm glad, too. By the way, do you have anything to eat?

Red: (*Taking some cookies out the basket*) Would you like some cookies?

Wolf: No, thanks. I don't eat cookies. I like chicken.

Red: Don't worry. I'll change the story again. Then you will like eating cookies. (*Checking the basket*) Oh, I lost my pen. What should I do?

Wolf: (*Dancing and crying*) Oh, no! I'm so tired and hungry now.

(*Andersen comes in.*)

Andersen: I think you need my help, right?

Red: Oh, Mr. Andersen. I'm so glad you're here.

Grandma: (*To Red*) Who's that?

Red: He is Mr. Andersen, the famous writer. Have you ever heard of "The Red Shoes"? 앞 문장에서 쓰인 'Have you …?'에 대해 조동사 'have'를 이용하여 답한 것   경험을 묻는 현재완료 구문

Grandma: Yes, I have. Is he the one who wrote that story?

Red: Right. (*To Andersen*) I changed the story, and the poor Wolf got tired and hungry. get+형용사: '…해지다'

Andersen: You can change the story again. 'you' 앞에 목적격 관계대명사 'which[that]'가 생략된 구문

Red: I'm sorry, but I lost the pen you gave to me. Please help me.

Andersen: No problem. I'll write a happy ending for everyone. Is that okay?

Red: That'll be great!

Andersen: All right. I'll use my pen here. "The kind Wolf stops dancing. He can enjoy cakes and cookies."

Wolf: (*Stopping dancing*) I can stop dancing! (*Eating cookies*) And I can eat cookies! Thank you very much. 'stop'은 목적어로 동명사를 취하는 동사

(*Everybody laughs and enjoys cookies together.*)

knock 두드리다

by the way 그런데, 그건 그렇고

📎 **확인문제**

● 다음 문장이 본문의 내용과 일치하면 T, 일치하지 <u>않으면</u> F를 쓰시오.

1 Grandma looks very happy and excited. ☐

2 Wolf thanks Red for pleasing Grandma. ☐

3 Wolf likes cookies but doesn't eat chicken. ☐

4 Wolf is so tired and hungry. ☐

5 Red can change the story again. ☐

6 Mr. Andersen wrote "The Red Shoes." ☐

● 우리말을 참고하여 빈칸에 알맞은 말을 쓰시오.

1 _____ Red Writing Hood

2 _____ 1: _____ _____ _____ the three little piggies' house

3 (Red _____ _____ _____ a basket of cakes and cookies.)

4 Red: Now I can see the three little piggies' house. I'll _____ _____ _____ here under the tree.

5 (Wolf walks in and _____ _____ the house.)

6 Wolf: Baby piggies! They look delicious. I'll eat them _____ _____.

7 (Wolf blows the house hard and it _____ _____.)

8 Red: Oh, that bad Wolf! What can I do _____ _____ him? Let me see. ... That's it! (To Wolf) Hey, you! I'll _____ _____ _____!

9 Wolf: What do you mean _____ _____?

10 Red: (_____ out a pen and _____ something) "There lived three big strong piggies in the house."

11 Wolf: You _____ _____ that!

12 (Wolf blows again, but the three big strong piggies _____ _____ _____ the house.)

13 Three Piggies: _____ _____! Why did you blow our house?

14 Wolf: Um ... I didn't. I just _____ _____ _____.

15 Three Piggies: Don't do that again here. _____ _____!

16 Wolf: Okay. I'm _____ _____.

17 (The piggies _____ _____ _____ the house.)

18 Wolf: I can't believe _____ _____. I'm so hungry! (Looking at Red's basket) What are those?

19 Red: These are cookies _____ Grandma.

20 Wolf: _____ does she live?

21 Red: She lives _____ _____ this road.

22 Wolf: (_____) Grandma is good _____ lunch, too. (To Red) See you later. (Wolf leaves.)

23 Red: Bye. (Talking _____ _____) Hmm .... He's going to Grandma's. I think I should change the story again. (Taking out the pen and writing something) Okay. If my story _____, Grandma will be safe. I'll follow him. (Red leaves.)

24 _____ 2: Grandma's house

25 (Wolf dances around Grandma. She looks very _____ and _____.)

1 빨간 모자

2 장면 1: 아기 돼지 삼 형제의 집 앞에서

3 (Red가 케이크와 과자가 든 바구니를 들고 등장한다.)

4 Red: 이제 아기 돼지 삼 형제의 집이 보인다. 여기 나무 아래에서 좀 쉬어야지.

5 (늑대가 걸어 들어와 집 안을 들여다본다.)

6 늑대: 새끼 돼지들이네! 맛있어 보인다. 점심으로 그들을 먹어야겠어.

7 (늑대가 집을 세게 불자 집이 흔들리고 있다.)

8 Red: 오, 저런 나쁜 늑대 같으니라고! 그를 멈추게 하려면 내가 뭘 할 수 있을까? 어디 보자. … 바로 그거야! (늑대에게) 이봐! 내가 이야기를 바꾸겠어!

9 늑대: 그게 무슨 말이야?

10 Red: (펜을 꺼내 뭔가를 쓰면서) "크고 힘센 아기 돼지 삼 형제가 그 집에 살고 있었다."

11 늑대: 그렇게 하면 안 돼!

12 (늑대가 다시 집을 분다. 그러나 크고 힘센 돼지 삼 형제가 집에서 나온다.)

13 돼지 삼 형제: 이봐, 거기! 왜 우리 집을 불고 있어?

14 늑대: 음… 그러지 않았어. 나는 그냥 코를 풀었을 뿐이야.

15 돼지 삼 형제: 여기서 다시는 그러지 마. 가 버려!

16 늑대: 알았어. 정말 미안해.

17 (돼지들은 집 안으로 다시 들어간다.)

18 늑대: 이런 일이 일어나다니 믿을 수가 없어. 나는 너무 배가 고파! (Red의 바구니를 보며) 그건 뭐야?

19 Red: 할머니께 드릴 과자들이야.

20 늑대: 어디 사시는데?

21 Red: 이 길의 끝에 사셔.

22 늑대: (혼잣말로) 할머니도 점심으로 좋지. (Red에게) 나중에 보자. (늑대가 떠난다.)

23 Red: 안녕. (혼잣말로) 흠…. 그는 할머니 댁으로 갈 거야. 이야기를 다시 바꿔야겠어. (펜을 꺼내서 뭔가를 쓰며) 좋아. 내 이야기가 제대로 돌아가면 할머니는 안전하실 거야. 그를 따라가 봐야지. (Red가 떠난다.)

24 장면 2: 할머니의 집

25 (늑대가 할머니 주변을 맴돌며 춤을 춘다. 할머니는 아주 행복하고 신나 보인다.)

26 Red: (Knocking on the door) Grandma, _____ _____ . Are you okay?

27 Grandma: (Laughing _____ and opening the door) Sure, Red. Come on in. I was watching Wolf _____ for me.

28 Red: Hey, Wolf. Thank you _____ _____ my grandmother.

29 Wolf: Well, _____ ....

30 Prince: (Opening the door and running in) Hey, you bad Wolf! (Prince _____ _____ Wolf.)

31 Red: No, no! Stop. He's not _____ .

32 Grandma: Right. Look. He is dancing _____ us.

33 Prince: Really? Wolf, I'm sorry. I'm glad you're kind _____ Grandma.

34 Wolf: Well, ... I'm glad, too. _____ _____ _____ , do you have anything to eat?

35 Red: (Taking some cookies out the basket) _____ _____ some cookies?

36 Wolf: _____ , _____ . I don't eat cookies. I like chicken.

37 Red: _____ _____ . I'll change the story again. Then you will like eating cookies. (Checking the basket) Oh, I lost my pen. _____ _____ _____ _____ ?

38 Wolf: (Dancing and crying) Oh, no! I'm so _____ and hungry now.

39 (Andersen comes in.)

40 Andersen: I _____ you need my help, right?

41 Red: Oh, Mr. Andersen. I'm _____ _____ you're here.

42 Grandma: (To Red) _____ that?

43 Red: He is Mr. Andersen, the famous writer. Have you ever _____ _____ "The Red Shoes"?

44 Grandma: Yes, I _____ . Is he the one who wrote that story?

45 Red: Right. (To Andersen) I _____ the story, and the poor Wolf _____ _____ and hungry.

46 Andersen: You can _____ _____ _____ again.

47 Red: I'm sorry, but I lost the pen _____ _____ . Please help me.

48 Andersen: _____ _____ . I'll write a happy ending for everyone. Is that okay?

49 Red: _____ be great!

50 Andersen: All right. I'll use my pen here. "The kind Wolf stops _____ . He can enjoy cakes and cookies."

51 Wolf: (Stopping dancing) I can _____ _____ ! (Eating cookies) And I can eat cookies! Thank you very much.

52 (Everybody laughs and _____ _____ _____ .)

26 Red: (문을 두드리며) 할머니. 저예요. 괜찮으세요?

27 할머니: (행복하게 웃으며 문을 열면서) 물론이지, Red야. 어서 들어와. 늑대가 나를 위해 춤추는 걸 보고 있었단다.

28 Red: 이봐. 늑대야. 우리 할머니를 기쁘게 해드려서 고마워.

29 늑대: 음. 그게 ….

30 왕자: (문을 열고 뛰어 들어오며) 이봐, 이 나쁜 늑대야! (왕자가 늑대에게 달려든다.)

31 Red: 아니, 아니에요! 멈춰요. 그는 위험하지 않아요.

32 할머니: 맞아. 보세요. 그가 우리를 위해 춤추고 있잖아요.

33 왕자: 정말요? 늑대야, 미안해. 네가 할머니께 잘해 드린다니 기쁘다.

34 늑대: 음… 나도 기뻐. 그런데. 먹을 것 좀 있어?

35 Red: (바구니에서 과자를 좀 꺼내며) 과자 좀 먹을래?

36 늑대: 고맙지만 됐어. 난 과자를 먹지 않아. 나는 닭고기가 좋아.

37 Red: 걱정하지 마. 내가 이야기를 다시 바꿔야겠네. 그러면 넌 과자 먹는 걸 좋아하게 될 거야. (바구니를 뒤지며) 오, 펜을 잃어버렸어. 어떻게 하지?

38 늑대: (춤을 추며 울부짖으며) 오, 안 돼! 난 지금 너무 피곤하고 배고파.

39 (Andersen이 들어온다.)

40 Andersen: 내 도움이 필요한 것 같은데, 맞지?

41 Red: 오, Andersen 씨. 여기 오셔서 너무 기뻐요.

42 할머니: (Red에게) 저 사람이 누구니?

43 Red: 저분은 유명한 작가 Andersen 씨예요. "빨간 구두"에 대해 들어 보신 적이 있죠?

44 할머니: 그래, 들어 봤지. 그 이야기를 쓴 사람이란 말이지?

45 Red: 맞아요. (Andersen에게) 제가 이야기를 바꿔서 저 불쌍한 늑대가 피곤하고 배고파졌어요.

46 Andersen: 너는 다시 이야기를 바꿀 수 있잖아.

47 Red: 죄송하지만, 제가 작가님이 주신 펜을 잃어버렸어요. 저 좀 도와주세요.

48 Andersen: 문제없지. 내가 모두에게 행복한 결말을 쓸게. 괜찮지?

49 Red: 아주 좋아요!

50 Andersen: 좋아. 여기 내 펜을 써야지. "그 친절한 늑대는 춤추기를 멈춘다. 그는 케이크와 과자를 즐겨 먹을 수 있다."

51 늑대: (춤을 멈추며) 춤을 멈출 수가 있다! (과자를 먹으며) 그리고 과자를 먹을 수 있어! 정말 고마워요.

52 (모두 웃으며 함께 과자를 맛있게 먹는다.)

● 우리말을 참고하여 본문을 영작하시오.

1 빨간 모자
➡ _____

2 장면 1: 아기 돼지 삼 형제의 집 앞에서
➡ _____

3 (Red가 케이크와 과자가 든 바구니를 들고 등장한다.)
➡ _____

4 Red: 이제 아기 돼지 삼 형제의 집이 보인다. 여기 나무 아래에서 좀 쉬어야지.
➡ _____

5 (늑대가 걸어 들어와 집 안을 들여다본다.)
➡ _____

6 늑대: 새끼 돼지들이네! 맛있어 보인다. 점심으로 그들을 먹어야겠어.
➡ _____

7 (늑대가 집을 세게 불자 집이 흔들리고 있다.)
➡ _____

8 Red: 오, 저런 나쁜 늑대 같으니라고! 그를 멈추게 하려면 내가 뭘 할 수 있을까? 어디 보자. … 바로 그거야! (늑대에게) 이봐! 내가 이야기를 바꾸겠어!
➡ _____

9 늑대: 그게 무슨 말이야?
➡ _____

10 Red: (펜을 꺼내 뭔가를 쓰면서) "크고 힘센 아기 돼지 삼 형제가 그 집에 살고 있었다."
➡ _____

11 늑대: 그렇게 하면 안 돼!
➡ _____

12 (늑대가 다시 집을 분다. 그러나 크고 힘센 돼지 삼 형제가 집에서 나온다.)
➡ _____

13 돼지 삼 형제: 이봐, 거기! 왜 우리 집을 불고 있어?
➡ _____

14 늑대: 음… 그러지 않았어. 나는 그냥 코를 풀었을 뿐이야.
➡ _____

15 돼지 삼 형제: 여기서 다시는 그러지 마. 가 버려!
➡ _____

16 늑대: 알았어. 정말 미안해.
➡ _____

17 (돼지들은 집 안으로 다시 들어간다.)
➡ _____

18 늑대: 이런 일이 일어나다니 믿을 수가 없어. 나는 너무 배가 고파! (Red의 바구니를 보며) 그건 뭐야?
➡ _____

19 Red: 할머니께 드릴 과자들이야.
➡ _____

20 늑대: 어디 사시는데?
➡ _____

21 Red: 이 길의 끝에 사셔.

22 늑대: (혼잣말로) 할머니도 점심으로 좋지. (Red에게) 나중에 보자. (늑대가 떠난다.)
➡ _____

23 Red: 안녕. (혼잣말로) 흠…. 그는 할머니 댁으로 갈 거야. 이야기를 다시 바꿔야겠어. (펜을 꺼내서 뭔가를 쓰며) 좋아. 내 이야기가 제대로 돌아가면 할머니는 안전하실 거야. 그를 따라가 봐야지. (Red가 떠난다.)
➡ _____

24 장면 2: 할머니의 집
➡ _____

25 (늑대가 할머니 주변을 맴돌며 춤을 춘다. 할머니는 아주 행복하고 신나 보인다.)
➡ _____

26 Red: (문을 두드리며) 할머니, 저예요. 괜찮으세요?
➡

27 할머니: (행복하게 웃으며 문을 열면서) 물론이지, Red야. 어서 들어와. 늑대가 나를 위해 춤추는 걸 보고 있었단다.
➡

28 Red: 이봐, 늑대야. 우리 할머니를 기쁘게 해드려서 고마워.
➡

29 늑대: 음, 그게 ….
➡

30 왕자: (문을 열고 뛰어 들어오며) 이봐, 이 나쁜 늑대야! (왕자가 늑대에게 달려든다.)
➡

31 Red: 아니, 아니에요! 멈춰요. 그는 위험하지 않아요.
➡

32 할머니: 맞아. 보세요. 그가 우리를 위해 춤추고 있잖아요.
➡

33 왕자: 정말요? 늑대야, 미안해. 네가 할머니께 잘해 드린다니 기쁘다.
➡

34 늑대: 음 … 나도 기뻐. 그런데, 먹을 것 좀 있어?
➡

35 Red: (바구니에서 과자를 좀 꺼내며) 과자 좀 먹을래?
➡

36 늑대: 고맙지만 됐어. 난 과자를 먹지 않아. 나는 닭고기가 좋아.
➡

37 Red: 걱정하지 마. 내가 이야기를 다시 바꿔야겠네. 그러면 넌 과자 먹는 걸 좋아하게 될 거야. (바구니를 뒤지며) 오, 펜을 잃어버렸어. 어떻게 하지?
➡

38 늑대: (춤을 추며 울부짖으며) 오, 안 돼! 난 지금 너무 피곤하고 배고파.
➡

39 (Andersen이 들어온다.)
➡

40 Andersen: 내 도움이 필요한 것 같은데, 맞지?
➡

41 Red: 오, Andersen 씨. 여기 오셔서 너무 기뻐요.
➡

42 할머니: (Red에게) 저 사람이 누구니?
➡

43 Red: 저분은 유명한 작가 Andersen 씨예요. "빨간 구두"에 대해 들어 보신 적이 있죠?
➡

44 할머니: 그래, 들어 봤지. 그 이야기를 쓴 사람이란 말이지?
➡

45 Red: 맞아요. (Andersen에게) 제가 이야기를 바꿔서 저 불쌍한 늑대가 피곤하고 배고파졌어요.
➡

46 Andersen: 너는 다시 이야기를 바꿀 수 있잖아.
➡

47 Red: 죄송하지만, 제가 작가님이 주신 펜을 잃어버렸어요. 저 좀 도와주세요.
➡

48 Andersen: 문제없지. 내가 모두에게 행복한 결말을 쓸게. 괜찮지?
➡

49 Red: 아주 좋아요!
➡

50 Andersen: 좋아. 여기 내 펜을 써야지. "그 친절한 늑대는 춤추기를 멈춘다. 그는 케이크와 과자를 즐겨 먹을 수 있다."
➡

51 늑대: (춤을 멈추며) 춤을 멈출 수가 있다! (과자를 먹으며) 그리고 과자를 먹을 수 있어! 정말 고마워요.
➡

52 (모두 웃으며 함께 과자를 맛있게 먹는다.)
➡

01 다음 짝지어진 단어의 관계가 같도록 빈칸에 알맞은 말을 쓰시오.

> thin : thick – d_____ : safe

[02~03] 다음 대화의 빈칸에 알맞은 것을 쓰시오.

02
> A: _____ you ever heard about the garage sale?
> B: No, I haven't. What is it?

03
> A: What time are you free every Sunday?
> B: _____ me see. I'm free after 2 p.m.

04 다음 빈칸에 공통으로 들어갈 말을 쓰시오.

> • Their songs are full of energy and are good _____ dancing.
> • Thank you _____ helping me.

05 다음 주어진 우리말에 맞게 빈칸을 채우시오. (철자가 주어진 것이 있으면 그 철자로 시작할 것)

(1) 나는 그가 혼잣말을 한다고 생각한다.
➡ I think he's talking to _____.
(2) 당신의 사진 아래에 이름을 쓰세요.
➡ Write your name _____ your picture.
(3) 내가 방을 떠나면 내 아기는 화를 낸다.
➡ My baby g_____ upset when I l_____ the room.

06 다음 빈칸에 알맞은 단어를 〈보기〉에서 골라 쓰시오. (필요하면 어형 변화를 할 것.)

> ┤ 보기 ├
> blow   check   knock   need

(1) Plants _____ light in order to survive.
(2) The first rule in solving any mystery is to _____ the facts.
(3) She _____ onto her coffee to cool it down when I saw her.
(4) We _____ at the door.

07 다음 빈칸을 어법에 알맞게 채우시오. (어휘가 주어진 경우 그 어휘를 활용할 것.)

(1) I was watching Wolf _____ for me. (dance)
(2) I have loved her _____ I first met her at the party.
(3) I needed a sheet of paper _____. (write)
(4) I can't believe _____ this happened.

08 다음 두 문장을 관계대명사를 이용하여 한 문장으로 연결하여 쓰시오.

(1) • I like the pen.
  • You gave it to me.
  ➡ _____
  _____

(2) • Mary had dinner with Sam.
  • Sam is her best friend.
  ➡ _____
  _____

(3) • Kate read the book.
  • It was about global warming.
  ➡ _____
  _____

(A)[Scene / Scenery] 1: In front of the three little piggies' house

(*Red comes in with a basket of cakes and cookies.*)

Red: Now I can see the three little piggies' house. I'll take a break here under the tree.

(*Wolf walks in and looks into the house.*)

Wolf: Baby piggies! They look (B)[delicious / deliciously]. I'll eat them ⓐ lunch.

(Wolf blows the house (C)[*hard / hardly*] and it is shaking.)

Red: Oh, that bad Wolf! What can I do to stop him? Let me see. ... That's it! (*To Wolf*) Hey, you! I'll change the story!

Wolf: ⓑ그게 무슨 말이야?

Red: (*Taking out a pen and writing something*) "There lived three big strong piggies in the house."

Wolf: You shouldn't do that!

09 위 글의 괄호 (A)~(C)에서 문맥이나 어법상 알맞은 낱말을 골라 쓰시오.

➡ (A) _____ (B) _____ (C) _____

10 위 글의 빈칸 ⓐ에 알맞은 말을 쓰시오.

➡ _____

11 위 글의 밑줄 친 ⓑ의 우리말에 맞게 주어진 어휘를 이용하여 6 단어로 영작하시오.

by

➡ _____

Red: (①*Taking some cookies out the basket*) Would you like some cookies?

Wolf: No, thanks. I don't eat cookies. I like chicken.

Red: Don't worry. I'll change the story again. ⓐThen you will like ⓑ _____ cookies. (②*Checking the basket*) Oh, I lost my pen. What should I do?

Wolf: (③*Dancing* and ④*crying*) Oh, no! I'm so ⑤tiring and hungry now.

(*Andersen comes in.*)

Andersen: I think you need my help, right?

Red: Oh, Mr. Andersen. I'm so glad you're here.

Grandma: (*To Red*) Who's that?

Red: He is Mr. Andersen, the famous writer. Have you ever heard of "The Red Shoes"?

12 위 글의 밑줄 친 ①~⑤ 중 어법상 틀린 것을 찾아 고치시오.

➡ _____

13 위 글의 밑줄 친 ⓐThen을 If를 사용하여 고치시오.

➡ _____

14 위 글의 빈칸 ⓑ에 eat을 알맞은 형태로 쓰시오.

➡ _____

15 다음 빈칸에 들어갈 알맞은 단어를 본문에서 찾아 넣어 Andersen에 대한 소개를 완성하시오.

Andersen is a _____ _____ who wrote "The Red Shoes."

단원별 예상문제

✏️ 출제율 95%

01

I have to _____ my nose all the time when I have a cold.

① fall   ② break   ③ blow
④ draw   ⑤ flow

✏️ 출제율 95%

02

Before _____ the train, make sure you have all your belongings with you.

① starting   ② getting   ③ making
④ finding   ⑤ leaving

✏️ 출제율 100%

03 다음 제시된 단어를 사용하여 자연스러운 문장을 만들 수 <u>없는</u> 것은? (형태 변화 가능)

| follow   need   please   shake |

① _____ the bottle before you open it.
② It _____ a new battery.
③ She did it to _____ him.
④ I think I will _____ her advice this time.
⑤ What time do you _____ working?

✏️ 출제율 85%

04 다음 대화의 빈칸에 알맞은 것을 쓰시오.

A: She's a busy bee.
B: _____ do you _____ _____ that?
A: She's a busy worker.

✏️ 출제율 95%

05 〈보기〉의 단어를 사용하여 문장을 만드시오.

┌─ 보기 ─┐
away   by   of   to

(1) _____ the way, will you be free tomorrow evening?
(2) He went _____ like a wind last night.
(3) The crazy man talked _____ himself all the time.
(4) Let's get out _____ here, and go to the movies.
(5) Have you ever heard _____ the new teacher?

✏️ 출제율 100%

06 다음 빈칸에 알맞은 말을 〈보기〉에서 골라 쓰시오.

┌─ 보기 ─┐
though   that   if

(1) We'll drive in the country _____ it's warm tomorrow.
(2) He supported his family _____ he was young.
(3) She told me _____ I should be more careful.

✏️ 출제율 90%

07 다음 문장에서 <u>잘못된</u> 부분을 바르게 고치시오.

(1) I didn't get better if I took the medicine.
(2) I heard Lisa opened the window.
(3) Abigail has met Andy in Seoul then.
(4) If you will find a four-leaf clover, you will have good luck.
(5) John is watering the plant which he bought it last week.

➡ (1) _____   (2) _____
   (3) _____   (4) _____
   (5) _____

08 다음 빈칸에 알맞은 말을 <u>모두</u> 고르시오.

> He will ask Ann the question _____ nobody answered.

① who   ② whose   ③ whom
④ which   ⑤ that

출제율 90%

09 다음 빈칸에 공통으로 알맞은 말을 쓰시오.

> • I want something _____.
> • We eat to live, not live _____.

➡ _____

출제율 95%

10 괄호 안에 주어진 어휘를 빈칸에 알맞게 쓰시오.

> Sean watched the girl _____ for the contest. (practice sing)

➡ _____

출제율 100%

11 다음 괄호 안에서 알맞은 것을 고르시오.

(1) (Though / Because) he is quite old, he enjoys playing soccer.

(2) I heard my friend (calling / called) my name.

(3) If you (open / will open) your umbrella in the house, you will have bad luck.

(4) I have (been / gone) to London twice.

(5) He is looking for creative ways (who/ which) can solve the problems.

[12~14] 다음 글을 읽고 물음에 답하시오.

> **Scene 1**: In front of the three little piggies' house
>
> (*Red comes in with a basket of cakes and cookies.*)
>
> Red: Now I can see the three little piggies' house. I'll take a break here under the tree.
>
> (*Wolf walks in and looks into the house.*)
>
> Wolf: Baby piggies! They look delicious. I'll eat ①them ⓐ lunch.
>
> (*Wolf blows the house hard and ②it is shaking.*)
>
> Red: Oh, that bad Wolf! What can I do ⓑto stop ③him? Let me see. ... That's it! (*To Wolf*) Hey, you! I'll change the story!
>
> Wolf: What do you mean ⓒ that?
>
> Red: (*Taking out a pen and writing something*) "There lived three big strong piggies in the house."
>
> Wolf: ④You shouldn't ⑤do that!

출제율 85%

12 위 글의 밑줄 친 ①~⑤가 가리키는 것에 대한 설명으로 옳지 <u>않은</u> 것을 고르시오.

① baby piggies를 가리킨다.
② the house를 가리킨다.
③ the wolf를 가리킨다.
④ Red를 가리킨다.
⑤ take out a pen을 가리킨다.

출제율 85%

13 위 글의 빈칸 ⓐ와 ⓒ에 들어갈 전치사가 바르게 짝지어진 것은?

① for – by   ② in – by
③ in – from   ④ for – to
⑤ on – to

14 위 글의 밑줄 친 ⓑto stop과 to부정사의 용법이 다른 것을 <u>모두</u> 고르시오. *출제율 90%*

① He works hard <u>to get</u> a good grade.

② It is easy <u>to acquire</u> a bad habit.

③ Ted got up early <u>to go</u> fishing.

④ She was happy <u>to see</u> the show.

⑤ Who was the first person <u>to invent</u> the airplane?

[15~19] 다음 글을 읽고 물음에 답하시오.

(*Wolf blows again, but the three big strong piggies come out of the house.*)

Three Piggies: Hey there! Why did you blow our house?

Wolf: Um ... I didn't. I just blew my nose.

Three Piggies: Don't ⓐdo that again here. Go away!

Wolf: Okay. I'm so sorry.

(*The piggies go back into the house.*)

Wolf: I can't believe this (A)[happened / was happened]. I'm so hungry! (*Looking at Red's basket*) What are those?

Red: These are cookies for Grandma.

Wolf: Where does she live?

Red: She lives at the end of this road.

Wolf: (*To* (B)[*him / himself*]) Grandma is good for lunch, too. (*To Red*) See you later. (*Wolf leaves.*)

Red: Bye. (*Talking to herself*) Hmm .... He's going to Grandma's. I think I should change the story again. (*Taking out the pen and writing something*) Okay. If my story ⓑworks, Grandma will be (C) [dangerous / safe]. I'll follow him. (*Red leaves.*)

15 위 글의 밑줄 친 ⓐdo that의 내용을 영어로 쓰시오. (3 단어) *출제율 100%*

➡ _____

16 위 글의 괄호 (A)~(C)에서 문맥이나 어법상 알맞은 낱말을 골라 쓰시오. *출제율 90%*

➡ (A) _____ (B) _____ (C) _____

17 위 글의 밑줄 친 ⓑworks와 같은 의미로 쓰인 것을 고르시오. *출제율 95%*

① He <u>works</u> for an engineering company.

② Jim is looking for <u>work</u>.

③ This medicine <u>works</u> on me.

④ I bought the complete <u>works</u> of Scott.

⑤ It was very hard <u>work</u>.

18 위 글의 마지막 부분에 어울리는 속담으로 적절한 것을 고르시오. *출제율 95%*

① The grass is greener on the other side of the fence.

② It never rains but it pours.

③ Nothing ventured, nothing gained.

④ Hunger is the best sauce.

⑤ There may be blue and better blue.

19 위 글의 내용과 일치하지 <u>않는</u> 것은?

① 늑대가 다시 집을 불고 있는데, 크고 힘센 돼지 삼 형제가 집에서 나온다.

② 늑대는 돼지 삼 형제의 집을 불고 있는 것이 아니라 코를 풀었을 뿐이라고 한다.

③ 늑대는 일어난 일을 믿을 수 없어 한다.

④ 늑대는 너무 배가 고파서 Red가 할머니께 드릴 과자들을 먹는다.

⑤ Red는 할머니가 안전하시도록 이야기를 다시 바꾸려고 한다.

[20~23] 다음 글을 읽고 물음에 답하시오.

Scene2: Grandma's house
(*Wolf dances around Grandma. She looks very* (A)[*happy / happily*] *and* (B)[*exciting / excited*].)

Red: (*Knocking on the door*) Grandma, it's me. Are you okay?

Grandma: (*Laughing* (C)[*happy / happily*] *and opening the door*) Sure, Red. Come on in. I was watching Wolf dance for me.

Red: Hey, Wolf. Thank you for @<u>pleasing</u> my grandmother.

Wolf: Well, that's ....

Prince: (*Opening the door and running in*) Hey, you bad Wolf! (*Prince jumps over Wolf.*)

Red: No, no! Stop. He's not dangerous.

Grandma: Right. Look. He is dancing for us.

Prince: Really? Wolf, I'm sorry. ⓑ<u>네가 할머니께 잘해 드린다니 기쁘다.</u>

Wolf: Well, ... I'm glad, too. _____ⓒ_____, do you have anything to eat?

20 위 글의 괄호 (A)~(C)에서 어법상 알맞은 낱말을 골라 쓰시오.

➡ (A) _____ (B) _____ (C) _____

21 위 글의 밑줄 친 @pleasing과 문법적 쓰임이 같은 것을 <u>모두</u> 고르시오.

① <u>Growing</u> plants is not easy.

② She finished <u>doing</u> the dishes.

③ Look at the <u>sleeping</u> baby.

④ I heard her <u>singing</u> in her room.

⑤ He came <u>running</u>.

22 위 글의 밑줄 친 ⓑ의 우리말에 맞게 한 단어를 보충하여, 주어진 어휘를 알맞게 배열하시오.

> kind / glad / you're / Grandma / I'm

➡ _____

23 위 글의 빈칸 ⓒ에 들어갈 알맞은 말을 고르시오.

① Therefore ② At last

③ As a result ④ By the way

⑤ In other words

[24~26] 다음 글을 읽고 물음에 답하시오.

Red: (*Taking some cookies out the basket*) Would you like some cookies?

Wolf: No, thanks. I don't eat cookies. I like chicken.

Red: Don't worry. I'll change the story again. @<u>Then you will like eating chicken.</u> (*Checking the basket*) Oh, I lost my pen. ⓑ<u>What should I do?</u>

Wolf: (*Dancing and crying*) Oh, no! I'm so tired and hungry now.

(*Andersen comes in.*)

Andersen: I think you need my help, right?

Red: Oh, Mr. Andersen. I'm so glad you're here.

Grandma: (*To Red*) Who's that?

Red: He is Mr. Andersen, the famous writer. ⓒ <u>Have you ever heard of "The Red Shoes"?</u>

24 위 글의 밑줄 친 ⓐ에서 흐름상 어색한 부분을 찾아 고치시오. (출제율 95%)

➡ _____

25 위 글의 밑줄 친 ⓑ에서 알 수 있는 'I'의 심경으로 가장 알맞은 것을 고르시오. (출제율 90%)

① bored   ② embarrassed

③ satisfied   ④ depressed

⑤ excited

26 위 글의 밑줄 친 ⓒ와 현재완료의 용법이 같은 것을 <u>모두</u> 고르시오. (출제율 100%)

① He <u>has gone</u> to New York.

② I <u>have</u> never <u>heard</u> the news.

③ She <u>has been</u> sick since yesterday.

④ <u>Have</u> you <u>seen</u> it yet?

⑤ How many times <u>have</u> you <u>read</u> it?

[27~31] 다음 글을 읽고 물음에 답하시오.

Grandma: *(To Red)* Who's that?

Red: He is Mr. Andersen, the famous writer. Have you ever heard of "The Red Shoes"?

Grandma: Yes, I ___ⓐ___ . Is he the one who wrote that story?

Red: Right. *(To Andersen)* I changed the story, and the poor Wolf got tired and hungry.

Andersen: You can change the story again.

Red: I'm sorry, ___ⓑ___ I lost the pen you gave to me. Please help me.

Andersen: No problem. I'll write a happy ending for everyone. Is that okay?

Red: That'll be great!

Andersen: All right. I'll use my pen here. "<u>ⓒ The kind Wolf stops to dance. He can enjoy cakes and cookies.</u>"

27 위 글의 빈칸 ⓐ에 들어갈 알맞은 말을 쓰시오. (출제율 95%)

➡ _____

28 위 글의 빈칸 ⓑ에 알맞은 것은? (출제율 90%)

① so   ② and

③ but   ④ for

⑤ though

29 위 글의 밑줄 친 ⓒ에서 어법상 틀린 부분을 찾아 고치시오. (출제율 100%)

➡ _____

30 위 글을 읽고 대답할 수 <u>없는</u> 질문은? (출제율 85%)

① What does Mr. Andersen do?

② Who changed the story of "The Red Shoes"?

③ Why did Red ask Mr. Andersen to help her?

④ Where did Red lose the pen Mr. Andersen had given to her?

⑤ How did Mr. Andersen change the story?

31 Who gave a pen to Red? Answer in English. (3 words) (출제율 95%)

➡ _____

Lesson 5

Shapes Around Us

의사소통 기능

- 능력 여부 묻기
  Do you know how to solve this puzzle?
- 열거하기
  First, draw a square. Then, draw a triangle.
  Finally, draw a circle.

언어 형식

- 의문사+to부정사
  I don't know **how to spin** this.
- 동사+목적어+형용사(목적격 보어) (5형식)
  Square decided to **make** the room **better**.

Words & Expressions

교과서

Key Words

- **boil**[bɔil] 동 끓이다
- **bookshelf**[búkʃelf] 명 책꽂이
- **carry**[kǽri] 동 옮기다
- **choose**[tʃuːz] 동 고르다, 선택하다
- **circle**[sə́ːrkl] 명 원
- **complain**[kəmpléin] 동 불평하다
- **control**[kəntróul] 동 통제하다, 조절하다
- **decide**[disáid] 동 결정하다
- **difficult**[dífikʌlt] 형 어려운
- **divide**[diváid] 동 나누다
- **dot**[dɑt] 명 점
- **draw**[drɔː] 동 (그림을) 그리다
- **dried fish** 마른 생선, 건어물
- **dried soup** 건조 수프
- **excited**[iksáitid] 형 흥분된
- **exercise**[éksərsàiz] 동 운동하다
- **face**[feis] 동 마주하다
- **finally**[fáinəli] 부 마지막으로
- **half**[hæf] 명 반, 절반
- **hanger**[hǽŋər] 명 옷걸이
- **hold**[hould] 동 잡고 있다, 지탱하다
- **hot pepper** (매운) 고추
- **hula hoop** 훌라후프
- **hurry**[hə́ːri] 동 서두르다
- **hurt**[həːrt] 동 다치게 하다
- **jacket**[dʒǽkit] 명 윗옷
- **mess**[mes] 명 혼잡, 혼란
- **move**[muːv] 명 움직임, 이동 동 움직이다
- **must**[məst] 조 ~임에 틀림없다
- **perfect**[pə́ːrfikt] 형 완벽한
- **plastic bag** 비닐봉지
- **pointy**[pɔ́inti] 형 끝이 뾰족한
- **press**[pres] 동 누르다
- **puzzle**[pʌ́zl] 명 퍼즐, 수수께끼
- **realize**[ríːəlàiz] 동 깨닫다, 알아차리다
- **reply**[riplái] 동 대답하다
- **roll**[roul] 동 구르다
- **round**[raund] 형 둥근
- **rush**[rʌʃ] 동 서두르다, 돌진하다
- **sauce**[sɔːs] 명 소스
- **shape**[ʃeip] 명 모양, 모습
- **share**[ʃɛər] 동 공유하다
- **shout**[ʃaut] 동 소리치다, 외치다
- **sick**[sik] 형 아픈
- **solve**[sɑlv] 동 풀다, 해결하다
- **spin**[spin] 동 돌리다, 회전시키다
- **spirit**[spírit] 명 영혼, 요정
- **square**[skwɛər] 명 사각형
- **stick**[stik] 명 막대기, 나뭇가지
- **tidy**[táidi] 형 잘 정돈된, 단정한, 깔끔한
- **triangle**[tráiæŋgl] 명 삼각형
- **used jeans** 낡은 청바지
- **vegetable**[védʒətəbl] 명 야채
- **water**[wɔ́ːtər] 동 물을 주다
- **wheel**[hwiːl] 명 바퀴
- **without**[wiðáut] 전 ~ 없이

Key Expressions

- **a bag of** 한 자루의, 한 봉지의
- **by oneself** 자기 혼자서
- **cut A into pieces** A를 조각으로 자르다
- **divide A into B** A를 B로 나누다
- **each other** 서로 (주로 둘 사이에 쓰임)
- **have to+동사원형** ~해야 한다
- **How about+동사원형-ing ~?** ~하는 게 어때?
- **how to+동사원형** ~하는 방법
- **in charge of ~** ~을 담당하여
- **in control** 담당하고 있는, 통제 중인
- **Let me see.**(= Let's see.) 어디 보자.
- **make a mess** 엉망으로 만들다
- **one another** (주로 셋 이상 사이에 쓰임) 서로
- **one by one** 하나씩, 차례대로
- **pick up ~** ~을 집다, ~을 들어올리다
- **press and hold** 길게 누르다
- **put A on B** A를 B에 놓다[두다, 뿌리다]
- **put on** 입다, 쓰다, 신다
- **take away ~** ~을 치우다
- **take out** 꺼내다, 끄집어내다, 가지고 나가다
- **the other side** 반대편
- **There lived+주어** ~가 살았다
- **what to+동사원형** 무엇을 ~할지
- **wrap up** 감싸다, 포장하다

Word Power

※ 서로 반대되는 뜻을 가진 어휘

- □ **together** (같이, 함께) ↔ **apart** (따로, 떨어져)
- □ **difficult** (어려운) ↔ **easy** (쉬운)
- □ **tidy** (잘 정돈된) ↔ **untidy** (어수선한)

- □ **divide** (분리하다) ↔ **join** (결합하다)
- □ **perfect** (완벽한) ↔ **imperfect** (불완전한)
- □ **without** (~ 없이) ↔ **with** (~이 있는, ~와 함께)

※ 서로 비슷한 뜻을 가진 어휘

- □ **solve** : **work out** (문제를 해결하다)
- □ **hurry** : **rush** (서두르다)
- □ **realize** : **be aware of** (~을 알게 되다)
- □ **decide** : **determine** (결정[결심]하다)
- □ **face** : **confront** (직면하다)

- □ **reply** : **respond** (대답하다)
- □ **mess** : **disorder** (혼잡, 혼란, 무질서)
- □ **choose** : **select** (고르다, 선택하다)
- □ **dot** : **spot** (점)
- □ **finally** : **lastly** (마지막으로)

English Dictionary

- □ **complain** 불평하다
  → to say that you are not satisfied with something
  무언가에 만족하지 않다고 말하다

- □ **control** 조절하다, 통제하다
  → to have the power to make it work in the way you want
  당신이 원하는 방식으로 작동하도록 하는 힘을 가지다

- □ **decide** 결정하다
  → to make a choice about what you are going to do
  당신이 하려는 것에 대해 선택을 하다

- □ **excited** 흥분한
  → feeling very happy and enthusiastic
  매우 행복하고 열광적으로 느끼는

- □ **hanger** 옷걸이
  → a curved piece of wire, wood or plastic on which clothes are hung while they are being stored
  옷이 보관되는 동안 걸려 있는 철사, 나무 또는 플라스틱의 휘어진 부품

- □ **hold** 잡고 있다, 지탱하다
  → to have something in your hands or arms
  손이나 팔로 무언가를 쥐고 있다

- □ **hula hoop** 훌라후프
  → a very large ring that you try to keep spinning round your body
  몸 주위로 계속 돌리는 매우 큰 고리

- □ **jacket** 재킷, 윗옷
  → a short coat that covers the upper part of the body
  몸의 윗부분을 덮는 짧은 코트

- □ **mess** 혼란, 혼잡
  → a situation in which a place is dirty or not neat
  장소가 더럽거나 단정하지 못한 상황

- □ **perfect** 완벽한
  → complete and correct in every way
  모든 면에서 완전하고 올바른

- □ **pointy** 끝이 뾰족한
  → having a point at the end
  끝에 뾰족한 끝을 가지고 있는

- □ **realize** 깨닫다, 알아차리다
  → to gradually begin to understand something that you did not know or notice before
  전에 알지 못하거나 알아차리지 못한 것을 서서히 이해하기 시작하다

- □ **reply** 대답하다
  → to answer someone by saying or writing something
  무언가를 말하거나 씀으로써 누군가에게 답하다

- □ **roll** 구르다
  → to move forward while turning over and over
  계속 회전하면서 앞으로 움직이다

- □ **rush** 서두르다, 돌진하다
  → to move quickly toward someone
  누군가를 향해 빠르게 움직이다

- □ **spirit** 요정
  → an imaginary creature with magic powers
  마법의 힘을 가진 상상의 생명체

- □ **wheel** 바퀴
  → a round object that turns around and around to make a car, bicycle, or other vehicle move
  차, 자전거 또는 다른 차량이 움직이도록 계속 도는 둥근 물체

01 다음 문장의 빈칸에 들어갈 말로 알맞은 것은?

> This bookshelf can't stand alone. Do you
> know how to _____ this problem?

① divide   ② move

③ draw   ④ solve

⑤ complain

서답형

02 다음 글의 빈칸에 주어진 영영풀이에 해당하는 말을 세 단어로 쓰시오.

> • Triangle was _____ the hangers and the plants.
> <영영 풀이> responsible for something or someone

➡ _____

03 다음 중 밑줄 친 단어의 우리말 뜻이 잘못된 것은?

① Their pointy leaves will hurt someone! 끝이 뾰족한

② Mike waters the flowers every day. 물을 주다

③ He complained that you two always made a mess. 불평했다

④ I don't know how to spin this. 돌리다

⑤ I try to make this room tidy. 지저분한

서답형

04 다음 우리말에 맞게 세 단어로 쓰시오. (시제를 맞추시오.)

> Circle은 둥근 것들을 돌보았다.
> ➡ Circle _____ the round things.

➡ _____

[05~06] 다음 영영풀이에 해당하는 단어를 고르시오.

05

> an imaginary creature with magic powers

① wheel   ② spirit

③ ghost   ④ dot

⑤ puzzle

06

> to have the power to make something
> work in the way you want

① decide   ② roll

③ control   ④ hold

⑤ reply

07 다음 빈칸에 들어갈 말로 가장 알맞은 것은?

> Do you know how to _____ a bear
> with three dots?

① hurry   ② remember

③ share   ④ draw

⑤ shout

08 다음 빈칸에 들어갈 단어가 알맞게 짝지어진 것은?

> • Do you know how to divide this _____ four equal pieces?
> • He picked _____ the square hula-hoop to exercise.

① off – of   ② as – as

③ for – to   ④ into – up

⑤ of – for

01 대화의 빈칸에 들어갈 단어를 주어진 철자로 시작하여 쓰시오.

A: Do you know how to draw a fish?
B: Sure. (A)F_____, draw a large square. Then, draw a triangle. (B)F_____, draw a small circle in the square.

➡ (A) _____ (B) _____

02 다음 우리말과 같은 표현이 되도록 문장의 빈칸을 채우시오.

(1) Mike의 방에는 세 도형 요정이 살았다.
➡ _____ _____ three shape _____ in Mike's room.

(2) 이 훌라후프를 치워, 그렇지 않으면 굴러가서 뭔가를 부술 거야!
➡ _____ this hula-hoop _____, _____ it will _____ and break something!

(3) 난 이 방을 정돈하려고 애쓰고 있어.
➡ I _____ _____ make this room _____.

(4) Triangle과 Circle은 서로를 쳐다보았다.
➡ Triangle and Circle looked at _____ _____.

03 다음 빈칸에 밑줄 친 단어와 같은 뜻을 가진 단어를 쓰시오. (주어진 철자로 쓸 것)

G: Do you know how to divide this cake into four e_____ pieces?
B: Let me see. How about dividing it this way? Then the pieces will be the same size and shape.

➡ _____

04 각 문장에 들어갈 단어를 <보기>의 영영풀이를 보고 쓰시오.

┌─ 보기 ─┐
(1) to make a choice about what you are going to do
(2) a situation in which a place is dirty or not neat
(3) to say that you are not satisfied with something
(4) complete and correct in every way

(1) I can't _____ which to choose.
(2) The kids made a _____ in the bathroom.
(3) They always _____ that they cannot find time to do what they want to do.
(4) She speaks _____ English.

05 <보기>에서 알맞은 단어를 골라 문장을 완성하시오. (필요하면 단어를 추가하거나 변형하여 쓰시오.)

┌─ 보기 ─┐
point / control / square / divide

(1) Triangle and Circle went out and Square was now _____. He made the hangers, plants, and all the round things _____.
(2) Take these plants away, or their _____ leaves will hurt someone!

Conversation

교과서

① 능력 여부 묻기

> **Do you know how to solve this puzzle?** 이 퍼즐을 어떻게 푸는지 아니?

- 'how to+동사원형'은 '~하는 방법, 어떻게 ~하는지'라는 의미로, 상대방의 능력을 묻거나 무언가를 하는 방법을 물을 때 'Do you know how to+동사원형 ~?'의 표현을 사용하며, 'Can you+동사원형 ~?'으로 바꿔 쓸 수 있다. 'how to+동사원형'은 'how+주어+should+동사원형 ~'으로 바꾸어 쓸 수 있다.

  - Do you know how to take a picture? 너는 사진을 어떻게 찍는지 아니?
    = Do you know how you should take a picture?
    = Can you take a picture? 너는 사진을 찍을 수 있니?

- **능력 여부를 묻는 말에 대한 대답**

  (1) 할 수 있다고 말할 때

  - Sure. 물론. / Yes, I can. 응, 할 수 있어. / Of course. 물론이지.
    Yes, I'm good at 명사/동사ing. 응, 나는 ~을 잘해.

  (2) 할 수 없다고 말할 때

  - No, I can't. 아니, 못해.
    = No, I'm not good at 명사/동사ing. 아니, 나는 ~을 잘 못해.
    = No, I don't know how to 동사원형. 아니, 나는 ~하는 방법을 몰라.

핵심 Check

1. 다음 우리말에 맞도록 빈칸에 들어갈 알맞은 것은?

너는 이 문제를 푸는 방법을 아니?

Do you know _____ to solve this problem?

① when   ② how   ③ what   ④ why   ⑤ where

2. 다음 대화의 밑줄 친 부분과 바꿔 쓸 수 있는 것은?

A: <u>Can you make paper airplanes?</u>

B: Sure. I'll show you how.

① Will you make paper airplanes?
② When will you learn how to make paper airplanes?
③ Do you know how to make paper airplanes?
④ How did you make paper airplanes?
⑤ How long have you learned how to make paper airplanes?

② 열거하기

First, draw a square. Then, draw a triangle. Finally, draw a circle.
먼저 사각형을 그려. 그러고 나서 삼각형을 그려. 마지막으로 원을 그려.

■ 어떤 것을 열거하거나 절차나 순서에 대해 말할 때 주로 First, Second, Third …(첫째, 둘째, 셋째 …) 를 사용해서 각 단계의 내용을 열거한다.
First of all[Above all/To begin with], Next, And then, Finally[Lastly](처음으로, 그 다음에, 그러고 나서, 마침내[마지막으로])를 사용할 수도 있다.

- A: Can you tell me how to use a microwave? 전자레인지 사용하는 법을 나한테 말해 주겠니?
  B: Sure. 물론이지.

  First, put the food in the microwave. Second, set the timer and push the start button. Finally, take the food out when the time is up. 먼저 전자레인지에 음식을 넣어. 둘째, 타이머를 정하고 시작 버튼을 눌러. 마지막으로, 시간이 다 되면 음식을 꺼내.

핵심 Check

3. 다음 대화의 빈칸에 알맞은 것은?

A: First, write the number '5' between the two eyes.

B: Okay, what's next?

A: _____

B: A circle? Okay.

① What do you mean?
② Next, write the number '6.'
③ Finally, draw the two eyes.
④ Second, draw a small circle under the number '5.'
⑤ First of all, draw a circle under the eyes.

4. 다음 대화의 빈칸에 알맞은 말은?

A: Do you know how to cook *ramyeon*?

B: Sure. First, boil some water. Then, put the *ramyeon* and dried soup mix.
   _____, boil for 4 more minutes.

① To begin with   ② Above all   ③ Finally
④ Second   ⑤ First of all

Get Ready 2

(1) **G:** This bookshelf can't stand alone. Do you know ❶how to solve this problem?

B: ❷Put some legs on the bottom.

(2) **G:** Do you know how to ❸divide this cake into four equal pieces?

B: ❹Let me see. … ❺How about dividing it this way? Then the pieces will be the same size and shape.

(3) **G:** This car doesn't move. Do you know how to move it?

B: Sure. Put wheels under the car.

(1)
G: 이 책꽂이는 혼자서 서 있을 수 없어. 이 문제를 어떻게 해결할지 아니?
B: 바닥에 다리를 몇 개 붙여.
(2)
G: 이 케이크를 네 개의 같은 조각으로 어떻게 나눌 수 있는지 아니?
B: 글쎄. … 이 방법으로 그것을 나누는 것은 어때? 그럼 그 조각들은 같은 크기에 같은 모양이 될 거야.
(3)
G: 이 차는 움직이지 않아. 어떻게 움직이게 할 수 있는지 아니?
B: 물론이지. 차 아래에 바퀴들을 붙여.

❶ 'how to+동사원형'은 '~하는 방법, 어떻게 ~하는지'라는 의미로, 상대방의 능력을 묻거나 무언가를 하는 방법을 묻는 표현이다.
❷ put A on B: A를 B에 두다
❸ divide A into B: A를 B로 나누다
❹ 생각할 시간을 필요로 할 때 사용하는 표현으로 '글쎄, 어디 보자'의 의미로 사용된다.
❺ How about -ing ~?: '~하는 게 어때?'라는 뜻으로 'What about -ing ~?'와 같이 제안을 하는 표현이다.

Check(√) True or False

(1) This bookshelf can stand alone if you put some legs on the bottom. T ☐ F ☐

(2) The boy knows how to divide the cake into the same size and shape. T ☐ F ☐

(3) The girl knows how to move this car. T ☐ F ☐

Start Off Listen & Talk A-1

G: These twelve sticks make four squares. Do you know ❶how to make three squares of the same size with three moves?

B: Sure. ❷First, move this stick here.

G: 이 12개의 막대기들은 사각형 4개를 만들어. 세 번 움직여서 어떻게 같은 크기의 사각형 3개를 만드는지 아니?
B: 물론이지. 먼저, 이 막대기를 여기로 옮겨.

❶ 'how to+동사원형'은 '~하는 방법, 어떻게 ~하는지'라는 의미로, 상대방의 능력을 묻거나 무언가를 하는 방법을 묻는 표현이다. 'how+주어+should+동사원형 ~'으로 바꾸어 쓸 수 있다.
❷ 열거를 할 때 사용하는 표현이다.

Check(√) True or False

(4) The girl wants to make three squares of the same size. T ☐ F ☐

(5) They are solving puzzles. T ☐ F ☐

Start Off Listen & Talk A-2

B: Here's a triangle with three pencils. Do you know ❶how to make three more triangles with three more pencils?

G: ❷Let me see. … It's too difficult for me. Can I break the pencils in half?

B: No, you can't.

❶ 'how to+동사원형'은 '~하는 방법, 어떻게 ~하는지'라는 의미로, 상대방의 능력을 묻거나 무언가를 하는 방법을 묻는 표현이다. 'how+주어+should+동사원형 ~'으로 바꾸어 쓸 수 있다.

❷ 생각할 시간을 필요로 할 때 사용하는 표현으로 '글쎄, 어디 보자'의 의미로 사용된다.

Start Off Listen & Talk B

B: Do you know ❶how to divide this into four equal pieces?

G: Sure. ❷First, divide it into three equal squares. Then, divide each square into four smaller squares. Finally, color three small squares in the inside corner of the L.

B: Oh, I can see three other L shapes around it! You're great!

❶ 'how to+동사원형'은 '~하는 방법, 어떻게 ~하는지'라는 의미로, 상대방의 능력을 묻거나 무언가를 하는 방법을 묻는 표현이다.

❷ 어떤 일을 하는 절차나 방법을 단계적으로 설명할 때, "First, … Then, … Finally, …"를 사용하여 각 단계의 내용을 열거한다.

Speak Up Look and talk.

A: Do you know ❶how to draw a fish with shapes?

B: Sure. First, draw a large square. Then, draw a triangle. Finally, draw a small circle in the square.

❶ 'how you should draw with shapes'로 바꿀 수 있다.

Speak Up Mission

G: Do you know how to make paper airplanes?

B: Sure. I'll show you ❶how.

❶ 여기서 how는 명사로 '방법'이라는 의미다.

Real-life Scene

B: Do you know ❶how to solve this puzzle?

G: What is it?

B: You must take a dog, a chicken, and a bag of rice across the river. The boat only carries you and one of the things at a time.

G: That's easy. I can ❷take them to the other side one by one.

B: But without you, the dog will kill the chicken, and the chicken will eat the rice.

G: Let me see. … ❸First, take the chicken and come back. Then, take the rice and come back with the chicken.

B: And?

G: After that, take the dog and come back. Finally, take the chicken.

B: You're great!

❶ 'how to+동사원형'은 '~하는 방법, 어떻게 ~하는지'라는 의미로, 'how you should solve this puzzle'로 바꾸어 쓸 수 있다.

❷ take A to B: A를 B로 데려가다

❸ 어떤 일을 하는 절차나 방법을 단계적으로 설명할 때, "First, … Then, … Finally, …"를 사용하여 각 단계의 내용을 열거한다.

Express Yourself A

1. B: Do you know how to make this?
   G: Sure. First, ❶cut off the leg from used jeans.
2. B: This looks great.
   G: I think so, too. Do you know how to make it?
   B: It's easy. First, put some rice on *gim*. Then, add some dried fish and hot peppers. Finally, ❷wrap it up and make a triangle.
3. B: Do you know how to fly this?
   G: Yes. I'll show you how. It has to face the wind. Hold it up like this.

❶ cut off: ~을 자르다

❷ wrap ~ up: ~을 싸다

Learning Diary Check Yourself

W: Excuse me. Do you know ❶how to draw a mouse with shapes?

M: Sure. First, draw a large triangle. Then, draw two dots and 6 lines. Finally, draw two small circles.

W: Thanks. I'll draw it ❷myself now.

❶ 'how you should draw a mouse with shapes'로 바꿀 수 있다.

❷ myself는 주어를 강조하는 재귀대명사이다.

• 다음 우리말과 일치하도록 빈칸에 알맞은 말을 쓰시오.

Get Ready 2

(1) **G:** This bookshelf can't stand _____. Do you know _____ _____ _____ this problem?

   B: _____ some legs _____ the _____.

(2) **G:** Do you know _____ _____ _____ this cake _____ four equal pieces?

   B: _____ me _____. … How about _____ it this way? Then the pieces will be the same size and shape.

(3) **G:** This car doesn't move. Do you know _____ _____ _____ it?

   B: Sure. _____ wheels under the car.

Start Off Listen & Talk A

1. **G:** These twelve sticks make four squares. Do you know _____ _____ _____ _____ three squares of the same size with three moves?

   B: Sure. _____, move this stick here.

2. **B:** Here's a triangle with three pencils. Do you know _____ _____ _____ three more triangles with three more pencils?

   G: Let me see. … It's too _____ for me. Can I break the pencils _____ _____?

   B: No, you can't.

Start Off Listen & Talk B

B: Do you know _____ _____ _____ this _____ four equal pieces?

G: Sure. _____, divide it into three _____ squares. _____, _____ each square _____ four smaller squares. _____, color three small squares in the inside corner of the L.

B: Oh, I can see three other L shapes around it! You're great!

Speak Up Look and talk.

A: Do you know _____ _____ _____ a fish with shapes?

B: Sure. _____, draw a large square. _____, draw a triangle. _____, draw a small circle in the square.

해석

(1) G: 이 책꽂이는 혼자서 서 있을 수 없어. 이 문제를 어떻게 해결할지 아니?
   B: 바닥에 다리를 몇 개 붙여.

(2) G: 이 케이크를 네 개의 같은 조각으로 어떻게 나눌 수 있는지 아니?
   B: 글쎄. … 이 방법으로 그것을 나누는 것은 어때? 그럼 그 조각들은 같은 크기에 같은 모양이 될 거야.

(3) G: 이 차는 움직이지 않아. 어떻게 움직이게 할 수 있는지 아니?
   B: 물론이지. 차 아래에 바퀴들을 붙여.

1. G: 이 12개 막대기들은 사각형 4개를 만들어. 세 번 움직여서 어떻게 같은 크기의 사각형 3개를 만드는지 아니?
   B: 물론이지. 먼저, 이 막대기를 여기로 옮겨.

2. B: 여기 연필 세 자루로 만든 삼각형이 하나 있어. 연필 세 자루를 더 추가해서 어떻게 삼각형 3개를 더 만드는지 아니?
   G: 글쎄.… 내게는 너무 어려워. 연필을 반으로 부러뜨려도 돼?
   B: 아니, 안 돼.

B: 이것을 4개의 같은 조각으로 나누는 방법을 아니?
G: 물론이지. 먼저, 그것을 3개의 같은 사각형으로 나눠. 그러고 나서, 각 사각형을 4개의 더 작은 사각형으로 나눠. 마지막으로, L자 모양의 안쪽 모서리에 있는 3개의 작은 사각형에 색칠해.
B: 오, 그 주변에 3개의 다른 L자 모양들이 보여! 너 대단하다!

A: 너는 도형들로 물고기를 그리는 방법을 알고 있니?
B: 물론. 먼저, 큰 사각형을 그려. 그러고 나서, 삼각형을 그려. 마지막으로, 사각형 안에 작은 원을 그려.

Speak Up Mission

G: Do you know _____ _____ _____ paper airplanes?

B: Sure. I'll show you _____.

Real-life Scene

B: Do you know _____ _____ _____ this puzzle?

G: What is it?

B: You must _____ a dog, a chicken, and a bag of rice across the river. The boat only carries you and one of the things _____ _____.

G: That's easy. I can _____ them _____ the other side _____ _____ _____.

B: But _____ you, the dog will kill the chicken, and the chicken will eat the rice.

G: Let me see. … _____, take the chicken and come back. _____, take the rice and come back with the chicken.

B: And?

G: After that, take the dog and come back. _____, take the chicken.

B: You're great!

Express Yourself A

1. B: Do you know _____ _____ _____ this?
   G: Sure. First, _____ _____ the leg from _____ jeans.

2. B: This looks great.
   G: I think so, too. Do you know _____ to make it?
   B: It's easy. _____, put some rice on *gim*. _____, add some _____ fish and hot peppers. _____, _____ it up and make a triangle.

3. B: Do you know _____ _____ fly this?
   G: Yes. I'll show you how. It has to _____ the wind. _____ it up like this.

Learning Diary Check Yourself

W: Excuse me. Do you know how _____ _____ a mouse with shapes?

M: Sure. _____, draw a large triangle. _____, draw two dots and 6 lines. _____, draw two small circles.

W: Thanks. I'll _____ it _____ now.

해석

G: 너는 종이 비행기를 어떻게 접는지 아니?

B: 물론이지. 내가 너에게 방법을 보여 줄게.

B: 이 퍼즐을 어떻게 푸는지 아니?

G: 그게 뭔데?

B: 너는 개, 닭, 쌀 한 자루를 강 건너로 옮겨야 해. 그 배는 한 번에 너와 그 것들 중 하나만 옮길 수 있어.

G: 그것은 쉬워. 난 반대편으로 그것들 을 하나씩 옮길 수 있어.

B: 하지만 네가 없으면, 개는 닭을 죽일 것이고, 닭은 쌀을 먹을 거야.

G: 어디 보자. … 먼저, 닭을 데려다 놓 고 돌아와. 그러고 나서, 쌀을 가져 다 놓고 닭을 데려와.

B: 그리고?

G: 그 후에, 개를 데려다 놓고 돌아와. 마지막으로, 닭을 데려가는 거야.

B: 너 대단하구나!

1. B: 이것을 어떻게 만드는지 아니?
   G: 물론이지. 먼저, 낡은 청바지에서 다리 부분을 잘라내.

2. B: 이것은 멋져 보여.
   G: 나도 그렇게 생각해. 그걸 어떻게 만드는지 아니?
   B: 그건 쉬워. 먼저, 김 위에 밥을 좀 얹어. 그러고 나서, 멸치와 매운 고추를 추가해. 마지막으로, 그것 을 모두 싸서 삼각형을 만들어.

3. B: 이것을 어떻게 날리는지 아니?
   G: 그래. 내가 너에게 방법을 보여 줄게. 그것은 바람을 마주해야만 해. 이렇게 그것을 들고 있어.

W: 실례합니다. 도형으로 쥐를 어떻게 그리는지 아세요?

M: 물론이죠. 먼저, 큰 삼각형을 그려 요. 그러고 나서, 점 두 개와 선 6개 를 그려요. 마지막으로, 작은 원 두 개를 그려요.

W: 감사합니다. 이제 제가 그것을 직접 그려 볼게요.

01 다음 대화의 빈칸에 들어갈 말은?

> G: This bookshelf can't stand alone. Do you know _____ this problem?
> B: Put some legs on the bottom.

① how solving   ② what to solve   ③ how to solve

④ when to solve   ⑤ where to solve

02 다음 대화의 빈칸에 들어갈 말로 알맞지 <u>않은</u> 것은?

> G: These twelve sticks make four squares. Do you know how to make three squares of the same size with three moves?
> B: Sure. _____, move this stick here.

① To begin with   ② First of all   ③ First

④ Above all   ⑤ Finally

03 다음 대화의 우리말에 맞게 부정사를 이용하여 4단어의 영어로 쓰시오.

> B: This looks great.
> G: I think so, too. Do you know <u>그것을 어떻게 만드는지</u>?
> B: It's easy. First, put some rice on *gim*. Then, add some dried fish and hot peppers. Finally, wrap it up and make a triangle.

➡ _____

04 다음 대화의 밑줄 친 우리말에 맞게 주어진 단어를 알맞은 순서로 배열하시오.

> G: Do you know <u>이 케이크를 네 개의 같은 조각으로 어떻게 나눌 수 있는지</u>?
> B: Let me see. ... How about dividing it this way? Then the pieces will be the same size and shape.

(divide / how / this cake / into / to / four / pieces / equal)

➡ _____

[01~02] 다음 대화를 읽고 물음에 답하시오.

> B: Here's a triangle with three pencils. Do you know _____(A)_____ with three more pencils?
>
> G: Let me see. ... It's too difficult for me. Can I break the pencils (B)반으로?
>
> B: No, you can't.

01 위 대화의 빈칸 (A)에 들어갈 말로 알맞은 것은?

① where to buy three more pencils

② how to draw a bear with a pencil

③ how to make three more triangles

④ how to make potato salad

⑤ how to use these triangles

서답형
02 위 대화의 밑줄 친 (B)의 우리말에 맞게 주어진 철자로 시작하여 쓰시오.

➡ i _____

[03~04] 다음 대화를 읽고 물음에 답하시오.

> B: Do you know _____?
>
> G: Yes. I'll show you how. It has to face the wind. Hold it up like this.

03 위 대화의 빈칸에 들어갈 말로 가장 적절한 것은?

① how to make it

② how to show this

③ when to fly this

④ how to fly this

⑤ where to fly this

서답형
04 위 문제의 답을 '주어+동사'가 있는 문장으로 바꾸어 쓰시오.

➡ _____

[05~06] 다음 대화를 읽고 물음에 답하시오.

> B: Do you know _____(A)_____
>
> G: Sure. ___(B)___, divide it into three equal squares. Then, divide each square into four smaller squares. ___(C)___, color three small squares in the inside corner of the L.
>
> B: Oh, I can see three other L shapes around it! You're great!

05 위 대화의 빈칸 (A)에 들어갈 말로 가장 알맞은 것은?

① how to make three squares of the same size with three moves?

② how to make paper airplanes?

③ how to draw a mouse with shapes?

④ how to divide this into four equal pieces?

⑤ how to draw a fish with shapes?

06 위 대화의 (B)와 (C)에 들어갈 말로 알맞은 것은?

① First – Finally

② Then – Next

③ First of all – Second

④ Above all – Three

⑤ One – The other

[07~09] 다음 대화를 읽고 물음에 답하시오.

> A: Do you know _____(A)_____?
> B: What is it?
> A: You must take a dog, a chicken, and a bag of rice across the river. (①) The boat only carries you and one of the things at a time.
> B: That's easy. I can take them to the other side ____(B)____. (②)
> A: But without you, the dog will kill the chicken, and the chicken will eat the rice.
> B: Let me see. ⋯ First, take the chicken and come back. (③) Then, take the rice and come back with the chicken. (④)
> A: And?
> B: (⑤) Finally, take the chicken.
> A: You're great!

07 위 대화의 빈칸 (A)에 들어갈 말로 알맞은 것은?

① how to make paper airplanes
② how to solve this puzzle
③ how to take a dog across the river
④ how to row a boat
⑤ how to come back with the chicken

08 위 대화의 빈칸 (B)에 들어갈 말로 알맞은 것은?

① each other   ② together
③ one by one   ④ one another
⑤ with me

09 위 대화의 (①)~(⑤)에서 다음 주어진 문장이 들어갈 위치로 알맞은 것은?

> After that, take the dog and come back.

①   ②   ③   ④   ⑤

10 다음 중 짝지어진 대화가 <u>어색한</u> 것을 고르시오.

① A: Do you know how to cook *ramyeon*?
  B: Sure.
② A: Do you know how to make paper cranes?
  B: Sure. I'll show you how.
③ A: Do you know how to fix this?
  B: That's not right.
④ A: Do you know how to divide this cake into four equal pieces?
  B: Let me see.
⑤ A: Can I help you?
  B: Yes, can you tell me where to sit?

[11~12] 다음 대화를 읽고 물음에 답하시오.

> G: Do you know how to draw a fish with ____(A)____s?
> B: Sure. First, draw a large square. ____(B)____, draw a triangle. Finally, draw a small circle in the square.

서답형
11 위 대화의 빈칸 (A)의 단어에 대한 영어 설명을 읽고 알맞은 단어를 쓰시오.

> an arrangement that is formed by joining lines together in a particular way or by the line or lines around its outer edge

➡ _____

12 위 대화의 빈칸 (B)에 들어갈 말로 알맞은 것을 <u>모두</u> 고르시오.

① Then   ② Third
③ Two   ④ Second
⑤ Next

[01~02] 다음 대화를 읽고 물음에 답하시오.

A: Do you know how to solve this puzzle?
B: What is it?
A: You must take a dog, a chicken, and a bag of rice ①across the river. The boat only carries you and one of the things ②at a time.
B: That's easy. I can take them to the other side ③one by one.
A: But ④with you, the dog will kill the chicken, and the chicken will eat the rice.
B: _____(A)_____ ... First, take the chicken and come back. Then, take the rice and come back with the chicken.
A: And?
B: After that, ⑤take the dog and come back. Finally, take the chicken.
A: You're great!

01 위 대화의 밑줄 친 ①~⑤ 중 어휘의 쓰임이 어색한 것을 찾아 바르게 고치시오.

➡ 번호: _____.

➡ 고쳐 쓰기: _____.

02 위 대화의 빈칸 (A)에 들어갈 표현을 주어진 영영풀이를 참고하여 세 단어로 쓰시오. (3 words)

used when you want to think carefully about something or are trying to remember

➡ _____

[03~04] 다음 대화를 읽고 물음에 답하시오.

A: 너는 도형들로 쥐를 그리는 방법을 알고 있니?
B: Sure. First, draw a large _____(a)_____. Then, draw two small _____(b)_____. Finally, draw _____(c)_____ and six _____(d)_____.

03 위 대화의 밑줄 친 우리말에 맞게 주어진 단어를 알맞은 순서로 배열하시오.

you / how / to / know / do / draw / a mouse / shapes / with

➡ _____

04 위 대화의 빈칸 (a)~(d)에 들어갈 말을 다음 그림을 보고 완성하시오.

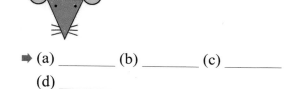

➡ (a) _____ (b) _____ (c) _____
(d) _____

05 다음 대화의 밑줄 친 우리말에 맞게 주어진 단어를 이용하여 4 단어의 영어로 쓰시오.

(how / move)

G: This car doesn't move. Do you know 그것을 어떻게 움직이게 하는지?
B: Sure. Put wheels under the car.

➡ _____

Grammar

① 의문사+to부정사

> • Do you know **how to solve** this problem? 이 문제를 어떻게 해결할지 아니?
> • Will you tell me **where to meet**? 어디서 만날지 내게 말해 줄래?

■ '의문사+to부정사'는 'what/when/where/how/whom + to부정사'의 형태로 쓰이며, 문장 속에서 주어, 목적어, 보어 역할을 하는 명사구로 사용되며, '…할지'라는 뜻을 나타낸다. 주로 동사의 목적어로 사용된다. 'why + to부정사'는 쓰이지 않는다.

  • **How to spend** money is very important. 〈주어〉 돈을 어떻게 쓰는지가 매우 중요하다.

  • I don't know **how to spin** this. 〈know의 목적어〉 이걸 어떻게 돌리는지 모르겠어.

의문사	to부정사	의미
what	to do	무엇을 해야 할지
whom	to meet	누구를 만나야 할지
which	to buy	어느 것을 사야 할지
when	to start	언제 출발해야 할지
where	to go	어디로 가야 할지
how	to fix	어떻게 고치는지

■ '의문형용사 + 명사 + to부정사'나 '의문부사 + 형용사 + to부정사' 형태로도 사용된다.

  • Can you tell me **which bus to take**? 어느 버스를 타야 할지 말해줄 수 있어?

  • I don't know **how much to buy**. 얼마나 많이 사야 할지 모르겠다.

■ '의문사+to부정사'는 '의문사 + 주어 + should[can] + 동사원형'으로 바꿔 쓸 수 있다.

  • I don't know **when to start**. 언제 출발해야 할지 모르겠어.
    = I don't know when I should start.

  • Do you know **how to fix** this? 이걸 어떻게 고칠 수 있는지 아니?
    = Do you know how you can fix this?

핵심 Check

1. 다음 우리말에 맞게 빈칸에 알맞은 말을 쓰시오.

  (1) 그걸 어떻게 움직이는지 아니?
    ➡ Do you know ＿＿＿＿ ＿＿＿＿ ＿＿＿＿ it?

  (2) 어디에 앉아야 할지 제게 말해 주시겠어요?
    ➡ Can you tell me ＿＿＿＿ ＿＿＿＿ ＿＿＿＿?

② 동사+목적어+형용사(목적격 보어)

• Square decided to **make** the room **better**. Square는 방을 더 낫게 만들기로 결심했다.

• I **found** math **interesting**. 나는 수학이 재미있다는 것을 알았다.

■ '주어 + 동사 + 목적어 + 목적격 보어'의 형식을 취하는 문장을 5형식 문장이라고 하며, 목적격 보어 자리에는 명사, 형용사, to부정사, 현재분사, 과거분사, 동사원형 등 다양한 형태가 올 수 있다. 이때, 목적격 보어는 목적어의 특징이나 상태 등을 설명하는 역할을 한다. 형용사를 목적격 보어로 취하는 동사에는 make, keep, find, get, leave, paint, think 등이 있다.

• His mom **made** him **a doctor**. 〈명사〉 그의 엄마는 그를 의사가 되도록 했다.

• That **made** me **happy**. 〈형용사〉 그게 나를 행복하게 했다.

• I **asked** him **to mail** the letter. 〈to부정사〉 나는 그에게 편지를 부쳐달라고 부탁했다.

• I've never **seen** him **singing** in public. 〈현재분사〉 나는 그가 사람들 앞에서 노래 부르는 걸 본 적이 없어.

• I **had** it **stolen** somewhere. 〈과거분사〉 어딘가에서 그것을 도난당했습니다.

• Her father didn't **let** her **go** to the party. 〈동사원형〉 그녀의 아버지는 그녀를 파티에 못 가게 하셨어.

■ 목적격 보어를 형용사가 아닌 부사로 쓰지 않도록 주의해야 한다.

• Everyone wonders if money can **make** us **happy**. 모든 사람들이 돈으로 행복해질 수 있는지 궁금해 한다.

• In the winter, it **keeps** your head **warm**. 겨울에는, 그것이 너의 머리를 계속 따뜻하도록 해준다.

■ 5형식 문장과 4형식 문장 비교

5형식 문장: 주어+동사+목적어+목적격 보어

• He **made** me **happy**. (me = happy) 그는 나를 행복하게 했다.

4형식 문장: 주어+동사+간접목적어+직접목적어

• He **made** me **a desk**. (me ≠ a desk) 그는 나에게 책상을 만들어 주었다.

핵심 Check

2. 다음 우리말에 맞게 빈칸에 알맞은 말을 쓰시오.

(1) 난 이 방을 정돈하려고 애쓰지만, 너희 둘은 항상 엉망으로 만들어.

➡ I try to make this room _____, but you two always make _____

_____.

(2) 숙제는 나를 지치게 만든다.

➡ My homework makes me _____.

01 다음 빈칸에 들어갈 알맞은 것은?

> • Do you know _____ to make paper airplanes?

① whom   ② who   ③ what

④ which   ⑤ how

02 다음 문장에서 어법상 어색한 부분을 바르게 고쳐 쓰시오.

(1) Can you tell me how cook spaghetti?

_____ ➡ _____

(2) I don't know when I to start.

_____ ➡ _____

(3) The story made me sadly.

_____ ➡ _____

(4) She asked him wait outside.

_____ ➡ _____

03 다음 우리말에 맞게 괄호 안에 주어진 단어를 빈칸에 바르게 배열하시오. (필요하면 어형을 바꿀 것)

(1) 그것이 계속 나를 들뜨게 했다. (me / excite / kept)

➡ It _____ _____ _____.

(2) 무엇을 사야 할지 모르겠어. (buy / what / to)

➡ I don't know _____ _____ _____.

(3) 열쇠를 어디에 두면 좋을지 모르겠다. (put / where / the / key / to)

➡ I am not sure _____ _____ _____ _____ _____.

04 다음 괄호 안에 주어진 단어를 어법에 맞게 빈칸에 쓰시오.

(1) I did not know whom _____ for the gift. (thank)

(2) We found the test _____. (difficult)

중요

01 다음 중 어법상 바르지 <u>않은</u> 것은?

① Do you know how to divide this cake into four equal pieces?
② I couldn't know where to buy the shirt.
③ Can you tell me whom to meet tomorrow?
④ The boy will ask her what to do it next.
⑤ Elle told him where to meet her when he left for the day.

서답형

02 주어진 어휘를 이용하여 다음 우리말을 영어로 쓰시오.

나는 그 책이 재미있다는 것을 알게 되었다.
(find, interesting.)

➡ _____

서답형

03 다음 괄호 안에서 알맞은 말을 고르시오.

(1) We asked her when (to start / starting) to paint the wall.
(2) We couldn't decide (what / why) to do, so we just waited.
(3) Christine didn't tell her husband (how / what) to use the washing machine.
(4) Regular exercising makes me (health / healthy).
(5) The bird's song made the man (happy / happily).

➡ (1) _____ (2) _____ (3) _____
(4) _____ (5) _____

[04~05] 다음 빈칸에 알맞은 말을 고르시오.

04

My sister _____ the living room clean.

① made ② charged
③ asked ④ begged
⑤ ordered

05

Jenny doesn't know _____ to make a bookmark.

① what ② how
③ that ④ whom
⑤ why

중요

06 주어진 문장의 밑줄 친 부분과 용법이 <u>다른</u> 것은?

He <u>made</u> the hangers, the plants, and all the round things square.

① Jogging in the morning <u>made</u> her keep in shape.
② My dog <u>made</u> me happy.
③ The Olympic Games <u>made</u> a lot of people excited.
④ Linsey <u>made</u> him wait for her for more than two hours.
⑤ Mom <u>made</u> me delicious gimbap last night.

서답형

07 다음 빈칸에 알맞은 말을 쓰시오.

Do you know how _____ ride a bike?

➡ _____

서답형

08 두 문장의 의미가 같도록 빈칸에 알맞은 말을 쓰시오.

(1) Now, do you all understand how to play this game?

= Now, do you all understand _____ _____ _____ _____ this game?

(2) Do you know how to make a bag out of used jeans?

= Do you know _____ _____ _____ _____ a bag out of used jeans?

(3) Tell me what to do.

= Tell me _____ _____ _____ _____.

중요

09 다음 중 어법상 어색한 문장을 고르시오.

① Doing the same work again and again makes me tire.

② The 2002 World Cup games made Korean people excited.

③ I knew how to make a kite.

④ Watching TV before going to bed can keep you awake.

⑤ Listening to music always makes us comfortable.

[10~11] 다음 우리말에 맞게 영작한 것을 고르시오.

10

그것은 나를 전보다 더 똑똑하게 만들었어.

① It made me smart than before.

② It made me smarter than before.

③ It made me smartly than before.

④ It made me more smartly than before.

⑤ It made me smartlier than before.

11

그들은 그 북을 어디에 놓아야 할지 몰랐다.

① They didn't know how to put the drum.

② They didn't know what to put the drum.

③ They didn't know where to put the drum.

④ They didn't know when to put the drum.

⑤ They didn't know which to put the drum.

중요

12 다음 빈칸에 적절하지 않은 것을 모두 고르시오.

I'd like to know _____ to go.

① how   ② where   ③ when
④ what   ⑤ why

서답형

13 다음 두 문장의 뜻이 같도록 빈칸에 알맞은 말을 쓰시오.

• I found the book interesting.
• I found that _____ _____ _____ _____.

서답형

14 우리말과 일치하도록 주어진 어휘를 이용하여 빈칸에 알맞은 말을 쓰시오.

(1) 그녀는 어느 옷을 사야 할지 알 수 없었다. (buy, dress)

➡ She didn't know _____ _____ _____ _____.

(2) 그 수학 시험이 모든 학생들을 불안하게 했다. (make, every, nervous)

➡ The math test _____ _____ _____ _____.

서답형

15 다음 문장에서 어법상 어색한 것을 바르게 고치시오.

(1) She couldn't decide where going to buy some bread.

_____ ➡ _____

(2) How to say greetings are important for Koreans.

_____ ➡ _____

(3) Harold didn't know what to help her at that time.

_____ ➡ _____

(4) Do you know how should draw a mouse with shapes?

_____ ➡ _____

(5) I found Stella very smartly.

_____ ➡ _____

(6) The baby made the mom happiness by smiling back.

_____ ➡ _____

(7) Doing a lot of homework makes me tiring.

_____ ➡ _____

중요

16 다음 밑줄 친 부분의 쓰임이 나머지 넷과 다른 것은?

① The teacher will tell Rick when to begin.
② Do you know how to make three squares of the same size with three moves?
③ Matilda asked Alex where to get those dresses.
④ He had no friends to support him.
⑤ Andrew couldn't decide what to do next for her.

서답형

17 다음 문장을 같은 뜻의 다른 문장으로 바꿔 쓸 때 빈칸을 두 단어로 채우시오.

> I watched the movie and I felt sad.
> → The movie made _____ .

➡ _____

서답형

18 주어진 어휘를 이용하여 다음 우리말을 두 가지로 영작하시오.

> 오늘 밤 파티를 위해 무엇을 사야 할지 내게 말해 줘. (tell, buy)

➡ _____
➡ _____

19 다음 중 어법상 틀린 것은?

① Watching a movie with a girl friend makes the movie more interested.
② Computer games make people around the world excited.
③ Playing soccer makes me happy.
④ Reading books for homework makes me bored.
⑤ Washing the dishes after dinner makes me tired.

20 다음 중 어법상 옳은 문장의 개수는?

> ⓐ I can make this room better all by myself.
> ⓑ Can you tell me where sit?
> ⓒ I don't know what doing.
> ⓓ Do you know how to fly this?
> ⓔ This jacket will keep you warmly.

① 1개   ② 2개   ③ 3개   ④ 4개   ⑤ 5개

01 다음 문장에서 어법상 <u>어색한</u> 것을 바르게 고쳐 다시 쓰시오.

(1) He showed what to draw a triangle that has three sides of the same length.

　➡ ＿＿＿＿＿＿＿＿＿＿＿＿＿＿＿
　＿＿＿＿＿＿＿＿＿＿＿＿＿＿＿

(2) When we to go there is not decided yet.

　➡ ＿＿＿＿＿＿＿＿＿＿＿＿＿＿＿
　＿＿＿＿＿＿＿＿＿＿＿＿＿＿＿

(3) Do you know why to share photos on the Internet?

　➡ ＿＿＿＿＿＿＿＿＿＿＿＿＿＿＿
　＿＿＿＿＿＿＿＿＿＿＿＿＿＿＿

(4) The bird's song makes him happily.

　➡ ＿＿＿＿＿＿＿＿＿＿＿＿＿＿＿
　＿＿＿＿＿＿＿＿＿＿＿＿＿＿＿

(5) At first, Sophie thought Nicholas honesty.

　➡ ＿＿＿＿＿＿＿＿＿＿＿＿＿＿＿
　＿＿＿＿＿＿＿＿＿＿＿＿＿＿＿

(6) We found *Alita: Battle Angel* very interested.

　➡ ＿＿＿＿＿＿＿＿＿＿＿＿＿＿＿
　＿＿＿＿＿＿＿＿＿＿＿＿＿＿＿

02 다음 빈칸을 어법에 맞게 채우시오.

> I'll tell you how to solve it.
> = I'll tell you how ＿＿＿ ＿＿＿ ＿＿＿ it.

03 다음 그림을 보고 괄호 안에 주어진 어휘를 이용하여 주어진 대화의 빈칸을 알맞게 채우시오.

(1)

> A: Do you like sandwiches?
> B: Yes, I do. Eating sandwiches makes ＿＿＿＿＿＿. (full)

　➡ ＿＿＿＿＿＿＿＿＿＿＿＿＿＿＿

(2)

> A: Does Minsu know ＿＿＿＿＿＿ *ramyeon*? (cook)
> B: Sure. He is a good cook.

　➡ ＿＿＿＿＿＿＿＿＿＿＿＿＿＿＿

04 괄호 안에 주어진 어휘를 이용하여 영작하시오.

(1) 너 이 꽃을 어떻게 기르는지 아니? (know, grow, this flower, 8 단어)

➡ _____

(2) 과자를 얼마나 많이 사야 할지 나에게 말해 줘. (tell, cookies, buy, 7 단어)

➡ _____

(3) 그들은 어느 길을 택할 것인가 결정할 수가 없었다. (decide, which, take, 7 단어)

➡ _____

(4) 내 낮은 성적이 엄마를 실망하게 했다. (poor, grade, make, disappoint, 7 단어)

➡ _____

(5) 우리는 그가 어리석다고 생각했다. (stupid, 4 단어)

➡ _____

(6) 이 선풍기가 여러분을 이번 여름에 시원하게 해 줄 것이다. (this fan, keep, cool, 8 단어)

➡ _____

05 주어진 어휘와 to부정사를 이용하여 자신의 문장을 쓰시오.

(1) how, make

➡ _____

(2) what, write

➡ _____

(3) where, put

➡ _____

(4) which, tell, read, book

➡ _____

06 우리말에 맞게 다음 빈칸에 알맞은 말을 쓰시오.

(1) 그는 그 책이 매우 재미있다는 것을 알았다.

➡ He found the book very _____.

(2) 밖에 나가면 햇볕 때문에 따뜻해질 거예요.

➡ If you go out, the sun will keep you _____.

(3) Romeo는 Juliet이 친절하다고 믿었다.

➡ Romeo believed Juliet _____.

(4) 그녀가 아이를 혼자 내버려두었다.

➡ She left her child _____.

07 두 문장이 같은 뜻이 되도록 빈칸에 알맞은 것을 쓰시오.

(1) I can't decide what to eat for lunch.
= I can't decide _____ _____ _____ _____ for lunch.

(2) Which dress to buy is a difficult decision for her to make.
= _____ _____ _____ _____ _____ is a difficult decision for her to make.

08 다음 문장을 주어진 어휘로 시작하는 문장으로 바꿔 쓰시오.

(1) When she got the present, she felt happy.

➡ The present made _____.

(2) When I heard the news, I got excited.

➡ Hearing the news _____.

Reading

Three Shape Spirits

There lived three shape spirits in Mike's room. Square controlled
the table, the bookshelf, and the window. Triangle was in charge of
the hangers and the plants. Circle took care of the round things. They
worked together to make a nice room for Mike.

One day Square decided to make the room better and shouted at
the other spirits.

"Take these plants away, or their pointy leaves will hurt someone!" he
said to Triangle.

"But Mike waters them every day," said Triangle.

"Take this hula hoop away, or it will roll and break something!" he
said to Circle.

"But Mike exercises with it every day," said Circle.

"I try to make this room tidy, but you two always make a mess,"
he complained.

Triangle and Circle looked at each other.

"So you think you can do it without us?" Triangle asked Square.

"Sure. I can make this room better all by myself," replied Square.

"Great! Then we can get some rest," Circle said to Square.

spirit 영혼. 요정
hanger 옷걸이
hula hoop 훌라후프
wheel 바퀴
pointy 끝이 뾰족한
control 통제하다. 조절하다
in charge of …을 담당하여
decide 결정하다
roll 구르다. 굴러가다
mess 혼란, 혼잡
complain 불평하다

확인문제

● 다음 문장이 본문의 내용과 일치하면 T, 일치하지 <u>않으면</u> F를 쓰시오.

1 Square controlled the table, the bookshelf, and the window. ☐

2 Circle took care of the hangers and the plants. ☐

3 Three shape spirits worked together to make a nice room for Mike. ☐

4 One day Triangle decided to make the room better. ☐

5 Mike exercises with the hula hoop every day. ☐

6 Square thinks he can do nothing without Triangle and Circle. ☐

Triangle and Circle went out and Square was now in control. He made the hangers, plants, and all the round things square. Then he looked around and smiled. "Much better!"

When Mike came home from school, he picked up a square hanger to hang his jacket on.

"What? This will not hold my clothes."

He went to water the plants and saw their square leaves.

"Poor things. ... They must be sick."

He picked up the square hula hoop to exercise.

"Hmm ... I don't know how to spin this."

He went to take out his bike and looked at the square wheels.

"Well, I can't ride this. I'll just have to walk." Then he hurried out of the house.

When the other spirits came back, Square rushed over to them. "Mike doesn't like his room. I don't know what to do," he said.

They looked at the hangers, the plants, and all the new square things.

Then they looked at one another, and Square realized his problem.

"Let's make this room great again," he said to the others, and the three spirits worked together once again.

clothes 옷, 의복
pick up 집다, 집어 들다
out of ~에서, ~ 밖으로
spin 돌리다, 회전하다
rush 서두르다, 돌진하다

확인문제

● 다음 문장이 본문의 내용과 일치하면 T, 일치하지 않으면 F를 쓰시오.

1 Square made the hangers, plants, and all the round things square. ☐

2 Mike picked up a triangular hanger to hang his jacket on. ☐

3 Mike doesn't know how to spin the square hula hoop. ☐

4 Mike went to take out his bike and looked at the round wheels. ☐

5 Square rushed over to the other spirits when they came back. ☐

6 Triangle and Circle said to Square, "Let's make this room great again." ☐

● 우리말을 참고하여 빈칸에 알맞은 말을 쓰시오.

1 Three Shape _____

2 _____ _____ three shape spirits in Mike's room.

3 Square _____ the table, the bookshelf, and the window.

4 Triangle _____ _____ _____ _____ the hangers and the plants.

5 Circle _____ _____ _____ the round things.

6 They _____ _____ to make a nice room for Mike.

7 One day Square decided _____ _____ _____ _____ _____ and shouted at the other spirits.

8 "_____ these plants _____, or their _____ leaves will hurt someone!" he said to Triangle.

9 "But Mike _____ _____ every day," said Triangle.

10 "_____ this hula hoop _____, or it will _____ _____ _____ something!" he said to Circle.

11 "But Mike _____ _____ _____ every day," said Circle.

12 "I try to make this room _____, but you two always _____ _____ _____," he complained.

13 Triangle and Circle _____ _____ each other.

14 "So you think you can do it _____ _____?" Triangle asked Square.

15 "Sure. I can make this room better _____ _____ _____," replied Square.

16 "Great! Then we can _____ _____ _____," Circle said to Square.

17 Triangle and Circle went out and Square was now _____ _____.

---

1 세 도형 요정들

2 Mike의 방에는 세 도형 요정이 살았다.

3 Square는 탁자, 책장, 그리고 창문을 담당했다.

4 Triangle은 옷걸이들과 식물들을 담당했다.

5 Circle은 둥근 것들을 돌보았다.

6 그들은 Mike에게 좋은 방을 만들어 주기 위해서 함께 일했다.

7 어느 날 Square는 방을 더 낫게 만들기로 결심하고 나머지 요정들에게 소리쳤다.

8 "이 식물들을 치워, 그렇지 않으면 그것들의 끝이 뾰족한 잎사귀들이 누군가를 다치게 할 거야!" 그가 Triangle에게 말했다.

9 "하지만 Mike가 매일 그들에게 물을 주는데." Triangle이 말했다.

10 "이 훌라후프를 치워, 그렇지 않으면 굴러가서 뭔가를 부술 거야!" 그가 Circle에게 말했다.

11 "하지만 Mike는 매일 그걸로 운동을 하는데." Circle이 말했다.

12 "난 이 방을 정돈하려고 애쓰지만, 너희 둘은 항상 엉망으로 만들어." 그가 불평했다.

13 Triangle과 Circle이 서로를 쳐다보았다.

14 "그래서 네 생각에는 네가 우리 없이 다 할 수 있다는 거야?" Triangle이 Square에게 물었다.

15 "물론이지. 난 완전히 혼자서 이 방을 더 낫게 만들 수 있어." Square가 대답했다.

16 "잘됐네! 그럼 우린 쉴 수 있겠어." Circle이 Square에게 말했다.

17 Triangle과 Circle이 밖으로 나갔고 이제 Square가 모든 것을 담당했다.

18 He made the hangers, plants, and all the round things _____.

19 Then he _____ _____ and smiled.

20 "_____ better!"

21 When Mike came home from school, he _____ _____ a square hanger _____ _____ his jacket _____.

22 "What? This will not _____ _____ _____."

23 He _____ _____ _____ the plants and saw their square leaves.

24 "Poor things. ... They _____ _____ sick."

25 He _____ _____ the square hula hoop _____ _____.

26 "Hmm ... I don't know _____ _____ _____ this."

27 He went _____ _____ _____ his bike and looked at the square wheels.

28 "Well, I can't ride this. I'll just _____ _____ walk."

29 Then he _____ _____ _____ the house.

30 When the other spirits came back, Square _____ _____ _____ them.

31 "Mike doesn't like his room. I don't know _____ _____ _____," he said.

32 They looked at the hangers, the plants, and _____ _____ _____ _____ _____.

33 Then they looked at _____ _____, and Square _____ his problem.

34 "Let's make this room _____ again," he said to _____ _____, and the three spirits worked together _____ _____.

---

18 그는 옷걸이들과 식물들과 모든 둥근 물건들을 사각형으로 만들었다.

19 그러고 나서 그는 주위를 둘러보고 미소 지었다.

20 "훨씬 좋군!"

21 Mike가 학교에서 집으로 왔을 때, 그는 재킷을 걸기 위해 사각형 옷걸이 하나를 집었다.

22 "뭐야? 이것은 내 옷을 걸고 있지 못할 거야."

23 그는 식물에 물을 주러 가서 그것들의 사각형 잎사귀들을 보았다.

24 "불쌍한 것들.… 그들은 병든 것이 틀림없어."

25 그는 운동을 하기 위해 사각형 훌라후프를 집어 들었다.

26 "흠… 이걸 어떻게 돌리는지 모르겠어."

27 그는 자전거를 꺼내러 가서 사각형 바퀴들을 보았다.

28 "음, 난 이걸 탈 수 없어. 그냥 걸어가야 할 것 같아."

29 그러고 나서 그는 서둘러 집을 나섰다.

30 다른 요정들이 돌아왔을 때, Square는 그들에게 달려갔다.

31 "Mike는 그의 방을 좋아하지 않아. 난 뭘 해야 할지 모르겠어." 그가 말했다.

32 그들은 옷걸이들, 식물들, 그리고 모든 새로 사각형이 된 물건들을 바라보았다.

33 그러고 나서 그들은 서로를 바라보았고, Square는 자신의 문제를 깨달았다.

34 "이 방을 다시 멋지게 만들자." 그가 나머지 요정들에게 말했고, 세 요정들은 다시 한 번 함께 일했다.

● 우리말을 참고하여 본문을 영작하시오.

1 세 도형 요정들
➡ _____

2 Mike의 방에는 세 도형 요정이 살았다.
➡ _____

3 Square는 탁자, 책장, 그리고 창문을 담당했다.
➡ _____

4 Triangle은 옷걸이들과 식물들을 담당했다.
➡ _____

5 Circle은 둥근 것들을 돌보았다.
➡ _____

6 그들은 Mike에게 좋은 방을 만들어 주기 위해서 함께 일했다.
➡ _____

7 어느 날 Square는 방을 더 낮게 만들기로 결심하고 나머지 요정들에게 소리쳤다.
➡ _____

8 "이 식물들을 치워, 그렇지 않으면 그것들의 끝이 뾰족한 잎사귀들이 누군가를 다치게 할 거야!" 그가 Triangle에게 말했다.
➡ _____

9 "하지만 Mike가 매일 그들에게 물을 주는데." Triangle이 말했다.
➡ _____

10 "이 훌라후프를 치워, 그렇지 않으면 굴러가서 뭔가를 부술 거야!" 그가 Circle에게 말했다.
➡ _____

11 "하지만 Mike는 매일 그걸로 운동을 하는데." Circle이 말했다.
➡ _____

12 "난 이 방을 정돈하려고 애쓰지만, 너희 둘은 항상 엉망으로 만들어." 그가 불평했다.
➡ _____

13 Triangle과 Circle이 서로를 쳐다보았다.
➡ _____

14 "그래서 네 생각에는 네가 우리 없이 다 할 수 있다는 거야?" Triangle이 Square에게 물었다.
➡ _____

15 "물론이지. 난 완전히 혼자서 이 방을 더 낮게 만들 수 있어." Square가 대답했다.
➡ _____

16 "잘됐네! 그럼 우린 쉴 수 있겠어." Circle이 Square에게 말했다.
➡ _____

17 Triangle과 Circle이 밖으로 나갔고 이제 Square가 모든 것을 담당했다.

➡ _____

18 그는 옷걸이들과 식물들과 모든 둥근 물건들을 사각형으로 만들었다.

➡ _____

19 그러고 나서 그는 주위를 둘러보고 미소 지었다.

➡ _____

20 "훨씬 좋군!"

➡ _____

21 Mike가 학교에서 집으로 왔을 때, 그는 재킷을 걸기 위해 사각형 옷걸이 하나를 집었다.

➡ _____

22 "뭐야? 이것은 내 옷을 걸고 있지 못할 거야."

➡ _____

23 그는 식물에 물을 주러 가서 그것들의 사각형 잎사귀들을 보았다.

➡ _____

24 "불쌍한 것들.… 그들은 병든 것이 틀림없어."

➡ _____

25 그는 운동을 하기 위해 사각형 훌라후프를 집어 들었다.

➡ _____

26 "흠… 이걸 어떻게 돌리는지 모르겠어."

➡ _____

27 그는 자전거를 꺼내러 가서 사각형 바퀴들을 보았다.

➡ _____

28 "음, 난 이걸 탈 수 없어. 그냥 걸어가야 할 것 같아."

➡ _____

29 그러고 나서 그는 서둘러 집을 나섰다.

➡ _____

30 다른 요정들이 돌아왔을 때, Square는 그들에게 달려갔다.

➡ _____

31 "Mike는 그의 방을 좋아하지 않아. 난 뭘 해야 할지 모르겠어." 그가 말했다.

➡ _____

32 그들은 옷걸이들, 식물들, 그리고 모든 새로 사각형이 된 물건들을 바라보았다.

➡ _____

33 그러고 나서 그들은 서로를 바라보았고, Square는 자신의 문제를 깨달았다.

➡ _____

34 "이 방을 다시 멋지게 만들자." 그가 나머지 요정들에게 말했고, 세 요정들은 다시 한 번 함께 일했다.

➡ _____

[01~03] 다음 글을 읽고 물음에 답하시오.

There lived three shape spirits in Mike's room. Square controlled the table, the bookshelf, and the window. Triangle was in ⓐcharge of the hangers and the plants. Circle took care of the round things. ⓑThey worked together to make a nice room for Mike.

01 위 글의 밑줄 친 ⓐcharge와 같은 의미로 쓰인 것을 고르시오.

① Delivery is free of charge.
② When did they charge at the enemy?
③ He took charge of the farm after his father's death.
④ Before use, charge the battery.
⑤ What did they charge for the repairs?

서답형

02 위 글의 밑줄 친 ⓑThey가 가리키는 것을 쓰시오.

➡ _____ 또는

_____

중요

03 위 글의 내용과 어울리는 속담을 모두 고르시오.

① Too many cooks spoil the broth.
② Two heads are better than one.
③ A stitch in time saves nine stitches.
④ Every cloud has a silver lining.
⑤ Many hands make light work.

[04~06] 다음 글을 읽고 물음에 답하시오.

One day Square decided to make the room better and shouted at (A)[another / the other] spirits.

"Take these plants away, or their pointy leaves will hurt someone!" he said to Triangle.

"But Mike waters them every day," said Triangle.

"Take this hula hoop away, or it will roll and break something!" he said to Circle.

"But Mike exercises with it every day," said Circle.

"I try ⓐto make this room (B)[messy / tidy], but you two always make a mess," he complained.

Triangle and Circle looked at each other.

"So you think you can do it (C)[with / without] us?" Triangle asked Square.

"Sure. I can make this room better all by myself," replied Square.

"Great! Then we can get some rest," Circle said to Square.

서답형

04 위 글의 괄호 (A)~(C)에서 문맥이나 어법상 알맞은 것을 골라 쓰시오.

➡ (A) _____ (B) _____ (C) _____

05 위 글의 밑줄 친 ⓐto make와 to부정사의 용법이 다른 것을 모두 고르시오.

① To help others makes me happy.
② I have no friend to help me.
③ I found it useless to meet her there.
④ To lose weight, he started jogging.
⑤ His fault is to talk too much.

06 위 글의 내용과 일치하지 <u>않는</u> 것은?

① Square는 방을 더 낮게 만들기로 결심했다.

② Mike는 매일 식물들에게 물을 준다.

③ 훌라후프가 굴러가서 뭔가를 부술 거라고 Circle이 말했다.

④ Square는 Triangle과 Circle이 방을 항상 엉망으로 만든다고 불평했다.

⑤ Square는 완전히 혼자서 이 방을 더 낮게 만들 수 있다고 대답했다.

[07~09] 다음 글을 읽고 물음에 답하시오.

Triangle and Circle went out and Square was now in control. ⓐ그는 옷걸이들과 식물들과 모든 둥근 물건들을 사각형으로 만들었다. Then he looked around and smiled. "Much better!"

When Mike came home from school, he picked up a square hanger to hang his jacket on.

"What? This will not hold my clothes."

He went to water the plants and saw their square leaves.

"Poor things. ... They ⓑ<u>must</u> be sick."

He picked up the square hula hoop to exercise.

"Hmm ... I don't know how to spin this."

He went to take out his bike and looked at the square wheels.

"Well, I can't ride this. I'll just have to walk." Then he hurried out of the house.

서답형

07 위 글의 밑줄 친 ⓐ의 우리말에 맞게 주어진 어휘를 이용하여 11 단어로 영작하시오.

the hangers, all the round things

➡ _____

_____

08 위 글의 밑줄 친 ⓑmust와 같은 의미로 쓰인 것을 <u>모두</u> 고르시오.

① All visitors <u>must</u> report to reception.

② You <u>must</u> be hungry after all that walking.

③ I <u>must</u> be going now.

④ You <u>must</u> do as you are told.

⑤ He <u>must</u> be at home. I see his car in his garage.

중요

09 위 글을 읽고 대답할 수 <u>없는</u> 질문은?

① After Triangle and Circle went out, who was in control?

② In what shape did Square make all the things in the room?

③ When Mike came home, why did he go to the plants?

④ How many plants with the square leaves were there?

⑤ Why did Mike have to walk?

[10~12] 다음 글을 읽고 물음에 답하시오.

When the other spirits came back, Square rushed over to them.

"Mike doesn't like his room. ⓐ난 뭘 해야 할지 모르겠어," he said.

They looked at the hangers, the plants, and all the new square things. Then they looked at one another, and Square realized his problem.

ⓑ"Let's make this room greatly again," he said to the others, and the three spirits worked together once again.

서답형

10 위 글의 밑줄 친 @의 우리말에 맞게 영작하시오.

➡ _____

_____

서답형

11 위 글의 밑줄 친 ⓑ에서 어법상 <u>틀린</u> 부분을 찾아 고치시오.

_____ ➡ _____

중요

12 위 글의 종류로 알맞은 것을 고르시오.

① review   ② article   ③ fable
④ legend   ⑤ poem

[13~15] 다음 글을 읽고 물음에 답하시오.

　One day Square decided to make the room better and shouted ___@___ ①the other spirits.
　"Take these plants away, or their pointy leaves will hurt someone!" he said to Triangle.
　"But Mike waters ②them every day," said Triangle.
　"Take this hula hoop away, or it will roll and break something!" he said to Circle.
　"But Mike exercises ___ⓑ___ it every day," said Circle.
　"I try to make this room tidy, but you two always make a mess," he complained.
　Triangle and Circle looked at ③each other.
　"So you think you can do it without ④us?" Triangle asked Square.
　"Sure. I can make this room better all by myself," replied Square.
　"Great! Then ⑤we can get some rest," Circle said to Square.

중요

13 밑줄 친 ①~⑤ 중에서 가리키는 대상이 나머지 넷과 <u>다른</u> 것은?

①　　②　　③　　④　　⑤

14 위 글의 빈칸 @와 ⓑ에 들어갈 전치사가 바르게 짝지어진 것은?

① at – with   ② to – on
③ to – from   ④ at – on
⑤ on – with

서답형

15 다음 문장에서 위 글의 내용과 <u>다른</u> 부분을 고쳐 문장을 다시 쓰시오.

> Triangle and Circle thought that they could make the room better all by themselves without Square.

➡ _____

_____

[16~18] 다음 글을 읽고 물음에 답하시오.

　When the other spirits came back, Square rushed over to them.
　"Mike doesn't like his room. I don't know what to do," he said.
　They looked at the hangers, the plants, and all the new square things. Then they looked at one another, and Square realized his problem.
　"Let's make this room great again," he said to ___@___, and the three spirits worked together once again.

　　　　　Adapted from *The Greedy Triangle*
　　　　　(Marilyn Burns, 2008)

16 위 글에서 알 수 있는 Square의 심경 변화로 가장 알맞은 것을 고르시오.

① excited → disappointed
② worried → hopeful
③ confident → excited
④ satisfied → depressed
⑤ worried → upset

17 위 글의 빈칸 ⓐ에 들어갈 알맞은 말을 고르시오.

① others
② the others
③ another
④ some
⑤ the other

18 위 글을 읽고 답할 수 <u>없는</u> 질문은?

① When the other spirits came back, what did Square do?
② Does Mike like his room?
③ How many new square things are there in the room?
④ Did Square make the room great again by himself?
⑤ Why did the three spirits work together once again?

[19~21] 다음 글을 읽고 물음에 답하시오.

"I try to make this room tidy, but ⓐ<u>you two</u> always make a mess," he ___ⓑ___ .
Triangle and Circle looked at each other.
"So you think you can do it without us?" Triangle asked Square.
"Sure. ⓒ<u>난 완전히 혼자서 이 방을 더 낮게 만들 수 있어</u>," replied Square.
"Great! Then we can get some rest," Circle said to Square.

서답형
19 위 글의 밑줄 친 ⓐ<u>you two</u>가 가리키는 것을 본문에서 찾아 쓰시오.

➡ _____

20 위 글의 빈칸 ⓑ에 들어갈 알맞은 말을 고르시오.

① praised
② required
③ allowed
④ complained
⑤ prevented

서답형
21 위 글의 밑줄 친 ⓒ의 우리말에 맞게 한 단어를 보충하여, 주어진 어휘를 알맞게 배열하시오.

> myself / this / all / make / room / can / I / by

➡ _____

[22~23] 다음 글을 읽고 물음에 답하시오.

Square for Mom
I made a square bag out of (A)[using / used] jeans.
My mom knew (B)[how / what] to wear with it.
ⓐ<u>그것은 엄마를 들뜨게 했어.</u>
That made me (C)[happy / happily].

22 위 글의 괄호 (A)~(C)에서 어법상 알맞은 낱말을 골라 쓰시오.

➡ (A) _____ (B) _____ (C) _____

23 위 글의 밑줄 친 ⓐ의 우리말에 맞게 주어진 어휘를 이용하여 영작하시오. (필요하면 변형할 것, 4 단어)

> excite, her

➡ _____

[01~03] 다음 글을 읽고 물음에 답하시오.

There lived three (A)[shape / shapes] spirits in Mike's room. Square (B)[controled / controlled] the table, the bookshelf, and the window. Triangle was (C)[in / on] charge of the hangers and the plants. Circle took care of the round things. They worked together to make a nice room ___ⓐ___ Mike.

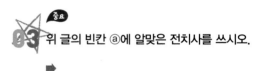

01 위 글의 괄호 (A)~(C)에서 문맥이나 어법상 알맞은 낱말을 골라 쓰시오.

➡ (A) _____ (B) _____ (C) _____

02 What did Square control? Answer in English in a full sentence.

➡ _____

03 위 글의 빈칸 ⓐ에 알맞은 전치사를 쓰시오.

➡ _____

[04~06] 다음 글을 읽고 물음에 답하시오.

Triangle and Circle went out and Square was now in control. He made the hangers, plants, and all the round things square. Then he looked around and smiled. "Much better!"

When Mike came home from school, he picked up a square hanger to hang his jacket on.

"What? This will not hold my (A)[cloths / clothes]."

He went to water the plants and saw their square leaves.

"Poor things. ... They (B)[must / have to] be sick."

He picked up the square hula hoop to exercise.

ⓐ"Hmm ... I don't know how to spin this."

He went to take out his bike and looked at the square wheels.

"Well, I can't ride this. I'll just (C)[must / have to] walk." Then he hurried out of the house.

04 위 글의 괄호 (A)~(C)에서 문맥이나 어법상 알맞은 낱말을 골라 쓰시오.

➡ (A) _____ (B) _____ (C) _____

05 물건들이 다음처럼 사각형으로 바뀐 것에 대한 Mike의 생각을 우리말로 쓰시오.

➡ 사각형 옷걸이:

_____

사각형 잎사귀들을 가진 식물들:

_____

06 위 글을 읽고 Mike가 밑줄 친 ⓐ처럼 말한 이유를 우리말로 쓰시오.

➡ _____

[07~09] 다음 글을 읽고 물음에 답하시오.

Triangle and Circle went out and Square was now in control. He made the hangers, plants, and all the round things square. Then he looked around and smiled. "Much better!"

When Mike came home from school, he picked up a square hanger to hang his jacket on.

"What? This will not hold my clothes."

He went to water the plants and saw their square leaves.

"Poor things. ... They must be sick."

He picked up the square hula hoop to exercise.

"Hmm ... ⓐI don't know how to spin this."

He went to take out his bike and looked at the square wheels.

"Well, I can't ride this. I'll just have to walk." Then he hurried out of the house.

07 위 글에서 Triangle이 담당하던 물건들을 Square가 어떻게 바꾸었는지 우리말로 쓰시오.

➡ (1) _____

(2) _____

중요

08 위 글의 밑줄 친 ⓐ를 다음과 같이 바꿔 쓸 때 빈칸에 들어갈 알맞은 말을 쓰시오.

➡ I don't know how _____ spin this.

09 위 글에서 Square가 Circle이 담당하던 물건들을 바꾼 것 때문에, Mike가 할 수 <u>없게</u> 된 것 두 가지를 우리말로 쓰시오.

➡ (1) _____

(2) _____

[10~11] 다음 글을 읽고 물음에 답하시오.

One day Square decided to make the room better and shouted at the other spirits.

"Take these plants away, or their pointy leaves will hurt someone!" he said to Triangle.

"But Mike waters them every day," said Triangle.

"ⓐTake this hula hoop away, or it will roll and break something!" he said to Circle.

"But Mike exercises with it every day," said Circle.

"I try to make this room tidy, but you two always make a mess," he complained.

Triangle and Circle looked at each other.

ⓑ"So you think you can do it with us?" Triangle asked Square.

"Sure. I can make this room better all by myself," replied Square.

"Great! Then we can get some rest," Circle said to Square.

10 위 글의 밑줄 친 ⓐ를 (1) If, (2) Unless를 사용하여 고치시오.

➡ (1) _____

_____

(2) _____

_____

11 위 글의 밑줄 친 ⓑ에서 흐름상 어색한 부분을 찾아 고치시오.

_____ ➡ _____

해석

Your Turn

1. **A:** Do you know how to cook *ramyeon*?
   '어떻게 ~하는지' '~하는 방법'으로 해석, 상대방의 능력이나 하는 방법을 물을 때 사용
   B: Sure. First, boil some water. Then, put the *ramyeon* and dried soup mix.
   어떤 일을 하는 절차나 방법을 단계적으로 설명할 때, "First. …
   Finally, boil for 4 more minutes.   Then. … Finally. …"를 사용하여 각 단계의 내용을 열거한다.

2. **A:** Do you know how to make potato salad?

   B: Sure. First, boil the potatoes. Then, cut them into pieces. Finally, put
   ~을 조각으로 자르다
   some sauce on them.

3. **A:** Do you know how to make sandwiches?

   B: Sure. First, put an egg on bread. Then, add some vegetables. Finally, put

   bread on top.
   맨 위에

구문해설 • boil 끓이다 • dried 건조된, 마른 • potato 감자
   • cut A into pieces A를 조각으로 자르다 • vegetable 야채, 채소

Express Yourself

Square for Mom
~을 위한
I made a square bag out of used jeans.
   (재료를 나타내어) …에서, …으로   낡은
My mom knew what to wear with it.
   = she should   = the bag
It made her excited.
   exciting(×)
That made me happy.
목적격보어 자리에 부사를 쓸 수 없고 형용사로 써야 한다.

구문해설 • jeans: 청바지 • wear: ~을 입다 • excited: 신이 난, 들뜬, 흥분한

Link to the World

Euclid taught math at the Library of Alexandria when Ptolemy I was the king
   접속사(~일 때)
of Egypt.

People call him "the father of math." He showed how to draw a triangle
call A B(A를 B라고 부르다)   의문사+to부정사(showed의 목적어)
that has three sides of the same length.
주격 관계대명사
He also showed how to find the center of the biggest circle in a triangle.
   의문사+to부정사(showed의 목적어)
One day, Ptolemy I asked, "Is there an easier way to study math?" Euclid
                        부정사(형용사적 용법)
replied, "There is no royal road to learning."
                전치사   동명사

구문해설 • royal road: 쉬운 방법, 지름길, 왕도

1. **A:** 너 라면을 요리할 줄 아니?
   B: 물론이지. 먼저, 약간의 물을 끓여. 그러고 나서, 라면과 건조 수프를 넣어. 마지막으로, 4분을 더 끓여.
2. **A:** 너 감자 샐러드를 만들 줄 아니?
   B: 물론이지. 먼저, 감자를 삶아. 그러고 나서, 감자를 여러 조각으로 잘라. 마지막으로, 그 위에 소스를 좀 뿌려.
3. **A:** 너 샌드위치를 만들 줄 아니?
   B: 물론이지. 먼저, 빵 위에 계란을 올려. 그러고 나서, 채소를 약간 추가해. 마지막으로, 빵을 맨 위에 올려.

엄마를 위한 사각형
난 낡은 청바지로 사각형 가방을 만들었어.
엄마는 그걸 들 때 뭘 입어야 할지 아셔.
그것은 엄마를 들뜨게 했어.
그게 나를 행복하게 했어.

유클리드는 프톨레마이오스 1세(Ptolemy I)가 이집트의 왕이었을 때 알렉산드리아 도서관에서 수학을 가르쳤다.
사람들은 그를 '수학의 아버지'라고 부른다. 그는 같은 길이의 세 변을 가진 삼각형을 어떻게 그리는지를 보여 주었다.
그는 또한 한 개의 삼각형 안에서 가장 큰 원의 중심을 어떻게 찾는지도 보여 주었다.
어느 날, 프톨레마이오스 1세가 "수학을 공부하는 더 쉬운 방법은 없나요?"라고 물었다.
유클리드는 "배움에 왕도는 없습니다."라고 응답했다.

Words & Expressions

01 다음 주어진 두 단어의 관계가 같도록 빈칸에 알맞은 단어를 쓰시오.

> hurry : rush = lastly : _____

02 다음 대화의 빈칸에 공통으로 들어갈 단어로 알맞은 것은?

> G: Do you know _____ to divide this cake into four equal pieces?
> B: Let me see... _____ about dividing it this way? Then the pieces will be the same size and shape.

① what[What]
② why[Why]
③ when[When]
④ who[Who]
⑤ how[How]

03 다음 글의 빈칸 ⓐ와 ⓑ에 들어갈 단어로 알맞은 것은?

> One day Square decided to make the room better and ⓐ_____ at the other spirits.
> "Take these plants away, or their pointy leaves will ⓑ_____ someone!" he said to Triangle.

① whispered – save
② shouted – hurt
③ shouted – take
④ hurried – reply
⑤ divided – control

04 빈칸에 들어갈 말로 알맞은 것은?

> • _____ : to become separated into smaller parts
> *e.g.* I know how to _____ this cake into four equal pieces.

① take
② divide
③ hold
④ carry
⑤ move

05 다음 영영풀이에 해당하는 것을 고르시오.

> to gradually begin to understand something that you did not know or notice before

① roll
② hang
③ perform
④ realize
⑤ remember

06 다음 밑줄 친 부분의 의미가 바르지 않은 것은?

① The boat only carries you and one of the things <u>at a time</u>. 한 번에
② I can take them to the other side <u>one by one</u>. 하나씩
③ I can make this room better all <u>by myself</u>. 저절로
④ He picked up a hanger to <u>hang</u> his jacket on. 걸다
⑤ He went to take out his bike and looked at the <u>square wheels</u>. 사각형 바퀴

Conversation

07 주어진 그림을 참고하여 대화의 빈칸에 들어갈 말로 알맞은 것을 고르시오.

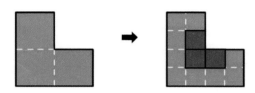

Ben: Do you know how to divide this into four equal pieces?

Jenny: Sure. First, divide it into three _____(A)_____ . Then, divide each square into four smaller squares. Finally, color three small squares in the inside corner of the L.

Ben: Oh, I can see ___(B)___ other L shapes around it! You're great!

① different triangles – two
② equal squares – four
③ equal circles – three
④ equal squares – three
⑤ different squares – four

08 대화의 빈칸에 들어갈 말의 순서로 알맞은 것은?

G: Do you know how to make this?
B: _____

(A) Finally, wrap it up and make a triangle.
(B) Then, add some dried fish and hot peppers.
(C) It's easy. First, put some rice on *gim*.

① (A) – (B) – (C)　② (B) – (A) – (C)
③ (B) – (C) – (A)　④ (C) – (A) – (B)
⑤ (C) – (B) – (A)

[09~10] 다음 대화를 읽고 물음에 답하시오.

(1)
W: Excuse me. Do you know ____(A)____ draw a mouse with shapes?
M: Sure. First, draw a large triangle. Then, draw two dots and 6 lines. Finally, draw two small circles.
W: Thanks. I'll draw it myself now.

(2)
A: Do you know ____(A)____ make potato salad?
B: Sure. (a)First, boil the potatoes. Then, cut them into pieces. Finally, put some sauce on them.

09 (1)과 (2)의 빈칸 (A)에 공통으로 들어갈 두 단어를 쓰시오.

➡ _____

10 위 대화의 밑줄 친 (a)의 의도로 알맞은 것은?

① 능력 묻기　　② 소개하기
③ 관심 묻기　　④ 열거하기
⑤ 동작 묘사

[11~12] 다음 대화의 빈칸에 들어갈 알맞은 표현은?

11

A: _____
B: Sure. First, put an egg on bread. Then, add some vegetables. Finally, put bread on top.

① Do you know how to make potato salad?
② Are you good at cooking?
③ Do you know how to cook *ramyeon*?
④ Why are you making sandwiches?
⑤ Do you know how to make sandwiches?

12

> G: Do you know how to make paper airplanes?
>
> B: _____

① No, you can't.
② Sure. I'll show you how.
③ Put some legs on the bottom.
④ Sure. Put wheels under the car.
⑤ Sure. Push the button here.

Grammar

13 다음 빈칸에 알맞은 말이 바르게 짝지어진 것은?

> • Mildred _____ her room bright.
> • It shows _____ to divide a square into seven pieces.

① made – how
② wanted – why
③ ordered – that
④ asked – what
⑤ forced – where

14 다음 중 어법상 어색한 문장은?

① I don't know what to do.
② I can't decide which car to buy.
③ She knew where to stop and where to pass.
④ Rose was wondering whom to meet that afternoon.
⑤ He wants to know when should begin the project.

15 다음 중 어법상 옳은 것은?

① Let's make her happily.
② Samantha looked very friendly.
③ The thick clothes keep me warmly.
④ Jogging early in the morning makes me health.
⑤ Rick painted his house greenly.

16 다음 주어진 단어를 이용하여 빈칸에 알맞은 말을 쓰시오.

> 어느 것을 먹어야 할지 결정하지 못하겠어.
> = I can't decide _____. (eat)

➡ _____

17 괄호 안에서 알맞은 것을 고르시오.

(1) He also showed (how / what) to find the center of the biggest circle in a triangle.
(2) Can you tell me where (sitting / to sit)?
(3) Do you know (how / why) to solve the puzzle in another way?
(4) I'm not sure how (I should / I) draw a bear with shapes.
(5) Try to make the poem (special / specially) using your imagination and creativity.
(6) The boys (founded / found) the movie exciting.

18 다음 글에서 어법상 잘못 쓰인 것을 찾아 알맞게 고치시오. (2곳)

> One day, Square wanted the other spirits to take the round or triangular things away to make the room better. Triangle and Circle left the room to get some rest and Square made the hangers, the plants, and the all round things square. However, Mike didn't like the newly changed things, and Square didn't know how to do. He realized his problem, and the three spirits worked together again.

➡ _____

➡ _____

Reading

[19~20] 다음 글을 읽고 물음에 답하시오.

> There lived three shape spirits in Mike's room. Square controlled the table, the bookshelf, and the window. Triangle was in charge of the hangers and the plants. Circle took care of the round things. They worked together ⓐto make a nice room for Mike.

19 아래 〈보기〉에서 위 글의 밑줄 친 ⓐto make와 문법적 쓰임이 같은 것의 개수를 고르시오.

┌─── 보기 ───┐
① He was pleased to make such a beautiful garden.
② She went shopping to make me a delicious lunch.
③ Please tell me the way to make a wooden table.
④ He must be foolish to make such a big mistake.
⑤ I tried to make a model airplane.
└──────────┘

① 1개 ② 2개 ③ 3개 ④ 4개 ⑤ 5개

20 위 글의 내용과 일치하지 <u>않는</u> 것은?

① Mike의 방에는 세 도형 요정이 살았다.
② Square는 탁자, 옷장, 그리고 창문을 담당했다.
③ Triangle은 옷걸이들과 식물들을 담당했다.
④ Circle은 둥근 것들을 돌보았다.
⑤ 세 도형 요정들은 Mike에게 좋은 방을 만들기 위해서 함께 일했다.

[21~23] 다음 글을 읽고 물음에 답하시오.

> One day Square decided to make the room better and shouted at the other spirits.
> "Take these plants away, or their pointy leaves will hurt someone!" he said to Triangle.
> "But Mike waters them every day," said Triangle.
> "Take this hula hoop away, ___ⓐ___ it will roll and break something!" he said to Circle.
> "But Mike exercises with it every day," said Circle.
> "I try to make this room tidy, but you two always make a mess," he complained.
> Triangle and Circle looked at each other.
> "So you think you can do it without us?" Triangle asked Square.
> "Sure. I can make this room better all ⓑby myself," replied Square.
> "Great! Then we can get some rest," Circle said to Square.

21 주어진 영영풀이에 해당하는 단어를 본문에서 찾아 쓰시오.

| neat and arranged in an organized way |

➡ _____

22 위 글의 빈칸 ⓐ에 알맞은 말을 쓰시오.

➡ _____

23 위 글의 밑줄 친 ⓑby myself와 바꿔 쓸 수 있는 한 단어를 쓰시오.

➡ _____

[24~26] 다음 글을 읽고 물음에 답하시오.

Triangle and Circle went out and Square was now ___ⓐ___ control. He made the hangers, plants, and all the round things square. Then he looked around and smiled. "Much better!"

When Mike came home from school, he picked up a square hanger to hang his jacket ___ⓑ___ .

"What? ①This will not hold my clothes."

He went to water the plants and saw ②their square leaves.

"Poor things. ... ③They must be sick."

He picked up the square hula-hoop to exercise.

"Hmm ... I don't know how to spin ④this."

He went to take out his bike and looked at the square wheels.

"Well, I can't ride ⑤this. I'll just have to walk." Then he hurried out of the house.

24 위 글의 빈칸 ⓐ와 ⓑ에 들어갈 전치사가 바르게 짝지어진 것은?

① in – on
② at – to
③ in – from
④ for – to
⑤ for – on

25 위 글의 밑줄 친 ①~⑤가 지칭하는 것이 옳지 <u>않은</u> 것은?

① a square hanger
② the plants
③ the plants
④ the square hula hoop
⑤ the square wheels

26 본문의 내용과 일치하도록 다음 빈칸 (A)와 (B)에 알맞은 단어를 쓰시오.

Mike couldn't do such things as hanging his jacket, spinning the hula hoop, and (A)_____ his bike because (B)_____ made the things square.

[27~28] 다음 글을 읽고 물음에 답하시오.

ⓐWhen the other spirits came back, Square rushed over to them.

"Mike doesn't like his room. I don't know what to do," he said.

They looked at the hangers, the plants, and all the new square things. Then they looked at one another, and Square realized ⓑhis problem.

"Let's make this room great again," he said to the others, and the three spirits worked together once again.

Adapted from *The Greedy Triangle*
(Marilyn Burns, 2008)

27 위 글의 밑줄 친 ⓐWhen과 같은 의미로 쓰인 것을 고르시오.

① I don't know when Mike went out.
② Do you remember when you saw it?
③ When did he promise to meet her?
④ He stays at home when it rains.
⑤ When can she come?

28 다음 빈칸에 알맞은 단어를 넣어 밑줄 친 ⓑhis problem에 대한 설명을 완성하시오.

Square made the hangers and the plants square, so Mike didn't _____ _____ _____ .

01 다음 짝지어진 단어의 관계가 같도록 빈칸에 알맞은 말을 쓰시오.

> perfect : imperfect = join : _____

02 우리말에 맞게 빈칸에 알맞은 단어를 쓰시오.

> • 먼저, 낡은 청바지에서 다리 부분을 잘라내.
>   (A) _____, _____ _____ the leg
>   from used jeans.
> • 마지막으로, 그것을 싸서 삼각형을 만들어.
>   (B) _____, _____ it _____ and
>   make a triangle.

03 다음 글의 괄호 안에 알맞은 말을 선택하시오.

> One day Square decided to make the room better and shouted at the other spirits.
> "Take these plants away, or their (A) [round / pointy] leaves will hurt someone!" he said to Triangle.
> "But Mike waters them every day," said Triangle.
> "Take this hula hoop away, or it will (B) [hang / roll] and break something!" he said to Circle.
> "But Mike exercises with it every day," said Circle.
> "I try to make this room tidy, but you two always make a mess," he (C)[complained / cheered].

	(A)	(B)	(C)
①	round	roll	complained
②	round	hang	cheered
③	pointy	roll	cheered
④	pointy	roll	complained
⑤	pointy	hang	complained

04 다음 영영풀이에 해당하는 단어는?

> a short coat that covers the upper part of the body

① plant　　② shirt　　③ jacket
④ space　　⑤ bottom

[05~06] 다음 대화를 읽고 물음에 답하시오.

> Boy: Do you know how to solve this puzzle?
> Girl: What is it?
> Boy: You must take a dog, a chicken, and a bag of rice across the river. The boat only carries you and one of the things at a time.
> Girl: That's easy. I can take them to the other side one by one.
> Boy: But without you, the dog will kill the chicken, and the chicken will eat the rice.
> Girl: Let me see. ... First, take the chicken and come back. Then, take the rice and come back with the chicken.
> Boy: And?
> Girl: After that, take the dog and come back. Finally, take the chicken.
> Boy: You're great!

05 다음 질문에 대한 답을 대화에서 찾아 영어로 쓰시오.

> Q: What's the problem if the girl takes the rice first?

➡ _____

06 위 대화를 읽고 답할 수 <u>없는</u> 질문은?

① Did the girl know the answer at first?

② What must be taken to the other side of the river?

③ Which must be taken across the river last?

④ When did the boy know the answer?

⑤ What will the chicken do if the girl takes the dog first?

[07~08] 다음 대화를 읽고 물음에 답하시오.

B: ⓐ<u>This</u> looks great.

G: I think so, too. Do you know how to make it?

B: It's easy. First, put some rice on *gim*. Then, add some dried fish and hot peppers. Finally, wrap it up and make a triangle.

07 위 대화의 밑줄 친 ⓐThis는 무엇을 가리키는가?

① a square kite

② a triangle *gimbap*

③ triangle sunglasses

④ a circle bookmark

⑤ a round bear

08 위 대화에서 언급된 것을 만들 때 재료로 언급되지 <u>않은</u> 것은?

① rice   ② *gim*

③ dried fish   ④ wrap

⑤ hot peppers

09 다음 두 사람의 대화가 <u>어색한</u> 것은?

① A: So you think you can do it without us?

　B: Sure!

② A: Do you know how to solve this puzzle?

　B: What is it?

③ A: Do you know how to cook *ramyeon*?

　B: Sure. First, put an egg on bread. Then, add some vegetables. Finally, put bread on top.

④ A: Do you know how to draw a bear with shapes?

　B: Sure. First, draw a large circle. Then, draw three small circles. Finally, draw three dots.

⑤ A: Do you know how to make three more triangles with three more pencils?

　B: Let me see. ... It's too difficult for me.

10 대화의 밑줄 친 우리말에 맞게 문장의 빈칸에 들어갈 알맞은 말을 고르시오.

B: Do you know how to fly this?

G: Yes. I'll show you how. <u>그것은 바람을 마주해야만 해.</u> Hold it up like this.

It has to _____ the wind.

① reply   ② visit

③ face   ④ move

⑤ control

11 다음 중 어법상 <u>어색한</u> 것은?

① He made the tables square.

② Julia painted the table brown.

③ This thick jacket kept me warm last winter.

④ The boy found the ants very strongly.

⑤ Don't get me wrong.

12 다음 그림을 보고 괄호 안에 주어진 어휘를 이용하여 빈칸에 알맞은 말을 쓰시오.

> A: Do you know _____ cookies? (bake)
>
> B: Yes, I do. I like baking cookies.

13 주어진 문장의 밑줄 친 부분과 용법이 <u>다른</u> 하나는?

> The pig <u>made</u> the tent dirty.

① The movie <u>made</u> me excited.

② The song <u>makes</u> me sad.

③ Her mom <u>made</u> her a dress.

④ Having regular exercise <u>makes</u> us healthy.

⑤ His joke <u>made</u> me laugh a lot.

14 다음 괄호 안에 주어진 단어를 어법에 맞게 빈칸에 한 단어씩 쓰시오.

(1) I didn't know where to fish.

= I didn't know _____ _____ _____ _____. (fish)

(2) Will you tell me _____ _____ _____ to the bus stop? (get)

= Will you tell me how I can get to the bus stop?

(3) Marie asked her mom _____ _____ _____ after. (look)

= Marie asked her mom whom she should look after.

(4) Please tell me which apple to choose.

= Please tell me _____ _____ _____ _____ _____. (choose)

[15~16] 다음 글을 읽고 물음에 답하시오.

> ⓐThere lived three shape spirits in Mike's room. Square controlled the table, the bookshelf, and the window. Triangle was in charge of the hangers and the plants. Circle took care of the round things. They worked together to make a nice room for Mike.

15 위 글의 밑줄 친 ⓐThere와 의미가 <u>다른</u> 것을 모두 고르시오.

① <u>There</u> are two people waiting outside.

② <u>There</u> seemed to be no doubt about it.

③ I hope we get <u>there</u> in time.

④ <u>There</u> is a book on the desk.

⑤ What were you doing <u>there</u>?

16 Who took care of the round things? Answer in English in two words.

➡ _____

[17~19] 다음 글을 읽고 물음에 답하시오.

Triangle and Circle went out and Square was now in control. He made the hangers, plants, and all the round things ___ⓐ___. Then he looked around and smiled. "Much better!"

When Mike came home from school, he picked up a square hanger ①to hang his jacket on.

"What? This will not hold my clothes."

He went ②to water the plants and saw their square leaves.

"Poor things. ... They must be sick."

He picked up the square hula hoop ③to exercise.

"Hmm ... I don't know how ④to spin this."

He went ⑤to take out his bike and looked at the square wheels.

"Well, I can't ride this. I'll just have to walk." Then he hurried out of the house.

ᐧ출제율90%
17 위 글의 빈칸 ⓐ에 들어갈 알맞은 말을 고르시오.

① pointy   ② triangle   ③ tidy
④ circle   ⑤ square

ᐧ출제율95%
18 밑줄 친 ①~⑤ 중에서 to부정사의 용법이 나머지 넷과 다른 것은?

①   ②   ③   ④   ⑤

ᐧ출제율95%
19 위 글의 내용과 일치하지 <u>않는</u> 것은?

① Triangle과 Circle이 밖으로 나갔고 이제 Square가 모든 것을 담당했다.
② Mike가 학교에서 집으로 왔을 때, 그는 옷걸이에 재킷을 걸었다.
③ Mike는 식물들이 병든 것이 틀림없다고 생각했다.
④ Mike는 사각형 훌라후프를 돌릴 수 없었다.
⑤ Mike는 자전거를 타는 대신 걸어가기로 했다.

[20~22] 다음 글을 읽고 물음에 답하시오.

Triangle Sunglasses

I made triangle sunglasses ⓐout of a paper box and a plastic bag.

My baby sister knew ⓑ언제 그걸 써야 할지.

They made her excited.

That made me happy.

ᐧ출제율95%
20 위 글의 밑줄 친 ⓐout of와 같은 의미로 쓰인 것을 고르시오.

① This robot was made <u>out of</u> an empty can.
② Two bears came <u>out of</u> the forest.
③ She did so <u>out of</u> curiosity.
④ He came <u>out of</u> a poor family.
⑤ <u>Out of</u> sight, <u>out of</u> mind.

ᐧ출제율95%
21 위 글의 밑줄 친 ⓑ의 우리말에 맞게 주어진 어휘를 이용하여 5 단어로 영작하시오.

put, on

➡ _____

ᐧ출제율95%
22 위 글을 읽고 알 수 <u>없는</u> 것을 고르시오.

① 삼각형 선글라스를 만든 사람
② 삼각형 선글라스의 재료
③ 삼각형 선글라스를 쓸 사람
④ 삼각형 선글라스를 써야 할 때
⑤ 글쓴이의 기분

01 다음은 상대방의 능력 여부를 묻는 말이다. 주어진 단어를 이용하여 대화의 내용에 어울리는 질문을 완성하시오.

> B: Do you know _____?
> G: Sure. First, divide it into three equal squares. Then, divide each square into four smaller squares. Finally, color three small squares in the inside corner of the L.
> B: Oh, I can see three other L shapes around it! You're great!

> how / divide / this / equal pieces

➡ _____

02 다음은 연을 날리는 방법에 대한 글이다. 주어진 문장을 순서대로 배열하여 절차를 말하는 대화를 완성하시오.

> • hold it up until it catches the wind
> • let the line out
> • stand with your back to the wind

> A: Do you know how to fly this?
> B: _____
> _____
> _____

03 다음 대화의 밑줄 친 우리말에 맞게 주어진 어휘를 이용하여 영어로 쓰시오.

> ┤ 보기 ├
> (A) (know / how / divide / this cake / pieces)
> (B) (how / divide / it / this)

> G: (A)이 케이크를 네 개의 같은 조각으로 어떻게 나눌 수 있는지 아니?
> B: Let me see. ... (B)이 방법으로 그것을 나누는 것은 어때? Then the pieces will be the same size and shape.

➡ (A) _____
_____

(B) _____

04 다음 우리말을 주어진 어휘를 이용하여 영작하시오.

(1) 연필 세 자루를 더 추가해서 어떻게 삼각형 3개를 더 만드는지 아니? (make, more, with)
➡ _____
_____

(2) 이 꽃들을 어디서 길러야 하는지 내게 알려 줘. (grow, let, these)
➡ _____

(3) 언제 출발해야 하는지 말해 줄 수 있어? (tell, can, start)
➡ _____

(4) 작은 검정색 원들이 그것을 완벽하게 만들었어. (perfect, make, the)
➡ _____

(5) 그것은 점심시간에 나를 배부르게 했지. (make, it, lunch time, full, at)
➡ _____

(6) 나의 아버지는 내가 정직하다고 믿는다. (father, believe)
➡ _____

One day Square decided (A)[to make / making] the room better and shouted at the other spirits.

"Take these plants away, ___ⓐ___ their (B) [pointing / pointy] leaves will hurt someone!" he said to Triangle.

"But Mike (C)[water / waters] them every day," said Triangle.

"Take this hula hoop away, or it will roll and break something!" he said to Circle.

"But Mike exercises with it every day," said Circle.

"I try to make this room tidy, but you two always make a mess," he complained.

Triangle and Circle looked at each other.

"So you think you can do it without us?" Triangle asked Square.

"Sure. I can make this room better all by myself," replied Square.

"Great! Then we can get some rest," Circle said to Square.

05 위 글의 빈칸 ⓐ에 들어갈 알맞은 말을 쓰시오.

➡ _____

06 위 글의 괄호 (A)~(C)에서 문맥이나 어법상 알맞은 낱말을 골라 쓰시오.

➡ (A) _____ (B) _____ (C) _____

중요
07 다음 질문에 대한 알맞은 대답을 주어진 단어로 시작하여 쓰시오. (6 단어)

Q: Why does Square tell Circle to take the hula hoop away?

A: Because _____ if Circle doesn't take it away.

➡ _____

Triangle and Circle went out and Square was now in control. He made the hangers, plants, and all the round things square. Then he looked around and smiled. "Much better!"

When Mike came home from school, he picked up a square hanger to hang his jacket on.

"What? This will not hold my clothes."

He went to water the plants and saw their square leaves.

"Poor things. ... They must be sick."

He picked up the square hula hoop to exercise.

"Hmm ... I don't know how to spin this."

He went to take out his bike and looked at the square wheels.

ⓐ"Well, I can't ride this. I'll just have to walk." Then he hurried out of the house.

중요
08 위 글에서 Circle이 담당하던 물건들을 Square가 어떻게 바꾸었는지 우리말로 쓰시오.

➡ (1) _____
   (2) _____

09 다음 문장에서 위 글의 내용과 <u>다른</u> 부분을 찾아서 <u>모두</u> 고치시오.

• When Mike came home from school, he hung jacket on a hanger, and rode his bike.

➡ _____

_____

10 위 글을 읽고 Mike가 밑줄 친 ⓐ처럼 말한 이유를 우리말로 쓰시오.

➡ _____

01 다음 주어진 어구를 이용하여 상대방의 능력을 묻는 질문과 그에 대한 절차를 설명하는 대화를 완성하시오.

<능력 묻기>

how to share a photo / how to make potato salad / how to make sandwiches

<절차 열거하기>

press and hold a photo, choose "Share.", choose an SNS /

boil the potatoes, cut them into pieces, put some sauce on them /

put an egg on bread, add some vegetables, put bread on top

(1) _____

_____

(2) _____

_____

(3) _____

_____

02 주어진 어휘를 이용하여 3문장 이상을 쓰시오.

what	how	when	where	whom	eat	take	go	put	meet

(1) _____

(2) _____

(3) _____

(4) _____

(5) _____

03 빈칸에 알맞은 말을 써서 문장을 완성하시오.

Triangle Sunglasses

I made triangle sunglasses (A)_____ a paper box and a plastic bag.

My baby sister knew (B)_____ to put them on.

They made her (C)_____.

That made me (D)_____.

단원별 모의고사

01 다음 단어에 대한 영어 설명이 <u>어색한</u> 것은?

① square: a flat shape with four sides of equal length and four angles of 90°

② reply: to answer someone by saying or writing something

③ excited: feeling very happy and relaxed

④ hold: to have something in your hands or arms

⑤ hula hoop: a very large ring that you try to keep spinning round your body

02 다음 짝지어진 단어의 관계가 같도록 빈칸에 알맞은 말을 쓰시오.

> dot : spot = choose : _____

03 다음 영영풀이에 해당하는 단어를 고르시오.

> to turn around and around, especially fast

① spin   ② move
③ hang   ④ roll
⑤ rush

04 대화의 빈칸에 들어갈 단어를 주어진 철자로 시작하여 쓰시오.

> G: Do you know how to divide this cake into four equal pieces?
>
> B: Let me see. ... How about dividing it this way? Then the pieces will be the s_____ size and shape.

➡ _____

05 빈칸 (A)와 (B)에 들어갈 알맞은 단어는?

> • Triangle was in (A)_____ of the hangers and the plants.
> • The three spirits are looking at one (B)_____.

    (A)   (B)
① care   – other
② control – each
③ control – other
④ charge – the other
⑤ charge – another

06 대화의 빈칸에 들어갈 말로 알맞은 것은?

> B: Here's a triangle with three pencils. Do you know how to make three more triangles with three more pencils?
>
> G: Let me see... _____ Can I break the pencils in half?
>
> B: No, you can't.

① Do you know how to do it?
② It's about how to make three more triangles.
③ It's too difficult for me.
④ I don't think you know the answer.
⑤ Sorry, I can't remember it.

07 다음 대화의 빈칸에 들어갈 말을 세 단어의 영어로 쓰시오.

> A: Do you know _____ a fish with shapes?
>
> B: Sure. First, draw a large square. Then, draw a triangle. Finally, draw a small circle in the square.

➡ _____

[08~09] 다음 대화를 읽고 물음에 답하시오.

> **Boy:** Do you know how to solve this puzzle?
>
> **Girl:** What is it?
>
> **Boy:** You must take a dog, a chicken, and a bag of rice across the river. The boat only carries you and one of the things __(a)__ a time.
>
> **Girl:** That's easy. I can take them to the other side one __(b)__ one.
>
> **Boy:** But without you, the dog will kill the chicken, and the chicken will eat the rice.
>
> **Girl:** Let me see. ... First, take the chicken and come back. Then, take the rice and come back with the chicken.
>
> **Boy:** And?
>
> **Girl:** After that, take the dog and come back. Finally, take the chicken.
>
> **Boy:** You're great!

08 위 대화의 (a)와 (b)에 알맞은 전치사로 짝지어진 것은?

① on – to
② at – by
③ for – in
④ from – with
⑤ with – for

09 위 대화의 내용과 일치하지 <u>않는</u> 것은?

① The boy and the girl are talking about a puzzle.
② Without the girl, the dog will kill the chicken.
③ Without the girl, the chicken will eat the rice.
④ The girl must carry a dog, rice, and a chicken together on the boat.
⑤ The girl finally solves the puzzle.

10 다음 대화에서 말한 퍼즐의 답으로 알맞은 것은?

> **B:** Do you know how to divide this into four equal pieces?
>
> **G:** Sure. First, divide it into three equal squares. Then, divide each square into four smaller squares. Finally, color three small squares in the inside corner of the L.
>
> **B:** Oh, I can see three other L shapes around it! You're great!

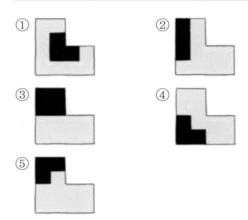

11 다음 두 사람의 대화가 <u>어색한</u> 것은?

① A: Do you know how to fly this kite?
　 B: Yes. I'll show you how.
② A: Excuse me. Do you know how to draw a mouse with shapes?
　 B: Sure.
③ A: Do you know how to solve this puzzle?
　 B: When is it?
④ A: Do you know how to solve the puzzle in another way?
　 B: Let me see.
⑤ A: Do you know how to cook *ramyeon*?
　 B: Sure. First, boil some water.

12 다음은 감자 샐러드를 만드는 방법에 관한 대화다. 빈칸에 어울리는 단어를 쓰시오.

> A: Do you know how to make potato salad?
> B: Sure. (A)_____, boil the potatoes. Then, cut them (B) _____ pieces. Finally, put some sauce (C)_____ them.

13 다음 그림을 보고 괄호 안에 주어진 어휘를 이용하여 빈칸에 알맞은 말을 쓰시오.

> A: Do you like cooking?
> B: Of course. Cooking makes _____. (excite)

14 다음 빈칸에 들어갈 말로 알맞지 <u>않은</u> 것을 <u>모두</u> 고르시오.

> I told him _____ to do it.

① what   ② when   ③ how
④ where   ⑤ why

15 다음 빈칸에 공통으로 들어갈 말로 가장 알맞은 것은?

> • Refrigerators _____ food cool.
> • City workers _____ them clean and green.

① need   ② require   ③ ask
④ force   ⑤ keep

16 다음 중 어법상 <u>어색한</u> 것을 고르시오.

① She painted the house bright.
② I taught him how could read English.
③ The bird kept the eggs warm.
④ I knew where to put the small four-leaf-clover.
⑤ I don't know what I should say to him.

17 다음 문장에서 어법상 <u>어색한</u> 것을 바르게 고쳐 다시 쓰시오.

(1) Do you know what make triangle sunglasses?
　➡ _____

(2) When to finish the works were an important issue.
　➡ _____

(3) Tell me whom I to meet.
　➡ _____

(4) The news made them sadly.
　➡ _____

(5) We found he honesty.
　➡ _____

[18~19] 다음 글을 읽고 물음에 답하시오.

> There lived three shape spirits in Mike's room. Square controlled the table, the bookshelf, and the window. Triangle was in charge of the hangers and the plants. Circle ⓐ <u>took care of</u> the round things. They worked together to make a nice room for Mike.

18 Who was in charge of the plants? Answer in English.

　➡ _____

19 위 글의 밑줄 친 ⓐtook care of와 바꿔 쓸 수 있는 것을 모두 고르시오.

① took after   ② cared for
③ looked like   ④ called for
⑤ looked after

[20~21] 다음 글을 읽고 물음에 답하시오.

One day Square decided to make the room better and shouted at the other spirits.

"Take these plants away, or their pointy leaves will hurt someone!" ①he said to Triangle.

"But Mike waters them every day," said Triangle.

ⓐ"Take this hula hoop away, and it will roll and break something!" he said to Circle.

"But Mike exercises with ②it every day," said Circle.

"③I try to make this room tidy, but you two always make a mess," he complained.

Triangle and Circle looked at each other.

"So ④you think you can do it without us?" Triangle asked Square.

"Sure. I can make this room better all by ⑤myself," replied Square.

"Great! Then we can get some rest," Circle said to Square.

20 밑줄 친 ①~⑤ 중에서 가리키는 대상이 나머지 넷과 다른 것은?

①   ②   ③   ④   ⑤

21 위 글의 밑줄 친 ⓐ에서 흐름상 어색한 부분을 찾아 고치시오.

＿＿＿＿＿＿＿   ➡   ＿＿＿＿＿＿＿

[22~23] 다음 글을 읽고 물음에 답하시오.

Triangle and Circle went out and Square was now in control. He made the hangers, plants, and all the round things square. Then he looked around and smiled. "Much better!"

When Mike came home from school, he picked up a square hanger to hang his jacket on.

"What? This will not hold my clothes."

He went to water the plants and (A)[saw / to see] their square leaves.

"Poor things. ... They must be sick."

He picked up the square hula hoop (B)[exercising / to exercise].

"Hmm ... I don't know (C)[how / what] to spin this."

He went to take out his bike and looked at the square wheels.

"Well, I can't ride this. I'll just have to walk." Then he hurried out of the house.

22 위 글의 괄호 (A)~(C)에서 문맥이나 어법상 알맞은 낱말을 골라 쓰시오.

➡ (A) ＿＿＿＿＿   (B) ＿＿＿＿＿   (C) ＿＿＿＿＿

23 위 글의 앞부분에서 알 수 있는 Square의 심경으로 가장 알맞은 것을 고르시오.

① bored   ② disappointed
③ satisfied   ④ ashamed
⑤ nervous

INSIGHT
on the textbook
교과서 파헤치기

※ 다음 영어를 우리말로 쓰시오.

01	alone	_____
02	bite	_____
03	careful	_____
04	dangerous	_____
05	direction	_____
06	clothes	_____
07	exist	_____
08	past	_____
09	far	_____
10	figure	_____
11	climber	_____
12	actually	_____
13	following	_____
14	fun	_____
15	safety	_____
16	real	_____
17	special	_____
18	remember	_____
19	climb	_____
20	scenery	_____
21	harmony	_____

22	behind	_____
23	someday	_____
24	join	_____
25	kind	_____
26	create	_____
27	balance	_____
28	later	_____
29	probably	_____
30	rule	_____
31	search	_____
32	touch	_____
33	skill	_____
34	yet	_____
35	hang up	_____
36	keep ~ in mind	_____
37	over there	_____
38	make noise	_____
39	be good for	_____
40	hear of	_____
41	for the first time	_____
42	for example	_____
43	go up	_____

※ 다음 우리말을 영어로 쓰시오.

01 활동적인, 활발한		22 담소하다, 채팅하다	
02 표지판, 간판		23 과거, 지난날	
03 축제		24 비결, 요령, 속임수	
04 인물, 모습		25 ~ 없이, ~하지 않고	
05 밀다		26 해변, 바닷가	
06 곳, 장소		27 경치, 풍경	
07 풀, 잔디		28 균형, 평형	
08 연습하다		29 조화, 화합	
09 조언, 충고		30 옷, 의복	
10 가까운, 친한		31 조심하는, 주의 깊은	
11 안전한		32 위험한	
12 포즈[자세]		33 안전, 안전성	
13 정보		34 특별한, 특수한	
14 길, 거리, 도로		35 예를 들면, 예를 들어	
15 바위, 암석		36 처음으로	
16 십대의		37 ~을 명심하다	
17 공주		38 ~에 좋다	
18 헐거워진, 풀린, 헐렁한		39 ~ 앞에	
19 거울		40 전화를 끊다	
20 헬멧		41 떠들다	
21 박물관, 미술관		42 ~에 대해 듣다	
		43 저쪽에, 저기에서	

※ 다음 영영풀이에 알맞은 단어를 <보기>에서 골라 쓴 후, 우리말 뜻을 쓰시오.

1 _____ : an artist who paints pictures: _____

2 _____ : able or likely to hurt or harm you: _____

3 _____ : moving around a lot or doing a lot of things: _____

4 _____ : an area of sand or stones beside the sea: _____

5 _____ : sit on a horse or bike and control its movements: _____

6 _____ : to talk to each other in an informal and friendly way: _____

7 _____ : a female member of a royal family, usually the daughter of a king or
                queen: _____

8 _____ : a road in a city, town, or village, usually with houses along it: _____

9 _____ : aged between thirteen and nineteen years old: _____

10 _____ : the things that people wear, such as shirts, coats, trousers, and dresses:
                _____

11 _____ : the hard substance which the Earth is made of: _____

12 _____ : a hat made of a strong material which you wear to protect your head:
                _____

13 _____ : what you think someone should do in a particular situation: _____

14 _____ : to move towards the top of something such as a tree, mountain, or
                ladder: _____

15 _____ : to use force to make something move away from you or away from its
                previous position: _____

16 _____ : a flat piece of glass which reflects light, so that when you look at it you
                can see yourself reflected in it: _____

보기			
beach	dangerous	chat	street
push	mirror	teenage	active
helmet	painter	ride	advice
clothes	climb	rock	princess

※ 다음 우리말과 일치하도록 빈칸에 알맞은 말을 쓰시오.

Get Ready - 2

1. G: Look _____ that boy. He's _____.

   B: He's _____ an MTB. Do you _____ _____ it?

   G: No. _____ is it?

   B: It's a _____ bike _____ _____ _____ a mountain.

2. G: Wait. _____ jump _____ the water _____.

   B: _____ _____ ?

   G: You _____ swim _____ a life jacket. _____ it _____.

3. G: _____ _____ the beautiful flowers _____ _____! I'd _____ _____ _____ a selfie _____ _____ them.

   B: You _____ go _____ there.

   G: Oh, _____.

4. B: I _____ _____ _____ the birds _____ the trees.

   G: You _____ _____ _____ too close to the _____.

   B: All _____, thanks.

Start Off - Listen & Talk A

1. G: Dad, _____ you _____ _____ _____ Kim Soyun, the rock _____?

   M: Yes, I've _____ her _____ _____.

   G: She's _____ _____ _____ at a _____ this Saturday. I _____ _____ _____ the camp.

   M: Okay, Miso, _____ you _____ _____ _____ too high.

   G: All _____. Thanks, Dad.

2. G: _____ you _____ of Rock Boys?

   M: _____, _____ _____.

   G: It's my _____ band. There's a _____ this Saturday. _____ _____ _____?

   M: Okay, Minju, but you _____ _____ _____ _____ too late.

   G: All _____. Thanks, Dad.

1. G: 저 소년을 봐. 그는 대단하다.
   B: 그는 MTB를 타고 있어. 넌 그것에 대해 알고 있니?
   G: 아니. 그게 뭐지?
   B: 그것은 산에서 타는 특별한 자전거야.

2. G: 기다려. 아직 물속으로 뛰어들지 마.
   B: 왜 안 돼?
   G: 구명조끼 없이 수영하면 안 돼. 이것을 입어.

3. G: 저기 있는 아름다운 꽃들을 봐! 그 꽃들 앞에서 셀피를 찍고 싶어.
   B: 거기 가면 안 돼.
   G: 아, 알았어.

4. B: 나는 나무에 있는 새들을 보고 싶어.
   G: 새들에게 너무 가까이 가지 마.
   B: 알았어, 고마워.

1. G: 아빠, 암벽 등반가인 김소윤에 대해 들어본 적 있으세요?
   M: 응, TV에서 봤어.
   G: 그녀가 이번 토요일에 캠프에서 암벽 등반을 가르쳐요. 저는 캠프에 참가하고 싶어요.
   M: 알았어, 미소야, 하지만 너무 높이 올라가면 안 돼.
   G: 알았어요. 고마워요, 아빠.

2. G: Rock Boys에 대해 들어보셨어요?
   M: 아니, 듣지 못했다.
   G: 그건 제가 제일 좋아하는 밴드에요. 이번 토요일에 콘서트가 있어요. 가도 돼요?
   M: 좋아, 민주야, 하지만 너무 늦게 집에 오면 안 돼.
   G: 알았어요. 고마워요, 아빠.

Start Off - Listen & Talk B

B: _____ you _____ _____ bird watching?

M: Sure. I _____ it _____ I was a child.

B: That's nice. Actually, I'm _____ it _____ _____ _____ this Saturday.

M: Are you? You _____ _____ warm clothes and _____ _____ _____.

B: Okay. What else _____ I _____ _____ _____?

M: You _____ _____ any noise _____ you watch the birds.

B: I'll _____ _____ _____ _____ _____. Thanks, Dad.

Step Up - Real-life Scene

Video Chat with Minjun from Jeju

A: Hello, Somin! _____ me! _____ you _____ _____?

B: Oh, _____, Minjun! What's _____?

A: This is so cool, _____ _____? We can video _____ on the phone! _____ you _____ _____ Jeju *Olle*?

B: _____, _____ _____. I really _____ to go there someday.

A: _____ _____? I'm on it now. Actually, I'm _____ _____ _____ _____ Seongsan Ilchulbong now.

B: That's _____!

A: Don't _____ _____. Enjoy the beautiful _____ with me.

B: _____ careful! You _____ _____ your cell phone _____ _____ _____.

A: Oh, _____. _____ you. I'll _____ you photos _____.

Express Yourself A

1. **G:** _____ _____ _____ _____ _____ Elvis Presley?

   B: _____, _____ _____. _____ is he?

   G: He was a _____ _____ _____ _____ and _____. We can see a _____ of Elvis here.

   B: _____ interesting. I want to _____ _____ with it.

   G: Okay. _____ _____.

2. **W:** You _____ _____ selfies here. Van Gogh's _____ is _____ you.

   B: _____ _____ _____, Mom. It's not his _____ painting. _____ I can take selfies _____ _____ _____ it.

   W: Really? Sounds interesting. _____ I take _____ here, too?

   B: Why _____?

B: 새 관찰에 대해 들어보셨어요?

M: 물론이지. 어렸을 때 해 봤어.

B: 그거 멋지네요. 사실, 전 이번 주 토요일에 처음으로 그것을 할 거예요.

M: 그래? 넌 따뜻한 옷과 먹을 것을 가져가야 해.

B: 알았어요. 그 밖에 또 무엇을 명심해야 하나요?

M: 너는 새들을 관찰할 때 아무 소리도 내지 말아야 해.

B: 그것을 명심할게요. 고마워요, 아빠.

제주에서 걸려온 민준과의 화상 채팅

A: 여보세요, 소민아! 나야! 나를 볼 수 있니?

B: 오, 안녕, 민준아! 무슨 일이니?

A: 이거 정말 멋지지 않니? 전화로 화상 채팅도 할 수 있어! 너 제주 올레에 대해 들어 본 적이 있니?

B: 응, 있어. 나는 언젠가 꼭 가 보고 싶어.

A: 그거 알아? 나 지금 올레에 있어. 사실은, 지금 성산 일출봉에 올라가려고 해.

B: 멋지다!

A: 끊지 마. 나와 함께 아름다운 경치를 즐겨.

B: 조심해! 걸을 때는 휴대폰을 사용해서는 안 돼.

A: 아, 맞다. 고마워. 나중에 사진 보내줄게.

1. **G:** 엘비스 프레슬리에 대해 들어 본 적 있니?

   B: 아니, 없어. 그는 누구인데?

   G: 그는 유명한 미국 가수이자 배우였어. 우리는 여기서 엘비스의 모형을 볼 수 있어.

   B: 재미있을 것 같다. 그것과 함께 사진을 찍고 싶어.

   G: 좋아. 가자.

2. **W:** 넌 여기서 셀피를 찍으면 안 돼. 반 고흐의 그림이 네 뒤에 있어.

   B: 엄마, 걱정하지 마세요. 그건 그의 진짜 그림이 아니에요. 그래서 그 앞에서 셀피를 찍을 수 있어요.

   W: 정말이지? 재미있겠다. 나도 여기서 셀피를 찍을 수 있을까?

   B: 물론이죠.

※ 다음 우리말에 맞도록 대화를 영어로 쓰시오.

Get Ready - 2

1. G: _____
   B: _____
   G: _____
   B: _____

2. G: _____
   B: _____
   G: _____

3. G: _____
   _____
   B: _____
   G: _____

4. B: _____
   G: _____
   B: _____

Start Off - Listen & Talk A

1. G: _____
   M: _____
   G: _____
   _____
   M: _____
   G: _____

2. G: _____
   M: _____
   G: _____
   M: _____
   G: _____

해석

1. G: 저 소년을 봐. 그는 대단하다.
   B: 그는 MTB를 타고 있어. 넌 그것에 대해 알고 있니?
   G: 아니. 그게 뭐지?
   B: 그것은 산에서 타는 특별한 자전거야.

2. G: 기다려. 아직 물속으로 뛰어들지 마.
   B: 왜 안 돼?
   G: 구명조끼 없이 수영하면 안 돼. 이것을 입어.

3. G: 저기 있는 아름다운 꽃들을 봐! 그 꽃들 앞에서 셀피를 찍고 싶어.
   B: 거기 가면 안 돼.
   G: 아, 알았어.

4. B: 나는 나무에 있는 새들을 보고 싶어.
   G: 새들에게 너무 가까이 가지 마.
   B: 알았어, 고마워.

1. G: 아빠, 암벽 등반가인 김소윤에 대해 들어 본 적 있으세요?
   M: 응, TV에서 봤어.
   G: 그녀가 이번 토요일에 캠프에서 암벽 등반을 가르쳐요. 저는 캠프에 참가하고 싶어요.
   M: 알았어, 미소야, 하지만 너무 높이 올라가면 안 돼.
   G: 알았어요. 고마워요, 아빠.

2. G: Rock Boys에 대해 들어보셨어요?
   M: 아니, 듣지 못했다.
   G: 그건 제가 제일 좋아하는 밴드에요. 이번 토요일에 콘서트가 있어요. 가도 돼요?
   M: 좋아, 민주야, 하지만 너무 늦게 집에 오면 안 돼.
   G: 알았어요. 고마워요, 아빠.

Start Off - Listen & Talk B

B: _____

M: _____

B: _____

M: _____

B: _____

M: _____

B: _____

Step Up - Real-life Scene

Video Chat with Minjun from Jeju

A: _____

B: _____

A: _____
_____

B: _____

A: _____
_____

B: _____

A: _____

B: _____

A: _____

Express Yourself A

1. G: _____

   B: _____

   G: _____
   _____

   B: _____

   G: _____

2. W: _____

   B: _____

   W: _____

   B: _____

B: 새 관찰에 대해 들어보셨어요?

M: 물론이지. 어렸을 때 해 봤어.

B: 그거 멋지네요. 사실, 전 이번 주 토요일에 처음으로 그것을 할 거예요.

M: 그래? 넌 따뜻한 옷과 먹을 것을 가져가야 해.

B: 알았어요. 그 밖에 또 무엇을 명심해야 하나요?

M: 너는 새들을 관찰할 때 아무 소리도 내지 말아야 해.

B: 그것을 명심할게요. 고마워요, 아빠.

제주에서 걸려온 민준과의 화상 채팅

A: 여보세요, 소민아! 나야! 나를 볼 수 있니?

B: 오, 안녕, 민준아! 무슨 일이니?

A: 이거 정말 멋지지 않니? 전화로 화상 채팅도 할 수 있어! 너 제주 올레에 대해 들어 본 적이 있니?

B: 응, 있어. 나는 언젠가 꼭 가 보고 싶어.

A: 그거 알아? 나 지금 올레에 있어. 사실은, 지금 성산 일출봉에 올라가려고 해.

B: 멋지다!

A: 끊지 마. 나와 함께 아름다운 경치를 즐겨.

B: 조심해! 걸을 때는 휴대폰을 사용해서는 안 돼.

A: 아, 맞다. 고마워. 나중에 사진 보내줄게.

1. G: 엘비스 프레슬리에 대해 들어 본 적 있니?

   B: 아니, 없어. 그는 누구인데?

   G: 그는 유명한 미국 가수이자 배우였어. 우리는 여기서 엘비스의 모형을 볼 수 있어.

   B: 재미있을 것 같다. 그것과 함께 사진을 찍고 싶어.

   G: 좋아. 가자.

2. W: 넌 여기서 셀피를 찍으면 안 돼. 반 고흐의 그림이 네 뒤에 있어.

   B: 엄마, 걱정하지 마세요. 그건 그의 진짜 그림이 아니에요. 그래서 그 앞에서 셀피를 찍을 수 있어요.

   W: 정말이지? 재미있겠다. 나도 여기서 셀피를 찍을 수 있을까?

   B: 물론이죠.

※ 다음 우리말과 일치하도록 빈칸에 알맞은 것을 골라 쓰시오.

1 _____ you _____ _____ of a "selfie"?
A. heard   B. ever   C. have

2 _____ you _____ a photograph of _____, it's a selfie.
A. yourself   B. take   C. when

3 The students from Minji's photo club _____ searched
information _____ selfies for one month.
A. about   B. for   C. have

4 _____ are some of their _____ about _____.
A. selfies   B. presentations   C. here

5 Did _____ in the past _____ selfies?
A. take   B. people

6 _____ it wasn't easy _____ that time, the _____ is yes.
A. answer   B. at   C. though

7 _____ _____ this photo _____ Princess Anastasia.
A. of   B. at   C. look

8 She _____ a mirror to _____ a picture of _____.
A. herself   B. take   C. used

9 She _____ _____.
A. nervous   B. looks

10 Can you _____ _____?
A. why   B. guess

11 Well, I _____ it was her _____ selfie.
A. first   B. think

12 And it was _____ the world's first _____ selfie _____.
A. teenage   B. ever   C. probably

13 You can _____ selfies _____ world-famous places _____
Big Ben and the Leaning Tower of Pisa.
A. like   B. at   C. take

14 To _____ great pictures, just do fun _____ and use camera
_____.
A. tricks   B. poses   C. take

15 You can _____ visit _____ museums to take _____
selfies.
A. fun   B. special   C. also

16 For _____, there _____ a _____ selfie museum in the
Philippines.
A. is   B. famous   C. example

17 It has special _____ to _____ selfies.
A. take   B. spots

18 You can _____ the paintings and _____ _____ inside them.
A. step   B. touch   C. even

19 Look _____ the _____ pictures.
A. following   B. at

20 _____ the boys are not really _____ horses, it looks _____
they are.
A. like   B. riding   C. though

1 여러분은 "셀피"에 대해 들어
본 적이 있나요?

2 여러분 자신의 사진을 찍을 때
그것이 셀피에요.

3 민지의 사진 동아리 학생들은
한 달 동안 셀피에 대한 정보를
찾았습니다.

4 여기 셀피에 대한 그들의 발표
내용이 있습니다.

5 과거의 사람들은 셀피를 찍었나
요?

6 그 때는 셀피를 찍는 것이 쉽지
않았지만, 답은 '그렇다'입니다.

7 아나스타샤 공주의 이 사진을
보세요.

8 그녀는 거울을 사용하여 자신의
사진을 찍었습니다.

9 그녀는 긴장되어 보입니다.

10 왜인지 추측할 수 있나요?

11 글쎄, 나는 그것이 그녀의 첫 번
째 셀피였다고 생각해요.

12 그리고 그것은 아마도 세계 최초
의 10대 소녀의 셀피였을 거예요.

13 여러분은 빅벤과 피사의 사탑과
같은 세계적으로 유명한 장소에
서 셀피를 찍을 수 있습니다.

14 멋진 사진을 찍기 위해서, 단지
재미있는 포즈를 취하고 카메라
기술을 이용하세요.

15 여러분은 또한 재미있는 셀피를
찍기 위해 특별한 박물관을 방
문할 수 있습니다.

16 예를 들어, 필리핀에는 유명한
셀피 박물관이 있습니다.

17 그곳은 셀피를 찍기 위한 특별한
장소들이 있습니다.

18 여러분은 그림들을 만질 수 있
고 심지어 그림들 안으로 들어
갈 수도 있어요.

19 다음 사진들을 보세요.

20 비록 그 소년들은 말을 타고 있
는 것은 아니지만, 말을 타고 있
는 것처럼 보입니다.

21 Though the man is just _____ a big _____, it looks like he is _____ the Mona Lisa.
A. painting   B. brush   C. holding

22 Selfie museums _____ in Korea, _____.
A. too   B. exist

23 I have _____ one in Chuncheon _____.
A. before   B. visited

24 Why _____ you go there _____?
A. yourself   B. don't

25 These selfies _____ great, _____ they a good idea?
A. were   B. but   C. look

26 I _____ think _____.
A. so   B. don't

27 They don't _____ _____.
A. safe   B. look

28 You _____ take special _____ when you take _____ in the wild or at high _____ like these.
A. places   B. selfies   C. care   D. should

29 A monkey could _____ you at any _____, or you _____ fall.
A. could   B. time   C. bite

30 Here _____ some _____ tips:
A. safety   B. are

31 1. _____ take selfies _____ you're _____.
A. walking   B. while   C. don't

32 2. _____ not _____ with or _____ wild animals.
A. near   B. pose   C. do

33 3. _____ take selfies _____ dangerous _____.
A. places   B. in   C. never

34 I think we can _____ selfies to _____ a _____ school life.
A. better   B. make   C. use

35 We _____ do good _____ at school and _____ selfies.
A. take   B. things   C. can

36 Then we can _____ the photos _____ our school _____.
A. website   B. on   C. post

37 I've _____ the _____ and flowers at school _____ one month.
A. for   B. plants   C. watered

38 I've _____ helped the teacher _____ the school library many _____.
A. times   B. at   C. also

39 _____ _____ my selfies of _____ things.
A. those   B. at   C. look

40 How _____ me to _____ a better school life?
A. create   B. joining   C. about

21 비록 그 남자는 단지 커다란 붓을 잡고 있지만, 모나리자를 그리고 있는 것처럼 보입니다.

22 한국에도 셀피 박물관이 있습니다.

23 나는 전에 춘천에 있는 한 박물관을 방문한 적이 있습니다.

24 여러분도 직접 그곳에 가는 게 어때요?

25 이 셀피들은 멋져 보이지만, 그것들은 좋은 생각이었나요?

26 난 그렇게 생각하지 않아요.

27 그것들은 안전해 보이지 않습니다.

28 여러분은 야생이나 이와 같이 높은 곳에서 셀피를 찍을 때 특별한 주의를 기울여야 합니다.

29 원숭이가 언제든지 당신을 물거나 또는 당신은 떨어질 수 있습니다.

30 여기 몇 가지 안전 수칙이 있습니다.

31 1. 걸으면서 셀피를 찍지 마세요.

32 2. 야생 동물들과 함께 또는 가까이에서 포즈를 취하지 마세요.

33 3. 위험한 곳에서는 절대 셀피를 찍지 마세요.

34 나는 우리가 더 나은 학교생활을 만들기 위해 셀피를 이용할 수 있다고 생각해요.

35 우리는 학교에서 좋은 일을 할 수 있고 셀피를 찍을 수도 있습니다.

36 그러고 나서 우리는 학교 웹사이트에 사진을 올릴 수 있어요.

37 나는 한 달 동안 학교에서 식물과 꽃에 물을 주었습니다.

38 나는 또한 학교 도서관에서 선생님을 여러 번 도왔습니다.

39 그런 것들에 대한 내 셀피를 보세요.

40 저와 함께 더 나은 학교생활을 만들어 보는 건 어때요?

※ 다음 우리말과 일치하도록 빈칸에 알맞은 말을 쓰시오.

1 _____ you _____ _____ _____ a "selfie"?

2 When you _____ a photograph _____ _____, it's a selfie.

3 The students from Minji's photo _____ have _____ _____ _____ about selfies _____ one month.

4 _____ are some of _____ _____ about selfies.

5 Did _____ in the past _____ _____?

6 _____ it _____ easy at that time, the _____ is yes.

7 _____ _____ this photo of Princess Anastasia.

8 She _____ a mirror _____ _____ a picture of _____.

9 She _____ _____.

10 _____ you _____ _____?

11 Well, I _____ it was _____ _____ _____ _____.

12 And it was _____ the world's first _____ selfie ever.

13 You _____ _____ _____ at world-famous places _____ Big Ben and the Leaning Tower of Pisa.

14 _____ _____ _____ great _____, just do fun _____ and _____ _____ _____.

15 You can _____ visit special museums to take _____ selfies.

16 For _____, there is a _____ selfie museum in the Philippines.

17 It _____ _____ _____ to _____ selfies.

18 You can _____ the paintings and _____ _____ inside them.

19 _____ _____ the _____ pictures.

20 _____ the boys are not really _____ horses, it _____ _____ they are.

1 여러분은 "셀피"에 대해 들어 본 적이 있나요?

2 여러분 자신의 사진을 찍을 때 그것이 셀피에요.

3 민지의 사진 동아리 학생들은 한 달 동안 셀피에 대한 정보를 찾았습니다.

4 여기 셀피에 대한 그들의 발표 내용이 있습니다.

5 과거의 사람들은 셀피를 찍었나요?

6 그 때는 셀피를 찍는 것이 쉽지는 않았지만, 답은 '그렇다'입니다.

7 아나스타샤 공주의 이 사진을 보세요.

8 그녀는 거울을 사용하여 자신의 사진을 찍었습니다.

9 그녀는 긴장되어 보입니다.

10 왜인지 추측할 수 있나요?

11 글쎄, 나는 그것이 그녀의 첫 번째 셀피였다고 생각해요.

12 그리고 그것은 아마도 세계 최초의 10대 소녀의 셀피였을 거예요.

13 여러분은 빅벤과 피사의 사탑과 같은 세계적으로 유명한 장소에서 셀피를 찍을 수 있습니다.

14 멋진 사진을 찍기 위해서, 단지 재미있는 포즈를 취하고 카메라 기술을 이용하세요.

15 여러분은 또한 재미있는 셀피를 찍기 위해 특별한 박물관을 방문할 수 있습니다.

16 예를 들어, 필리핀에는 유명한 셀피 박물관이 있습니다.

17 그곳은 셀피를 찍기 위한 특별한 장소들이 있습니다.

18 여러분은 그림들을 만질 수 있고 심지어 그림들 안으로 들어갈 수도 있어요.

19 다음 사진들을 보세요.

20 비록 그 소년들은 말을 타고 있는 것은 아니지만, 말을 타고 있는 것처럼 보입니다.

21 Though the man is _____ _____ a big _____, it _____ _____ he is _____ the Mona Lisa.

22 Selfie museums _____ in Korea, _____.

23 I _____ _____ one in Chuncheon _____.

24 _____ _____ you go there _____?

25 These selfies _____ great, _____ were they a good idea?

26 I _____ _____ _____.

27 They _____ _____ _____.

28 You _____ _____ _____ _____ when you take selfies in the wild or at high _____ _____ these.

29 A monkey _____ _____ you _____ _____ _____, or you _____ _____.

30 _____ _____ some _____ _____:

31 1. Don't _____ selfies _____ _____ _____.

32 2. Do _____ _____ with or near _____ animals.

33 3. _____ _____ _____ in dangerous _____.

34 I think we can _____ selfies to make a _____ school life.

35 We can do good _____ at school and _____ selfies.

36 Then we _____ _____ the photos on our school _____.

37 I've _____ the plants and flowers at _____ for one month.

38 I've _____ _____ the teacher _____ the school library _____ _____.

39 _____ _____ my selfies of _____ things.

40 _____ _____ joining me to _____ a better school life?

---

21 비록 그 남자는 단지 커다란 붓을 잡고 있지만, 모나리자를 그리고 있는 것처럼 보입니다.

22 한국에도 셀피 박물관이 있습니다.

23 나는 전에 춘천에 있는 한 박물관을 방문한 적이 있습니다.

24 여러분도 직접 그곳에 가는 게 어때요?

25 이 셀피들은 멋져 보이지만, 그것들은 좋은 생각이었나요?

26 난 그렇게 생각하지 않아요.

27 그것들은 안전해 보이지 않습니다.

28 여러분은 야생이나 이와 같이 높은 곳에서 셀피를 찍을 때 특별한 주의를 기울여야 합니다.

29 원숭이가 언제든지 당신을 물거나 또는 당신은 떨어질 수 있습니다.

30 여기 몇 가지 안전 수칙이 있습니다.

31 1. 걸으면서 셀피를 찍지 마세요.

32 2. 야생 동물들과 함께 또는 가까이에서 포즈를 취하지 마세요.

33 3. 위험한 곳에서는 절대 셀피를 찍지 마세요.

34 나는 우리가 더 나은 학교생활을 만들기 위해 셀피를 이용할 수 있다고 생각해요.

35 우리는 학교에서 좋은 일을 할 수 있고 셀피를 찍을 수도 있습니다.

36 그리고 나서 우리는 학교 웹사이트에 사진을 올릴 수 있어요.

37 나는 한 달 동안 학교에서 식물과 꽃에 물을 주었습니다.

38 나는 또한 학교 도서관에서 선생님을 여러 번 도왔습니다.

39 그런 것들에 대한 내 셀피를 보세요.

40 저와 함께 더 나은 학교생활을 만들어 보는 건 어떨까요?

※ 다음 문장을 우리말로 쓰시오.

1 Have you ever heard of a "selfie"? When you take a photograph of yourself, it's a selfie.

➡ _____

2 The students from Minji's photo club have searched for information about selfies for one month.

➡ _____

3 Here are some of their presentations about selfies.

➡ _____

4 Did people in the past take selfies?

➡ _____

5 Though it wans't easy at that time. the answer is yes.

➡ _____

6 Look at this photo of Princess Anastasia. She used a mirror to take a picture of herself.

➡ _____

7 She looks nervous. Can you guess why?

➡ _____

8 Well, I think it was her first selfie.

➡ _____

9 And it was probably the world's first teenage selfie ever.

➡ _____

10 You can take selfies at world-famous places like Big Ben and the Leaning Tower of Pisa.

➡ _____

11 To take great pictures, just do fun poses and use camera tricks.

➡ _____

12 You can also visit special museums to take fun selfies.

➡ _____

13 For example, there is a famous selfie museum in the Philippines.

➡ _____

14 It has special spots to take selfies.

➡ _____

15 You can touch the paintings and even step inside them.

➡ _____

16 Look at the following pictures.

➡ _____

17 Though the boys are not really riding horses, it looks like they are.

➡ _____

18 Though the man is just holding a big brush, it looks like he is painting the Mona Lisa.

➡ _____

19 Selfie museums exist in Korea, too. I have visited one in Chuncheon before.

➡ _____

20 Why don't you go there yourself? These selfies look great, but were they a good idea?

➡ _____

21 I don't think so. They don't look safe.

➡ _____

22 You should take special care when you take selfies in the wild or at high places like these.

➡ _____

23 A monkey could bite you at any time, or you could fall.

➡ _____

24 Here are some safety tips:

➡ _____

25 Don't take selfies while you're walking.

➡ _____

26 Do not pose with or near wild animals.

➡ _____

27 Never take selfies in dangerous places.

➡ _____

28 I think we can use selfies to make a better school life.

➡ _____

29 We can do good things at school and take selfies.

➡ _____

30 Then we can post the photos on our school website.

➡ _____

31 I've watered the plants and flowers at school for one month.

➡ _____

32 I've also helped the teacher at the school library many times.

➡ _____

33 Look at my selfies of those things.

➡ _____

34 How about joining me to create a better school life?

➡ _____

※ 다음 괄호 안의 단어들을 우리말에 맞도록 바르게 배열하시오.

1 (you / have / ever / of / heard / "selfie"? / a // when / take / you / photograph / of / a / yourself, / a / selfie. / it's)
➡ _____

2 (students / the / from / photo / Minji's / club / searched / have / information / for / about / selfies / month. / one / for)
➡ _____

3 (are / here / of / some / their / presentations / selfies. / about)
➡ _____

4 (people / did / in / past / the / selfies? / take)
➡ _____

5 (it / though / wasn't / easy / that / at / time, / yes. / is / answer / the)
➡ _____

6 (at / look / photo / this Princess / of / Anastasia. // used / she / mirror / a / take / to / picture / a / herself. / of)
➡ _____

7 (looks / she / nervous. // you / can / guess / why?)
➡ _____

8 (well, / think / I / was / it / selfie. / first / her)
➡ _____

9 (and / was / it / the / probably / world's / teenage / first / ever. / selfie)
➡ _____

10 (you / take / can / selfies / at / places / world-famous / like / Big / Ben / and / Pisa. / of / Tower / the / Leaning)
➡ _____

11 (take / great / to / pictures, / do / just / poses / fun / and / tricks. / camera / use)
➡ _____

12 (you / also / can / visit / museums / special / selfies. / take / to / fun)
➡ _____

13 (example, / for / is / there / famous / a / selfie / in / museum / Philippines. / the)
➡ _____

14 (has / it / spots / special / selfies. / take / to)
➡ _____

15 (can / you / touch / paintings / the / and / step / even / them. / inside)
➡ _____

16 (at / look / the / pictures. / following)
➡ _____

1 여러분은 "셀피"에 대해 들어 본 적이 있나요? 여러분 자신의 사진을 찍을 때 그것이 셀피에 요.

2 민지의 사진 동아리 학생들은 한 달 동안 셀피에 대한 정보를 찾았습니다.

3 여기 셀피에 대한 그들의 발표 내용이 있습니다.

4 과거의 사람들은 셀피를 찍었나 요?

5 그 때는 셀피를 찍는 것이 쉽지는 않았지만. 답은 '그렇다'입니다.

6 아나스타샤 공주의 이 사진을 보세요. 그녀는 거울을 사용하 여 자신의 사진을 찍었습니다.

7 그녀는 긴장되어 보입니다. 왜 인지 추측할 수 있나요?

8 글쎄. 나는 그것이 그녀의 첫 번 째 셀피였다고 생각해요.

9 그리고 그것은 아마도 세계 최초 의 10대 소녀의 셀피였을 거예요.

10 여러분은 빅벤과 피사의 사탑과 같은 세계적으로 유명한 장소에 서 셀피를 찍을 수 있습니다.

11 멋진 사진을 찍기 위해서, 단지 재미있는 포즈를 취하고 카메라 기술을 이용하세요.

12 여러분은 또한 재미있는 셀피를 찍기 위해 특별한 박물관을 방 문할 수 있습니다.

13 예를 들어. 필리핀에는 유명한 셀피 박물관이 있습니다.

14 그곳은 셀피를 찍기 위한 특별한 장소들이 있습니다.

15 여러분은 그림들을 만질 수 있 고 심지어 그림들 안으로 들어 갈 수도 있어요.

16 다음 사진들을 보세요.

17 (the / though / boys / are / really / not / horses, / riding / looks / it / like / are. / they)
➡ _____

18 (the / man / though / is / holding / just / big / a / brush, / it / like / looks / is / he / painting / Lisa. / Mona / the)
➡ _____

19 (museums / selfie / in / exist / too. / Korea, // have / I / visited / in / one / before. / Chuncheon)
➡ _____

20 (you / don't / why / go / yourself? / there // selfies / these / great, / look / but / they / were / idea? / good / a)
➡ _____

21 (don't / so. / I / think // don't / they / safe. / look)
➡ _____.

22 (you / take / should / care / special / when / take / you / selfies / the / in / wild / or / high / at / these. / places / like)
➡ _____

23 (monkey / a / bite / could / you / at / time, / any / or / fall. / could / you)
➡ _____

24 (are / here / safety / tips: / some)
➡ _____

25 (selfies / don't / take / while / walking. / you're)
➡ _____

26 (pose / not / do / with / or / animals. / near / wild)
➡ _____

27 (take / never / selfies / places. / dangerous / in)
➡ _____

28 (we / think / I / use / can / selfies / make / to / a / school / better / life.)
➡ _____

29 (we / do / can / things / good / school / at / and / selfies. / take)
➡ _____

30 (then / we / post / can / photos / the / on / website. / school / our)
➡ _____

31 (I've / the / plants / watered / and / flowers / school / at / month. / one / for)
➡ _____

32 (I've / helped / also / teacher / the / at / school / the / library / times. / many)
➡ _____

33 (at / my / look / selfies / things. / those / of)
➡ _____

34 (about / how / joining / to / me / create / a / life? / school / better)
➡ _____

17 비록 그 소년들은 말을 타고 있는 것은 아니지만, 말을 타고 있는 것처럼 보입니다.

18 비록 그 남자는 단지 커다란 붓을 잡고 있지만, 모나리자를 그리고 있는 것처럼 보입니다.

19 한국에도 셀피 박물관이 있습니다. 나는 전에 춘천에 있는 한 박물관을 방문한 적이 있습니다.

20 여러분도 직접 그곳에 가는 게 어때요? 이 셀피들은 멋져 보이지만, 그것들은 좋은 생각이었나요?

21 난 그렇게 생각하지 않아요. 그것들은 안전해 보이지 않습니다.

22 여러분은 야생이나 이와 같이 높은 곳에서 셀피를 찍을 때 특별한 주의를 기울여야 합니다.

23 원숭이가 언제든지 당신을 물거나 또는 당신은 떨어질 수 있습니다.

24 여기 몇 가지 안전 수칙이 있습니다.

25 걸으면서 셀피를 찍지 마세요.

26 야생 동물들과 함께 또는 가까이에서 포즈를 취하지 마세요.

27 위험한 곳에서는 절대 셀피를 찍지 마세요.

28 나는 우리가 더 나은 학교생활을 만들기 위해 셀피를 이용할 수 있다고 생각해요.

29 우리는 학교에서 좋은 일을 할 수 있고 셀피를 찍을 수도 있습니다.

30 그리고 나서 우리는 학교 웹사이트에 사진을 올릴 수 있어요.

31 나는 한 달 동안 학교에서 식물과 꽃에 물을 주었습니다.

32 나는 또한 학교 도서관에서 선생님을 여러 번 도왔습니다.

33 그런 것들에 대한 내 셀피를 보세요.

34 저와 함께 더 나은 학교생활을 만들어 보는 건 어떨까요?

※ 다음 우리말을 영어로 쓰시오.

1 여러분은 "셀피"에 대해 들어 본 적이 있나요? 여러분 자신의 사진을 찍을 때 그것이 셀피에요.
➡ _____

2 민지의 사진 동아리 학생들은 한 달 동안 셀피에 대한 정보를 찾았습니다.
➡ _____

3 여기 셀피에 대한 그들의 발표 내용이 있습니다.
➡ _____

4 과거의 사람들은 셀피를 찍었나요?
➡ _____

5 그 때는 셀피를 찍는 것이 쉽지는 않았지만. 답은 '그렇다'입니다.
➡ _____

6 아나스타샤 공주의 이 사진을 보세요. 그녀는 거울을 사용하여 자신의 사진을 찍었습니다.
➡ _____

7 그녀는 긴장되어 보입니다. 왜인지 추측할 수 있나요?
➡ _____

8 글쎄, 나는 그것이 그녀의 첫 번째 셀피였다고 생각해요.
➡ _____

9 그리고 그것은 아마도 세계 최초의 10대 소녀의 셀피였을 거예요.
➡ _____

10 여러분은 빅벤과 피사의 사탑과 같은 세계적으로 유명한 장소에서 셀피를 찍을 수 있습니다.
➡ _____

11 멋진 사진을 찍기 위해서, 단지 재미있는 포즈를 취하고 카메라 기술을 이용하세요.
➡ _____

12 여러분은 또한 재미있는 셀피를 찍기 위해 특별한 박물관을 방문할 수 있습니다.
➡ _____

13 예를 들어, 필리핀에는 유명한 셀피 박물관이 있습니다.
➡ _____

14 그곳은 셀피를 찍기 위한 특별한 장소들이 있습니다.
➡ _____

15 여러분은 그림들을 만질 수 있고 심지어 그림들 안으로 들어갈 수도 있어요.
➡ _____

16 다음 사진들을 보세요.
➡ _____

17 비록 그 소년들은 말을 타고 있는 것은 아니지만, 말을 타고 있는 것처럼 보입니다.

➡ _____

18 비록 그 남자는 단지 커다란 붓을 잡고 있지만, 모나리자를 그리고 있는 것처럼 보입니다.

➡ _____

19 한국에도 셀피 박물관이 있습니다. 나는 전에 춘천에 있는 한 박물관을 방문한 적이 있습니다.

➡ _____

20 여러분도 직접 그곳에 가는 게 어때요? 이 셀피들은 멋져 보이지만, 그것들은 좋은 생각이었나요?

➡ _____

21 난 그렇게 생각하지 않아요. 그것들은 안전해 보이지 않습니다.

➡ _____

22 여러분은 야생이나 이와 같이 높은 곳에서 셀피를 찍을 때 특별한 주의를 기울여야 합니다.

➡ _____

23 원숭이가 언제든지 당신을 물거나 또는 당신은 떨어질 수 있습니다.

➡ _____

24 여기 몇 가지 안전 수칙이 있습니다.

➡ _____

25 걸으면서 셀피를 찍지 마세요.

➡ _____

26 야생 동물들과 함께 또는 가까이에서 포즈를 취하지 마세요.

➡ _____

27 위험한 곳에서는 절대 셀피를 찍지 마세요.

➡ _____

28 나는 우리가 더 나은 학교생활을 만들기 위해 셀피를 이용할 수 있다고 생각해요.

➡ _____

29 우리는 학교에서 좋은 일을 할 수 있고 셀피를 찍을 수도 있습니다.

➡ _____

30 그러고 나서 우리는 학교 웹사이트에 사진을 올릴 수 있어요.

➡ _____

31 나는 한 달 동안 학교에서 식물과 꽃에 물을 주었습니다.

➡ _____

32 나는 또한 학교 도서관에서 선생님을 여러 번 도왔습니다.

➡ _____

33 그런 것들에 대한 내 셀피를 보세요.

➡ _____

34 저와 함께 더 나은 학교생활을 만들어 보는 건 어떨까요?

➡ _____

※ 다음 우리말과 일치하도록 빈칸에 알맞은 말을 쓰시오.

Express Yourself-C

1. _____ you _____ of the pyramids in Egypt?

2. Though I _____ never _____ _____ _____ Egypt before,
   I'm standing _____ _____ _____ a pyramid in this picture.

3. I _____ it at the selfie _____.

1. 여러분은 이집트의 피라미드에 대해 들어 본 적이 있나요?
2. 나는 전에 이집트에 가 본 적이 없지만, 이 사진에서 나는 피라미드 앞에 서 있어요.
3. 나는 이 사진을 셀피 박물관에서 찍었어요.

Project-Step 2

1. Fire _____ _____

2. _____ you _____ _____ fire safety rules?

3. _____ there's a fire, you can _____ _____.

4. You _____ _____ the elevator.

5. You should _____ the teacher's _____.

1. 화재 안전 수칙
2. 당신은 화재 안전 수칙에 대해 들어 본 적이 있습니까?
3. 불이 났지만, 당신은 안전할 수 있어요.
4. 엘리베이터를 타지 마세요.
5. 선생님의 지시에 따라야 해요.

Link to the World

1. BMX Bike _____

2. _____ a BMX bike _____ very _____.

3. You can try _____ _____ _____.

4. You can _____ the bike _____ and _____ with the bike.

5. _____ it's not _____, it's very _____.

6. You _____ _____ _____ standing skills.

7. _____ you try _____ skills, _____ is very important.

8. But _____ _____. You _____ _____ a helmet and gloves.

9. Also, you _____ _____ too fast _____ you're _____.

1. BMX 자전거 타기
2. BMX 자전거를 타는 것은 매우 흥미롭다.
3. 여러분은 많은 기술을 시도할 수 있다.
4. 여러분은 자전거를 자유롭게 돌릴 수 있고 심지어 자전거와 함께 점프할 수도 있다.
5. 쉽지는 않지만, 매우 흥미롭다.
6. 여러분은 서 있는 기술과 함께 시작하면 된다.
7. 서 있는 기술을 시도할 때, 균형을 잡는 것이 매우 중요하다.
8. 하지만 조심해라! 헬멧과 장갑을 착용해야 한다.
9. 또한, 자전거를 탈 때는 너무 빨리 가지 말아야 한다.

※ 다음 우리말을 영어로 쓰시오.

Express Yourself-C

1. 여러분은 이집트의 피라미드에 대해 들어 본 적이 있나요?

   ➡ _____

2. 나는 전에 이집트에 가 본 적이 없지만, 이 사진에서 나는 피라미드 앞에 서 있어요.

   ➡ _____

3. 나는 이 사진을 셀피 박물관에서 찍었어요.

   ➡ _____

Project - Step 2

1. 화재 안전 수칙

   ➡ _____

2. 당신은 화재 안전 수칙에 대해 들어 본 적이 있습니까?

   ➡ _____

3. 불이 났지만, 당신은 안전할 수 있어요.

   ➡ _____

4. 엘리베이터를 타지 마세요.

   ➡ _____

5. 선생님의 지시에 따라야 해요.

   ➡ _____

Link to the World

1. BMX 자전거 타기

   ➡ _____

2. BMX 자전거를 타는 것은 매우 흥미롭다.

   ➡ _____

3. 여러분은 많은 기술을 시도할 수 있다.

   ➡ _____

4. 여러분은 자전거를 자유롭게 돌릴 수 있고 심지어 자전거와 함께 점프할 수도 있다.

   ➡ _____

5. 쉽지는 않지만, 매우 흥미롭다.

   ➡ _____

6. 여러분은 서 있는 기술과 함께 시작하면 된다.

   ➡ _____

7. 서 있는 기술을 시도할 때, 균형을 잡는 것이 매우 중요하다.

   ➡ _____

8. 하지만 조심해라! 헬멧과 장갑을 착용해야 한다.

   ➡ _____

9. 또한, 자전거를 탈 때는 너무 빨리 가지 말아야 한다.

   ➡ _____

※ 다음 영어를 우리말로 쓰시오.

01 remember

02 practice

03 grade

04 super

05 move

06 February

07 special

08 field trip

09 funny

10 cook

11 far

12 delicious

13 memory

14 medal

15 nursing home

16 secret

17 lose

18 sunlight

19 bring

20 laughter

21 hen

22 whisper

23 aunt

24 bounce

25 hairpin

26 traditional

27 thick

28 competition

29 neighbor

30 perform

31 alone

32 puppet

33 together

34 precious

35 thank A for B

36 What about+-ing ~?

37 the same as ~

38 go into

39 one by one

40 remember+-ing

41 cut holes

42 thanks to

43 look like+명사

※ 다음 우리말을 영어로 쓰시오.

01 함께, 같이 _____

02 판자, 널빤지 _____

03 다시, 한 번 더 _____

04 입다, 쓰다, 착용하다 _____

05 두꺼운 _____

06 양호 선생님 _____

07 앨범 _____

08 재미있는 _____

09 대회, 경쟁 _____

10 날다, 비행하다 _____

11 혼자, 홀로 _____

12 (경기의) 판, 회 _____

13 꼭두각시, 인형 _____

14 과학 _____

15 가장 좋아하는 _____

16 사람 _____

17 이웃 (사람) _____

18 만화 _____

19 닦다, 청소하다 _____

20 귀중한 _____

21 갓 낳은, 신선한 _____

22 전에 _____

23 공연하다 _____

24 눈물 _____

25 머리핀 _____

26 학년, 성적 _____

27 속삭이다 _____

28 기억, 추억 _____

29 햇빛 _____

30 ~을 튀기다 _____

31 웃음 _____

32 맛있는 _____

33 연습하다 _____

34 특별한 _____

35 ~한 것을 기억하다 _____

36 ~처럼 보이다 _____

37 ~으로 들어가다 _____

38 ~ 덕분에 _____

39 ~와 똑같은 _____

40 결혼하다 _____

41 B 때문에 A에게 감사하다 _____

42 하나씩, 차례차례 _____

43 ~을 보고 미소 짓다 _____

※ 다음 영영풀이에 알맞은 단어를 <보기>에서 골라 쓴 후, 우리말 뜻을 쓰시오.

1 _____ : to speak very quietly: _____

2 _____ : best liked or most enjoyed: _____

3 _____ : a drop of salty liquid that flows from the eye: _____

4 _____ : not ordinary or usual: _____

5 _____ : a pin that is worn in your hair: _____

6 _____ : the act or sound of laughing: _____

7 _____ : someone who lives near you: _____

8 _____ : the action or sound of laughing: _____

9 _____ : to move up or away after hitting a surface: _____

10 _____ : someone's ability to remember things, places, experiences, etc.:

_____

11 _____ : one of the levels in a school with children of similar age: _____

12 _____ : something that is kept hidden or that is known about by only a few

people: _____

13 _____ : an empty space in an object, usually with an opening to the object's

surface: _____

14 _____ : of great value because of being rare, expensive, or important: _____

15 _____ : to do something to entertain people by acting a play or playing a piece

of music: _____

16 _____ : a toy in the shape of a person or animal that you can move with strings

or by putting your hand inside: _____

보기			
perform	tear	special	precious
whisper	hairpin	puppet	laughter
grade	bounce	hole	hen
favorite	memory	secret	neighbor

※ 다음 우리말과 일치하도록 빈칸에 알맞은 말을 쓰시오.

Get Ready

1. **G:** _____ are you, Ms. Hwang? We _____ TV together _____ _____. _____ you _____ that?

   M: Sure, Jieun. I _____ a great time _____ you.

2. **M:** Hi, Minjun. So, you _____ _____ _____ _____ in the board _____ _____. _____ _____ again now.

   B: Okay. _____ _____. Is this right?

   M: Yes. You _____ _____.

3. **G:** Hello, Mr. Yang. _____ _____ Minji. Do you _____ _____?

   M: Sure, Minji. Thank you _____ _____.

Start Off Listen & Talk A

1. **G:** Do you _____ Mr. Kim, _____ _____ _____ teacher?

   B: _____ _____. He _____ super _____ _____.

   G: _____ what? He _____ _____ a new school in February _____ _____.

   B: I _____ _____ that. _____ him together.

   G: Okay. _____ _____.

2. **B:** _____ you _____ Ms. Lee?

   G: Ms. Lee? _____ is _____?

   B: She was _____ _____ _____ English teacher.

   G: Now I _____. She _____ _____ _____ _____ pop songs in her class.

   B: She was a _____ _____, _____.

Start Off Listen & Talk B

B: Do you _____ Ms. Kang, the _____ _____?

G: Sure. She was _____ _____ _____.

B: _____ _____? She's _____ _____ next month.

G: Wow! What _____ we _____ for her?

B: _____ _____ _____. What _____ _____ a special album?

G: That's a _____ _____.

---

1. G: 황 여사님, 안녕하세요? 우리 지난 주말에 함께 TV를 봤어요. 기억하세요?
   W: 물론이지, 지은아. 너랑 즐거운 시간을 보냈지.

2. M: 안녕, 민준아. 자, 지난번에 판자에 구멍 뚫는 걸 배웠지. 지금 다시 연습해 보자.
   B: 네. 어디 보자. 이렇게 하는 게 맞나요?
   M: 그래, 모두 기억하고 있구나.

3. G: 안녕하세요, 양 선생님. 저 민지예요. 저 기억하세요?
   M: 물론이지, 민지야. 전화 줘서 고맙다.

1. G: 6학년 때 선생님이셨던 김 선생님 기억나니?
   B: 물론이지. 그분은 엄청나게 두꺼운 안경을 쓰고 계셨는데.
   G: 있지. 그분이 올해 2월에 새 학교로 옮기셨대.
   B: 몰랐어. 함께 찾아뵙자.
   G: 응. 좋은 생각이야.

2. B: 너 이 선생님 기억나니?
   G: 이 선생님? 누구신데?
   B: 4학년 때 영어 선생님이셨어.
   G: 이제 기억난다. 그분은 수업시간에 팝송을 많이 가르쳐 주셨지.
   B: 춤도 잘 추셨어.

   B: 학교 보건 선생님이셨던 강 선생님 기억하니?
   G: 물론이지. 그분은 우리 모두에게 친절하셨잖아.
   B: 있지. 그분이 다음 달에 결혼하신대.
   G: 와. 그분에게 우리 뭘 해드릴까?
   B: 어디 보자. 특별한 앨범을 만들어 드리는 게 어떨까?
   G: 좋은 생각이야.

Speak Up Look and talk.

A: Do you remember the field trip _____ _____ ?
B: _____ _____. We played fun games.
A: I have some _____ _____ from it _____ my phone.
B: That's _____!

Speak Up Mission

A: Do you _____ _____ _____ ?
B: _____ _____ _____. It's _____ 3. Right?
A: That's _____. / That's _____ _____. It's _____ _____.

Real-life Scene

G: Do you remember Ms. Park, the old lady _____ _____ _____ ?
B: _____ _____. We _____ her a birthday party _____.
G: And she _____ *japchae* for us. She _____ some chicken _____ it.
B: Right. It was _____. And we _____ card games _____. Do you _____ _____ ?
G: Yes. She _____ all the _____. She's really _____ _____ games.
B: When _____ we _____ _____ see her next, Mina?
G: _____ _____ _____. Next Saturday.
B: _____ _____ some pictures with her _____ _____.
G: _____ _____, Junsu.

Express Yourself

1. G: _____ _____ _____ the hot air balloon? We _____ it in Turkey.
   M: Of course. It _____ _____ an elephant.
2. G: Do you remember the rock?
   M: Is it the _____ _____ _____ ?
   G: Right.
   M: I _____ it. It _____ _____ a queen's head.

Learning Diary Check Yourself

B: Do you remember the _____ _____ last year?
G: _____ _____. We _____ super _____.
B: I have some _____ _____ from it _____ my phone.
G: That's _____!

A: 작년에 간 체험학습 기억하니?
B: 물론이지. 우리 신나는 게임을 했잖아.
A: 내 휴대 전화에 그때 찍은 재미있는 사진이 좀 있어.
B: 멋지다!

A: 내 생일 기억하니?
B: 어디 보자. 6월 3일이지. 그렇지?
A: 맞아. / 아니야. 6월 13일이야.

G: 혼자 사시는 할머니, 박 여사님 기억하니?
B: 물론이지. 작년에 우리가 생신 잔치를 해 드렸잖아.
G: 그리고 그분이 우리를 위해 잡채 요리를 해주셨지. 안에 닭고기를 넣으셨어.
B: 맞아. 맛있었어. 그러고 나서 함께 카드 게임도 했는데. 그거 기억나?
G: 응. 그분이 모든 판을 다 이기셨지. 게임을 정말 잘하셔.
B: 미나야, 다음에 언제 그분을 뵈러 갈 거야?
G: 어디 보자. 다음 주 토요일.
B: 이번에는 그분과 같이 사진을 몇 장 찍자.
G: 좋은 생각이다, 준수야.

1. G: 그 열기구 기억나? 터키에서 탔었지.
   M: 물론이지. 그것은 코끼리처럼 생겼었지.

2. G: 그 바위 기억나?
   M: 대만에 있는 거지?
   G: 맞아.
   M: 기억나지. 그것은 여왕의 머리처럼 생겼었지.

B: 작년에 한 노래 경연 대회 기억하니?
G: 물론이지. 우리 엄청나게 연습했잖아.
B: 내 휴대 전화에 그때 찍은 재미있는 사진이 좀 있어.
G: 멋지다!

※ 다음 우리말에 맞도록 대화를 영어로 쓰시오.

Get Ready

1. G: _____

   W: _____

2. M: _____

   B: _____

   M: _____

3. G: _____

   M: _____

Start Off Listen & Talk A

1. G: _____

   B: _____

   G: _____

   B: _____

   G: _____

2. B: _____

   G: _____

   B: _____

   G: _____

   B: _____

Start Off Listen & Talk B

B: _____

G: _____

B: _____

G: _____

B: _____

G: _____

해석

1. G: 황 여사님, 안녕하세요? 우리 지난 주말에 함께 TV를 봤어요. 기억하세요?
   W: 물론이지, 지은아. 너랑 즐거운 시간을 보냈지.

2. M: 안녕, 민준아. 자, 지난번에 판자에 구멍 뚫는 걸 배웠지. 지금 다시 연습해 보자.
   B: 네. 어디 보자. 이렇게 하는 게 맞나요?
   M: 그래, 모두 기억하고 있구나.

3. G: 안녕하세요, 양 선생님. 저 민지예요. 저 기억하세요?
   M: 물론이지, 민지야. 전화 줘서 고맙다.

1. G: 6학년 때 선생님이셨던 김 선생님 기억나니?
   B: 물론이지. 그분은 엄청나게 두꺼운 안경을 쓰고 계셨는데.
   G: 있지. 그분이 올해 2월에 새 학교로 옮기셨대.
   B: 몰랐어. 함께 찾아뵙자.
   G: 응. 좋은 생각이야.

2. B: 너 이 선생님 기억나니?
   G: 이 선생님? 누구신데?
   B: 4학년 때 영어 선생님이셨어.
   G: 이제 기억난다. 그분은 수업시간에 팝송을 많이 가르쳐 주셨지.
   B: 춤도 잘 추셨어.

B: 학교 보건 선생님이셨던 강 선생님 기억하니?
G: 물론이지. 그분은 우리 모두에게 친절하셨잖아.
B: 있지. 그분이 다음 달에 결혼하신대.
G: 와. 그분에게 우리 뭘 해드릴까?
B: 어디 보자. 특별한 앨범을 만들어 드리는 게 어떨까?
G: 좋은 생각이야.

Speak Up Look and talk.

A: _____
B: _____
A: _____
B: _____

A: 작년에 간 체험학습 기억하니?
B: 물론이지. 우리 신나는 게임을 했잖아.
A: 내 휴대 전화에 그때 찍은 재미있는 사진이 좀 있어.
B: 멋지다!

Speak Up Mission

A: _____
B: _____
A: _____

A: 내 생일 기억하니?
B: 어디 보자. 6월 3일이지. 그렇지?
A: 맞아. / 아니야. 6월 13일이야.

Real-life Scene

G: _____
B: _____
G: _____
B: _____
G: _____
B: _____
G: _____
B: _____
G: _____

G: 혼자 사시는 할머니, 박 여사님 기억하니?
B: 물론이지. 작년에 우리가 생신 잔치를 해 드렸잖아.
G: 그리고 그분이 우리를 위해 잡채 요리를 해주셨지. 안에 닭고기를 넣으셨어.
B: 맞아. 맛있었어. 그러고 나서 함께 카드 게임도 했는데. 그거 기억나?
G: 응. 그분이 모든 판을 다 이기셨지. 게임을 정말 잘하셔.
B: 미나야, 다음에 언제 그분을 뵈러 갈 거야?
G: 어디 보자. 다음 주 토요일.
B: 이번에는 그분과 같이 사진을 몇 장 찍자.
G: 좋은 생각이다, 준수야.

Express Yourself

1. G: _____
   M: _____
2. G: _____
   M: _____
   G: _____
   M: _____

1. G: 그 열기구 기억나? 터키에서 탔었지.
   M: 물론이지. 그것은 코끼리처럼 생겼었지.

2. G: 그 바위 기억나?
   M: 대만에 있는 거지?
   G: 맞아.
   M: 기억나지. 그것은 여왕의 머리처럼 생겼었지.

Learning Diary Check Yourself

B: _____
G: _____
B: _____
G: _____

B: 작년에 한 노래 경연 대회 기억하니?
G: 물론이지. 우리 엄청나게 연습했잖아.
B: 내 휴대 전화에 그때 찍은 재미있는 사진이 좀 있어.
G: 멋지다!

※ 다음 우리말과 일치하도록 빈칸에 알맞은 것을 골라 쓰시오.

1 _____ a _____?
  A. Memory   B. What's

2 Wilfrid Gordon Parker was a _____ boy _____ lived _____ to a nursing home.
  A. little   B. next   C. who

3 He liked _____ the people _____ lived _____.
  A. there   B. who   C. all

4 But his _____ person was Ms. Nancy Gordon Cooper because her middle name was the _____ as _____.
  A. his   B. favorite   C. same

5 He told _____ _____ his _____.
  A. all   B. secrets   C. her

6 _____ day, Wilfrid's parents were _____ _____ Ms. Cooper.
  A. about   B. one   C. talking

7 "_____ old _____," said _____ mother.
  A. lady   B. poor   C. his

8 "_____ is she a poor _____ lady?" _____ Wilfrid.
  A. asked   B. why   C. old

9 "_____ she's _____ her _____," said his father.
  A. memory   B. lost   C. because

10 "_____ a memory?" _____ Wilfrid.
  A. asked   B. what's

11 "It is _____ you _____," said his father.
  A. remember   B. something

12 Wilfrid wanted to know _____, _____ he went to his _____.
  A. so   B. more   C. neighbors

13 Ms. Jordan was _____ the _____.
  A. sunlight   B. enjoying

14 "What's a _____?" he _____.
  A. asked   B. memory

15 "_____, my _____," she said.
  A. warm   B. child   C. something

16 Ms. Mitchell was _____ a _____.
  A. reading   B. cartoon

17 "What's a _____?" he _____.
  A. asked   B. memory

18 "_____ that _____ you _____," she said.
  A. laughter   B. something   C. brings

19 Mr. Hunter _____ _____ his _____.
  A. was   B. medal   C. cleaning

1 추억이란 무엇일까?

2 Wilfrid Gordon Parker는 요양원 옆에 사는 어린 소년이었다.

3 그는 그곳에 사는 모든 사람들을 좋아했다.

4 하지만 그가 가장 좋아하는 사람은 Nancy Gordon Cooper 할머니였는데, 그 이유는 그녀의 가운데 이름이 그의 것과 같았기 때문이었다.

5 그는 자기의 모든 비밀을 그녀에게 말했다.

6 어느 날, Wilfrid의 부모님은 Cooper 할머니에 관해 이야기를 하고 있었다.

7 "불쌍한 분." 그의 어머니가 말했다.

8 "왜 불쌍한 분이세요?"라고 Wilfrid가 물었다.

9 "왜냐하면 그분은 기억을 잃으셨거든." 그의 아버지가 말했다.

10 "기억이 뭐예요?" Wilfrid가 물었다.

11 "그것은 네가 기억하는 것이란다."라고 그의 아버지가 말했다.

12 Wilfrid는 더 알고 싶어서, 그의 이웃들에게 갔다.

13 Jordan 할머니는 햇볕을 즐기고 있었다.

14 "기억이 뭐예요?" 그가 물었다.

15 "따뜻한 거란다, 아가야." 그녀가 말했다.

16 Mitchell 할머니는 만화책을 읽고 있었다.

17 "기억이 뭐예요?" 그가 물었다.

18 "너에게 웃음을 가져다주는 것이란다." 그녀가 말했다.

19 Hunter 할아버지는 자신의 메달을 닦고 있었다.

20 "It's _____ as _____ _____ gold, young man," he said.

A. as　　　　B. precious　　　C. something

21 So Wilfrid _____ _____ home to _____ _____ memories for Ms. Cooper.

A. for　　　B. back　　　C. went　　　D. look

22 He _____ _____ the hen house and _____ a fresh, warm egg _____ under a hen.

A. took　　　B. from　　　C. into　　　D. went

23 _____, he _____ _____ his sock puppet.

A. for　　　B. next　　　C. looked

24 It _____ _____ laughter _____ his parents.

A. brought　　　B. to　　　C. always

25 _____, he _____ his football _____ his toy box.

A. found　　　B. finally　　　C. in

26 It was _____ _____ as _____ to him.

A. gold　　　B. precious　　　C. as

27 Wilfrid _____ to Ms. Cooper and _____ her the things one _____ one.

A. by　　　B. gave　　　C. went

28 "_____ a strange, sweet child!" thought Ms. Cooper, "He's _____ all these wonderful _____."

A. brought　　　B. what　　　C. things

29 Then she started _____ _____ her _____.

A. past　　　B. remember　　　C. to

30 She _____ the warm egg and _____ _____ Wilfrid, "Long _____, I found a small blue egg in my aunt's garden."

A. whispered　　　B. held　　　C. ago　　　D. to

31 She smiled _____ the sock puppet and _____ _____ a puppet show _____ her sister.

A. performing　　　B. at　　　C. for　　　D. remembered

32 "My sister _____ _____ _____," said Ms. Cooper.

A. lot　　　B. laughed　　　C. a

33 She _____ the football _____ Wilfrid and _____ him.

A. remembered　　　B. bounced　　　C. to

34 "Wilfrid? Wilfrid Gordon Parker! _____ _____!"

A. friend　　　B. my

35 She _____ _____ their secrets _____ by one.

A. remembered　　　B. one　　　C. also

36 The two smiled _____ _____ _____.

A. at　　　B. other　　　C. each

37 Ms. Cooper _____ her memory _____ thanks to the little boy _____ the same middle name _____ hers.

A. got　　　B. with　　　C. back　　　D. as

---

20 "그건 금처럼 소중한 거지, 어린 친구."라고 그가 말했다.

21 그래서 Wilfrid는 Cooper 할머니께 드릴 기억들을 찾으러 집으로 돌아갔다.

22 그는 닭장 안으로 들어가서 암탉이 품고 있던 신선하고 따뜻한 달걀을 꺼냈다.

23 다음으로, 그는 자신의 양말 인형을 찾았다.

24 그것은 항상 그의 부모님께 큰 웃음을 안겨 드렸다.

25 마지막으로, 그는 자신의 장난감 상자 속에서 축구공을 찾아냈다.

26 그것은 그에게는 금만큼이나 소중했다.

27 Wilfrid는 Cooper 할머니께 가서 그녀에게 물건들을 하나씩 드렸다.

28 "이상하면서도 귀여운 아이구나! 이 멋진 물건들을 다 가져오다니 말이야."라고 Cooper 할머니는 생각했다.

29 그러다가 그녀는 자신의 과거를 기억해 내기 시작했다.

30 그녀는 따뜻한 달걀을 쥐고 Wilfrid에게, "오래 전에, 나는 나의 이모님 댁 정원에서 작고 푸른 알을 찾았단다."라고 속삭였다.

31 그녀는 양말 인형을 보며 미소를 짓다가 자기 여동생에게 인형극을 공연해 주었던 것을 기억해 냈다.

32 "내 여동생이 엄청나게 웃었지." 라고 Cooper 할머니가 말했다.

33 그녀는 축구공을 바닥에 튀게 해서 Wilfrid에게 던져 주다가 그를 기억해 냈다.

34 "Wilfrid? Wilfrid Gordon Parker! 내 친구!"

35 그녀는 또한 그들만의 비밀을 하나씩 기억해 냈다.

36 두 사람은 서로 바라보며 미소 지었다.

37 Cooper 할머니는 가운데 이름이 자신의 것과 같은 어린 소년 덕분에 기억을 다시 찾게 되었다.

※ 다음 우리말과 일치하도록 빈칸에 알맞은 말을 쓰시오.

1 _____ a Memory?

2 Wilfrid Gordon Parker was _____ _____ _____ who _____ _____ _____ a nursing home.

3 He liked _____ the people _____ _____ there.

4 But his _____ _____ was Ms. Nancy Gordon Cooper _____ her middle name was _____ _____ _____ _____.

5 He _____ _____ all his _____.

6 One day, Wilfrid's parents were _____ _____ Ms. Cooper.

7 "_____ _____ _____," _____ his mother.

8 "_____ is she a _____ old lady?" _____ Wilfrid.

9 "_____ she's _____ her memory," _____ his father.

10 "What's a _____?" _____ Wilfrid.

11 "It is _____ _____ _____," said his father.

12 Wilfrid _____ _____ know more, so he _____ to his neighbors.

13 Ms. Jordan _____ _____ the sunlight.

14 "What's a memory?" _____ _____.

15 "_____ _____, my child," she said.

16 Ms. Mitchell _____ _____ a cartoon.

17 "_____ _____ _____?" he asked.

18 "Something that _____ _____ _____," she said.

1 추억이란 무엇일까?

2 Wilfrid Gordon Parker는 요양원 옆에 사는 어린 소년이었다.

3 그는 그곳에 사는 모든 사람들을 좋아했다.

4 하지만 그가 가장 좋아하는 사람은 Nancy Gordon Cooper 할머니였는데, 그 이유는 그녀의 가운데 이름이 그의 것과 같았기 때문이었다.

5 그는 자기의 모든 비밀을 그녀에게 말했다.

6 어느 날, Wilfrid의 부모님은 Cooper 할머니에 관해 이야기를 하고 있었다.

7 "불쌍한 분." 그의 어머니가 말했다.

8 "왜 불쌍한 분이세요?"라고 Wilfrid가 물었다.

9 "왜냐하면 그분은 기억을 잃으셨거든." 그의 아버지가 말했다.

10 "기억이 뭐예요?" Wilfrid가 물었다.

11 "그것은 네가 기억하는 것이란다."라고 그의 아버지가 말했다.

12 Wilfrid는 더 알고 싶어서, 그의 이웃들에게 갔다.

13 Jordan 할머니는 햇볕을 즐기고 있었다.

14 "기억이 뭐예요?" 그가 물었다.

15 "따뜻한 거란다, 아가야." 그녀가 말했다.

16 Mitchell 할머니는 만화책을 읽고 있었다.

17 "기억이 뭐예요?" 그가 물었다.

18 "너에게 웃음을 가져다주는 것이란다." 그녀가 말했다.

19 Mr. Hunter _____ _____ his medal.

20 "It's something _____ _____ _____ gold, young man," he said.

21 So Wilfrid _____ _____ home _____ _____ _____ memories for Ms. Cooper.

22 He _____ _____ the hen house and took a fresh, warm egg _____ _____ _____ _____ _____.

23 Next, he _____ _____ his sock puppet.

24 It _____ _____ to his parents.

25 Finally, he _____ his football _____ his toy box.

26 It was _____ precious _____ _____ to him.

27 Wilfrid _____ _____ Ms. Cooper and gave her the things _____ _____ _____.

28 "_____ a strange, sweet child!" _____ Ms. Cooper, "He's _____ all these wonderful things."

29 Then she _____ _____ _____ her past.

30 She _____ the warm egg and _____ to Wilfrid, "Long ago, I _____ a small blue egg in my aunt's garden."

31 She _____ _____ the sock puppet and _____ _____ a puppet show for her sister.

32 "My sister _____ _____ _____," said Ms. Cooper.

33 She _____ the football _____ Wilfrid and remembered him.

34 "Wilfrid? Wilfrid Gordon Parker! _____ _____!"

35 She also _____ their _____ one by one.

36 The two smiled _____ _____ _____.

37 Ms. Cooper got her memory back _____ _____ the little boy with _____ _____ middle name _____ hers.

19 Hunter 할아버지는 자신의 메달을 닦고 있었다.

20 "그건 금처럼 소중한 거지, 어린 친구."라고 그가 말했다.

21 그래서 Wilfrid는 Cooper 할머니께 드릴 기억들을 찾으러 집으로 돌아갔다.

22 그는 닭장 안으로 들어가서 암탉이 품고 있던 신선하고 따뜻한 달걀을 꺼냈다.

23 다음으로, 그는 자신의 양말 인형을 찾았다.

24 그것은 항상 그의 부모님께 큰 웃음을 안겨 드렸다.

25 마지막으로, 그는 자신의 장난감 상자 속에서 축구공을 찾아냈다.

26 그것은 그에게는 금만큼이나 소중했다.

27 Wilfrid는 Cooper 할머니께 가서 그녀에게 물건들을 하나씩 드렸다.

28 "이상하면서도 귀여운 아이구나! 이 멋진 물건들을 다 가져오다니 말이야."라고 Cooper 할머니는 생각했다.

29 그러다가 그녀는 자신의 과거를 기억해 내기 시작했다.

30 그녀는 따뜻한 달걀을 쥐고 Wilfrid에게, "오래 전에, 나는 나의 이모님 댁 정원에서 작고 푸른 알을 찾았단다."라고 속삭였다.

31 그녀는 양말 인형을 보며 미소를 짓다가 자기 여동생에게 인형극을 공연해 주었던 것을 기억해 냈다.

32 "내 여동생이 엄청나게 웃었지."라고 Cooper 할머니가 말했다.

33 그녀는 축구공을 바닥에 튀게 해서 Wilfrid에게 던져 주다가 그를 기억해 냈다.

34 "Wilfrid? Wilfrid Gordon Parker! 내 친구!"

35 그녀는 또한 그들만의 비밀을 하나씩 기억해 냈다.

36 두 사람은 서로 바라보며 미소 지었다.

37 Cooper 할머니는 가운데 이름이 자신의 것과 같은 어린 소년 덕분에 기억을 다시 찾게 되었다.

※ 다음 문장을 우리말로 쓰시오.

1 What's a Memory?

➡ _____

2 Wilfrid Gordon Parker was a little boy who lived next to a nursing home.

➡ _____

3 He liked all the people who lived there.

➡ _____

4 But his favorite person was Ms. Nancy Gordon Cooper because her middle name was the same as his.

➡ _____

5 He told her all his secrets.

➡ _____

6 One day, Wilfrid's parents were talking about Ms. Cooper.

➡ _____

7 "Poor old lady," said his mother.

➡ _____

8 "Why is she a poor old lady?" asked Wilfrid.

➡ _____

9 "Because she's lost her memory," said his father.

➡ _____

10 "What's a memory?" asked Wilfrid.

➡ _____

11 "It is something you remember," said his father.

➡ _____

12 Wilfrid wanted to know more, so he went to his neighbors.

➡ _____

13 Ms. Jordan was enjoying the sunlight.

➡ _____

14 "What's a memory?" he asked.

➡ _____

15 "Something warm, my child," she said.

➡ _____

16 Ms. Mitchell was reading a cartoon.

➡ _____

17 "What's a memory?" he asked.

➡ _____

18 "Something that brings you laughter," she said.

➡ _____

19 Mr. Hunter was cleaning his medal.

➡ _____

20 "It's something as precious as gold, young man," he said.

➡ _____

21 So Wilfrid went back home to look for memories for Ms. Cooper.

➡ _____

22 He went into the hen house and took a fresh, warm egg from under a hen.

➡ _____

23 Next, he looked for his sock puppet.

➡ _____

24 It always brought laughter to his parents.

➡ _____

25 Finally, he found his football in his toy box.

➡ _____

26 It was as precious as gold to him.

➡ _____

27 Wilfrid went to Ms. Cooper and gave her the things one by one.

➡ _____

28 "What a strange, sweet child!" thought Ms. Cooper, "He's brought all these wonderful things."

➡ _____

29 Then she started to remember her past.

➡ _____

30 She held the warm egg and whispered to Wilfrid, "Long ago, I found a small blue egg in my aunt's garden."

➡ _____

31 She smiled at the sock puppet and remembered performing a puppet show for her sister.

➡ _____

32 "My sister laughed a lot," said Ms. Cooper.

➡ _____

33 She bounced the football to Wilfrid and remembered him.

➡ _____

34 "Wilfrid? Wilfrid Gordon Parker! My friend!"

➡ _____

35 She also remembered their secrets one by one.

➡ _____

36 The two smiled at each other.

➡ _____

37 Ms. Cooper got her memory back thanks to the little boy with the same middle name as hers.

➡ _____

※ 다음 괄호 안의 단어들을 우리말에 맞도록 바르게 배열하시오.

1 (Memory? / a / What's)
➡ _____

2 (Gordon / Wilfrid / Parker / a / was / boy / little / lived / who / to / next / home. / nursing / a)
➡ _____

3 (liked / he / the / all / who / people / there. / lived)
➡ _____

4 (his / but / person / favorite / was / Nancy / Ms. / Cooper / Gordon / because / middle / her / was / name / the / as / his. / same)
➡ _____

5 (told / he / all / her / secrets. / his)
➡ _____

6 (day, / one / parents / Wilfrid's / talking / were / about / Cooper. / Ms.)
➡ _____

7 (old / "poor / lady," / his / mother. / said)
➡ _____

8 (is / "why / she / a / old / poor / lady?" / Wilfrid. / asked)
➡ _____

9 (she's / "because / her / lost / memory," / father. / his / said)
➡ _____

10 (a / "what's / memory?" / Wilfrid. / asked)
➡ _____

11 (is / "it / something / remember," / you / father. / his / said)
➡ _____

12 (wanted / Wilfrid / know / to / more, / he / so / to / went / neighbors. / his)
➡ _____

13 (Jordan / Ms. / enjoying / was / sunlight. / the)
➡ _____

14 (a / "what's / memory?" / asked. / he)
➡ _____

15 (warm, / "something / child," / my / said. / she)
➡ _____

16 (Mitchell / Ms. / reading / was / cartoon. / a)
➡ _____

17 (a / "what's / memory?" / asked. / he)
➡ _____

18 (that / "something / birngs / laughter," / you / said. / she)
➡ _____

1 추억이란 무엇일까?

2 Wilfrid Gordon Parker는 요양원 옆에 사는 어린 소년이었다.

3 그는 그곳에 사는 모든 사람들을 좋아했다.

4 하지만 그가 가장 좋아하는 사람은 Nancy Gordon Cooper 할머니였는데, 그 이유는 그녀의 가운데 이름이 그의 것과 같았기 때문이었다.

5 그는 자기의 모든 비밀을 그녀에게 말했다.

6 어느 날, Wilfrid의 부모님은 Cooper 할머니에 관해 이야기를 하고 있었다.

7 "불쌍한 분." 그의 어머니가 말했다.

8 "왜 불쌍한 분이세요?"라고 Wilfrid가 물었다.

9 "왜냐하면 그분은 기억을 잃으셨거든." 그의 아버지가 말했다.

10 "기억이 뭐예요?" Wilfrid가 물었다.

11 "그것은 네가 기억하는 것이란다."라고 그의 아버지가 말했다.

12 Wilfrid는 더 알고 싶어서, 그의 이웃들에게 갔다.

13 Jordan 할머니는 햇볕을 즐기고 있었다.

14 "기억이 뭐예요?" 그가 물었다.

15 "따뜻한 거란다, 아가야." 그녀가 말했다.

16 Mitchell 할머니는 만화책을 읽고 있었다.

17 "기억이 뭐예요?" 그가 물었다.

18 "너에게 웃음을 가져다주는 것이란다." 그녀가 말했다.

19 (Hunter / Mr. / cleaning / was / medal. / his)
➡ _____

20 (something / "it's / precious / as / gold, / as / man," / young / said. / he)
➡ _____

21 (Wilfrid / so / back / went / home / look / to / memories / for / Cooper. / for / Ms.)
➡ _____

22 (went / he / into / hen / the / house / took / and / fresh, / a / egg / warm / under / hen. / a / from)
➡ _____

23 (next, / looked / he / for / puppet. / sock / his)
➡ _____

24 (always / it / laughter / brought / parents. / his / to)
➡ _____

25 (finally, / found / he / football / his / in / box. / toy / his)
➡ _____

26 (was / it / precious / as / to / gold / him. / as)
➡ _____

27 (Wilfrid / to / went / Cooper / Ms. / gave / and / her / things / the / one. / by / one)
➡ _____

28 (a / "what / strange, / child!" / sweet / Ms. / thought / Cooper, / "he's / all / brought / things." / wonderful / these)
➡ _____

29 (she / then / to / started / her / remember / past.)
➡ _____

30 (held / she / warm / the / egg / and / to / whispered / Wilfrid, / ago, / "long / found / I / small / a / egg / blue / in / garden." / aunt's / my)
➡ _____

31 (smiled / she / the / at / puppet / sock / and / performing / remembered / puppet / a / show / her / sister. / for)
➡ _____

32 ("my / laughed / sister / lot," / a / Cooper. / Ms. / said)
➡ _____

33 (bounced / she / football / the / Wilfrid / to / him. / and / remembered)
➡ _____

34 ("Wilfrid? / Gordon / Wilfrid / Parker! / friend!" / my)
➡ _____

35 (also / she / remembered / secrets / their / one. / by / one)
➡ _____

36 (two / the / smiled / at / other. / each)
➡ _____

37 (Cooper / Ms. / her / got / memory / thanks / back / to / little / the / boy / with / same / the / name / middle / hers. / as)
➡ _____

19 Hunter 할아버지는 자신의 메달을 닦고 있었다.

20 "그건 금처럼 소중한 거지, 어린 친구."라고 그가 말했다.

21 그래서 Wilfrid는 Cooper 할머니께 드릴 기억들을 찾으러 집으로 돌아갔다.

22 그는 닭장 안으로 들어가서 암탉이 품고 있던 신선하고 따뜻한 달걀을 꺼냈다.

23 다음으로, 그는 자신의 양말 인형을 찾았다.

24 그것은 항상 그의 부모님께 큰 웃음을 안겨 드렸다.

25 마지막으로, 그는 자신의 장난감 상자 속에서 축구공을 찾아냈다.

26 그것은 그에게는 금만큼이나 소중했다.

27 Wilfrid는 Cooper 할머니께 가서 그녀에게 물건들을 하나씩 드렸다.

28 "이상하면서도 귀여운 아이구나! 이 멋진 물건들을 다 가져오다니 말이야."라고 Cooper 할머니는 생각했다.

29 그러다가 그녀는 자신의 과거를 기억해 내기 시작했다.

30 그녀는 따뜻한 달걀을 쥐고 Wilfrid에게, "오래 전에, 나는 나의 이모님 댁 정원에서 작고 푸른 알을 찾았단다."라고 속삭였다.

31 그녀는 양말 인형을 보며 미소를 짓다가 자기 여동생에게 인형극을 공연해 주었던 것을 기억해 냈다.

32 "내 여동생이 엄청나게 웃었지."라고 Cooper 할머니가 말했다.

33 그녀는 축구공을 바닥에 튀게 해서 Wilfrid에게 던져 주다가 그를 기억해 냈다.

34 "Wilfrid? Wilfrid Gordon Parker! 내 친구!"

35 그녀는 또한 그들만의 비밀을 하나씩 기억해 냈다.

36 두 사람은 서로 바라보며 미소 지었다.

37 Cooper 할머니는 가운데 이름이 자신의 것과 같은 어린 소년 덕분에 기억을 다시 찾게 되었다.

※ 다음 우리말을 영어로 쓰시오.

1 추억이란 무엇일까?
➡ _____

2 Wilfrid Gordon Parker는 요양원 옆에 사는 어린 소년이었다.
➡ _____

3 그는 그곳에 사는 모든 사람들을 좋아했다.
➡ _____

4 하지만 그가 가장 좋아하는 사람은 Nancy Gordon Cooper 할머니였는데, 그 이유는 그녀의 가운데 이름이 그의 것과 같았기 때문이었다.
➡ _____

5 그는 자기의 모든 비밀을 그녀에게 말했다.
➡ _____

6 어느 날, Wilfrid의 부모님은 Cooper 할머니에 관해 이야기를 하고 있었다.
➡ _____

7 "불쌍한 분." 그의 어머니가 말했다.
➡ _____

8 "왜 불쌍한 분이세요?"라고 Wilfrid가 물었다.
➡ _____

9 "왜냐하면 그분은 기억을 잃으셨거든." 그의 아버지가 말했다.
➡ _____

10 "기억이 뭐예요?" Wilfrid가 물었다.
➡ _____

11 "그것은 네가 기억하는 것이란다."라고 그의 아버지가 말했다.
➡ _____

12 Wilfrid는 더 알고 싶어서, 그의 이웃들에게 갔다.
➡ _____

13 Jordan 할머니는 햇볕을 즐기고 있었다.
➡ _____

14 "기억이 뭐예요?" 그가 물었다.
➡ _____

15 "따뜻한 거란다, 아가야." 그녀가 말했다.
➡ _____

16 Mitchell 할머니는 만화책을 읽고 있었다.
➡ _____

17 "기억이 뭐예요?" 그가 물었다.
➡ _____

18 "너에게 웃음을 가져다주는 것이란다." 그녀가 말했다.
➡ _____

19 Hunter 할아버지는 자신의 메달을 닦고 있었다.
➡ _____

20 "그건 금처럼 소중한 거지, 어린 친구."라고 그가 말했다.
➡ _____

21 그래서 Wilfrid는 Cooper 할머니께 드릴 기억들을 찾으러 집으로 돌아갔다.
➡ _____

22 그는 닭장 안으로 들어가서 암탉이 품고 있던 신선하고 따뜻한 달걀을 꺼냈다.
➡ _____

23 다음으로, 그는 자신의 양말 인형을 찾았다.
➡ _____

24 그것은 항상 그의 부모님께 큰 웃음을 안겨 드렸다.
➡ _____

25 마지막으로, 그는 자신의 장난감 상자 속에서 축구공을 찾아냈다.
➡ _____

26 그것은 그에게는 금만큼이나 소중했다.
➡ _____

27 Wilfrid는 Cooper 할머니께 가서 그녀에게 물건들을 하나씩 드렸다.
➡ _____

28 "이상하면서도 귀여운 아이구나! 이 멋진 물건들을 다 가져오다니 말이야."라고 Cooper 할머니는 생각했다.

29 그러다가 그녀는 자신의 과거를 기억해 내기 시작했다.
➡ _____

30 그녀는 따뜻한 달걀을 쥐고 Wilfrid에게, "오래 전에, 나는 나의 이모님 댁 정원에서 작고 푸른 알을 찾았단다."라고 속삭였다.
➡ _____
_____

31 그녀는 양말 인형을 보며 미소를 짓다가 자기 여동생에게 인형극을 공연해 주었던 것을 기억해 냈다.
➡ _____

32 "내 여동생이 엄청나게 웃었지."라고 Cooper 할머니가 말했다.
➡ _____

33 그녀는 축구공을 바닥에 튀게 해서 Wilfrid에게 던져 주다가 그를 기억해 냈다.
➡ _____

34 "Wilfrid? Wilfrid Gordon Parker! 내 친구!"
➡ _____

35 그녀는 또한 그들만의 비밀을 하나씩 기억해 냈다.
➡ _____

36 두 사람은 서로 바라보며 미소 지었다.
➡ _____

37 Cooper 할머니는 가운데 이름이 자신의 것과 같은 어린 소년 덕분에 기억을 다시 찾게 되었다.
➡ _____
_____

※ 다음 우리말과 일치하도록 빈칸에 알맞은 말을 쓰시오.

Express Yourself

1. _____ May 29, 2017, we _____ _____ India.
2. This is a _____ _____ _____ _____ in the market.
3. I'll _____ _____ the experience.
4. We _____ _____ of Korean _____ _____.
5. We _____ them at the _____ festival.
6. _____ June 7, 2017, we _____ _____ Laos.
7. We met a _____ _____ _____ _____ a beautiful dress.
8. I'll _____ _____ the _____.
9. We _____ a rock. It _____ _____ a queen's head.

1. 2017년 5월 29일에 우리는 인도에 갔다.
2. 이것은 우리가 시장에서 산 그림이다.
3. 나는 그 경험을 결코 잊지 못할 것이다.
4 우리는 한국 전통 무용수들의 사진을 찍었다.
5. 우리는 그들을 마을 축제에서 보았다.
6. 2017년 6월 7일에 우리는 라오스에 도착했다.
7. 우리는 아름다운 옷을 입고 있는 한 소녀를 만났다.
8. 나는 그 경험을 결코 잊지 못할 것이다.
9. 우리는 바위를 보았다. 그것은 여왕의 머리처럼 생겼다.

Do It Yourself

1. I'd _____ _____ _____ you about a student teacher I can't forget.
2. _____ _____ is Ms. Jeon.
3. _____ _____ _____ you're great, Miso! _____ _____ _____ _____.
4. This is the bookmark that she gave to me _____ _____ _____ _____.
5. When I _____ _____, I always _____ _____ this.

1. 나는 잊을 수 없는 교생 선생님에 대해서 너희들에게 말하고 싶다.
2. 그분은 전 선생님이시다.
3. "네가 훌륭하다는 걸 잊지 마. 미소야! 계속 목적하는 것을 해보렴."
4. 이건 그분이 마지막 날 내게 주신 책갈피다.
5. 나는 스트레스를 받을 때면, 언제나 이것을 본다.

Link to the World

1. There are a lot of _____ _____ who _____ _____ and talents.
2. Mr. Kim in Busan is a smart farmer and _____ people _____ _____.
3. Ms. Lee was a science teacher _____ _____ _____.
4. Now she _____ in a park _____ _____ children about plants and birds.
5. In Ms. Choi's _____ _____, young people _____ _____ _____ gimchi and Korean hot pepper sauce.

1. 자신의 지식과 재능을 나누는 활동적인 어르신들이 많이 계시다.
2. 부산의 김 선생님은 스마트 농부이신데 사람들에게 농사에 관한 것을 가르치신다.
3. 이 선생님은 이전에 과학 선생님이셨다.
4. 지금은 공원에서 일하시며 아이들에게 식물과 새에 관해서 가르치신다.
5. 최 여사님의 요리 교실에서는 젊은이들이 김치와 한국의 고추장을 만드는 것을 배운다.

※ 다음 우리말을 영어로 쓰시오.

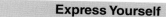
Express Yourself

1. 2017년 5월 29일에 우리는 인도에 갔다.
   ➡ _____

2. 이것은 우리가 시장에서 산 그림이다.
   ➡ _____

3. 나는 그 경험을 결코 잊지 못할 것이다.
   ➡ _____

4. 우리는 한국 전통 무용수들의 사진을 찍었다.
   ➡ _____

5. 우리는 그들을 마을 축제에서 보았다.
   ➡ _____

6. 2017년 6월 7일에 우리는 라오스에 도착했다.
   ➡ _____

7. 우리는 아름다운 옷을 입고 있는 한 소녀를 만났다.
   ➡ _____

8. 나는 그 경험을 결코 잊지 못할 것이다.
   ➡ _____

9. 우리는 바위를 보았다. 그것은 여왕의 머리처럼 생겼다.
   ➡ _____
   _____

Do It Yourself

1. 나는 잊을 수 없는 교생 선생님에 대해서 너희들에게 말하고 싶다.
   ➡ _____

2. 그분은 전 선생님이시다.
   ➡ _____

3. "네가 훌륭하다는 걸 잊지 마. 미소야! 계속 목적하는 것을 해보렴."
   ➡ _____

4. 이건 그분이 마지막 날 내게 주신 책갈피다.
   ➡ _____

5. 나는 스트레스를 받을 때면, 언제나 이것을 본다.
   ➡ _____
   _____

Link to the World

1. 자신의 지식과 재능을 나누는 활동적인 어르신들이 많이 계시다.
   ➡ _____

2. 부산의 김 선생님은 스마트 농부이신데 사람들에게 농사에 관한 것을 가르치신다.
   ➡ _____

3. 이 선생님은 이전에 과학 선생님이셨다.
   ➡ _____

4. 지금은 공원에서 일하시며 아이들에게 식물과 새에 관해서 가르치신다.
   ➡ _____

5. 최 여사님의 요리 교실에서는 젊은이들이 김치와 한국의 고추장을 만드는 것을 배운다.
   ➡ _____

※ 다음 영어를 우리말로 쓰시오.

01	lose		21	together	
02	need		22	under	
03	please		23	writer	
04	check		24	famous	
05	follow		25	shake	
06	stop		26	by the way	
07	dangerous		27	get + 형용사	
08	end		28	blow one's nose	
09	scene		29	Let me see.	
10	excited		30	be good for	
11	front		31	take out	
12	basket		32	No problem.	
13	safe		33	out of	
14	hood		34	look into	
15	knock		35	talk to oneself	
16	laugh		36	should not+동사원형	
17	blow		37	take a break	
18	leave		38	look at	
19	piggy		39	go away	
20	road		40	thank A for B	

※ 다음 우리말을 영어로 쓰시오.

01 웃다

02 함께

03 ~ 아래에

04 작가

05 (입으로) 불다

06 따라가다, 뒤따르다

07 ~을 기쁘게 하다

08 (~하는 것을) 그만두게 하다

09 길, 도로

10 정면, 앞

11 유명한

12 pig의 애칭

13 흔들리다

14 잃어버리다

15 점검하다

16 ~을 필요로 하다

17 위험한

18 바구니

19 안전한

20 (외투 등에 달린) 모자

21 끝, 마지막

22 장면, 광경

23 두드리다

24 신난

25 떠나다

26 ~을 들여다보다

27 ~의 밖으로

28 ~에 좋다

29 그럼요, 전혀 문제 되지 않아요

30 ~을 보다

31 ~을 꺼내다

32 가 버리다, 사라지다

33 ~해선 안 된다

34 어디 보자., 글쎄.

35 그런데, 그건 그렇고

36 B에 대해 A에게 감사하다

37 휴식을 취하다

38 코를 풀다

39 혼잣말하다

40 ~에 대해 들어 본 적 있니?

※ 다음 영영풀이에 알맞은 단어를 <보기>에서 골라 쓴 후, 우리말 뜻을 쓰시오.

1 _____ : to go away from a place or a person: _____

2 _____ : to send air out from your mouth: _____

3 _____ : the last part of a period of time, event, activity, or story: _____

4 _____ : known about by many people in many places: _____

5 _____ : to go, walk, drive, etc behind or after someone else: _____

6 _____ : to make someone happy or satisfied: _____

7 _____ : not likely to cause any physical injury or harm: _____

8 _____ : someone who writes books, stories, etc especially as a job: _____

9 _____ : the part of something that faces you: _____

10 _____ : a hard flat surface for vehicles, people, and animals to travel on:
_____

11 _____ : to be unable to find something or someone: _____

12 _____ : likely to injure or harm someone, or to damage or destroy something:
_____

13 _____ : to not continue, or to make someone or something not continue:
_____

14 _____ : to make the sounds and movements of your face that show you are happy
or think something is funny: _____

15 _____ : a part of a coat, jacket, etc that you can pull up to cover your head:
_____

16 _____ : to hit a door or window with your closed hand to attract the attention of
the people inside: _____

보기			
knock	leave	follow	dangerous
end	hood	stop	front
laugh	famous	road	writer
safe	blow	please	lose

※ 다음 우리말과 일치하도록 빈칸에 알맞은 것을 골라 쓰시오.

1 Little _____ Writing _____
A. Hood   B. Red

2 _____ 1: In _____ of the three _____ piggies' house
A. front   B. scene   C. little

3 (Red comes _____ _____ a _____ of cakes and cookies.)
A. basket   B. in   C. with

4 Red: Now I can see the three little piggies' house. I'll _____
a _____ here _____ the tree.
A. take   B. under   C. break

5 (Wolf _____ in and _____ _____ the house.)
A. looks   B. walks   C. into

6 Wolf: Baby piggies! They _____ delicious. I'll eat them
_____ _____.
A. look   B. lunch   C. for

7 (Wolf _____ the house _____ and it is _____.)
A. shaking   B. hard   C. blows

8 Red: Oh, that bad Wolf! What can I do to _____ him?
_____ me _____. ... That's it! (To Wolf) Hey, you! I'll
_____ the story!
A. change   B. see   C. stop   D. let

9 Wolf: _____ do you _____ that?
A. by   B. mean   C. what

10 Red: (_____ out a pen and _____ something) "There
_____ three big strong piggies in the house."
A. writing   B. lived   C. taking

11 Wolf: You _____ _____ that!
A. do   B. shouldn't

12 (Wolf _____ again, _____ the three big strong piggies
come _____ _____ the house.)
A. of   B. but   C. out   D. blows

13 Three Piggies: Hey _____! _____ did you _____ our
house?
A. there   B. blow   C. why

14 Wolf: Um ... I _____. I just _____ my _____.
A. didn't   B. nose   C. blew

15 Three Piggies: _____ do that again here. _____ _____!
A. away   B. don't   C. go

16 Wolf: Okay. I'm _____ _____.
A. sorry   B. so

17 (The piggies _____ _____ _____ the house.)
A. into   B. back   C. go

---

1 빨간 모자

2 장면 1: 아기 돼지 삼 형제의 집 앞에서

3 (Red가 케이크와 과자가 든 바구니를 들고 등장한다.)

4 Red: 이제 아기 돼지 삼 형제의 집이 보인다. 여기 나무 아래에서 좀 쉬어야지.

5 (늑대가 걸어 들어와 집 안을 들여다본다.)

6 늑대: 새끼 돼지들이네! 맛있어 보인다. 점심으로 그들을 먹어야겠어.

7 (늑대가 집을 세게 불자 집이 흔들리고 있다.)

8 Red: 오, 저런 나쁜 늑대 같으니라고! 그를 멈추게 하려면 내가 뭘 할 수 있을까? 어디 보자. … 바로 그거야! (늑대에게) 이봐! 내가 이야기를 바꾸겠어!

9 늑대: 그게 무슨 말이야?

10 Red: (펜을 꺼내 뭔가를 쓰면서) "크고 힘센 아기 돼지 삼 형제가 그 집에 살고 있었다."

11 늑대: 그렇게 하면 안 돼!

12 (늑대가 다시 집을 분다. 그러나 크고 힘센 돼지 삼 형제가 집에서 나온다.)

13 돼지 삼 형제: 이봐, 거기! 왜 우리 집을 불고 있어?

14 늑대: 음… 그러지 않았어. 나는 그냥 코를 풀었을 뿐이야.

15 돼지 삼 형제: 여기서 다시는 그러지 마. 가 버려!

16 늑대: 알았어. 정말 미안해.

17 (돼지들은 집 안으로 다시 들어간다.)

18 Wolf: I can't _____ this _____. I'm so hungry! (Looking _____ Red's basket) What are those?
    A. at   B. happened   C. believe

19 Red: _____ are cookies _____ Grandma.
    A. for   B. these

20 Wolf: _____ does she _____?
    A. live   B. where

21 Red: She _____ _____ the _____ of this road.
    A. end   B. at   C. lives

22 Wolf: (To _____) Grandma is good _____ lunch, too. (To Red) See you _____. (Wolf leaves.)
    A. for   B. himself   C. later

23 Red: Bye. (Talking to _____) Hmm …. He's going to Grandma's. I think I should change the story again. (Taking out the pen and writing something) Okay. If my story _____, Grandma will be _____. I'll _____ him. (Red leaves.)
    A. works   B. safe   C. follow   D. herself

24 _____ 2: Grandma's _____
    A. house   B. scene

25 (Wolf dances _____ Grandma. She looks very _____ and _____.)
    A. happy   B. excited   C. around

26 Red: (_____ _____ the door) Grandma, _____ me. Are you okay?
    A. on   B. knocking   C. it's

27 Grandma: (Laughing _____ and _____ the door) Sure, Red. Come on in. I was watching Wolf _____ for me.
    A. dance   B. happily   C. opening

28 Red: Hey, Wolf. _____ you _____ _____ my grandmother.
    A. thank   B. pleasing   C. for

29 Wolf: _____, _____ ….
    A. that's   B. well

30 Prince: (Opening the door and _____ in) Hey, you bad Wolf! (Prince _____ _____ Wolf.)
    A. running   B. over   C. jumps

31 Red: No, no! Stop. He's _____ _____.
    A. dangerous   B. not

32 Grandma: Right. Look. He is _____ _____ us.
    A. for   B. dancing

33 Prince: Really? Wolf, I'm sorry. I'm _____ you're _____ _____ Grandma.
    A. glad   B. to   C. kind

34 Wolf: Well, … I'm glad, _____. _____ the _____, do you have _____ to eat?
    A. too   B. anything   C. way   D. by

---

18 늑대: 이런 일이 일어나다니 믿을 수가 없어. 나는 너무 배가 고파! (Red의 바구니를 보며) 그건 뭐야?

19 Red: 할머니께 드릴 과자들이야.

20 늑대: 어디 사시는데?

21 Red: 이 길의 끝에 사셔.

22 늑대: (혼잣말로) 할머니도 점심으로 좋지. (Red에게) 나중에 보자. (늑대가 떠난다.)

23 Red: 안녕. (혼잣말로) 흠…. 그는 할머니 댁으로 갈 거야. 이야기를 다시 바꿔야겠어. (펜을 꺼내서 뭔가를 쓰며) 좋아. 내 이야기가 제대로 돌아가면 할머니는 안전하실 거야. 그를 따라가 봐야지. (Red가 떠난다.)

24 장면 2: 할머니의 집

25 (늑대가 할머니 주변을 맴돌며 춤을 춘다. 할머니는 아주 행복하고 신나 보인다.)

26 Red: (문을 두드리며) 할머니, 저예요. 괜찮으세요?

27 할머니: (행복하게 웃으며 문을 열면서) 물론이지, Red야. 어서 들어와. 늑대가 나를 위해 춤추는 걸 보고 있었단다.

28 Red: 이봐, 늑대야. 우리 할머니를 기쁘게 해드려서 고마워.

29 늑대: 음, 그게 ….

30 왕자: (문을 열고 뛰어 들어오며) 이봐, 이 나쁜 늑대야! (왕자가 늑대에게 달려든다.)

31 Red: 아니, 아니에요! 멈춰요. 그는 위험하지 않아요.

32 할머니: 맞아. 보세요. 그가 우리를 위해 춤추고 있잖아요.

33 왕자: 정말요? 늑대야, 미안해. 네가 할머니께 잘해 드린다니 기쁘다.

34 늑대: 음… 나도 기뻐. 그런데, 먹을 것 좀 있어?

35 Red: (Taking some cookies _____ the basket) _____ you _____ some cookies?
    A. out   B. like   C. would

36 Wolf: No, _____ . I _____ eat cookies. I _____ chicken.
    A. don't   B. thanks   C. like

37 Red: _____ worry. I'll change the story again. Then you will like _____ cookies. (Checking the basket) Oh, I _____ my pen. What _____ I do?
    A. eating   B. don't   C. should   D. lost

38 Wolf: (Dancing and _____) Oh, no! I'm so _____ and _____ now.
    A. tired   B. crying   C. hungry

39 (Andersen _____ _____ .)
    A. in   B. comes

40 Andersen: I _____ you _____ my help, _____ ?
    A. need   B. right   C. think

41 Red: Oh, Mr. Andersen. I'm _____ _____ you're _____ .
    A. glad   B. so   C. here

42 Grandma: (_____ Red) Who's _____ ?
    A. that   B. to

43 Red: He is Mr. Andersen, the _____ writer. Have you ever _____ _____ "The Red Shoes"?
    A. of   B. famous   C. heard

44 Grandma: Yes, I _____ . Is he the _____ who _____ that story?
    A. one   B. have   C. wrote

45 Red: Right. (To Andersen) I _____ the story, and the poor Wolf _____ _____ and hungry.
    A. changed   B. tired   C. got

46 Andersen: You _____ _____ the story _____ .
    A. change   B. again   C. can

47 Red: I'm sorry, but I _____ the pen you _____ to me. Please _____ me.
    A. help   B. gave   C. lost

48 Andersen: No _____ . I'll write a happy _____ for everyone. Is that _____ ?
    A. ending   B. problem   C. okay

49 Red: _____ _____ great!
    A. be   B. that'll

50 Andersen: All right. I'll use my pen here. "The kind Wolf _____ . He _____ _____ cakes and cookies."
    A. can   B. dancing   C. enjoy   D. stops

51 Wolf: (Stopping dancing) I can _____ _____ ! (Eating cookies) And I _____ _____ cookies! Thank you very much.
    A. eat   B. dancing   C. can   D. stop

52 (Everybody _____ and _____ cookies _____ .)
    A. together   B. enjoys   C. laughs

---

35 Red: (바구니에서 과자를 좀 꺼내며) 과자 좀 먹을래?

36 늑대: 고맙지만 됐어. 난 과자를 먹지 않아. 나는 닭고기가 좋아.

37 Red: 걱정하지 마. 내가 이야기를 다시 바꿔야겠네. 그러면 넌 과자 먹는 걸 좋아하게 될 거야. (바구니를 뒤지며) 오, 펜을 잃어버렸어. 어떻게 하지?

38 늑대: (춤을 추며 울부짖으며) 오, 안 돼! 난 지금 너무 피곤하고 배고파.

39 (Andersen이 들어온다.)

40 Andersen: 내 도움이 필요한 것 같은데, 맞지?

41 Red: 오, Andersen 씨. 여기 오셔서 너무 기뻐요.

42 할머니: (Red에게) 저 사람이 누구니?

43 Red: 저분은 유명한 작가 Andersen 씨예요. "빨간 구두"에 대해 들어 보신 적이 있죠?

44 할머니: 그래, 들어 봤지. 그 이야기를 쓴 사람이란 말이지?

45 Red: 맞아요. (Andersen에게) 제가 이야기를 바꿔서 저 불쌍한 늑대가 피곤하고 배고파졌어요.

46 Andersen: 너는 다시 이야기를 바꿀 수 있잖아.

47 Red: 죄송하지만, 제가 작가님이 주신 펜을 잃어버렸어요. 저 좀 도와주세요.

48 Andersen: 문제없지. 내가 모두에게 행복한 결말을 쓸게. 괜찮지?

49 Red: 아주 좋아요!

50 Andersen: 좋아. 여기 내 펜을 써야지. "그 친절한 늑대는 춤추기를 멈춘다. 그는 케이크와 과자를 즐겨 먹을 수 있다."

51 늑대: (춤을 멈추며) 춤을 멈출 수가 있다! (과자를 먹으며) 그리고 과자를 먹을 수 있어! 정말 고마워요.

52 (모두 웃으며 함께 과자를 맛있게 먹는다.)

※ 다음 우리말과 일치하도록 빈칸에 알맞은 말을 쓰시오.

1   Little _____ Writing _____

2   _____ 1: _____ _____ _____ the three _____ piggies' house

3   (Red _____ _____ _____ a basket of cakes and cookies.)

4   Red: Now I _____ _____ the three little piggies' house. I'll _____ _____ here _____ the tree.

5   (Wolf _____ _____ and _____ _____ the house.)

6   Wolf: Baby piggies! They _____ _____. I'll eat them _____ _____.

7   (Wolf _____ the house _____ and it _____ _____.)

8   Red: Oh, that bad Wolf! What can I do _____ _____ him? _____ _____ _____ _____. ... That's it! (To Wolf) Hey, you! I'll _____ _____!

9   Wolf: _____ do you _____ _____ that?

10 Red: (_____ _____ a pen and _____ _____) "_____ _____ three big strong piggies in the house."

11 Wolf: You _____ _____ that!

12 (Wolf _____ again, but the three big strong piggies _____ _____ the house.)

13 Three Piggies: Hey _____! _____ _____ you _____ our house?

14 Wolf: Um ... I _____. I _____ _____ my _____.

15 Three Piggies: _____ _____ that again here. _____ _____!

16 Wolf: Okay. I'm _____ _____.

17 (The piggies _____ _____ _____ the house.)

1   빨간 모자

2   장면 1: 아기 돼지 삼 형제의 집 앞에서

3   (Red가 케이크와 과자가 든 바구니를 들고 등장한다.)

4   Red: 이제 아기 돼지 삼 형제의 집이 보인다. 여기 나무 아래에서 좀 쉬어야지.

5   (늑대가 걸어 들어와 집 안을 들여다본다.)

6   늑대: 새끼 돼지들이네! 맛있어 보인다. 점심으로 그들을 먹어야겠어.

7   (늑대가 집을 세게 불자 집이 흔들리고 있다.)

8   Red: 오, 저런 나쁜 늑대 같으니라고! 그를 멈추게 하려면 내가 뭘 할 수 있을까? 어디 보자. … 바로 그거야! (늑대에게) 이봐! 내가 이야기를 바꾸겠어!

9   늑대: 그게 무슨 말이야?

10 Red: (펜을 꺼내 뭔가를 쓰면서) "크고 힘센 아기 돼지 삼 형제가 그 집에 살고 있었다."

11 늑대: 그렇게 하면 안 돼!

12 (늑대가 다시 집을 분다. 그러나 크고 힘센 돼지 삼 형제가 집에서 나온다.)

13 돼지 삼 형제: 이봐, 거기! 왜 우리 집을 불고 있어?

14 늑대: 음… 그러지 않았어. 나는 그냥 코를 풀었을 뿐이야.

15 돼지 삼 형제: 여기서 다시는 그러지 마. 가 버려!

16 늑대: 알았어. 정말 미안해.

17 (돼지들은 집 안으로 다시 들어간다.)

18 Wolf: I _____ this _____. I'm so hungry! (_____ _____ Red's basket) What are those?

19 Red: _____ are cookies _____ Grandma.

20 Wolf: _____ she _____?

21 Red: She _____ _____ _____ _____ of this road.

22 Wolf: (To _____) Grandma is good _____ _____, _____. (To Red) See you _____. (Wolf leaves.)

23 Red: Bye. (Talking to _____) Hmm …. He's _____ _____ Grandma's. I think I should change the story again. (Taking out the pen and writing something) Okay. If my story _____, Grandma will be _____. I'll _____ him. (Red leaves.)

24 _____ 2: Grandma's _____

25 (Wolf _____ _____ Grandma. She _____ very _____ and _____.)

26 Red: (_____ _____ the door) Grandma, _____ me. Are you _____?

27 Grandma: (Laughing _____ and _____ the door) Sure, Red. Come on in. I was _____ Wolf _____ for me.

28 Red: Hey, Wolf. _____ you _____ _____ my grandmother.

29 Wolf: _____, _____ ….

30 Prince: (Opening the door and _____ _____) Hey, you bad Wolf! (Prince _____ _____ Wolf.)

31 Red: No, no! Stop. He's _____ _____.

32 Grandma: Right. Look. He _____ _____ us.

33 Prince: Really? Wolf, I'm sorry. I'm _____ you're _____ _____ Grandma.

34 Wolf: Well, … I'm glad, too. _____ _____ _____, do you _____ _____ _____ _____?

---

18 늑대: 이런 일이 일어나다니 믿을 수가 없어. 나는 너무 배가 고파! (Red의 바구니를 보며) 그건 뭐야?

19 Red: 할머니께 드릴 과자들이야.

20 늑대: 어디 사시는데?

21 Red: 이 길의 끝에 사셔.

22 늑대: (혼잣말로) 할머니도 점심으로 좋지. (Red에게) 나중에 보자. (늑대가 떠난다.)

23 Red: 안녕. (혼잣말로) 흠…. 그는 할머니 댁으로 갈 거야. 이야기를 다시 바꿔야겠어. (펜을 꺼내서 뭔가를 쓰며) 좋아. 내 이야기가 제대로 돌아가면 할머니는 안전하실 거야. 그를 따라가 봐야지. (Red가 떠난다.)

24 장면 2: 할머니의 집

25 (늑대가 할머니 주변을 맴돌며 춤을 춘다. 할머니는 아주 행복하고 신나 보인다.)

26 Red: (문을 두드리며) 할머니. 저예요. 괜찮으세요?

27 할머니: (행복하게 웃으며 문을 열면서) 물론이지. Red야. 어서 들어와. 늑대가 나를 위해 춤추는 걸 보고 있었단다.

28 Red: 이봐, 늑대야. 우리 할머니를 기쁘게 해드려서 고마워.

29 늑대: 음, 그게 ….

30 왕자: (문을 열고 뛰어 들어오며) 이봐, 이 나쁜 늑대야! (왕자가 늑대에게 달려든다.)

31 Red: 아니, 아니에요! 멈춰요. 그는 위험하지 않아요.

32 할머니: 맞아. 보세요. 그가 우리를 위해 춤추고 있잖아요.

33 왕자: 정말요? 늑대야, 미안해. 네가 할머니께 잘해 드린다니 기쁘다.

34 늑대: 음… 나도 기뻐. 그런데 먹을 것 좀 있어?

35 Red: (_____ some cookies _____ _____ _____)
_____ you _____ some cookies?

36 Wolf: _____, _____. I _____ eat cookies. I _____
chicken.

37 Red: _____ _____. I'll change the story again. Then you will
like _____ cookies. (Checking the basket) Oh, I _____ my
pen. _____ _____ _____ _____?

38 Wolf: (Dancing and _____) Oh, no! I'm _____ _____ and
_____ now.

39 (Andersen _____ _____.)

40 Andersen: I _____ you _____ my _____, _____?

41 Red: Oh, Mr. Andersen. I'm _____ _____ you're _____.

42 Grandma: (_____ Red) _____ _____?

43 Red: He is Mr. Andersen, the _____ writer. _____ you
_____ _____ _____ "The Red Shoes"?

44 Grandma: Yes, I _____. Is he the _____ who _____ that
story?

45 Red: Right. (To Andersen) I _____ the story, and the poor Wolf
_____ _____ and _____.

46 Andersen: You _____ _____ the story _____.

47 Red: I'm sorry, but I _____ the pen you _____ to me. Please
_____ _____.

48 Andersen: No _____. I'll write _____ _____ _____
_____ everyone. Is that _____?

49 Red: _____ _____ _____!

50 Andersen: All right. I'll use my pen here. "The kind Wolf _____
_____. He _____ _____ cakes and cookies."

51 Wolf: (Stopping dancing) I can _____ _____! (Eating
cookies) And I _____ _____ cookies! Thank you very much.

52 (Everybody _____ and _____ cookies _____.)

35 Red: (바구니에서 과자를 좀 꺼내며) 과자 좀 먹을래?

36 늑대: 고맙지만 됐어. 난 과자를 먹지 않아. 나는 닭고기가 좋아.

37 Red: 걱정하지 마. 내가 이야기를 다시 바꿔야겠네. 그러면 넌 과자 먹는 걸 좋아하게 될 거야. (바구니를 뒤지며) 오, 펜을 잃어버렸어. 어떻게 하지?

38 늑대: (춤을 추며 울부짖으며) 오, 안 돼! 난 지금 너무 피곤하고 배고파.

39 (Andersen이 들어온다.)

40 Andersen: 내 도움이 필요한 것 같은데, 맞지?

41 Red: 오, Andersen 씨. 여기 오셔서 너무 기뻐요.

42 할머니: (Red에게) 저 사람이 누구니?

43 Red: 저분은 유명한 작가 Andersen 씨예요. "빨간 구두"에 대해 들어 보신 적이 있죠?

44 할머니: 그래, 들어 봤지. 그 이야기를 쓴 사람이란 말이지?

45 Red: 맞아요. (Andersen에게) 제가 이야기를 바꿔서 저 불쌍한 늑대가 피곤하고 배고파졌어요.

46 Andersen: 너는 다시 이야기를 바꿀 수 있잖아.

47 Red: 죄송하지만, 제가 작가님이 주신 펜을 잃어버렸어요. 저 좀 도와주세요.

48 Andersen: 문제없지. 내가 모두에게 행복한 결말을 쓸게. 괜찮지?

49 Red: 아주 좋아요!

50 Andersen: 좋아. 여기 내 펜을 써야지. "그 친절한 늑대는 춤추기를 멈춘다. 그는 케이크와 과자를 즐겨 먹을 수 있다."

51 늑대: (춤을 멈추며) 춤을 멈출 수가 있다! (과자를 먹으며) 그리고 과자를 먹을 수 있어! 정말 고마워요.

52 (모두 웃으며 함께 과자를 맛있게 먹는다.)

1 Little Red Writing Hood
➡ _____

2 Scene 1: In front of the three little piggies' house
➡ _____

3 (Red comes in with a basket of cakes and cookies.)
➡ _____

4 Red: Now I can see the three little piggies' house. I'll take a break here under the tree.
➡ _____

5 (Wolf walks in and looks into the house.)
➡ _____

6 Wolf: Baby piggies! They look delicious. I'll eat them for lunch.
➡ _____

7 (Wolf blows the house hard and it is shaking.)
➡ _____

8 Red: Oh, that bad Wolf! What can I do to stop him? Let me see. ... That's it! (To Wolf) Hey, you! I'll change the story!
➡ _____
➡ _____

9 Wolf: What do you mean by that?
➡ _____

10 Red: (Taking out a pen and writing something) "There lived three big strong piggies in the house."
➡ _____

11 Wolf: You shouldn't do that!
➡ _____

12 (Wolf blows again, but the three big strong piggies come out of the house.)
➡ _____

13 Three Piggies: Hey there! Why did you blow our house?
➡ _____

14 Wolf: Um ... I didn't. I just blew my nose.
➡ _____

15 Three Piggies: Don't do that again here. Go away!
➡ _____

16 Wolf: Okay. I'm so sorry.
➡ _____

17 (The piggies go back into the house.)
➡ _____

18 Wolf: I can't believe this happened. I'm so hungry! (Looking at Red's basket) What are those?
➡ _____

19 Red: These are cookies for Grandma.
➡ _____

20 Wolf: Where does she live?
➡ _____

21 Red: She lives at the end of this road.
➡ _____

22 Wolf: (To himself) Grandma is good for lunch, too. (To Red) See you later. (Wolf leaves.)
➡ _____

23 Red: Bye. (Talking to herself) Hmm .... He's going to Grandma's. I think I should change the story again. (Taking out the pen and writing something) Okay. If my story works, Grandma will be safe. I'll follow him. (Red leaves.)
➡ _____
_____

24 Scene2: Grandma's house
➡ _____

25 (Wolf dances around Grandma. She looks very happy and excited.)
➡ _____

26 Red: (Knocking on the door) Grandma, it's me. Are you okay?
➡ _____

27 Grandma: (Laughing happily and opening the door) Sure, Red. Come on in. I was watching Wolf dance for me.
➡ _____

28 Red: Hey, Wolf. Thank you for pleasing my grandmother.
➡ _____

29 Wolf: Well, that's ....
➡ _____

30 Prince: (Opening the door and running in) Hey, you bad Wolf! (Prince jumps over Wolf.)
➡ _____

31 Red: No, no! Stop. He's not dangerous.
➡ _____

32 Grandma: Right. Look. He is dancing for us.
➡ _____

33 Prince: Really? Wolf, I'm sorry. I'm glad you're kind to Grandma.
➡ _____

34 Wolf: Well, ... I'm glad, too. By the way, do you have anything to eat?
➡ _____

35 Red: (Taking some cookies out the basket) Would you like some cookies?
➡ _____

36 Wolf: No, thanks. I don't eat cookies. I like chicken.
➡ _____

37 Red: Don't worry. I'll change the story again. Then you will like eating cookies. (Checking the basket) Oh, I lost my pen. What should I do?

➡ _____

_____

38 Wolf: (Dancing and crying) Oh, no! I'm so tired and hungry now.

➡ _____

39 (Andersen comes in.)

➡ _____

40 Andersen: I think you need my help, right?

➡ _____

41 Red: Oh, Mr. Andersen. I'm so glad you're here.

➡ _____

42 Grandma: (To Red) Who's that?

➡ _____

43 Red: He is Mr. Andersen, the famous writer. Have you ever heard of "The Red Shoes"?

➡ _____

44 Grandma: Yes, I have. Is he the one who wrote that story?

➡ _____

45 Red: Right. (To Andersen) I changed the story, and the poor Wolf got tired and hungry.

➡ _____

46 Andersen: You can change the story again.

➡ _____

47 Red: I'm sorry, but I lost the pen you gave to me. Please help me.

➡ _____

48 Andersen: No problem. I'll write a happy ending for everyone. Is that okay?

➡ _____

49 Red: That'll be great!

➡ _____

50 Andersen: All right. I'll use my pen here. "The kind Wolf stops dancing. He can enjoy cakes and cookies."

➡ _____

51 Wolf: (Stopping dancing) I can stop dancing! (Eating cookies) And I can eat cookies! Thank you very much.

➡ _____

52 (Everybody laughs and enjoys cookies together.)

➡ _____

※ 다음 괄호 안의 단어들을 우리말에 맞도록 바르게 배열하시오.

1 (Red / Little / Hood / Writing)
➡ _____

2 (scene 1: / of / front / in / three / the / little / house. / piggies')
➡ _____

3 ((comes / Red / with / in / of / basket / a / cookies. / and / cakes))
➡ _____

4 (Red: / I / now / see / can / three / the / house / piggies' / little // take / I'll / break / a / under / tree. / here / the)
➡ _____
_____

5 ((walks / Wolf / and / in / into / house. / the / into / looks))
➡ _____

6 (Wolf: / piggies! / baby // look / they / delicious. // I'll / for / eat / lunch. / them)
➡ _____

7 ((blows / Wolf / house / the / and / hard / shaking. / is / it))
➡ _____

8 (Red: / oh, / bad / that / Wolf! // can / what / do / I / stop / to / him? // me / see. / let / ... // it! / that's / (to / Wolf) / you! / hey, // change / I'll / story! / the)
➡ _____
_____
_____

9 (Wolf: / do / what / mean / you / that? / by)
➡ _____

10 (Red: / (taking / a / out / pen / and / something) / writing // "there / three / lived / strong / big / piggies / house." / the / in)
➡ _____
_____

11 (Wolf: / shouldn't / you / that! / do)
➡ _____

12 ((Wolf / again, / blows / but / three / the / big / piggies / strong / out / come / house. / the / of))
➡ _____
_____

13 (piggies: / three / there! / hey // did / why / blow / house? / our / you)
➡ _____

14 (Wolf: / um / ... / didn't. / I // just / I / nose. / my / blew)
➡ _____

15 (piggies: / three / do / don't / that / here. / again // away! / go)
➡ _____

16 (Wolf: okay. // sorry. / so / I'm)
➡ _____

17 ((piggies / the / back / go / house. / the / into))
➡ _____

1 빨간 모자

2 장면 1: 아기 돼지 삼 형제의 집 앞에서

3 (Red가 케이크와 과자가 든 바구니를 들고 등장한다.)

4 Red: 이제 아기 돼지 삼 형제의 집이 보인다. 여기 나무 아래에서 좀 쉬어야지.

5 (늑대가 걸어 들어와 집 안을 들여다본다.)

6 늑대: 새끼 돼지들이네! 맛있어 보인다. 점심으로 그들을 먹어야겠어.

7 (늑대가 집을 세게 불자 집이 흔들리고 있다.)

8 Red: 오. 저런 나쁜 늑대 같으니라고! 그를 멈추게 하려면 내가 뭘 할 수 있을까? 어디 보자. … 바로 그거야! (늑대에게) 이봐! 내가 이야기를 바꾸겠어!

9 늑대: 그게 무슨 말이야?

10 Red: (펜을 꺼내 뭔가를 쓰면서) "크고 힘센 아기 돼지 삼 형제가 그 집에 살고 있었다."

11 늑대: 그렇게 하면 안 돼!

12 (늑대가 다시 집을 분다. 그러나 크고 힘센 돼지 삼 형제가 집에서 나온다.)

13 돼지 삼 형제: 이봐, 거기! 왜 우리 집을 불고 있어?

14 늑대: 음… 그러지 않았어. 나는 그냥 코를 풀었을 뿐이야.

15 돼지 삼 형제: 여기서 다시는 그러지 마. 가 버려!

16 늑대: 알았어. 정말 미안해.

17 (돼지들은 집 안으로 다시 들어간다.)

18 (Wolf: / can't / I / believe / happened. / this // hungry! / so / I'm // (looking / Red's / at / basket) // those? / are / what)
➡ _____

19 (Red: / are / these / cookies / Grandma. / for)
➡ _____

20 (Wolf: / does / where / live? / she)
➡ _____

21 (Red: / lives / she / the / at / of / end / road. / this)
➡ _____

22 (Wolf: / (to / himself) // is / Grandma / good / is / lunch, / too. / for // (to / red) / you / see / later. // (Wolf / leaves.)
➡ _____

23 (Red: / bye. // (talking / herself) / to // hmm / .... / going / he's / Grandma's. / to // think / I / should / I / change / story / the / again. // (taking / the / out / pen / and / something) / writing // okay. // my / if / story / works, / will / Grandma / safe. / be // him. / follow / I'll // (Red / leaves.)
➡ _____
_____
_____

24 (scene 2: / house / Grandma's)
➡ _____

25 ((dances / Wolf / Grandma. / around // looks / she / very / excited. / and / happy)
➡ _____

26 (Red: / on / (knocking / the / on / door) // Grandma, / me. / it's // okay? / you / are)
➡ _____

27 (Grandma: / (laughing / and / happily / the / opening / door) // Red. / sure, // in. / on / come // was / I / watching / dance / Wolf / me. / for)
➡ _____

28 (Red: Wolf. / hey, // you / thank / pleasing / for / grandmother. / my)
➡ _____

29 (Wolf: / that's / .... / well,)
➡ _____

30 (Prince: / (opening / door / the / running / and / in) // you / hey, / Wolf! / bad // (Prince / over / jumps / Wolf.)
➡ _____

31 (Red: no! / no, // stop. // not / he's / dangerous.)
➡ _____

32 (Grandma: / right. // look. // is / he / dancing / us. / for)
➡ _____

33 (Prince: / really? // I'm / Wolf, / sorry. // glad / I'm / kind / you're / Grandma. / to)
➡ _____

34 (Wolf: / ... / well, / glad, / I'm / too. // the / by / way, / you / have / do / anything / eat? / to)
➡ _____

18 늑대: 이런 일이 일어나다니 믿을 수가 없어. 나는 너무 배가 고파! (Red의 바구니를 보며) 그건 뭐야?

19 Red: 할머니께 드릴 과자들이야.

20 늑대: 어디 사시는데?

21 Red: 이 길의 끝에 사셔.

22 늑대: (혼잣말로) 할머니도 점심으로 좋지. (Red에게) 나중에 보자. (늑대가 떠난다.)

23 Red: 안녕. (혼잣말로) 흠…. 그는 할머니 댁으로 갈 거야. 이야기를 다시 바꿔야겠어. (펜을 꺼내서 뭔가를 쓰며) 좋아. 내 이야기가 제대로 돌아가면 할머니는 안전하실 거야. 그를 따라가 봐야지. (Red가 떠난다.)

24 장면 2: 할머니의 집

25 (늑대가 할머니 주변을 맴돌며 춤을 춘다. 할머니는 아주 행복하고 신나 보인다.)

26 Red: (문을 두드리며) 할머니. 저예요. 괜찮으세요?

27 할머니: (행복하게 웃으며 문을 열면서) 물론이지, Red야. 어서 들어와. 늑대가 나를 위해 춤추는 걸 보고 있었단다.

28 Red: 이봐. 늑대야. 우리 할머니를 기쁘게 해드려서 고마워.

29 늑대: 음, 그게….

30 왕자: (문을 열고 뛰어 들어오며) 이봐, 이 나쁜 늑대야! (왕자가 늑대에게 달려든다.)

31 Red: 아니, 아니에요! 멈춰요. 그는 위험하지 않아요.

32 할머니: 맞아. 보세요. 그가 우리를 위해 춤추고 있잖아요.

33 왕자: 정말요? 늑대야. 미안해. 네가 할머니께 잘해 드린다니 기쁘다.

34 늑대: 음… 나도 기뻐. 그런데. 먹을 것 좀 있어?

35 (Red: / (taking / cookies / some / the / out / basket) // you / like / would / cookies? / some)
➡ _____

36 (Wolf: / thanks. / no, // don't / I / cookies. / eat // chicken. / like / I)
➡ _____

37 (Red: / worry. / don't // change / I'll / story / again. / the // you / then / like / will / cookies. / eating // (checking / basket / the) // oh, / lost / my / I / pen. // should / what / do? / I)
➡ _____

38 (Wolf: / (dancing / and / crying) / no! / oh, // so / I'm / hungry / and / now. / tired)
➡ _____

39 ((comes / Andersen / in.))
➡ _____

40 (Andersen: / think / I / need / you / right? / help, / my)
➡ _____

41 (Red: / Mr. / oh, / Andersen. // so / I'm / here. / you're / glad)
➡ _____

42 (Grandma: / (to / red) // that? / who's)
➡ _____

43 (Red: / is / he / Andersen, / Mr. / famous / the / writer. // you / have / heard / ever / of / Shoes"? / Red / "The)
➡ _____

44 (Grandma: / have. / I / yes, // he / is / one / the / who / story? / that / wrote)
➡ _____

45 (Red: / right. // (to / Adnersen) // changed / I / story, / the / and / poor / the / got / Wolf / tired / hungry. / and)
➡ _____

46 (Andersen: / can / you / change / story / again. / the)
➡ _____

47 (Red: / sorry, / I'm / but / lost / I / pen / the / gave / you / me. / to // me. / help / please)
➡ _____

48 (Andersen: / problem. / no // write / I'll / happy / a / ending / everyone. / for // okay? / that / is)
➡ _____

49 (Red: / be / that'll / great!)
➡ _____

50 (Andersen: / right. / all // use / I'll / pen / my / here. // kind / "the / dancing. / stops / Wolf // can / he / cakes / cookies." / and / enjoy)
➡ _____

51 (Wolf: / (stopping / dancing) // can / I / dancing! / stop / (eating / cookies) // and / can / I / cookies! / eat // you / thank / much. / very)
➡ _____

52 ((laughs / everybody / enjoys / and / together. / cookies))
➡ _____

35 Red: (바구니에서 과자를 좀 꺼내며) 과자 좀 먹을래?

36 늑대: 고맙지만 됐어. 난 과자를 먹지 않아. 나는 닭고기가 좋아.

37 Red: 걱정하지 마. 내가 이야기를 다시 바꿔야겠네. 그러면 넌 과자 먹는 걸 좋아하게 될 거야. (바구니를 뒤지며) 오, 펜을 잃어버렸어. 어떻게 하지?

38 늑대: (춤을 추며 울부짖으며) 오, 안 돼! 난 지금 너무 피곤하고 배고파.

39 (Andersen이 들어온다.)

40 Andersen: 내 도움이 필요한 것 같은데, 맞지?

41 Red: 오, Andersen 씨. 여기 오셔서 너무 기뻐요.

42 할머니: (Red에게) 저 사람이 누구니?

43 Red: 저분은 유명한 작가 Andersen 씨예요. "빨간 구두"에 대해 들어 보신 적이 있죠?

44 할머니: 그래, 들어 봤지. 그 이야기를 쓴 사람이란 말이지?

45 Red: 맞아요. (Andersen에게) 제가 이야기를 바꿔서 저 불쌍한 늑대가 피곤하고 배고파졌어요.

46 Andersen: 너는 다시 이야기를 바꿀 수 있잖아.

47 Red: 죄송하지만, 제가 작가님이 주신 펜을 잃어버렸어요. 저 좀 도와주세요.

48 Andersen: 문제없지. 내가 모두에게 행복한 결말을 쓸게. 괜찮지?

49 Red: 아주 좋아요!

50 Andersen: 좋아. 여기 내 펜을 써야지. "그 친절한 늑대는 춤추기를 멈춘다. 그는 케이크와 과자를 즐겨 먹을 수 있다."

51 늑대: (춤을 멈추며) 춤을 멈출 수가 있다! (과자를 먹으며) 그리고 과자를 먹을 수 있어! 정말 고마워요.

52 (모두 웃으며 함께 과자를 맛있게 먹는다.)

※ 다음 우리말을 영어로 쓰시오.

1 빨간 모자

➡ _____

2 장면 1: 아기 돼지 삼 형제의 집 앞에서

➡ _____

3 (Red가 케이크와 과자가 든 바구니를 들고 등장한다.)

➡ _____

4 Red: 이제 아기 돼지 삼 형제의 집이 보인다. 여기 나무 아래에서 좀 쉬어야지.

➡ _____

5 (늑대가 걸어 들어와 집 안을 들여다본다.)

➡ _____

6 늑대: 새끼 돼지들이네! 맛있어 보인다. 점심으로 그들을 먹어야겠어.

➡ _____

7 (늑대가 집을 세게 불자 집이 흔들리고 있다.)

➡ _____

8 Red: 오, 저런 나쁜 늑대 같으니라고! 그를 멈추게 하려면 내가 뭘 할 수 있을까? 어디 보자. ⋯ 바로 그거야! (늑대에게) 이봐! 내가 이야기를 바꾸겠어!

➡ _____

_____

9 늑대: 그게 무슨 말이야?

➡ _____

10 Red: (펜을 꺼내 뭔가를 쓰면서) "크고 힘센 아기 돼지 삼 형제가 그 집에 살고 있었다."

➡ _____

11 늑대: 그렇게 하면 안 돼!

➡ _____

12 (늑대가 다시 집을 분다. 그러나 크고 힘센 돼지 삼 형제가 집에서 나온다.)

➡ _____

13 돼지 삼 형제: 이봐, 거기! 왜 우리 집을 불고 있어?

➡ _____

14 늑대: 음⋯ 그러지 않았어. 나는 그냥 코를 풀었을 뿐이야.

➡ _____

15 돼지 삼 형제: 여기서 다시는 그러지 마. 가 버려!

➡ _____

16 늑대: 알았어. 정말 미안해.

➡ _____

17 (돼지들은 집 안으로 다시 들어간다.)

➡ _____

18 늑대: 이런 일이 일어나다니 믿을 수가 없어. 나는 너무 배가 고파! (Red의 바구니를 보며) 그건 뭐야?

➡ _____

19 Red: 할머니께 드릴 과자들이야.

➡ _____

20 늑대: 어디 사시는데?

➡ _____

21 Red: 이 길의 끝에 사셔.

➡ _____

22 늑대: (혼잣말로) 할머니도 점심으로 좋지. (Red에게) 나중에 보자. (늑대가 떠난다.)

➡ _____

23 Red: 안녕. (혼잣말로) 흠…. 그는 할머니 댁으로 갈 거야. 이야기를 다시 바꿔야겠어. (펜을 꺼내서 뭔가를 쓰며) 좋아. 내 이야기가 제대로 돌아가면 할머니는 안전하실 거야. 그를 따라가 봐야지. (Red가 떠난다.)

➡ _____

_____

_____

24 장면 2: 할머니의 집

➡ _____

25 (늑대가 할머니 주변을 맴돌며 춤을 춘다. 할머니는 아주 행복하고 신나 보인다.)

➡ _____

26 Red: (문을 두드리며) 할머니, 저예요. 괜찮으세요?

➡ _____

27 할머니: (행복하게 웃으며 문을 열면서) 물론이지, Red야. 어서 들어와. 늑대가 나를 위해 춤추는 걸 보고 있었단다.

➡ _____

_____

28 Red: 이봐, 늑대야. 우리 할머니를 기쁘게 해드려서 고마워.

➡ _____

29 늑대: 음, 그게 ….

➡ _____

30 왕자: (문을 열고 뛰어 들어오며) 이봐, 이 나쁜 늑대야! (왕자가 늑대에게 달려든다.)

➡ _____

31 Red: 아니, 아니에요! 멈춰요. 그는 위험하지 않아요.

➡ _____

32 할머니: 맞아. 보세요. 그가 우리를 위해 춤추고 있잖아요.

➡ _____

33 왕자: 정말요? 늑대야, 미안해. 네가 할머니께 잘해 드린다니 기쁘다.

➡ _____

34 늑대: 음 … 나도 기뻐. 그런데, 먹을 것 좀 있어?

➡ _____

35 Red: (바구니에서 과자를 좀 꺼내며) 과자 좀 먹을래?
➡ _____

36 늑대: 고맙지만 됐어. 난 과자를 먹지 않아. 나는 닭고기가 좋아.
➡ _____

37 Red: 걱정하지 마. 내가 이야기를 다시 바꿔야겠네. 그러면 넌 과자 먹는 걸 좋아하게 될 거야.
(바구니를 뒤지며) 오, 펜을 잃어버렸어. 어떻게 하지?
➡ _____

38 늑대: (춤을 추며 울부짖으며) 오, 안 돼! 난 지금 너무 피곤하고 배고파.
➡ _____

39 (Andersen이 들어온다.)
➡ _____

40 Andersen: 내 도움이 필요한 것 같은데, 맞지?
➡ _____

41 Red: 오, Andersen 씨. 여기 오셔서 너무 기뻐요.
➡ _____

42 할머니: (Red에게) 저 사람이 누구니?
➡ _____

43 Red: 저분은 유명한 작가 Andersen 씨예요. "빨간 구두"에 대해 들어 보신 적이 있죠?
➡ _____

44 할머니: 그래, 들어 봤지. 그 이야기를 쓴 사람이란 말이지?
➡ _____

45 Red: 맞아요. (Andersen에게) 제가 이야기를 바꿔서 저 불쌍한 늑대가 피곤하고 배고파졌어요.
➡ _____

46 Andersen: 너는 다시 이야기를 바꿀 수 있잖아.
➡ _____

47 Red: 죄송하지만, 제가 작가님이 주신 펜을 잃어버렸어요. 저 좀 도와주세요.
➡ _____

48 Andersen: 문제없지. 내가 모두에게 행복한 결말을 쓸게. 괜찮지?
➡ _____

49 Red: 아주 좋아요!
➡ _____

50 Andersen: 좋아. 여기 내 펜을 써야지. "그 친절한 늑대는 춤추기를 멈춘다. 그는 케이크와
과자를 즐겨 먹을 수 있다."
➡ _____

51 늑대: (춤을 멈추며) 춤을 멈출 수가 있다! (과자를 먹으며) 그리고 과자를 먹을 수 있어!
정말 고마워요.
➡ _____

52 (모두 웃으며 함께 과자를 맛있게 먹는다.)
➡ _____

※ 다음 영어를 우리말로 쓰시오.

01	circle	
02	shape	
03	roll	
04	excited	
05	boil	
06	pointy	
07	share	
08	press	
09	bookshelf	
10	perfect	
11	exercise	
12	solve	
13	hurry	
14	plastic bag	
15	divide	
16	choose	
17	stick	
18	hanger	
19	mess	
20	round	
21	triangle	

22	difficult	
23	complain	
24	square	
25	control	
26	hurt	
27	shout	
28	spirit	
29	spin	
30	realize	
31	finally	
32	water	
33	rush	
34	tidy	
35	one another	
36	wrap up	
37	take away	
38	in charge of ~	
39	by oneself	
40	divide A into B	
41	in control	
42	cut A into pieces	
43	the other side	

※ 다음 우리말을 영어로 쓰시오.

01 끓이다

02 통제하다, 조절하다

03 다치게 하다

04 모양, 모습

05 마주하다

06 마지막으로

07 고르다, 선택하다

08 막대기, 나뭇가지

09 불평하다

10 옷걸이

11 삼각형

12 풀다, 해결하다

13 소리치다, 외치다

14 끝이 뾰족한

15 옮기다

16 공유하다

17 구르다

18 책꽂이

19 완벽한

20 둥근

21 잘 정돈된, 단정한

22 나누다

23 서두르다

24 회전시키다

25 영혼, 요정

26 대답하다

27 혼잡, 혼란

28 깨닫다, 알아차리다

29 물을 주다

30 서두르다, 돌진하다

31 ~ 없이

32 퍼즐, 수수께끼

33 사각형

34 움직임, 이동

35 A를 B로 나누다

36 하나씩, 차례대로

37 ~을 집다

38 ~을 치우다

39 A를 B에 놓다[두다]

40 감싸다, 포장하다

41 ~을 담당하여

42 (주로 셋 이상 사이에 쓰임) 서로

43 자기 혼자서

※ 다음 영영풀이에 알맞은 단어를 <보기>에서 골라 쓴 후, 우리말 뜻을 쓰시오.

1 _____ : having a point at the end: _____

2 _____ : an imaginary creature with magic powers: _____

3 _____ : to move forward while turning over and over: _____

4 _____ : complete and correct in every way: _____

5 _____ : feeling very happy and enthusiastic: _____

6 _____ : to make a choice about what you are going to do: _____

7 _____ : a situation in which a place is dirty or not neat: _____

8 _____ : to say that you are not satisfied with something: _____

9 _____ : to answer someone by saying or writing something: _____

10 _____ : to have something in your hands or arms: _____

11 _____ : to move quickly toward someone: _____

12 _____ : a very large ring that you try to keep spinning round your body:

_____

13 _____ : to have the power to make it work in the way you want: _____

14 _____ : to gradually begin to understand something that you did not know or

notice before: _____

15 _____ : a curved piece of wire, wood or plastic on which clothes are hung while

they are being stored: _____

16 _____ : a round object that turns around and around to make a car, bicycle, or

other vehicle move: _____

보기			
complain	roll	mess	control
hanger	hold	realize	perfect
spirit	decide	hula hoop	pointy
rush	wheel	reply	excited

※ 다음 우리말과 일치하도록 빈칸에 알맞은 말을 쓰시오.

Get Ready 2

(1) G: This bookshelf _____ _____ _____. Do you know _____ _____ _____ this problem?

B: _____ some legs _____ the _____.

(2) G: Do you know _____ _____ _____ this cake _____ four _____ _____?

B: _____ me _____. ... How about _____ it this way? Then the pieces will be _____ _____ _____ _____ and _____.

(3) G: This car _____ _____. Do you know _____ _____ _____ it?

B: Sure. _____ _____ under the car.

(1) G: 이 책꽂이는 혼자서 서 있을 수 없어. 이 문제를 어떻게 해결할지 아니?
B: 바닥에 다리를 몇 개 붙여.

(2) G: 이 케이크를 네 개의 같은 조각으로 어떻게 나눌 수 있는지 아니?
B: 글쎄. … 이 방법으로 그것을 나누는 것은 어때? 그럼 그 조각들은 같은 크기에 같은 모양이 될 거야.

(3) G: 이 차는 움직이지 않아. 어떻게 움직이게 할 수 있는지 아니?
B: 물론이지. 차 아래에 바퀴들을 붙여.

Start Off Listen & Talk A

1. G: These twelve sticks make four squares. Do you know _____ _____ _____ _____ _____ of the same size _____ _____ _____?

B: Sure. _____, _____ _____ _____ here.

2. B: Here's a triangle _____ three pencils. Do you know _____ _____ _____ three more triangles with three more pencils?

G: Let me see. ... It's _____ _____ _____ me. _____ I _____ the pencils _____ _____?

B: No, _____ _____.

1. G: 이 12개 막대기들은 사각형 4개를 만들어. 세 번 움직여서 어떻게 같은 크기의 사각형 3개를 만드는지 아니?
B: 물론이지. 먼저, 이 막대기를 여기로 옮겨.

2. B: 여기 연필 세 자루로 만든 삼각형이 하나 있어. 연필 세 자루를 더 추가해서 어떻게 삼각형 3개를 더 만드는지 아니?
G: 글쎄. … 내게는 너무 어려워. 연필을 반으로 부러뜨려도 돼?
B: 아니, 안 돼.

Start Off Listen & Talk B

B: Do you know _____ _____ _____ _____ this _____ four equal _____?

G: Sure. _____, _____ it _____ three _____ squares. _____, _____ each square _____ four smaller squares. _____, color three small squares in the inside corner of the L.

B: Oh, I can see three _____ L shapes _____ it! You're great!

B: 이것을 4개의 같은 조각으로 나누는 방법을 아니?
G: 물론이지. 먼저, 그것을 3개의 같은 사각형으로 나눠. 그리고 나서, 각 사각형을 4개의 더 작은 사각형으로 나눠. 마지막으로, L자 모양의 안쪽 모서리에 있는 3개의 작은 사각형에 색칠해.
B: 오, 그 주변에 3개의 다른 L자 모양들이 보여! 너 대단하다!

Speak Up Look and talk.

A: Do you know _____ _____ _____ a fish with shapes?

B: Sure. _____, draw a large square. _____, draw a triangle. _____, draw a small circle _____ _____.

A: 너는 도형들로 물고기를 그리는 방법을 알고 있니?
B: 물론. 먼저, 큰 사각형을 그려. 그리고 나서, 삼각형을 그려. 마지막으로, 사각형 안에 작은 원을 그려.

Speak Up Mission

G: Do you know _____ _____ _____ paper airplanes?

B: Sure. I'll _____ _____ _____.

Real-life Scene

B: Do you know _____ _____ _____ this puzzle?

G: What is it?

B: You must _____ a dog, a chicken, and a bag of rice _____ _____ _____. The boat _____ _____ you and one of the things _____ _____ _____.

G: That's easy. I can _____ them _____ the _____ _____ _____ _____ _____.

B: But _____ you, the dog will kill the chicken, and the chicken will _____ _____ _____.

G: Let me see. … _____, take the chicken and come back. _____, take the rice and _____ _____ _____ the chicken.

B: And?

G: After that, take the dog and come back. _____, take the chicken.

B: You're great!

Express Yourself A

1. B: Do you know _____ _____ _____ this?
   G: Sure. First, _____ the leg from _____ _____.

2. B: This _____ _____.
   G: I think so, too. Do you know _____ _____ _____ it?
   B: It's easy. _____, put some rice on *gim*. _____, add some _____ fish and hot peppers. _____, _____ _____ _____ and _____ _____ _____.

3. B: Do you know _____ _____ _____ this?
   G: Yes. I'll show you how. It _____ _____ _____ the wind. _____ it _____ like this.

Learning Diary Check Yourself

W: Excuse me. Do you know _____ _____ _____ a mouse _____ _____?

M: Sure. _____, draw a large _____. _____, draw two _____ and 6 lines. _____, draw two _____ _____.

W: Thanks. I'll _____ it _____ now.

G: 너는 종이 비행기를 어떻게 접는지 아니?

B: 물론이지. 내가 너에게 방법을 보여 줄게.

B: 이 퍼즐을 어떻게 푸는지 아니?

G: 그게 뭔데?

B: 너는 개, 닭, 쌀 한 자루를 강 건너로 옮겨야 해. 그 배는 한 번에 너와 그 것들 중 하나만 옮길 수 있어.

G: 그것은 쉬워. 난 반대편으로 그것들을 하나씩 옮길 수 있어.

B: 하지만 네가 없으면, 개는 닭을 죽일 것이고, 닭은 쌀을 먹을 거야.

G: 어디 보자. … 먼저, 닭을 데려다 놓고 돌아와. 그리고 나서, 쌀을 가져다 놓고 닭을 데려와.

B: 그리고?

G: 그 후에, 개를 데려다 놓고 돌아와. 마지막으로, 닭을 데려가는 거야.

B: 너 대단하구나!

1. B: 이것을 어떻게 만드는지 아니?
   G: 물론이지. 먼저, 낡은 청바지에서 다리 부분을 잘라내.

2. B: 이것은 멋져 보여.
   G: 나도 그렇게 생각해. 그걸 어떻게 만드는지 아니?
   B: 그건 쉬워. 먼저, 김 위에 밥을 좀 얹어. 그리고 나서, 멸치와 매운 고추를 추가해. 마지막으로, 그것을 모두 싸서 삼각형을 만들어.

3. B: 이것을 어떻게 날리는지 아니?
   G: 그래. 내가 너에게 방법을 보여 줄게. 그것은 바람을 마주해야만 해. 이렇게 그것을 들고 있어.

W: 실례합니다. 도형으로 쥐를 어떻게 그리는지 아세요?

M: 물론이죠. 먼저, 큰 삼각형을 그려요. 그리고 나서, 점 두 개와 선 6개를 그려요. 마지막으로, 작은 원 두 개를 그려요.

W: 감사합니다. 이제 제가 그것을 직접 그려 볼게요.

※ 다음 우리말에 맞도록 대화를 영어로 쓰시오.

Get Ready 2

(1) G: _____

B: _____

(2) G: _____

B: _____
_____

(3) G: _____

B: _____

Start Off Listen & Talk A

1. G: _____

B: _____

2. B: _____
_____

G: _____

B: _____

Start Off Listen & Talk B

B: _____

G: _____

B: _____

Speak Up Look and talk.

A: _____

B: _____
_____

(1) G: 이 책꽂이는 혼자서 서 있을 수 없어. 이 문제를 어떻게 해결할지 아니?
B: 바닥에 다리를 몇 개 붙여.

(2) G: 이 케이크를 네 개의 같은 조각으로 어떻게 나눌 수 있는지 아니?
B: 글쎄. … 이 방법으로 그것을 나누는 것은 어때? 그럼 그 조각들은 같은 크기에 같은 모양이 될 거야.

(3) G: 이 차는 움직이지 않아. 어떻게 움직이게 할 수 있는지 아니?
B: 물론이지. 차 아래에 바퀴들을 붙여.

1. G: 이 12개 막대기들은 사각형 4개를 만들어. 세 번 움직여서 어떻게 같은 크기의 사각형 3개를 만드는지 아니?
B: 물론이지. 먼저, 이 막대기를 여기로 옮겨.

2. B: 여기 연필 세 자루로 만든 삼각형이 하나 있어. 연필 세 자루를 더 추가해서 어떻게 삼각형 3개를 더 만드는지 아니?
G: 글쎄. … 내게는 너무 어려워. 연필을 반으로 부러뜨려도 돼?
B: 아니, 안 돼.

B: 이것을 4개의 같은 조각으로 나누는 방법을 아니?
G: 물론이지. 먼저, 그것을 3개의 같은 사각형으로 나눠. 그리고 나서, 각 사각형을 4개의 더 작은 사각형으로 나눠. 마지막으로, L자 모양의 안쪽 모서리에 있는 3개의 작은 사각형에 색칠해.
B: 오, 그 주변에 3개의 다른 L자 모양들이 보여! 너 대단하다!

A: 너는 도형들로 물고기를 그리는 방법을 알고 있니?
B: 물론. 먼저, 큰 사각형을 그려. 그리고 나서, 삼각형을 그려. 마지막으로, 사각형 안에 작은 원을 그려.

Speak Up Mission

G: _____

B: _____

Real-life Scene

B: _____

G: _____

B: _____

_____

G: _____

B: _____

G: _____

B: _____

G: _____

B: _____

Express Yourself A

1. B: _____

   G: _____

2. B: _____

   G: _____

   B: _____

3. B: _____

   G: _____

Learning Diary Check Yourself

W: _____

M: _____

W: _____

G: 너는 종이 비행기를 어떻게 접는지 아니?

B: 물론이지. 내가 너에게 방법을 보여 줄게.

B: 이 퍼즐을 어떻게 푸는지 아니?

G: 그게 뭔데?

B: 너는 개, 닭, 쌀 한 자루를 강 건너로 옮겨야 해. 그 배는 한 번에 너와 그것들 중 하나만 옮길 수 있어.

G: 그것은 쉬워. 난 반대편으로 그것들을 하나씩 옮길 수 있어.

B: 하지만 네가 없으면, 개는 닭을 죽일 것이고, 닭은 쌀을 먹을 거야.

G: 어디 보자. … 먼저, 닭을 데려다 놓고 돌아와. 그러고 나서, 쌀을 가져다 놓고 닭을 데려와.

B: 그리고?

G: 그 후에, 개를 데려다 놓고 돌아와. 마지막으로, 닭을 데려가는 거야.

B: 너 대단하구나!

1. B: 이것을 어떻게 만드는지 아니?

   G: 물론이지. 먼저, 낡은 청바지에서 다리 부분을 잘라내.

2. B: 이것은 멋져 보여.

   G: 나도 그렇게 생각해. 그걸 어떻게 만드는지 아니?

   B: 그건 쉬워. 먼저, 김 위에 밥을 좀 얹어. 그러고 나서, 멸치와 매운 고추를 추가해. 마지막으로, 그것을 모두 싸서 삼각형을 만들어.

3. B: 이것을 어떻게 날리는지 아니?

   G: 그래. 내가 너에게 방법을 보여 줄게. 그것은 바람을 마주해야만 해. 이렇게 그것을 들고 있어.

W: 실례합니다. 도형으로 쥐를 어떻게 그리는지 아세요?

M: 물론이죠. 먼저, 큰 삼각형을 그려요. 그러고 나서, 점 두 개와 선 6개를 그려요. 마지막으로, 작은 원 두 개를 그려요.

W: 감사합니다. 이제 제가 그것을 직접 그려 볼게요.

※ 다음 우리말과 일치하도록 빈칸에 알맞은 것을 골라 쓰시오.

1 Three _____ _____
A. Spirits   B. Shape

2 _____ _____ three shape _____ in Mike's room.
A. spirits   B. lived   C. there

3 Square _____ the table, the _____, and the _____.
A. bookshelf   B. controlled   C. window

4 Triangle was in _____ of the _____ and the _____
A. hangers   B. charge   C. plants

5 Circle _____ _____ of the _____ things.
A. care   B. round   C. took

6 They _____ _____ to make a nice room _____ Mike.
A. together   B. for   C. worked

7 One day Square _____ to make the room _____ and _____ at the other spirits.
A. better   B. shouted   C. decided

8 "_____ these plants _____, or their _____ leaves will hurt someone!" he said to Triangle.
A. away   B. take   C. pointy

9 "But Mike _____ them _____ _____," said Triangle.
A. every   B. waters   C. day

10 "_____ this hula hoop _____, or it will _____ and _____ something!" he said to Circle.
A. away   B. break   C. take   D. roll

11 "But Mike _____ _____ it _____ day," said Circle.
A. with   B. every   C. exercises

12 "I try to make this room _____, but you two always make a _____," he _____.
A. complained   B. tidy   C. mess

13 Triangle and Circle _____ _____ each _____.
A. other   B. at   C. looked

14 "So you _____ you can do it _____ us?" Triangle _____ Square.
A. without   B. think   C. asked

15 "Sure. I can make this room _____ all _____ _____," replied Square.
A. better   B. myself   C. by

16 "Great! Then we can _____ some _____," Circle _____ to Square.
A. get   B. said   C. rest

17 Triangle and Circle _____ _____ and Square was now _____ _____.
A. out   B. control   C. went   D. in

1 세 도형 요정들

2 Mike의 방에는 세 도형 요정이 살았다.

3 Square는 탁자, 책장, 그리고 창문을 담당했다.

4 Triangle은 옷걸이들과 식물들을 담당했다.

5 Circle은 둥근 것들을 돌보았다.

6 그들은 Mike에게 좋은 방을 만들어 주기 위해서 함께 일했다.

7 어느 날 Square는 방을 더 낫게 만들기로 결심하고 나머지 요정들에게 소리쳤다.

8 "이 식물들을 치워, 그렇지 않으면 그것들의 끝이 뾰족한 잎사귀들이 누군가를 다치게 할 거야!" 그가 Triangle에게 말했다.

9 "하지만 Mike가 매일 그들에게 물을 주는데." Triangle이 말했다.

10 "이 훌라후프를 치워, 그렇지 않으면 굴러가서 뭔가를 부술 거야!" 그가 Circle에게 말했다.

11 "하지만 Mike는 매일 그걸로 운동을 하는데." Circle이 말했다.

12 "난 이 방을 정돈하려고 애쓰지만, 너희 둘은 항상 엉망으로 만들어." 그가 불평했다.

13 Triangle과 Circle이 서로를 쳐다보았다.

14 "그래서 네 생각에는 네가 우리 없이 다 할 수 있다는 거야?" Triangle이 Square에게 물었다.

15 "물론이지. 난 완전히 혼자서 이 방을 더 낫게 만들 수 있어." Square가 대답했다.

16 "잘됐네! 그럼 우린 쉴 수 있겠어." Circle이 Square에게 말했다.

17 Triangle과 Circle이 밖으로 나갔고 이제 Square가 모든 것을 담당했다.

18 He made the _____, plants, and all the _____ things _____.

    A. square   B. hangers   C. round

19 Then he _____ _____ and _____.

    A. around   B. looked   C. smiled

20 "_____ _____!"

    A. better   B. much

21 When Mike came home from school, he _____ _____ a square hanger to _____ his jacket _____.

    A. hang   B. up   C. on   D. picked

22 "What? This will not _____ my _____."

    A. clothes   B. hold

23 He _____ to _____ the plants and saw their square _____.

    A. leaves   B. water   C. went

24 "_____ things. ... They _____ _____ sick."

    A. be   B. poor   C. must

25 He _____ _____ the square hula hoop _____.

    A. to   B. picked   C. exercise   D. up

26 "Hmm ... I don't know _____ _____ _____ this."

    A. to   B. how   C. spin

27 He went to _____ _____ his bike and _____ _____ the square wheels.

    A. out   B. at   C. looked   D. take

28 "Well, I can't _____ this. I'll just _____ _____ walk."

    A. have   B. ride   C. to

29 Then he _____ _____ _____ the house.

    A. out   B. hurried   C. of

30 When the _____ spirits came _____, Square rushed _____ to them.

    A. back   B. over   C. other

31 "Mike _____ like his room. I don't know _____ _____ _____," he said.

    A. what   B. doesn't   C. do   D. to

32 They looked at the _____, the plants, and _____ the new _____ things.

    A. square   B. all   C. hangers

33 Then they looked at _____ _____, and Square _____ his problem.

    A. realized   B. another   C. one

34 "Let's make this room _____ again," he said to the _____, and the three spirits worked together _____ _____.

    A. once   B. others   C. great   D. again

18 그는 옷걸이들과 식물들과 모든 둥근 물건들을 사각형으로 만들었다.

19 그러고 나서 그는 주위를 둘러보고 미소 지었다.

20 "훨씬 좋군!"

21 Mike가 학교에서 집으로 왔을 때, 그는 재킷을 걸기 위해 사각형 옷걸이 하나를 집었다.

22 "뭐야? 이것은 내 옷을 걸고 있지 못할 거야."

23 그는 식물에 물을 주러 가서 그것들의 사각형 잎사귀들을 보았다.

24 "불쌍한 것들.… 그들은 병든 것이 틀림없어."

25 그는 운동을 하기 위해 사각형 훌라후프를 집어 들었다.

26 "흠… 이걸 어떻게 돌리는지 모르겠어."

27 그는 자전거를 꺼내러 가서 사각형 바퀴들을 보았다.

28 "음, 난 이걸 탈 수 없어. 그냥 걸어가야 할 것 같아."

29 그러고 나서 그는 서둘러 집을 나섰다.

30 다른 요정들이 돌아왔을 때, Square는 그들에게 달려갔다.

31 "Mike는 그의 방을 좋아하지 않아. 난 뭘 해야 할지 모르겠어." 그가 말했다.

32 그들은 옷걸이들, 식물들, 그리고 모든 새로 사각형이 된 물건들을 바라보았다.

33 그러고 나서 그들은 서로를 바라보았고, Square는 자신의 문제를 깨달았다.

34 "이 방을 다시 멋지게 만들자." 그가 나머지 요정들에게 말했고, 세 요정들은 다시 한 번 함께 일했다.

Step2

※ 다음 우리말과 일치하도록 빈칸에 알맞은 말을 쓰시오.

1 Three _____

2 _____ three _____ _____ in Mike's room.

3 Square _____ the table, the _____, and the window.

4 Triangle _____ _____ _____ the hangers and the plants.

5 Circle _____ _____ the _____ _____.

6 They _____ _____ a nice room for Mike.

7 One day Square decided _____ _____ _____ _____ and _____ _____ the other spirits.

8 "_____ these plants _____, or their _____ _____ will hurt someone!" he said to Triangle.

9 "But Mike _____ _____ _____ _____," said Triangle.

10 "_____ this hula hoop _____, or it will _____ _____ something!" he said to Circle.

11 "But Mike _____ _____ _____ every day," said Circle.

12 "I _____ _____ make this room _____, but you two always _____ _____ _____," he _____.

13 Triangle and Circle _____ _____ _____ _____.

14 "So you think you can do it _____ _____?" Triangle asked Square.

15 "Sure. I can _____ this room _____ _____ _____," replied Square.

16 "Great! Then we can _____ _____," Circle said to Square.

17 Triangle and Circle _____ _____ and Square was now _____ _____.

1 세 도형 요정들

2 Mike의 방에는 세 도형 요정이 살았다.

3 Square는 탁자, 책장, 그리고 창문을 담당했다.

4 Triangle은 옷걸이들과 식물들을 담당했다.

5 Circle은 둥근 것들을 돌보았다.

6 그들은 Mike에게 좋은 방을 만들어 주기 위해서 함께 일했다.

7 어느 날 Square는 방을 더 낫게 만들기로 결심하고 나머지 요정들에게 소리쳤다.

8 "이 식물들을 치워. 그렇지 않으면 그것들의 끝이 뾰족한 잎사귀들이 누군가를 다치게 할 거야!" 그가 Triangle에게 말했다.

9 "하지만 Mike가 매일 그들에게 물을 주는데." Triangle이 말했다.

10 "이 훌라후프를 치워. 그렇지 않으면 굴러가서 뭔가를 부술 거야!" 그가 Circle에게 말했다.

11 "하지만 Mike는 매일 그걸로 운동을 하는데." Circle이 말했다.

12 "난 이 방을 정돈하려고 애쓰지만, 너희 둘은 항상 엉망으로 만들어." 그가 불평했다.

13 Triangle과 Circle이 서로를 쳐다보았다.

14 "그래서 네 생각에는 네가 우리 없이 다 할 수 있다는 거야?" Triangle이 Square에게 물었다.

15 "물론이지. 난 완전히 혼자서 이 방을 더 낫게 만들 수 있어." Square가 대답했다.

16 "잘됐네! 그럼 우린 쉴 수 있겠어." Circle이 Square에게 말했다.

17 Triangle과 Circle이 밖으로 나갔고 이제 Square가 모든 것을 담당했다.

18 He _____ the hangers, plants, and all the round things _____.

19 Then he _____ _____ and _____.

20 "_____ _____!"

21 When Mike _____ _____ from school, he _____ _____ a square hanger _____ _____ his jacket _____.

22 "What? This will not _____ _____ _____."

23 He _____ _____ _____ the plants and saw their square leaves.

24 "Poor things. ... They _____ _____ sick."

25 He _____ _____ the square hula hoop _____ _____.

26 "Hmm ... I don't know _____ _____ _____ this."

27 He went _____ _____ _____ his bike and _____ _____ the square wheels.

28 "Well, I _____ _____ this. I'll just _____ _____ walk."

29 Then he _____ _____ _____ the house.

30 When the _____ spirits _____ _____, Square _____ _____ _____ them.

31 "Mike doesn't like his room. I don't know _____ _____ _____," he said.

32 They _____ _____ the hangers, the plants, and _____ _____ _____ _____ _____.

33 Then they looked at _____ _____, and Square _____ his problem.

34 "Let's make this room _____ again," he said to _____ _____, and the three spirits worked together _____ _____.

18 그는 옷걸이들과 식물들과 모든 둥근 물건들을 사각형으로 만들었다.

19 그러고 나서 그는 주위를 둘러보고 미소 지었다.

20 "훨씬 좋군!"

21 Mike가 학교에서 집으로 왔을 때, 그는 재킷을 걸기 위해 사각형 옷걸이 하나를 집었다.

22 "뭐야? 이것은 내 옷을 걸고 있지 못할 거야."

23 그는 식물에 물을 주러 가서 그것들의 사각형 잎사귀들을 보았다.

24 "불쌍한 것들.… 그들은 병든 것이 틀림없어."

25 그는 운동을 하기 위해 사각형 훌라후프를 집어 들었다.

26 "흠… 이걸 어떻게 돌리는지 모르겠어."

27 그는 자전거를 꺼내러 가서 사각형 바퀴들을 보았다.

28 "음, 난 이걸 탈 수 없어. 그냥 걸어가야 할 것 같아."

29 그러고 나서 그는 서둘러 집을 나섰다.

30 다른 요정들이 돌아왔을 때, Square는 그들에게 달려갔다.

31 "Mike는 그의 방을 좋아하지 않아. 난 뭘 해야 할지 모르겠어." 그가 말했다.

32 그들은 옷걸이들, 식물들, 그리고 모든 새로 사각형이 된 물건들을 바라보았다.

33 그러고 나서 그들은 서로를 바라보았고, Square는 자신의 문제를 깨달았다.

34 "이 방을 다시 멋지게 만들자." 그가 나머지 요정들에게 말했고, 세 요정들은 다시 한 번 함께 일했다.

※ 다음 문장을 우리말로 쓰시오.

1 Three Shape Spirits

➡ _____

2 There lived three shape spirits in Mike's room.

➡ _____

3 Square controlled the table, the bookshelf, and the window.

➡ _____

4 Triangle was in charge of the hangers and the plants.

➡ _____

5 Circle took care of the round things.

➡ _____

6 They worked together to make a nice room for Mike.

➡ _____

7 One day Square decided to make the room better and shouted at the other spirits.

➡ _____

8 "Take these plants away, or their pointy leaves will hurt someone!" he said to Triangle.

➡ _____

9 "But Mike waters them every day," said Triangle.

➡ _____

10 "Take this hula hoop away, or it will roll and break something!" he said to Circle.

➡ _____

11 "But Mike exercises with it every day," said Circle.

➡ _____

12 "I try to make this room tidy, but you two always make a mess," he complained.

➡ _____

13 Triangle and Circle looked at each other.

➡ _____

14 "So you think you can do it without us?" Triangle asked Square.

➡ _____

15 "Sure. I can make this room better all by myself," replied Square.

➡ _____

16 "Great! Then we can get some rest," Circle said to Square.

➡ _____

17 Triangle and Circle went out and Square was now in control.

➡ _____

18 He made the hangers, plants, and all the round things square.

➡ _____

19 Then he looked around and smiled.

➡ _____

20 "Much better!"

➡ _____

21 When Mike came home from school, he picked up a square hanger to hang his jacket on.

➡ _____

22 "What? This will not hold my clothes."

➡ _____

23 He went to water the plants and saw their square leaves.

➡ _____

24 "Poor things. ... They must be sick."

➡ _____

25 He picked up the square hula hoop to exercise.

➡ _____

26 "Hmm ... I don't know how to spin this."

➡ _____

27 He went to take out his bike and looked at the square wheels.

➡ _____

28 "Well, I can't ride this. I'll just have to walk."

➡ _____

29 Then he hurried out of the house.

➡ _____

30 When the other spirits came back, Square rushed over to them.

➡ _____

31 "Mike doesn't like his room. I don't know what to do," he said.

➡ _____

32 They looked at the hangers, the plants, and all the new square things.

➡ _____

33 Then they looked at one another, and Square realized his problem.

➡ _____

34 "Let's make this room great again," he said to the others, and the three spirits worked together once again.

➡ _____

※ 다음 괄호 안의 단어들을 우리말에 맞도록 바르게 배열하시오.

1 (Shape / Three / Spirits)
➡ _____

2 (lived / there / shape / three / in / spirits / room. / Mike's)
➡ _____

3 (controlled / the / Square / table, / bookshelf, / the / and / window. / the)
➡ _____

4 (was / Triangle / charge / in / of / hangers / the / plants. / the / and)
➡ _____

5 (took / Circle / of / care / the / things. / round)
➡ _____

6 (worked / they / to / together / make / nice / a / Mike. / for / room)
➡ _____

7 (day / one / decided / Square / make / to / room / the / and / better / shouted / the / at / spirits. / other)
➡ _____

8 (these / "take / away, / plants / or / pointy / their / will / leaves / someone!" / hurt / said / he / Triangle. / to)
➡ _____

9 (Mike / "but / them / waters / day," / every / Triangle. / said)
➡ _____

10 (this / "take / away, / hula hoop / it / or / roll / will / break / and / something!" / said / he / Circle. / to)
➡ _____

11 (Mike / "but / with / exercises / it / day," / every / Circle. / said)
➡ _____

12 (try / "I / to / this / make / tidy, / room / but / two / you / make / always / mess," / a / complained. / he)
➡ _____

13 (Circle / and / Triangle / at / looked / other. / each)
➡ _____

14 (you / "so / think / can / you / do / without / it / us?" / Square. / asked / Triangle)
➡ _____

15 ("sure. // can / I / this / make / better / room / by / all / myself," / Square. / replied)
➡ _____

16 ("great! // we / then / get / can / rest," / some / to / Circle / Square. / said)
➡ _____

17 (Circle / and / Triangle / out / went / and / was / Square / control. / in / now)
➡ _____

1 세 도형 요정들

2 Mike의 방에는 세 도형 요정이 살았다.

3 Square는 탁자, 책장, 그리고 창문을 담당했다.

4 Triangle은 옷걸이들과 식물들을 담당했다.

5 Circle은 둥근 것들을 돌보았다.

6 그들은 Mike에게 좋은 방을 만들어 주기 위해서 함께 일했다.

7 어느 날 Square는 방을 더 낫게 만들기로 결심하고 나머지 요정들에게 소리쳤다.

8 "이 식물들을 치워, 그렇지 않으면 그것들의 끝이 뾰족한 잎사귀들이 누군가를 다치게 할 거야!" 그가 Triangle에게 말했다.

9 "하지만 Mike가 매일 그들에게 물을 주는데." Triangle이 말했다.

10 "이 훌라후프를 치워, 그렇지 않으면 굴러가서 뭔가를 부술 거야!" 그가 Circle에게 말했다.

11 "하지만 Mike는 매일 그걸로 운동을 하는데." Circle이 말했다.

12 "난 이 방을 정돈하려고 애쓰지만, 너희 둘은 항상 엉망으로 만들어." 그가 불평했다.

13 Triangle과 Circle이 서로를 쳐다보았다.

14 "그래서 네 생각에는 네가 우리 없이 다 할 수 있다는 거야?" Triangle이 Square에게 물었다.

15 "물론이지. 난 완전히 혼자서 이 방을 더 낫게 만들 수 있어." Square가 대답했다.

16 "잘됐네! 그럼 우린 쉴 수 있겠어." Circle이 Square에게 말했다.

17 Triangle과 Circle이 밖으로 나갔고 이제 Square가 모든 것을 담당했다.

18 (made / he / hangers, / the / and / plants, / all / round / the / square. / things)

➡ _____

19 (he / then / around / looked / smiled. / and)

➡ _____

20 (better!" / "much)

➡ _____

21 (Mike / when / home / came / school, / from / picked / up / he / hanger / square / a / hang / to / on. / jacket / his)

➡ _____

22 ("what? // will / this / hold / clothes." / my / not)

➡ _____

23 (went / he / water / to / plants / the / and / their / leaves. / saw / square)

➡ _____

24 (things. / "poor // ... / must / they / sick." / be)

➡ _____

25 (picked / he / up / square / the / to / hula hoop / exercise.)

➡ _____

26 ("hmm / ... / don't / I / know / to / how / this." / spin)

➡ _____

27 (went / he / take / to / his / out / bike / and / at / looked / wheels. / square / the)

➡ _____

28 (I / "well, / can't / this. / ride // just / I'll / walk." / to / have)

➡ _____

29 (he / then / out / hurried / of / house. / the)

➡ _____

30 (the / when / spirits / other / back, / came / rushed / Square / them. / to / over)

➡ _____

31 (doesn't / "Mike / his / like / room. // don't / I / know / to / what / do," / said. / he)

➡ _____

32 (looked / they / at / hangers, / the / plants, / and / all / new / the / things. / square)

➡ _____

33 (they / then / at / looked / another, / one / and / realized / Square / problem. / his)

➡ _____

34 (make / "let's / room / this / again," / great / said / he / the / to / others, / and / three / the / worked / spirits / again. / once / together)

➡ _____

18 그는 옷걸이들과 식물들과 모든 둥근 물건들을 사각형으로 만들었다.

19 그러고 나서 그는 주위를 둘러보고 미소 지었다.

20 "훨씬 좋군!"

21 Mike가 학교에서 집으로 왔을 때, 그는 재킷을 걸기 위해 사각형 옷걸이 하나를 집었다.

22 "뭐야? 이것은 내 옷을 걸고 있지 못할 거야."

23 그는 식물에 물을 주러 가서 그것들의 사각형 잎사귀들을 보았다.

24 "불쌍한 것들.… 그들은 병든 것이 틀림없어."

25 그는 운동을 하기 위해 사각형 훌라후프를 집어 들었다.

26 "흠… 이걸 어떻게 돌리는지 모르겠어."

27 그는 자전거를 꺼내러 가서 사각형 바퀴들을 보았다.

28 "음. 난 이걸 탈 수 없어. 그냥 걸어가야 할 것 같아."

29 그러고 나서 그는 서둘러 집을 나섰다.

30 다른 요정들이 돌아왔을 때, Square는 그들에게 달려갔다.

31 "Mike는 그의 방을 좋아하지 않아. 난 뭘 해야 할지 모르겠어." 그가 말했다.

32 그들은 옷걸이들, 식물들, 그리고 모든 새로 사각형이 된 물건들을 바라보았다.

33 그러고 나서 그들은 서로를 바라보았고, Square는 자신의 문제를 깨달았다.

34 "이 방을 다시 멋지게 만들자." 그가 나머지 요정들에게 말했고, 세 요정들은 다시 한 번 함께 일했다.

※ 다음 우리말을 영어로 쓰시오.

1 세 도형 요정들

➡ _____

2 Mike의 방에는 세 도형 요정이 살았다.

➡ _____

3 Square는 탁자, 책장, 그리고 창문을 담당했다.

➡ _____

4 Triangle은 옷걸이들과 식물들을 담당했다.

➡ _____

5 Circle은 둥근 것들을 돌보았다.

➡ _____

6 그들은 Mike에게 좋은 방을 만들어 주기 위해서 함께 일했다.

➡ _____

7 어느 날 Square는 방을 더 낮게 만들기로 결심하고 나머지 요정들에게 소리쳤다.

➡ _____

8 "이 식물들을 치워, 그렇지 않으면 그것들의 끝이 뾰족한 잎사귀들이 누군가를 다치게 할 거야!" 그가 Triangle에게 말했다.

➡ _____

9 "하지만 Mike가 매일 그들에게 물을 주는데." Triangle이 말했다.

➡ _____

10 "이 훌라후프를 치워, 그렇지 않으면 굴러가서 뭔가를 부술 거야!" 그가 Circle에게 말했다.

➡ _____

11 "하지만 Mike는 매일 그걸로 운동을 하는데." Circle이 말했다.

➡ _____

12 "난 이 방을 정돈하려고 애쓰지만, 너희 둘은 항상 엉망으로 만들어." 그가 불평했다.

➡ _____

13 Triangle과 Circle이 서로를 쳐다보았다.

➡ _____

14 "그래서 네 생각에는 네가 우리 없이 다 할 수 있다는 거야?" Triangle이 Square에게 물었다.

➡ _____

15 "물론이지. 난 완전히 혼자서 이 방을 더 낮게 만들 수 있어." Square가 대답했다.

➡ _____

16 "잘됐네! 그럼 우린 쉴 수 있겠어." Circle이 Square에게 말했다.

➡ _____

17 Triangle과 Circle이 밖으로 나갔고 이제 Square가 모든 것을 담당했다.

➡ _____

18 그는 옷걸이들과 식물들과 모든 둥근 물건들을 사각형으로 만들었다.

➡ _____

19 그러고 나서 그는 주위를 둘러보고 미소 지었다.

➡ _____

20 "훨씬 좋군!"

➡ _____

21 Mike가 학교에서 집으로 왔을 때, 그는 재킷을 걸기 위해 사각형 옷걸이 하나를 집었다.

➡ _____

22 "뭐야? 이것은 내 옷을 걸고 있지 못할 거야."

➡ _____

23 그는 식물에 물을 주러 가서 그것들의 사각형 잎사귀들을 보았다.

➡ _____

24 "불쌍한 것들.… 그들은 병든 것이 틀림없어."

➡ _____

25 그는 운동을 하기 위해 사각형 훌라후프를 집어 들었다.

➡ _____

26 "흠… 이걸 어떻게 돌리는지 모르겠어."

➡ _____

27 그는 자전거를 꺼내러 가서 사각형 바퀴들을 보았다.

➡ _____

28 "음, 난 이걸 탈 수 없어. 그냥 걸어가야 할 것 같아."

➡ _____

29 그러고 나서 그는 서둘러 집을 나섰다.

➡ _____

30 다른 요정들이 돌아왔을 때, Square는 그들에게 달려갔다.

➡ _____

31 "Mike는 그의 방을 좋아하지 않아. 난 뭘 해야 할지 모르겠어." 그가 말했다.

➡ _____

32 그들은 옷걸이들, 식물들, 그리고 모든 새로 사각형이 된 물건들을 바라보았다.

➡ _____

33 그러고 나서 그들은 서로를 바라보았고, Square는 자신의 문제를 깨달았다.

➡ _____

34 "이 방을 다시 멋지게 만들자." 그가 나머지 요정들에게 말했고, 세 요정들은 다시 한 번 함께 일했다.

➡ _____

※ 다음 우리말과 일치하도록 빈칸에 알맞은 말을 쓰시오.

Your Turn

1. A: Do you know _____ _____ _____ *ramyeon*?

   B: Sure. _____, boil some water. _____, put the *ramyeon* and dried soup mix. _____, boil for 4 _____ _____.

2. A: Do you know _____ _____ _____ potato salad?

   B: Sure. First, _____ the potatoes. Then, _____ them pieces. Finally, _____ some sauce _____ them.

3. A: Do you know _____ _____ _____ _____?

   B: Sure. First, _____ an egg _____ _____. Then, _____ some vegetables. Finally, _____ bread _____ _____.

1. A: 너 라면을 요리할 줄 아니?
   B: 물론이지. 먼저, 약간의 물을 끓여. 그러고 나서, 라면과 건조 수프를 넣어. 마지막으로, 4분을 더 끓여.
2. A: 너 감자 샐러드를 만들 줄 아니?
   B: 물론이지. 먼저, 감자를 삶아. 그러고 나서, 감자를 여러 조각으로 잘라. 마지막으로, 그 위에 소스를 좀 뿌려.
3. A: 너 샌드위치를 만들 줄 아니?
   B: 물론이지. 먼저, 빵 위에 계란을 올려. 그러고 나서, 채소를 약간 추가해. 마지막으로, 빵을 맨 위에 올려.

Express Yourself

1. _____ for Mom

2. I made a square bag _____ _____ _____ _____.

3. My mom knew _____ _____ _____ _____ it.

4. It _____ her _____. That _____ me _____.

1. 엄마를 위한 사각형
2. 난 낡은 청바지로 사각형 가방을 만들었어.
3. 엄마는 그걸 걸칠 때 뭘 입어야 할지 아셔.
4. 그것은 엄마를 들뜨게 했어. 그게 나를 행복하게 했어.

Link to the World

1. Euclid _____ math _____ the Library of Alexandria _____ Ptolemy 1 was the king of Egypt.

2. People _____ him "the _____ of _____."

3. He showed _____ _____ _____ a triangle that has _____ _____ of the _____ _____.

4. He also showed _____ _____ _____ the center of _____ _____ _____ in a triangle.

5. _____ _____, Ptolemy 1 asked, "Is there _____ _____ _____ _____ _____ math?"

6. Euclid replied, "There is no _____ _____ _____ _____ _____."

1. 유클리드는 프톨레마이오스 1세(Ptolemy I)가 이집트의 왕이었을 때 알렉산드리아 도서관에서 수학을 가르쳤다.
2. 사람들은 그를 '수학의 아버지'라고 부른다.
3. 그는 같은 길이의 세 변을 가진 삼각형을 어떻게 그리는지를 보여 주었다.
4. 그는 또한 한 삼각형 안에서 가장 큰 원의 중심을 어떻게 찾는지도 보여 주었다.
5. 어느 날, 프톨레마이오스 1세가 "수학을 공부하는 더 쉬운 방법은 없나요?" 하고 물었다.
6. 유클리드는 "배움에 왕도는 없습니다."라고 응답했다.

※ 다음 우리말을 영어로 쓰시오.

Your Turn

1. A: 너 라면을 요리할 줄 아니?
➡ _____

B: 물론이지. 먼저, 약간의 물을 끓여. 그러고 나서, 라면과 건조 수프를 넣어. 마지막으로, 4분을 더 끓여.
➡ _____

2. A: 너 감자 샐러드를 만들 줄 아니?
➡ _____

B: 물론이지. 먼저, 감자를 삶아. 그러고 나서, 감자를 여러 조각으로 잘라. 마지막으로, 그 위에 소스를 좀 뿌려.
➡ _____

3. A: 너 샌드위치를 만들 줄 아니?
➡ _____

B: 물론이지. 먼저, 빵 위에 계란을 올려. 그러고 나서, 채소를 약간 추가해. 마지막으로, 빵을 맨 위에 올려.
➡ _____

Express Yourself

1. 엄마를 위한 사각형
➡ _____

2. 난 낡은 청바지로 사각형 가방을 만들었어.
➡ _____

3. 엄마는 그걸 걸칠 때 뭘 입어야 할지 아셔.
➡ _____

4. 그것은 엄마를 들뜨게 했어. 그게 나를 행복하게 했어.
➡ _____

Link to the World

1. 유클리드는 프톨레마이오스 1세(Ptolemy I)가 이집트의 왕이었을 때 알렉산드리아 도서관에서 수학을 가르쳤다.
➡ _____

2. 사람들은 그를 '수학의 아버지'라고 부른다.
➡ _____

3. 그는 같은 길이의 세 변을 가진 삼각형을 어떻게 그리는지를 보여 주었다.
➡ _____

4. 그는 또한 한 삼각형 안에서 가장 큰 원의 중심을 어떻게 찾는지도 보여 주었다.
➡ _____

5. 어느 날, 프톨레마이오스 1세가 "수학을 공부하는 더 쉬운 방법은 없나요?" 하고 물었다.
➡ _____

6. 유클리드는 "배움에 왕도는 없습니다."라고 응답했다.
➡ _____

영어 기출 문제집

1학기

정답 및 해설

천재 | 정사열

중 2

영어 기출 문제집

1학기

정답 및 해설

천재 | 정사열

중 2

Be Active, Be Safe!

핵심 Check
p.10~11

1 (1) Have, read / have   (2) Have, heard / haven't

2 (1) shouldn't use, sorry   (2) Don't / not / shouldn't

   (3) think, cold / better not drink

시험대비 실력평가
p.08

01 ⑤   02 ②   03 ④   04 careless

05 ③   06 teenage   07 make   08 ②

01 ①, ②, ③, ④는 모두 clothes(옷)에 속한다.

02 for the first time: 처음으로 / look at: ~을 보다

03 대개 그것을 따라 집들이 있는, 도시나 읍 또는 마을의 도로: street(길, 도로)

04 반의어의 관계이다. 기억하다 : 잊다 = 주의 깊은 : 부주의한

05 over there: 저기에

06 열세 살에서 열아홉 살 사이의 나이인: teenage(십대의)

07 make noise: 떠들다, 소란 피우다

08 out of: ~에서 / lots of: 많은

교과서 대화문 익히기

📎 Check(√) True or False
p.12

1 T   2 F   3 T   4 F

서술형 시험대비
p.09

01 (1) colorful   (2) princess   (3) safe

02 (1) for example   (2) had, fun   (3) look at

03 (1) during   (2) Even   (3) following   (4) someday

04 (1) actually   (2) advice   (3) dangerous

05 (1) good at   (2) hear of   (3) look for   (4) keep in mind

06 (1) (r)ide   (2) (c)limb   (3) (p)ast

01 (1) 명사에 -ful을 붙이면 형용사가 된다. (2) 남성명사에 -ess를 붙이면 여성명사가 된다. (3) 반의어 관계이다. 위험한 : 안전한 = 강한 : 약한

02 (1) for example: 예를 들면 (2) have a lot of fun: 아주 재미있게 지내다 (3) look at: ~을 보다

03 (1) during: ~ 중에 (2) even: ~도, ~조차 (3) following: 다음에 나오는 (4) someday: 언젠가

04 (1) actually: 실제로, 사실 / actual: 실제의 (2) advice: 충고 / advise: 충고하다 (3) dangerous: 위험한 / danger: 위험

05 (1) be good at: ~을 잘하다 (2) hear of: ~에 대해 듣다 (3) look for: ~을 찾다 (4) keep in mind: ~을 명심하다

06 (1) ride: 타다 (2) climb: 오르다 (3) past: 과거

교과서 확인학습
p.14~15

Get Ready - 2

1 at, great / riding, know / What / special, riding

2 Don't, into / Why / shouldn't, without, Put, on

3 Look, over, like, take, front / over / okay

4 watch, in / up, birds / right

Start Off - Listen & Talk A

1 ever, climber / seen, on / climbing, camp, join / but, climb / right

2 Have, heard / haven't / favorite, concert, Can / shouldn't, too / right

Start Off - Listen & Talk B

heard of / when / doing, for / should bring / should, keep / shouldn't, when / in mind

Step Up - Real-life Scene

It's, see / hi, up / isn't, chat, heard / want / Guess, going / great / up, scenery / Be, use, while / right. Thank, send, later

Express Yourself A

1 heard, haven't, Who / singer, actor, figure / Sounds, take / Let's

2 take, painting / worry, real, So, front / Can, selfies, not

---

시험대비 기본평가
p.16

01 better not   02 ③   03 ②   04 ③

01 금지를 나타낼 때는 should not[shouldn't]이나 had better not 을 쓴다.

02 '~에 가 본 적 있니?'라고 경험을 물을 때는 Have you been ~? 표현을 사용한다. '전에'는 before로 쓴다.

03 B의 답변으로 보아, 빈칸에는 금지를 나타내는 should not을 사용한 문장이 들어가야 한다.

04 현재완료로 경험을 묻는 말에 부정으로 답할 때는 No, I haven't.라고 한다.

시험대비 실력평가

p.17~18

01 ⑤	02 Have, ever / have	03 ③
04 ④	05 ④	06 heard	07 ②
08 ①, ③	09 ⑤	10 ④	11 ⑤
12 Actually	13 scenery	14 ⑤	

01 금지의 표현은 명령문 「Don't+동사원형 ~.」을 쓰거나 You shouldn't + 동사원형 ~. / You'd better not + 동사원형 ~ 을 쓸 수 있다.

02 경험을 묻는 현재완료를 쓴다.

03 넌 여기서 셀피를 찍으면 안 돼. 반 고흐의 그림이 네 뒤에 있어. - 엄마, 걱정하지 마세요. 그건 그의 진짜 그림이 아니에요. 그래서 그 앞에서 셀피를 찍을 수 있어요. - 정말이지? 재미있겠다. 나도 여기서 셀피를 찍을 수 있을까? - 물론이죠.

04 영화를 본 경험이 있는지 묻는 말에 본 적 없다고 답하며 '너는 봤니?'라고 상대방에게 되묻는 표현이다. 대화의 흐름상 현재완료형으로 물어야 하므로 ④ Have you (seen it)?가 적절하다.

05 B가 자기의 행동을 사과하고 있으므로 잘못된 행동을 금지하는 말이 와야 알맞다. ④ leave computers on: 컴퓨터를 켠 채로 두다

06 현재완료이므로 'have+과거분사'의 형이 알맞다.

07 on TV: 텔레비전으로

08 금지의 표현인 must not, should not, had better not가 들어가 야 한다.

09 ⑤ 암벽 등반을 반대한 것이 아니라 너무 높이 올라가지 말라고 말했다.

10 What is up?: 무슨 일 있니?

11 부가의문문이므로 is의 부정형인 isn't가 오고, this는 인칭대명 사 it으로 바꾼다.

12 문장 전체를 수식하는 부사가 되어야 한다.

13 여러분 주위에서 볼 수 있는 땅, 물, 식물들: scenery(경치, 풍경)

14 ⑤ 민준이가 얼마나 많은 사진을 소민에게 보낼지는 위 대화를 통해 알 수 없다.

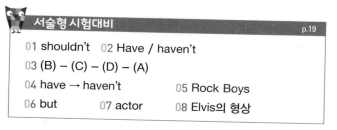

서술형 시험대비

p.19

01 shouldn't	02 Have / haven't
03 (B) – (C) – (D) – (A)	
04 have → haven't	05 Rock Boys
06 but	07 actor	08 Elvis의 형상

01 금지를 나타낼 때는 should not[shouldn't]나 must not[mustn't] 등을 쓸 수 있다.

02 경험을 나타내는 현재완료 문장이다.

03 저 소년을 봐. 그는 대단하다. - 그는 MTB를 타고 있어. 넌 그 것에 대해 알고 있니? - 아니. 그게 뭐지? - 산에 오르기 위한 특 별한 자전거야.

04 No로 시작하는 부정문이므로 haven't로 고쳐야 한다.

05 It은 인칭대명사로 앞에 나온 단수명사를 받는다. Rock Boys는 그룹의 명칭이므로 단수 취급한다.

06 앞뒤의 내용이 반대되는 개념이므로 but이 알맞다.

07 연극이나 영화에서 연기하는 것이 직업인 사람: actor(배우)

08 it은 위 문장의 a figure of Elvis를 받는다.

교과서
Grammar

핵심 Check

p.20~21

1 (1) done (2) have / eaten (3) has lived (4) for
2 (1) Though (2) Though (3) Though (4) Although

시험대비 기본평가

p.22

01 (1) has been (2) been (3) finished
(4) has just finished (5) arrived (6) did you reach

02 (1) Because → Though / Although
(2) since → though / although
(3) As → Though / Although

03 (1) He has been sick in bed since last Friday.
(2) How long have you known Miss Smith?
(3) Have you ever read the Christmas Carol?
(4) My father hasn't read the newspaper yet.

01 (1) 부사구 since ~가 있으므로 현재완료가 맞다. (2) '~에 다 녀오다'=have been to (3) two hours ago와 같이 명백한 과 거 시점을 나타내는 부사구가 있으므로 현재완료가 아닌 과거시 제로 써야 한다. (4) just와 함께 '이제 막 마쳤다'라는 의미이므 로 현재완료가 맞다. (5) yesterday와 같이 명백한 과거 시점

을 나타내는 부사가 있으므로 현재완료가 아닌 과거시제로 써야
한다. (6) 의문사 when은 특정 시점에 대해 묻는 의문사이므로
현재완료와 함께 쓸 수 없다.

02 '비록 ~이지만'의 의미를 나타내는 접속사 though나 although
를 사용해야 한다.

03 (1) 계속 용법의 현재완료이다. (2) 계속 용법의 현재완료이다.
(3) 경험 용법의 현재완료이다. (4) 완료 용법의 현재완료이다.

01 ⑤   02 ⑤   03 ④
04 T(t)hough   05 have   06 ①, ④   07 ④
08 Though the traffic was heavy, we arrived on
time. / We arrived on time though the traffic was
heavy.   09 ④   10 ④   11 not
12 ③   13 since   14 ①   15 ②
16 Although[Even though/Though] he played well,
he lost the soccer game.   17 ③   18 ④
19 ②   20 has been absent   21 yet
22 ②   23 ④

01 계속을 나타내는 현재완료이다.

02 though: 비록 ~이지만

03 계속을 나타내는 현재완료이다.

04 though: ~이지만(접속사); 그러나, 하지만(부사)

05 「have+p.p.」로 현재완료 시제로 쓰인 문장이다.

06 whether: ~인지 아닌지 / as though: 마치 ~처럼

07 현재완료의 경험 용법이 사용된 문장에서 빈도부사 never는
have와 been 사이에 위치해야 한다.

08 though로 시작하는 부사절은 주절의 앞이나 뒤에 올 수 있다.

09 계속을 나타내는 현재완료이다.

10 although: 비록 ~이지만

11 앞 문장이 현재완료 결과의 문장이므로 '나의 엄마는 쇼핑에 가고
여기 없다.'의 뜻이 되어야 한다.

12 though는 but을 써서 같은 의미로 바꿔 쓸 수 있다.

13 '~한 이래로'는 since로 나타낸다.

14 빈칸 뒤의 내용이 '나는 잠을 자지 않으려고 노력했다'의 의미이
므로 문맥상 졸렸다는 내용이 들어가야 한다.

15 현재완료형으로 물었으므로 현재완료형으로 대답해야 한다.

16 Because는 Though[Even though/Although] 등의 양보 접
속사로 바꿔 써야 한다.

17 though는 '비록 ~이지만'의 뜻으로 although, even though
등과 같은 의미로 사용된다.

18 ④와 같이 when ~이 명백한 과거의 시점을 나타낼 때는 현재
완료 시제는 쓸 수 없다. (has been → was)

19 ② though를 이유를 나타내는 접속사 as나 because로 고쳐야

자연스럽다.

20 결석을 얼마나 오랫동안 했는지 물었으므로 현재완료(have+p.p.)
로 쓴다.

21 yet: 1. 이미, 벌써(의문문) 2. 아직(부정문)

22 첫 번째 빈칸에는 양보의 접속사 though, although, even
though 등이 들어가고, 두 번째 빈칸에는 이유의 접속사 as,
because 등이 들어간다.

23 ④의 has gone은 '~에 가고 없다'는 의미의 현재완료 결과 용
법이다. 나머지는 모두 현재완료 경험의 용법으로 쓰였다.

01 (1) have, finished   (2) has not returned
    (3) has gone to
02 (1) Though[Although]   (2) though[although]
03 (1) has gone → went   (2) already → yet
04 T(t)hough
05 (1) has seen → saw   (2) is → has been
06 (1) He has been to Italy many times.
    (2) I have been very busy these days.
    (3) I have never visited Paris before.
07 (1) before   (2) that   (3) since   (4) because   (5) if
    (6) though
08 (1) I went to London four years ago.
    (2) When did you see a white lion?
    (3) I often played with her when I was a child.
    (4) He was ill in bed last month.
09 (1) Because → Although / Though
    (2) as → although / though
10 (1) He has lived in New York since 1970.
    (2) Have you finished reading this story yet?
    (3) I have seen the movie once.
11 (A)lthough

01 (1) 현재완료 완료 용법 (2) yet은 과거에서 현재까지 아직 완료
되지 않은 상태를 말한다. (3) 현재완료 결과 용법

02 양보의 접속사는 though, although, even though 등이 쓰인다.

03 (1) 과거를 나타내는 부사구가 있으므로 현재완료 시제가 아니라
과거시제를 써야 한다. (2) 부정문에서 '아직'의 뜻으로는 yet을
쓴다.

04 though가 문장 끝에 올 때는 부사로 '그러나, 하지만'의 뜻으로 쓰
인다.

05 (1) 과거를 나타내는 부사구가 있으므로 현재완료 시제가 아니라
과거시제를 써야 한다. (2) 계속을 나타내는 현재완료가 알맞다.

06 (1) 현재완료 경험 용법 (2) 일정한 기간을 나타내는 부사구
(these days)는 현재완료와 함께 쓰일 수 있다. (3) 현재완료 경

험 용법

07 (1) before: ~하기 전에 (2) so ~ that ...: 아주 ~해서 …하다
   (3) since: ~부터, ~한 이래 (4) because: ~이기 때문에 (5)
   if: 만일 ~한다면 (6) though: 비록 ~이지만

08 (1) 과거 시점을 나타내는 four years ago가 있으므로 과거시
   제로 쓴다. (2) when은 과거의 특정 시점을 묻는 표현이므로
   과거시제로 써야 한다. (3) when 이하의 절이 과거의 특정 시
   점을 나타내므로 과거시제로 쓴다. (4) '지난달(last month)'이
   라는 명백한 과거 시점이 있으므로 과거시제로 나타낸다.

09 '비록 ~이지만'의 의미를 나타내는 접속사 though나 although
   를 사용해야 한다.

10 (1) 현재완료 계속 용법 (2) 현재완료 완료 용법 (3) 현재완료
   경험 용법

11 although: 비록 ~이지만(= though, even though)

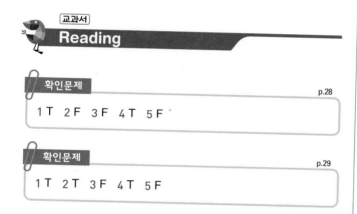

Reading 교과서

확인문제
p.28

1 T 2 F 3 F 4 T 5 F

확인문제
p.29

1 T 2 T 3 F 4 T 5 F

교과서 확인학습 A
p.30~31

01 Have, heard   02 take, yourself
03 club, for, for 04 Here, about 05 people, take
06 Though, answer   07 Look
08 used, herself   09 nervous
10 why   11 think, first
12 probably, teenage   13 take, like
14 take, tricks   15 also, fun
16 example, famous   17 special, take
18 touch, even   19 following
20 Though, riding, like
21 just, brush, painting 22 exist
23 visited, before 24 don't, yourself 25 look, but
26 so   27 safe
28 should, when, places
29 could, time, fall   30 safety
31 take, while   32 pose, wild   33 Never, places
34 use, better   35 things, take 36 post, website

37 watered, school   38 also, at, times
39 at, those   40 about, create

교과서 확인학습 B
p.32~33

1 Have you ever heard of a "selfie"? When you take
  a photograph of yourself, it's a selfie.

2 The students from Minji's photo club have
  searched for information about selfies for one
  month.

3 Here are some of their presentations about
  selfies.

4 Did people in the past take selfies?

5 Though it wasn't easy at that time. the answer is
  yes.

6 Look at this photo of Princess Anastasia. She
  used a mirror to take a picture of herself.

7 She looks nervous. Can you guess why?

8 Well, I think it was her first selfie.

9 And it was probably the world's first teenage
  selfie ever.

10 You can take selfies at world-famous places like
   Big Ben and the Leaning Tower of Pisa.

11 To take great pictures, just do fun poses and use
   camera tricks.

12 You can also visit special museums to take fun
   selfies.

13 For example. there is a famous selfie museum in
   the Philippines.

14 It has special spots to take selfies.

15 You can touch the paintings and even step
   inside them.

16 Look at the following pictures.

17 Though the boys are not really riding horses, it
   looks like they are.

18 Though the man is just holding a big brush, it
   looks like he is painting the Mona Lisa.

19 Selfie museums exist in Korea, too. I have visited
   one in Chuncheon before.

20 Why don't you go there yourself? These selfies look
   great, but were they a good idea?

21 I don't think so. They don't look safe.

22 You should take special care when you take
   selfies in the wild or at high places like these.

23 A monkey could bite you at any time, or you

could fall.

24 Here are some safety tips:

25 Don't take selfies while you're walking.

26 Do not pose with or near wild animals.

27 Never take selfies in dangerous places.

28 I think we can use selfies to make a better school life.

29 We can do good things at school and take selfies.

30 Then we can post the photos on our school website.

31 I've watered the plants and flowers at school for one month.

32 I've also helped the teacher at the school library many times.

33 Look at my selfies of those things.

34 How about joining me to create a better school life?

시험대비 실력평가
p.34~37

01 ③	02 ④	03 ③	04 ⑤
05 ②	06 her → herself		07 여러분은

그녀가 왜 긴장돼 보이는지 추측할 수 있나요? 08 ⑤

09 ⑤	10 ②	11 ③	12 ①, ④
13 ③	14 Why	15 ②	16 ③
17 ②	18 여러분은 야생이나 이와 같이 높은 곳에서		

셀피를 찍을 때 특별한 주의를 기울여야 합니다. 19 ⑤

20 ⑤ 21 그러고 나서 우리는 학교 웹사이트에 사진을 올릴 수 있다. 22 ① 23 What

24 ⑤	25 ①	26 ①, ④	27 ③
28 ①	29 She used a mirror to take a picture		

of herself. 30 ③

01 '~할 때'의 뜻을 나타내는 접속사 when이 알맞다.

02 search for: ~을 찾다 / for+수사가 붙은 기간

03 ⓓ, ③ 1문형 ① 3문형 ② 2문형 ④ 5문형 ⑤ 4문형

04 마지막 문장에 민지의 사진 동아리 학생들의 셀피에 대해 수집한 정보가 제시될 것이라고 서술하고 있다.

05 거울로 셀피를 찍은 Anastasia 공주의 사진을 보라는 뜻이므로 과거에도 셀피를 찍었다고 서술하는 문장 다음에 와야 한다.

06 전차사 of의 목적어가 주어 자신이므로 재귀대명사를 써야 한다.

07 why 뒤에는 she looks nervous가 생략된 것이다.

08 주어진 문장의 It은 a famous selfie museum을 받는다.

09 ⓐ와 ⑤는 전치사로 쓰였고, 나머지는 모두 동사로 쓰였다.

10 빈칸 뒤에 special museums에 대한 구체적인 예가 나오고 있다.

11 위 글은 셀피를 찍기 위한 재미있는 장소를 소개하고 있다.

12 문맥상 '비록 ~이지만'의 뜻인 양보의 접속사가 알맞다.

13 exist: ~에 있다, 존재하다

14 Why don't you ~?: ~하지 그래?

15 ② 소년들은 말을 타고 있는 것처럼 보인다고 언급되어 있다.

16 위험한 장소에서 셀피를 찍을 때는 주의해야 한다는 문장 앞에 와야 한다.

17 상반되는 절을 연결해 주는 접속사 but이 알맞다.

18 should: ~해야 한다 / like: ~와 같은

19 '~하는 동안'의 뜻인 while이 알맞다.

20 ⓐ, ⑤ 목적을 나타내는 부사적 용법 ①, ③, ④ 명사적 용법 ② 형용사적 용법

21 then: 그 다음에 / post: 올리다

22 for+수사가 붙은 기간

23 How[What] about -ing?: ~하는 게 어때?

24 ⑤ 소윤이가 왜 선생님을 도왔는지는 알 수 없다.

25 hear of: ~에 대해 듣다 / take a photograph of: ~의 사진을 찍다

26 ⓒ, ①, ④ 계속 ② 경험 ③ 완료 ⑤ 결과

27 문맥상 '비록 ~이지만'의 뜻인 though가 알맞다.

28 look at: ~을 보다

29 to take a picture of: ~의 사진을 찍기 위해

30 ③ 민지는 Anastasia 공주가 처음으로 셀피를 찍었다고 생각한다.

서술형 시험대비
p.38~39

01 여러분은 빅벤과 피사의 사탑과 같은 세계적으로 유명한 장소에서 셀피를 찍을 수 있습니다. 02 poses

03 For 04 필리핀에 있는 유명한 셀피 박물관

05 I can go to special museums to take fun selfies.

06 at 07 비록 그 소년들은 말을 타고 있는 것은 아니지만, 말을 타고 있는 것처럼 보입니다. 08 a selfie museum 09 yourself 10 they were a good idea 11 safely → safe 12 at

13 dangerous 14 야생 동물이 물거나 높은 데서 떨어질 위험이 있기 때문이다. 15 나는 우리가 더 나은 학교생활을 만들기 위해 셀피를 이용할 수 있다고 생각해요.

16 watered 17 for 18 about

01 like: ~와 같은

02 예를 들면 당신을 사진 찍거나 그릴 때 당신이 서 있거나, 앉거나, 또는 누워 있거나 하는 특별한 방법: pose(자세, 포즈)

03 for example: 예를 들면

06 look at: ~을 보다

07 it looks like (that) ~: ~처럼 보이다

08 부정대명사 one은 앞에 나온 'a+보통명사'를 받는다.

09 주어진 you를 강조하는 재귀대명사로 고쳐야 한다.

10 so는 지시대명사로 앞 문장에 나온 긍정의 내용을 받는다.

11 감각동사 look의 보어로 형용사가 와야 한다.

12 at any time: 어느 때고

13 danger의 형용사형으로 고쳐야 한다.

15 I think 뒤에는 명사절을 이끄는 접속사 that이 생략되었다.

16 현재완료 구문이므로 water의 과거분사형인 watered로 고쳐야 한다.

17 for+수사가 붙은 기간

18 How about -ing?: ~하는 게 어때요?

영역별 핵심문제   p.41~45

01 ②	02 ③	03 past	04 ④
05 ⑤	06 for	07 hang up	08 H(h)ave
09 ③	10 ④	11 this → it	12 what
13 careful	14 ⑤	15 ④	16 ③
17 ④	18 ④	19 Although it was cold,	

19 Although it was cold, there were a lot of people in the park.   20 ③

21 ④	22 ④	23 ②	24 ③
25 ①	26 Even if[though]		27 exciting
28 ④	29 ③	30 ②	31 ④

32 a famous selfie museum (in the Philippines)

33 비록 그 남자는 단지 커다란 붓을 잡고 있지만, 모나리자를 그리고 있는 것처럼 보입니다.   34 ①

35 ③   36 safety   37 ②, ④

01 ①, ③, ④, ⑤는 반의어의 관계이고, ②는 유의어의 관계이다.

02 • Kate는 그에게서 아직 편지를 받지 못했다. • 그가 몸을 돌려 뒤를 보았다. • 그는 그 장소를 어려움 없이 찾았다. • 그가 또 무슨 다른 말을 했나요?

03 과거 : 현재 : 미래

04 be good for: ~에 좋다

05 어떤 사람을 속이기 위해 의도된 행위: trick(속임수, 장난)

06 for the first time: 처음으로 / for example: 예를 들면

07 hang up: 전화를 끊다

08 경험을 묻고 대답하는 대화이다.

09 You'd better not + 동사원형 ~은 '~하지 않는 게 좋겠다.'라는 의미로 금지하는 표현이다.

10 What's up?: 무슨 일이니? / hang up: 전화를 끊다

11 this는 부가의문문에서 인칭대명사 it으로 바뀐다.

12 Guess what?: 있잖아., 알겠니?

13 be동사 다음은 보어 자리이므로 형용사가 되어야 한다. care에 -ful을 붙이면 형용사형이 된다.

14 문맥상 '~하는 동안'의 뜻인 while이 알맞다.

15 ④ 소민은 민준에게 걷는 동안은 전화기를 사용하지 말라고 충고했다.

16 과거에서 지금까지의 경험을 나타내는 문장이므로 현재완료

(have+p.p.) 시제로 써야 한다.

17 though: 비록 ~이지만

18 계속을 나타내는 현재완료이다.

19 although: 비록 ~이지만

20 ③ last week라는 특정 과거 시점이 있으므로 현재완료가 아니라 과거시제로 써야 한다. (have climbed → climbed)

21 although: 비록 ~이지만(= though, even though)

22 have[has] gone to ~: ~에 갔다(그래서 여기 없다) 결과를 나타내는 현재완료이다.

23 보기, ② 경험 ①, ④ 계속 ③ 완료 ⑤ 결과

24 ③ though를 이유를 나타내는 접속사 as나 because로 고쳐야 한다.

25 ① ~ ago라는 과거 시점이 있으므로 과거시제 went가 맞다.

26 though: 비록 ~이지만(= although, even though)

27 사물이 사람을 흥미 있게 하는 것이므로 현재분사형의 형용사를 써야 한다.

28 '많은'의 뜻이지만 뒤에 복수명사가 오므로 much는 쓸 수 없다.

29 문맥상 '~할 때'의 뜻인 when이 알맞다.

30 ② BMX의 가격은 언급되지 않았다.

31 for example: 예를 들면

32 it은 인칭대명사로 앞에 나온 단수명사를 받는다.

33 it looks like (that): ~처럼 보이다

34 Why don't you ~?: ~하지 그래요?

35 ③ 그림들에 손을 댈 수 있다고 언급되어 있다.

36 safe: 안전한 / safety: 안전

37 since와 as though는 양보를 나타내는 접속사가 아니다.

단원별 예상문제   p.46~49

01 ④	02 ②	03 arrival	04 ④
05 in mind	06 ④	07 ④	08 ④
09 bird watching	10 ③		11 ②

12 새를 관찰할 때 아무 소리도 내지 않는 것   13 ⑤

14 ③	15 ⑤	16 has lived	17 I have

17 I have not seen him since I was eleven.   18 ②

19 ④	20 ⑤	21 ③	22 ④

23 과거 사람들이 셀피를 찍는 것   24 ⑤

25 Anastasia가 처음으로 셀피를 찍고 있었기 때문이라고 생각한다.   26 ④   27 excited → exciting

28 ②, ③	29 but	30 ①	31 careful

01 ④는 유의어 관계이고 나머지는 남성명사 - 여성명사 관계이다.

02 be fond of: ~을 좋아하다 / in front of: ~ 앞에

03 동사 : 명사의 관계이다.

04 ④는 push(밀다)의 영영풀이이다.

05 keep in mind: ~을 명심하다, ~을 잊지 않다

06 shouldn't는 '~해서는 안 된다'의 뜻으로 금지를 나타낼 때 쓰

는 표현이다.

07 No, I haven't.로 답했으므로 현재완료를 이용해서 경험을 묻는 질문이 와야 알맞다.

08 주어진 문장은 그밖에 또 무엇을 명심해야 하느냐고 묻는 질문이므로 새들을 관찰할 때 아무 소리도 내지 말아야 한다는 문장 앞에 와야 한다.

09 it은 앞에 나온 단수명사를 받는다.

10 for the first time: 처음으로

11 make noise: 떠들다

12 that은 앞에 나온 문장의 내용을 받는다.

13 ⑤ 소년은 처음으로 들새 관찰을 하는 것이므로 취미라고 말할 수 없다.

14 현재완료의 경험 용법이 사용된 문장에서 빈도부사 never는 have[has]와 been 사이에 위치해야 한다.

15 although: 비록 ~이지만

16 since 이하가 과거에서 현재에 이르는 기간을 말하므로 현재완료의 계속 용법이 필요하다.

17 since는 현재완료 시제와 함께 쓰이므로 didn't see는 have not seen이 되어야 한다.

18 though는 but을 써서 같은 의미로 바꿔 쓸 수 있다.

19 시계를 잃어버려 현재 가지고 있지 않다는 것을 나타낸다. 결과를 나타내는 현재완료이다.

20 ⑤ Because 대신에 Though 또는 Although를 써야 한다.

21 ③의 has gone은 '~에 가고 없다'는 의미의 현재완료 결과 용법이다. 나머지는 모두 현재완료 경험 용법으로 쓰였다.

22 이유를 묻는 문장이므로 그녀가 긴장하고 있는 것처럼 보인다는 문장 다음에 와야 한다.

23 it은 앞에 나온 문장의 내용을 받는다.

24 ⑥, ⑤ 목적을 나타내는 부사적 용법 ①, ③ 명사적 용법 ②, ④ 형용사적 용법

26 주어진 문장은 헬멧과 장갑을 착용하라는 뜻이므로 주의하라는 문장 다음에 와야 한다.

27 사물이 사람을 흥분시키는 것이므로 현재분사형의 형용사를 써야 한다.

28 much는 양을 나타내는 명사에 쓰인다. a few는 '조금'이라는 뜻이다.

29 though와 but은 같은 뜻의 문장으로 바꿔 쓸 수 있다.

30 문맥상 '~할 때'의 뜻인 when이 알맞다.

31 be동사의 보어인 형용사형을 써야 한다.

서술형 실전문제
p.50~51

01 climber　　02 seen　　03 She will teach rock climbing at a camp.　　04 (B) – (C) – (D) – (A)
05 (1) Peter has lived in Peking since 2010.

(2) Tom has been in hospital for a week.

(3) My mother has gone shopping.

06 (1) Though it was windy, it wasn't very cold.

(2) Although Tim often annoyed Anne, she was fond of him.

(3) You must do it though you don't like it.

07 (1) has gone → went　　(2) have you seen → did you see

(3) have often played → often played

08 heard　　09 you → yourself　　10 for

11 자기 자신의 사진을 직접 찍는 것이다.　　12 to make

13 take　　14 plants　　15 joining

01 스포츠나 취미로 바위나 산을 오르는 사람: climber(등반가)

02 현재완료 구문이므로 see의 과거분사로 고쳐야 한다.

04 잠깐, 지민. - 왜? - 저 표지판 좀 봐. 여기서 사진 찍으면 안 돼. - 아, 알았어.

05 현재완료(have+p.p.)를 이용해 문장을 완성한다. (1) 현재완료의 계속 용법 (2) 현재완료의 계속 용법 (3) 현재완료의 결과 용법

07 (1) 과거 시점을 나타내는 last year가 있으므로 과거시제로 쓴다. (2) 의문사 when으로 시작하므로 과거시제로 쓴다. (3) when 이하의 부사절이 과거의 특정 시점을 나타내므로 과거시제로 쓴다.

08 현재완료이므로 hear의 과거분사를 쓴다.

09 전치사 of의 목적어가 주어 자신이므로 재귀대명사를 써야 한다.

10 search for: ~을 찾다 / for+수사가 붙은 기간

12 목적을 나타내는 부사적 용법의 to부정사가 알맞다.

13 take selfies: 셀피를 찍다

14 줄기, 잎, 뿌리를 가지고 있으며 땅에서 자라는 살아 있는 것, 특히 나무나 덤불보다 작은 것: plant(식물)

15 전치사 다음에는 동명사형을 써야 한다.

창의사고력 서술형 문제
p.52

|모범답안|

01 (1) I have just sent an e-mail to Jane.

(2) Kate has just cleaned her room.

(3) Mike has already finished his job.

(4) Have you taken your medicine yet?

(5) Mary hasn't sung yet.

(6) You haven't studied enough yet.

(7) Has Tom done his homework yet?

02 (1) Though my mother was sick, she tried to clean the house. / My mother tried to clean the house though she was sick.

(2) Although the food smelled delicious, I didn't feel like eating it. / I didn't feel like eating the

8　정답 및 해설

food although it smelled delicious.

(3) Even though I was sick, I didn't want to go to hospital. / I didn't want to go to hospital even though I was sick.

단원별 모의고사
p.53~56

01 ④	02 ②	03 ④	04 pull
05 of	06 ②	07 ②	08 ⑤
09 ③	10 ③	11 What else should I keep in mind?	
		12 ①	13 ②
14 ④	15 ③	16 ①	17 ④
18 have lost	19 ②, ④	20 ③	21 ①
22 ②	23 He or she took it at the selfie museum.		24 나는 이 셀피들이 좋은 생각이었다고 생각하지 않습니다.
		25 ①	26 ③
27 ③	28 rules	29 ④	30` fire, elevator

01 be good for: ~에 좋다

02 다른 사람들이나 다른 것들보다 더 좋거나 더 중요한: 특별한 (special)

03 during: ~ 중에, ~ 동안 / else 또[그 밖의] 다른, 다른

04 반의어 관계이다. 안전한 : 위험한 = 밀다 : 끌다

05 hear of: ~에 대해 소식을 듣다 / lots of: 많은

06 너 말을 타본 적 있니? - 응, 있어. 너는 언제? - 아니, 난 없어. 말 타는 거 어땠어? - 재미있었지만, 조금 무섭기도 했어.

07 Have you ever+과거분사 ~?에 대한 응답은 Yes, I have. / No, I haven't.이다. 빈칸 다음의 말로 보아 부정의 대답이 와야 한다.

08 You'd better not+동사원형 ~은 '~하지 않는 게 좋겠다'는 뜻으로 금지하는 표현이므로 You shouldn't + 동사원형 ~.으로 바꿔 쓸 수 있다.

09 hear of: ~에 관해 듣다 / for the first time: 처음으로

10 ⓒ, ③ 형용사적 용법 ①, ④ 명사적 용법 ②, ⑤ 부사적 용법

11 else는 '또[그 밖의] 다른'의 뜻으로 의문대명사 what 뒤에 위치한다.

12 문맥상 '~할 때'의 뜻을 나타내는 when이 알맞다.

13 ② 소년이 들새 관찰을 좋아하는지는 언급되지 않았다.

14 완료를 나타내는 현재완료의 부정문이다.

15 even though: 비록 ~이지만(= though, although)

16 ① ~ ago라는 과거 시점이 있으므로 과거시제 went가 맞다.

17 though: 비록 ~이지만

18 열쇠를 잃어버린 결과가 현재까지 영향을 미치므로 현재완료의 결과 용법으로 나타낸다.

19 though: 비록 ~이지만 (= although, even though)

20 과거에서 지금까지의 경험을 나타내는 문장이므로 현재완료 (have+p.p.) 시제로 써야 한다.

21 hear of: ~에 관해 듣다 / in front of: ~ 앞에서

22 ⓑ, ② 경험 ①, ④ 계속 ③ 완료 ⑤ 결과

23 셀피를 박물관에서 찍었다고 언급되어 있다.

24 so는 지시대명사로 앞 문장의 they were a good idea를 받는다.

25 문맥상 '안전한'이 알맞다.

26 '아니면, 또는'의 뜻으로 선택을 나타내는 접속사 or가 알맞다.

27 ③ 원숭이가 사람을 잘 따르는지는 알 수 없다.

28 당신이 할 수 있는 일과 할 수 없는 일을 알려주는 지침: rule(규칙)

29 문맥상 '비록 ~이라도'의 뜻으로 양보를 나타내는 접속사가 알맞다.

Lesson 4

Memories in Your Heart

Conversation

핵심 Check p.62~63

1 ② 2 ① 3 ③ 4 think

교과서 대화문 익히기

Check(√) True or False p.64

1 T 2 T 3 T 4 F

시험대비 실력평가 p.60

01 special 02 secrets 03 ④ 04 ②
05 ⑤ 06 super 07 ③ 08 ④

01 둘은 반의어 관계다. 두꺼운 : 얇은 – 일반적인 : 특별한
02 숨겨져 있거나 극소수의 사람들에 의해 알려져 있는 것은 '비밀(secret)'이다. 'all the+복수명사'이므로 secrets가 적절하다.
03 laughter는 명사로 '웃음'이다. '웃다'는 laugh이다.
04 눈에서 흐르는 짠 액체 방울: 눈물
05 희귀하거나 비싸거나 중요하기 때문에 매우 소중한: 귀중한
06 부사 hard를 수식하는 강조어로 '매우'의 의미를 가지는 super가 적절하다.
07 '그녀는 그에게 축구공을 튀겼다'는 의미가 자연스럽다.
08 그의 축구공은 그에게 금만큼 소중하다(precious)는 의미가 자연스럽고, 어린 '소년 덕분에'의 의미로 thanks to가 적절하다.

서술형 시험대비 p.61

01 (1) one by one (2) laughter (3) lost
02 (1) remember, past (2) under, hen (3) hot air, looked like 03 (1) take (2) remember
04 (1) whisper (2) neighbor (3) bounce (4) special
05 (1) (c)ut (2) (g)et married (3) (t)hrow (4) (s)ock puppet

01 (1) 그녀에게 물건을 하나씩 주었다. (2) '그의 양말 인형은 항상 그의 부모님에게 큰 웃음을 안겨 드렸다.' 동사의 목적어 자리에 사용되기 때문에 동사 laugh를 명사 형태로 바꾸어야 한다. (3) '기억을 잃다'는 의미로 동사 lose를 사용해야 하고, she has[she's] 뒤에 사용되므로 과거분사 lost가 적절하다.
02 (1) remember: 기억하다, past: 과거 (2) from under: ~ 아래에서, hen: 암탉 (3) hot air balloon: 열기구, look like: ~처럼 보이다
03 (1) bring '가져오다' ↔ take '가져가다' (2) forget '잊다' ↔ remember '기억하다'
04 (1) 매우 조용히 말하다 (2) 당신 근처에 사는 사람 (3) 표면을 치고 나서 위로 또는 멀리 이동하다 (4) 평범하거나 일반적이지 않은

교과서 확인학습 p.66~67

Get Ready
1 How, remember / had a great time
2 cut, practice / Let's see
3 This is / for calling

Start Off Listen & Talk A
1 wore super / Guess what, moved / Let's
2 remember / Who / grade / remember, taught / good

Start Off Listen & Talk B
school nurse / Guess what, getting married / shall we / Let me see, making

Speak Up Look and talk.
field trip / played / funny, on

Speak Up Mission
Let me see

Real-life Scene
who, alone / threw / for, put, in / played, together / won, rounds, good / are, going to / Let me see / Let's take

Express Yourself
1 rode / looked like
2 one / looked like

Learning Diary Check Yourself
singing competition / super / funny

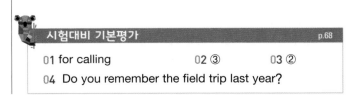

시험대비 기본평가 p.68

01 for calling 02 ③ 03 ②
04 Do you remember the field trip last year?

01 'thank A for B: B 때문에 A에게 감사하다'는 뜻으로 전치사 for 뒤에 동명사 calling이 적절하다.

02 나머지는 생각할 시간을 달라는 표현이고, ③번은 생각할 시간 요청을 수락할 때 사용하는 표현이다.

03 빈칸 뒤의 내용으로 보아 G는 Ms. Lee를 기억하고 있다는 것을 알 수 있다.

04 일반동사 의문문으로 '조동사+주어+동사원형 ~?' 형태로 사용한다.

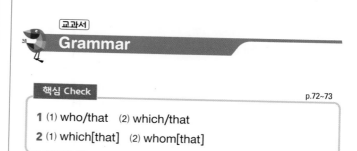

시험대비 실력평가
p.69~70

01 ③	02 making a special album	03 ③
04 ⑤	05 ①	06 looked like
07 ②	08 ③	09 ⑤ 10 ③
11 remember		12 calling

01 대화를 시작할 때나 대화의 화제를 바꿀 때 사용하는 표현으로 '있잖아'라는 뜻의 'Guess what?'이 적절하다.

02 What about은 뒤에 명사나 동명사를 사용해야 한다.

03 밑줄 친 super는 부사로 '매우, 극도로'의 의미를 가진다. ③번은 부사로 사용이 되었고, 나머지는 형용사로 '멋진, 굉장한'의 의미를 가진다.

04 Ben과 Jenny는 함께 김 선생님을 방문하기로 했다.

05 글의 흐름상 상대방의 기억을 묻는 remember가 자연스럽다.

06 '~처럼 보이다'의 의미로 look이 명사와 함께 사용될 때는 전치사 like가 필요하다.

07 빈칸에는 선행사 the old lady(사람)를 수식하는 절을 이끌고, lives의 주어 역할을 하는 주격 관계대명사 who가 적절하다.

08 (B) '파티를 열다'는 의미로 동사 throw, have, give, hold를 사용한다. 과거형이 적절하다. (C) 동사 cook은 간접목적어 앞에 전치사 for를 사용한다.

09 Let me see.는 상대방에게 생각할 시간을 요청할 때 사용하는 표현으로 '언제 그녀를 방문할 거니?'라는 물음 다음인 (⑤)에 오는 것이 자연스럽다.

10 ③은 내 생일을 기억하느냐는 질문에 '그것은 틀렸어. 7월 26일이다'라고 대답하는 것은 어색하다.

11 어떤 정보를 생각해 내거나 또는 어떤 정보를 기억 속에 보존하다 : remember(기억하다)

12 전치사 for 뒤에는 명사나 동명사가 와야 한다. 동사 call을 동명사로 바꾸어야 한다.

서술형 시험대비
p.71

01 Do you remember Ms. Lee?　**02** ④, bad → good　**03** Let me see[think].　**04** Guess what?　**05** What about making a special album?

---

01 상대방의 기억 여부를 묻는 표현으로 remember가 일반 동사이므로 조동사 Do로 시작하는 의문문을 완성한다.

02 ④번 앞 문장에 그녀가 모든 판을 이겼다고 했기 때문에 bad를 good으로 바꾸어야 한다.

03 어떤 일에 대해 주의 깊게 생각하고 싶거나 기억하려고 애쓸 때 사용하는 표현

04 흥미롭거나 놀라운 일을 누군가에게 말하기 전에 사용하는 표현

05 What about + -ing?' 구문을 이용하여 영작한다.

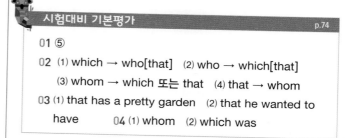

교과서
Grammar

핵심 Check
p.72~73

1 (1) who/that　(2) which/that
2 (1) which[that]　(2) whom[that]

시험대비 기본평가
p.74

01 ⑤

02 (1) which → who[that]　(2) who → which[that]
　(3) whom → which 또는 that　(4) that → whom

03 (1) that has a pretty garden　(2) that he wanted to have　**04** (1) whom　(2) which was

01 선행사가 The girl로 사람이며 is singing의 주어 역할을 할 수 있는 주격 관계대명사 who나 that이 적절하다.

02 (1) 선행사가 사람이므로 which를 who나 that으로 고쳐야 한다. (2) 선행사가 사물이므로 who를 which나 that으로 고쳐야 한다. (3) wrote의 목적어 역할을 해야 하며 선행사가 사물이므로 whom을 which나 that으로 고쳐야 한다. (4) 전치사 with의 목적어 역할을 해야 하며 선행사가 사람이므로 that을 whom으로 고쳐야 한다. that은 전치사 다음에 사용할 수 없다.

03 (1) 선행사가 사물이고 주격이므로 which나 that을 쓴다. (2) 선행사가 사물이고 목적격이므로 which나 that을 쓴다.

04 (1) 목적격 관계대명사는 흔히 생략된다. (2) 주격 관계대명사는 생략할 수 없으나 뒤에 분사가 오는 경우 '주격 관계대명사 +be동사'를 생략할 수 있다.

시험대비 실력평가
p.75~77

01 ②　**02** This is the book (which[that]) I am looking for.　**03** ④　**04** (1) which　(2) who
(3) that　(4) which　(5) whom　(6) who　(7) that

11

05 ⑤　　　　06 ②　　　　07 (1) which　(2) who is
08 ①　　　　09 ①, ②, ④　10 ③　　　11 ①
12 ⑤　　　　13 (1) that looked like an elephant
(2) which I took a rest　(3) whom I can trust
14 ③　　　　15 ②, ④
16 (1) This is the man who[whom/that] I met
yesterday.
(2) I don't know the girl who[that] is singing.
(3) Julie bought a computer which[that] she likes
very much yesterday.
(4) He completed drawing two pictures
which[that] look very similar.
(5) Mary took a picture of a man and his dog that
were crossing the road.
(6) Mike needs a friend who[whom/that] he wants
to play with. 또는 Mike needs a friend with
whom he wants to play.
17 watched the movie that Steve talked about to her
last week

01 모두 주격이나 목적격으로 사용된 관계대명사 that이 들어갈 수
있지만 ②번은 소유격 관계대명사 whose가 들어가야 한다.
02 for의 목적어 역할을 해야 하며 선행사가 사물이므로 which나
that을 쓴다. 또한 목적격 관계대명사이므로 생략해도 좋다.
03 ④ 선행사가 사람인 a cousin이므로 which가 아니라 who가
되어야 한다.
04 (1) 선행사가 사물이므로 which (2) 선행사가 사람이므로
who (3) 선행사가 사물이므로 that (4) 전치사가 관계대명사
바로 앞에 있으므로 which (5) 선행사가 사람이므로 whom
(6) who를 목적격 whom 대신 쓸 수 있지만 whom을 who
대신 쓰지는 않는다. (7) 선행사가 '사람+동물[사물]'인 경우에
는 반드시 관계대명사 that을 써야 한다.
05 ⑤번은 접속사이지만 나머지는 모두 관계대명사이다.
06 주격 관계대명사의 선행사가 사람이면 who나 that을 쓰고 사물
이면 which나 that을 쓴다.
07 목적격 관계대명사와 '주격 관계대명사+be동사'는 생략할 수 있
다.
08 관계대명사는 접속사와 대명사의 역할을 하므로 목적격 관계대
명사가 생략된 ①번은 목적어로 쓰인 it이 없어야 한다.
09 사람을 선행사로 받는 목적격 관계대명사는 whom과 that이다.
또한 whom 대신 who를 쓸 수 있다.
10 선행사가 사물이므로 which나 that을 이용하고 목적격이므로
목적어로 쓰인 it은 쓰지 말아야 한다.
11 ③번에서는 who를 which나 that으로 바꿔야 하고, ②, ④,
⑤에서는 관계대명사는 접속사와 대명사 역할을 하므로 it이 없
어야 한다.

12 관계대명사의 선행사가 사람이면 who, whom이나 that을 쓰
고 사물이면 which나 that을 쓴다. 전치사가 관계대명사 바로
앞에 있을 때는 that을 쓰지 않는다.
13 관계대명사의 선행사가 사람이면 who, whom이나 that을 쓰고
사물이면 which나 that을 쓴다. 전치사가 관계대명사 바로 앞에
있을 때는 that을 쓰지 않는다.
14 ③ 전치사가 관계대명사 바로 앞에 있으므로 that이 아니라
which를 써야 한다.
15 주어진 문장과 ②, ④번의 who는 주격 관계대명사이다. ①, ⑤
번은 목적격 관계대명사이고, ③번은 의문대명사이다.
16 관계대명사의 선행사가 사람이면 who, whom이나 that을 쓰고
사물이면 which나 that을 쓴다. 선행사가 '사람+동물'이면 that
을 쓴다. 전치사가 관계대명사 바로 앞에 있을 때는 that을 쓰지
않는다.
17 목적격 관계대명사 다음에는 '주어+동사'가 이어진다.

01 (1) Sejong was a great King who[that] invented
Hangeul.
(2) An elephant is an animal which[that] has a
long nose.
(3) Sharon met a man who[whom, that] she loved
very much.
(4) Tony bought a nice bag which[that] he gave to
Karen.
(5) There are Ms. Han and her cats that are playing
together.
02 (1) which Melanie works　(2) which Melanie works
(3) that Melanie works　(4) Melanie works at
03 (1) who is sitting on a wheelchair
(2) who is playing cards
(3) that is sleeping on the chair
04 (1) who → which[that]　(2) which → who[that]
(3) whom → who[that]　(4) were → was
(5) it 삭제
05 (1) You can create a scene.
(2) He bought them at the shop.
(3) I took them yesterday.
(4) It can be my friend.
06 (1) She has a son of whom she is very proud. /
She has a son whom she is very proud of.
(2) Do you like the dog which is jumping near the
piano?
(3) This is the hospital which I was born in. /
This is the hospital in which I was born.

07 (1) There are a lot of active seniors who[that] share their knowledge and talents.

(2) What is the title of the film which[that] you saw yesterday?

(3) Emma bought a dress which[that] looked very expensive.

(4) The woman who is wearing nice glasses is talking on the phone.

(5) The computer which Mom bought for me last week is really cool.

08 (1) Adelene saves money to buy a computer that she wants.

(2) I have a friend who helps me a lot.

(3) Sam met a man that he worked with two years ago.

01 (1), (3) 선행사가 사람이므로 주격에는 관계대명사 who나 that을, 목적격에는 who나 whom 또는 that을 써야 한다. (2), (4) 선행사가 사물이므로 관계대명사 which나 that을 써야 한다. (5) 선행사가 '사람+동물'이므로 관계대명사 that을 써야 한다.

02 선행사가 사물이므로 which나 that을 쓴다. 전치사를 관계대명사 앞으로 옮길 수 있으나 관계대명사 that은 전치사 다음에 쓸 수 없다. 목적격 관계대명사는 생략 가능하다.

03 관계대명사를 이용하여 질문을 완성한다. 주격 관계대명사일 경우 선행사가 사람이면 who, 사물이면 which가 쓰이며 선행사에 상관없이 that을 쓸 수도 있다.

04 (1) 선행사가 사물이므로 관계대명사 which나 that (2) 선행사가 사람이므로 관계대명사 who나 that (3) 목적격 관계대명사 whom대신 who를 쓸 수 있지만 주격 관계대명사 who 대신에 whom을 쓸 수 없다. (4) a scarf가 선행사이므로 was가 되어야 한다. (5) 관계대명사가 접속사와 대명사의 역할을 하므로 it을 삭제해야 한다.

05 선행사가 사람이면 관계대명사는 who나 that, 사물이나 동물이면 which나 that을 쓴다. 목적격 관계대명사일 경우 whom[who]이나 that, which나 that을 쓴다.

06 (1) 선행사가 사람이고 목적격이므로 whom을 쓴다. (2) 선행사가 동물이고 주격이므로 which를 쓴다. (3) 선행사가 사물이고 목적격이므로 which를 쓴다.

07 (1) 선행사가 사람이고 주격이므로 who나 that을 써야 한다. (2) 선행사가 사물이고 목적격이므로 which나 that을 써야 한다. (3) 선행사가 사물이고 주격이므로 which나 that을 써야 한다. (4) 관계대명사절의 수식을 받는 선행사가 The woman이므로 단수가 적절하다. (5) 관계대명사는 접속사와 대명사의 역할을 하므로 목적어로 쓴 it을 삭제해야 한다.

08 (1) 원하는 컴퓨터: a computer that she wants (2) 나를 도와주는 친구: a friend who helps me (3) 관계대명사 that은 전치사 다음에 쓸 수 없다.

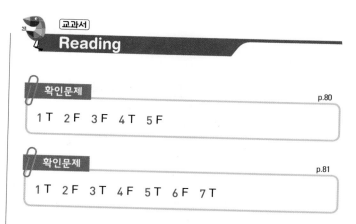

Reading

확인문제   p.80

1 T 2 F 3 F 4 T 5 F

확인문제   p.81

1 T 2 F 3 T 4 F 5 T 6 F 7 T

교과서 확인학습 A   p.82~83

01 What's   02 who, next to
03 who lived there
04 his favorite person, the same as his
05 all his secrets   06 were talking about
07 Poor old lady   08 Why, asked
09 Because she's lost   10 What's
11 something you remember
12 to know more   13 was enjoying
14 he asked   15 Something warm
16 was reading   17 What's a memory
18 brings you laughter   19 cleaning his medal
20 as precious as gold   21 to look for memories
22 went into, from under   23 Next, looked for
24 brought, to   25 Finally
26 as precious as gold   27 one by one
28 all these wonderful things
29 to remember   30 held, whispered to
31 smiled at, performing, for
32 a lot   33 bounced the football
34 My friend   35 one by one
36 each other   37 got, back, with, as hers

교과서 확인학습 B   p.84~85

1 What's a Memory?

2 Wilfrid Gordon Parker was a little boy who lived next to a nursing home.

3 He liked all the people who lived there.

4 But his favorite person was Ms. Nancy Gordon Cooper because her middle name was the same as his.

5 He told her all his secrets.

6 One day. Wilfrid's parents were talking about Ms. Cooper.

7 "Poor old lady," said his mother.

8 "Why is she a poor old lady?" asked Wilfrid.

9 "Because she's lost her memory," said his father.

10 "What's a memory?" asked Wilfrid.

11 "It is something you remember," said his father.

12 Wilfrid wanted to know more, so he went to his neighbors.

13 Ms. Jordan was enjoying the sunlight.

14 "What's a memory?" he asked.

15 "Something warm, my child," she said.

16 Ms. Mitchell was reading a cartoon.

17 "What's a memory?" he asked.

18 "Something that brings you laughter," she said.

19 Mr. Hunter was cleaning his medal.

20 "It's something as precious as gold, young man," he said.

21 So Wilfrid went back home to look for memories for Ms. Cooper.

22 He went into the hen house and took a fresh, warm egg from under a hen.

23 Next, he looked for his sock puppet.

24 It always brought laughter to his parents.

25 Finally, he found his football in his toy box.

26 It was as precious as gold to him.

27 Wilfrid went to Ms. Cooper and gave her the things one by one.

28 "What a strange, sweet child!" thought Ms. Cooper, "He's brought all these wonderful things."

29 Then she started to remember her past.

30 She held the warm egg and whispered to Wilfrid, "Long ago, I found a small blue egg in my aunt's garden."

31 She smiled at the sock puppet and remembered performing a puppet show for her sister.

32 "My sister laughed a lot," said Ms. Cooper.

33 She bounced the football to Wilfrid and remembered him.

34 "Wilfrid? Wilfrid Gordon Parker! My friend!"

35 She also remembered their secrets one by one.

36 The two smiled at each other.

37 Ms. Cooper got her memory back thanks to the little boy with the same middle name as hers.

시험대비 실력평가

p.86~89

01 ①, ④　　02 her middle name was the same as his　　03 his middle name

04 knowing → to know　　05 ②

06 Something that(또는 which) brings you laughter

07 ①, ③　　08 ④　　09 from under a hen

10 ⑤　　11 very　　12 this → these

13 middle　　14 ⓑ she has　ⓒ What is

15 ③　　16 ①, ④　　18 ③

17 Ms. Jordan → Ms. Mitchell

19 thanks to　20 hers　　21 ⑤

22 (A) 따뜻한 달걀　(B) 자신의 양말 인형　(C) 축구공

23 from under a hen　　24 ④　　25 ③

26 a fresh egg, a sock puppet, and his precious football　　27 ⑤

01 선행사가 사람이므로 주격 관계대명사 that이나 who가 적절하다.

02 'Ms. Cooper의 가운데 이름이 자신의 이름과 같기' 때문이었다.

03 '그의 가운데 이름'을 가리킨다.

04 want는 목적어로 to부정사를 쓰는 것이 적절하다.

05 이 글은 '추억이란 무엇인가?'에 관해 Wilfrid가 알아보는 내용이므로, 제목으로는 ②번 '추억이란 무엇인가?'가 적절하다.

06 'that'이나 'which'를 보충하면 된다.

07 ⓐ와 ②, ④, ⑤는 부사적 용법, ① 명사적 용법, ③ 형용사적 용법

08 ⓑ Cooper 할머니께 드릴 기억이라고 해야 하므로 for가 적절하다. ⓒ '그에게는'이라고 해야 하므로 to가 적절하다.

09 암탉이 '품고 있던' 신선하고 따뜻한 달걀을 꺼냈다. from under: ~ 밑에서

10 give는 to를 사용하여 3형식으로 고친다. gave the things 'to' her one by one

11 감탄문을 평서문으로 고칠 때, very를 사용하는 것이 적절하다.

12 뒤에 복수 명사(things)가 나오므로 지시형용사도 복수로 쓰는 것이 적절하다.

13 Wilfrid Gordon Parker와 Ms. Nancy Gordon Cooper는 둘 다 '가운데' 이름이 Gordon으로 서로 같다.

14 ⓑ she's lost는 she has lost의 줄임말이며, '결과' 용법으로 쓰인 현재완료이다.

15 'Wilfrid'가 'Cooper 할머니'에게 자신의 모든 비밀을 말했다.

16 ⓐ와 ②, ③, ⑤번은 현재분사, ①, ④번은 동명사

17 만화책을 읽고 있으면서 기억이란 너에게 웃음을 가져다주는 것이라고 말한 사람은 'Mitchell 할머니'이다.

18 이 글은 기억에 관해 Wilfrid의 이웃들이 정의를 내리는 내용에 관한 글이므로, 주제는 '기억의 의미'가 적절하다.

19 thanks to: ~ 덕분에

20 '그녀의 것'과 같은 가운데 이름이라고 해야 하므로 소유대명사로 쓰는 것이 적절하다.

21 ⑤ 이 글은 Cooper 할머니가 자신의 이름과 같은 가운데 이름을 가진 어린 소년 덕분으로 기억을 다시 찾게 되었다는 내용의 글이다.

22 ⓐ 닭장에서 신선하고 '따뜻한 달걀'을 가져왔다. ⓑ '자신의 양말 인형'이 그의 부모님에게 언제나 웃음을 가져다주었다. ⓒ '축구공'은 그에게 금만큼 소중했다.

23 from under: ~ 밑에서

24 ④ 축구공이 Wilfrid에게 금만큼 소중한 이유는 알 수 없다. ① Wilfrid가 집으로 돌아간 이유는 Cooper 할머니께 드릴 기억들을 찾기 위해서이다. ② Wilfrid가 닭장에 간 이유는 따뜻한 달걀을 꺼내기 위해서이다. ③ Wilfrid의 부모님에게 항상 큰 웃음을 안겨 드리는 것은 Wilfrid의 양말 인형이다. ⑤ Cooper 할머니를 위해 찾은 따뜻한 달걀, 양말 인형, 축구공이다.

25 ③번 다음 문장의 내용은 주어진 문장으로 인해 Wilfrid가 하게 된 행동을 말하는 것이므로 ③번이 적절하다.

26 '신선한 달걀', '양말 인형', 그리고 '그의 소중한 축구공'을 가리킨다.

27 ⑤ 축구공이 왜 Wilfrid에게 소중한지는 대답할 수 없다. ① Yes. get along well with: ~와 잘 지내다, ② Ms. Nancy Gordon Cooper. ③ They say that Ms. Cooper has lost her memory. ④ No.

서술형 시험대비 p.90~91

01 ③ him → his
02 It is something that(또는 which) you remember
03 the same middle name
04 she's lost her memory 05 doesn't have
06 A memory
07 (a) warm egg (b) laughter (c) football
(d) precious 08 (A) home (B) for (C) brought
09 Wilfrid's[his] sock puppet
10 whispered   11 remembered
performing a puppet show for her sister
12 first → middle

01 'his middle name'을 가리키도록 소유대명사로 고치는 것이 적절하다.

02 목적격 관계대명사 'that 또는 which'가 생략되어 있다.

03 Wilfrid는 Cooper 할머니의 가운데 이름이 그의 것과 같았기 때문에 그녀를 가장 좋아했다.

04 '그녀가 기억을 잃었기' 때문이다.

05 has lost: 과거에 잃어버려서 그 결과 지금 가지고 있지 않다

06 '기억'을 가리킨다.

07 ⓐ 그는 달걀이 따뜻하기 때문에 닭장에 가서 신선하고 '따뜻한 달걀'을 가져왔다. ⓑ 그는 자신의 양말 인형이 그의 부모님에게

항상 '웃음'을 안겨 드렸기 때문에 자신의 양말 인형을 찾았다. ⓒ 그는 축구공이 그에게 금만큼 '소중'하기 때문에 자신의 장난감 상자 속에서 '축구공'을 찾았다.

08 (A) home이 부사로 쓰여 '집에[으로]'라는 뜻이므로 전치사 없이 바로 home을 쓰는 것이 적절하다. (B) 기억을 '찾기' 위해라고 해야 하므로 for가 적절하다. look at: ~을 보다, look for: ~을 찾다, (C) 웃음을 '안겨 드렸다'고 해야 하므로 brought가 적절하다. take: ~을 가지고 가다

09 Wilfrid의 부모들은 '그의 양말 인형'을 볼 때 항상 웃으셨다.

10 whisper: 속삭이다, 오직 한 사람만 당신의 말을 들을 수 있도록 하기 위하여 목 대신 숨을 사용하여 아주 조용하게 말하는 것. held와 시제를 일치시켜서 과거시제로 쓰면 된다.

11 'performing'을 보충하면 된다.

12 Cooper 할머니와 Wilfrid는 '가운데' 이름이 같다.

영역별 핵심문제 p.93~97

01 special   02 ⑤   03 ④   04 ③
05 next   06 ②   07 ④   08 ④
09 looked like 10 ⓐ the hot air balloon ⓑ the rock
11 the old lady who lives alone   12 ③
13 ①, ③, ⑤ 14 ③   15 This is the bookmark.
She gave it to me on the last day.
16 (1) Jiwon is wearing the ribbon which[that] Mira bought for her.
(2) Harry chats with the man who[whom, that] he made friends with on line.
(3) Ginseng is a food which[that] can make you stay healthy.
(4) We saw many children who[that] were playing soccer together.
17 ②   18 ①   19 ②   20 ③
21 ①, ③   22 ⑤
23 It's something as precious as gold   24 ②
25 ⑤   26 ③
27 (A) Next (B) What (C) past
28 His football   29 ②   30 ③

01 반의어 관계다. 함께 : 따로 ↔ 일반적인 : 특별한

02 ⓐ는 형용사 thick을 수식하는 '매우'의 의미를 가지는 부사 super가 적절하다. ⓑ는 '있잖아'라는 의미로 흥미롭거나 놀라운 일을 말하기 전에 화제를 전환할 때 사용하는 Guess what이 적절하다.

03 ④ look for는 '~을 찾다'는 뜻이다.

04 연기를 하거나 음악을 연주함으로써 사람을 즐겁게 하는 일을 하다

05 next to: ~ 바로 옆에

06 Nancy의 중간 이름이 Wilfrid의 중간 이름과 같았다. '~와 똑같은'의 의미로 the same as가 적절하다.

07 ④번은 생각할 시간을 요청하는 표현이 아니다.

08 (C) 작년의 노래 경연대회를 기억하는지 여부를 묻고 → (A) 물론이지라는 긍정의 대답과 열심히 연습했다는 내용이 이어지고 → (B) 휴대 전화에 그때 찍은 재미있는 사진이 있다는 내용이 오고 → (D) 마지막으로 '멋지다!'라는 표현으로 대화를 마무리하는 것이 적절하다.

09 두 대화의 빈칸은 '~처럼 보이다'는 look like가 적절하다. 둘 다 과거의 기억에 대한 대화이므로 과거형을 사용한다.

10 it은 앞의 단수명사를 가리키는 인칭대명사로 ⓐ는 열기구를 ⓑ는 바위를 가리킨다.

11 the old lady를 수식하는 주격 관계대명사절을 뒤에 사용한다.

12 ⓒ put A in B 형태로 'A를 B에 넣다'는 의미로 전치사 in은 적절하지만 '닭고기를 잡채에 넣다'는 의미로 japchae를 가리키는 단수 대명사인 it이 적절하다.

13 동사 met의 목적어가 없으므로 목적격 관계대명사가 필요하다. 선행사가 사람이므로 who, whom, that을 쓸 수 있으며 생략할 수도 있다.

14 ③번은 목적격 관계대명사이지만 나머지는 모두 주격 관계대명사이다.

15 선행사가 사물이므로 관계대명사 that으로 연결한 문장이다.

16 (1) bought의 목적어로 쓰인 it을 관계대명사 which나 that으로 (2) with의 목적어로 쓰인 him을 who나 whom, that으로 (3) 주어로 쓰인 It을 which나 that으로 (4) 주어로 쓰인 They를 who나 that으로 연결한다.

17 모두 주격이나 목적격으로 사용된 관계대명사 that이 들어갈 수 있지만 ②번은 소유격 관계대명사 whose가 들어가야 한다.

18 ① 목적격 whom 대신 who를 쓸 수 있지만 who 대신 whom을 쓸 수는 없다.

19 ① I like Christine from whom I got a letter. ③ Dan has two dogs which have brown hair. ④ We saw a rock that looked like a queen's head. ⑤ A computer is a thing that we do many things with.

20 ③ Mom bought me a present that I liked very much.

21 ⓐ와 ①, ③은 명사적 용법, ②와 ⑤는 부사적 용법, ④는 형용사적 용법

22 ⑤는 Hunter 할아버지를 가리키고, 나머지는 다 Wilfrid를 가리킨다.

23 as ~ as 사이에 precious를 쓰면 된다.

24 ⓑ의 his는 '소유대명사'이고, 나머지는 다 '소유격'이다.

25 ⑤번 다음 문장의 It에 주목한다. 주어진 문장의 a memory를 가리키므로 ⑤번이 적절하다.

26 ⓐ와 ③번은 결과 용법, ① 경험 용법, ②와 ④ 계속 용법, ⑤

완료 용법

27 (A) 먼저 닭장에 갔고 '그 다음' 양말 인형을 찾았다고 해야 하므로 Next가 적절하다. to begin with: 우선, 먼저, (B) 명사가 있으므로 감탄문을 만들 때 What이 적절하다. What+a + 형용사+명사! / How+형용사[부사]! (C) '과거'를 기억해내기 시작했다고 해야 하므로 past가 적절하다.

28 '그의 축구공'을 가리킨다.

29 ② the same ... as ~: ~와 (똑)같은 ..., ① usual: 흔히 하는 [있는], 평상시의, 보통의, ⑤ similar: 비슷한

30 ③ 'Cooper 할머니'가 축구공을 바닥에 튀게 해서 'Wilfrid'에게 던져 주었다.

단원별 예상문제
p.98~101

01 special **02** (A) won (B) who[that], next to
03 ④ **04** ③ **05** ⑤ **06** ④
07 ④ **08** ② **09** ① **10** ①
11 ③ **12** ④ **13** ③
14 (1) Jieun is the girl whom[who, that] I like the best.
(2) These are the pictures which[that] were taken by my brother.
15 (A) Something warm (B) you (C) as
16 ②, ⑤ **17** ⑤ **18** ③
19 He found it in his toy box.
20 one by one 또는 one after another
21 How strange and sweet this[the] child is!
22 ①, ⑤ **23** ② **24** ④
25 Ms. Cooper and Wilfrid's

01 유의어 관계이다. 맛있는 = 특별한

02 (A) 메달을 따다는 의미로 동사 win의 과거형 won이 적절하다. (B) 선행사가 사람인 a little boy를 수식하는 관계대명사절을 이끄는 who가 적절하고, '~ 옆에'는 next to가 적절하다.

03 활동적인 노후 생활에 관한 글이므로 (A)에는 그들의 지식과 재능을 나누는(share) 노인들이 많다가 적절하고, (B)는 이전에 과학 선생님이었기 때문에 아이들에게 식물과 새에 관해 가르치기(teach) 위해 공원에서 일한다가 적절하다. (C)에는 농사에 관해 가르치기 때문에 농부(farmer)가 적절하다.

04 물체의 빈 공간, 대개 물체의 표면에 있는 틈[구멍]

05 Ben은 Ms. Park과 함께 사진을 찍자고 Ariel에게 제안하고 있다.

06 주어진 문장은 '어디 보자.'라고 생각할 시간을 요구하는 B의 대답 앞에 오는 것이 적절하다.

07 ④ let은 목적어 뒤에 동사원형을 취하는 동사다.

08 '물론이지. 우리는 재미있는 게임을 했어.'라는 B의 대답으로 보아 ②가 가장 자연스럽다.

09 선생님이 새 학교로 옮기셨다는 말에 ①이 가장 어울리는 대답이다.

10 ⓐ B의 대답으로 보아 Mr. Kim을 기억하는지 묻는 말이 자연스럽다. ⓑ 동사원형 visit과 함께 사용할 수 있는 '~하자'는 제안의 표현으로 Let's가 자연스럽다.

11 ③번만 목적격 관계대명사이고 나머지는 다 주격 관계대명사이다.

12 선행사가 사람과 사물이므로 관계대명사는 that을 써야 한다.

13 선행사가 사람과 사물, 주격과 목적격일 경우에 모두 쓰이는 관계대명사는 that이 적절하다.

14 (1) like의 목적어가 없으므로 목적격 관계대명사를 써야 한다.
   (2) 선행사가 사물이므로 that이나 which를 써야 한다.

15 (A) -thing으로 끝나는 말은 형용사가 뒤에서 수식해야 하므로 Something warm이 적절하다. (B) '간접목적어+직접목적어'의 순서로 쓸 때는 전치사가 필요 없으므로 you가 적절하다. (C) 동등비교는 as ~ as 사이에 형용사의 원급을 써야 하므로 as가 적절하다. 부정문일 때는 not so ~ as도 가능하다.

16 ⓐ와 ②, ⑤번은 관계대명사, ① 지시대명사, ③ 접속사, ④ 지시형용사

17 Hunter 할아버지는 '기억은 금처럼 소중한 것'이라고 말했다.

18 ⓐ와 ③ 마침내, 마지막으로, ① 처음에는, ② 게다가, ④ 그러므로, ⑤ 무엇보다도, 특히

19 그의 장난감 상자 속에서 축구공을 찾았다.

20 one by one 또는 one after another: 하나하나씩[차례차례]

21 What+a+형용사+명사(+주어 + 동사)! How+형용사[부사](+주어+동사)!

22 ①과 ⑤는 ⓒ에 해당하는 물건들을 찾은 장소이다.

23 ②번 다음 문장의 내용은 주어진 문장 끝에서 Cooper 할머니가 Wilfrid를 기억한 다음에 하는 말이므로 ②번이 적절하다.

24 ⓐ smile at: ~을 보고 미소 짓다, ⓒ 가운데 이름이 자신의 것과 같은(자신의 이름과 같은 가운데 이름을 '가진') 어린 소년

25 Cooper 할머니와 Wilfrid가 공동으로 소유한 것을 나타낼 때는 끝에 's를 붙이는 것이 적절하다.

---

01 Do you remember the singing competition
02 threw a part, cooked, delicious, card games / next Saturday, take pictures
03 (A) She's getting married next month.
   (B) What about making a special album?
04 (1) This is a picture which[that] we bought at the market.
   (2) That is the house which[that] Tom was born in.
   또는 That is the house in which Tom was born.

---

   (3) Marilyn is talking with a man who[that] is wearing a thick coat.
05 As Wilfrid wanted to know more, he went to his neighbors.
06 something warm / something that brings you laughter / something as precious as gold
07 meaning   08 to perform → performing
09 Ms. Cooper and Wilfrid
10 thanks to the little boy with the same middle name as hers

01 과거의 일을 기억하는지 물을 때 'Do you remember ~?'를 이용한다.

03 (A) be동사와 일반동사 get을 함께 이용하여 현재진행형을 만든다. 현재진행형이 미래의 일을 나타낼 때 사용될 수 있다. 결혼하다는 표현은 get married이다. (B) what about은 뒤에 동명사(-ing)를 사용한다.

04 (1) 선행사가 사물이고 목적격이므로 which나 that을 이용한다. (2) 관계대명사가 전치사의 목적격일 경우 전치사는 관계사절의 끝이나 관계대명사 앞에 올 수 있다. that은 전치사 다음에 쓸 수 없으며 목적격 관계대명사는 흔히 생략된다. (3) 선행사가 사람이고 주격이므로 who나 that을 이용한다.

05 so를 없애고 As를 맨 앞에 쓰면 된다.

06 Jordan 할머니는 '따뜻한 것'이라고 말했다. Mitchell 할머니는 '너에게 웃음을 가져다주는 것'이라고 말했다. Hunter 할아버지는 '금처럼 소중한 것'이라고 말했다.

07 Wilfrid는 기억에 대해 더 알기를 원했기 때문에 그의 세 명의 이웃에게 기억의 '의미'에 대해 물었다.

08 remember+to부정사: '미래'에 해야 할 일을 기억하다, remember+동명사: '과거'에 했던 일을 기억하다

09 Cooper 할머니와 Wilfrid를 가리킨다.

10 thanks to: ~ 덕분으로, hers: 그녀의 것

|모범답안|

01 (1) A: We rode a hot air balloon in Turkey. Do you remember that?
   B: Of course. It looked like an elephant.
   (2) A: We took pictures of Korean traditional dancers in Korea. Do you remember that?
   B: Sure. We saw them at the town festival.
   (3) A: We saw a rock in Taiwan. Do you remember that?
   B: Of course. It looked like a queen's head.

02 (1) that helps people in need
   (2) that I can be proud of
   (3) that I can look back on with pride
   (4) that can support a lot of people
   (5) that I like

03 (A) that   (B) that[which]   (C) stressed   (D) at

단원별 모의고사
p.105~108

01 ③	02 enter	03 ①
04 the field trip	05 ⑤	06 ③
07 Let's see.	08 ③	09 ④	10 ③
11 ⑤	12 ③	13 ②, ④	14 ①, ⑤
15 ③	16 ②	17 bring → brings
18 ④	19 It always brought his parents laughter.	20 remembering	21 ③
22 ③	23 her middle name	

01 ③번의 super는 'very, extremely'와 같은 뜻으로 '매우'라는 강조의 뜻을 가진다. 'a main meal eaten in the evening'은 supper(저녁식사)를 설명한 것이다.

02 유의어 관계이다. 대답하다 = 들어가다

03 일부 사람들이 이름과 성 사이에 가지고 있는 이름. ②와 ③은 '성'을 의미하고, ④는 '별명', ⑤는 '이름'을 의미한다.

04 it은 단수 명사를 가리키는 대명사이기 때문에 단수 명사인 the field trip을 가리킨다.

05 (A) smile at: ~을 보고 웃다 (B) remember+동명사(-ing): ~한 것을 기억하다

06 빈칸 뒤 G의 말로 보아 선생님을 기억하고 있다는 것을 알 수 있다.

07 상대방에게 생각할 시간을 요청할 때 사용하는 표현으로 Let's see.가 적절하다.

08 '그것 기억나니?'라는 물음은 사람에 대한 기억을 묻는 것이 아니라 어떤 일에 대한 기억을 묻는 것임을 알 수 있다.

10 ③ 긍정의 대답을 하고 나서 기억나지 않는다고 말하는 것은 어색하다.

11 언제 특별 앨범을 만들지는 대화에 언급되어 있지 않다.

12 (A)는 흥미롭거나 놀라운 일을 말하기 전에 '있잖아'의 의미로 사용이 되는 Guess what?이 자연스럽고, (B)는 생각할 시간을 요청하는 표현인 Let me see.가 적절하다.

13 ①, ③, ⑤는 접속사로 쓰인 that이고, ②와 ④는 관계대명사이다.

14 선행사가 사람이고 주격이므로 who나 that을 써야 한다.

15 ③ 선행사가 사람과 사물이므로 관계대명사는 that을 써야 한다.

16 ⓐ와 ②, ④번은 현재분사, 나머지는 다 동명사

17 선행사가 단수 Something이므로 'brings'로 고치는 것이 적절하다.

18 ④ Hunter 할아버지가 왜 메달을 받았는지는 대답할 수 없다. ① Because he wanted to know more about memory. ② Ms. Jordan did. ③ She was reading a cartoon. ⑤ He said that it is something as precious as gold.

19 to를 없애고 '간접목적어+직접목적어'의 순서로 쓰면 된다.

20 start는 목적어로 to부정사와 동명사를 둘 다 취할 수 있다.

21 ③ Wilfrid에게 축구공은 금만큼이나 소중했다.

22 ③ one by one = one after another: 하나하나씩[차례차례], ① 나란히, ② 서로서로, ④ 자주, 매번, ⑤ 점점, 더욱

23 '그녀의 가운데 이름'을 가리킨다.

Little Red Writing Hood

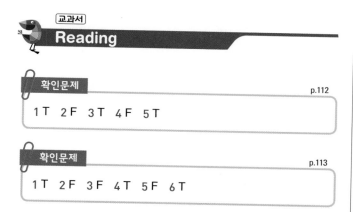

Reading 교과서

확인문제	p.112

1 T 2 F 3 T 4 F 5 T

확인문제	p.113

1 T 2 F 3 F 4 T 5 F 6 T

교과서 확인학습 A
p.114~115

01 Little	02 Scene, In front of
03 comes in with	04 take a break
05 looks into	06 for lunch
07 is shaking	08 to stop, change the story
09 by that	10 Taking, writing
11 shouldn't do	12 come out of
13 Hey there	14 blew my nose
15 Go away	16 so sorry
17 go back into	18 this happened
19 for	20 Where
21 at the end of	22 To himself, for
23 to herself, works	24 Scene
25 happy, excited	26 it's me
27 happily, dance	28 for pleasing
29 that's	30 jumps over
31 dangerous	32 for
33 to	34 By the way
35 Would you like	36 No, thanks
37 Don't worry, What should I do	
38 tired	40 think
41 so glad	42 Who's
43 heard of	44 have
45 changed, got tired	46 change the story
47 you gave to me	48 No problem
49 That'll	50 dancing
51 stop dancing	52 enjoys cookies together

교과서 확인학습 B
p.116~117

1 Little Red Writing Hood

2 Scene 1: In front of the three little piggies' house

3 (Red comes in with a basket of cakes and cookies.)

4 Red: Now I can see the three little piggies' house. I'll take a break here under the tree.

5 (Wolf walks in and looks into the house.)

6 Wolf: Baby piggies! They look delicious. I'll eat them for lunch.

7 (Wolf blows the house hard and it is shaking.)

8 Red: Oh, that bad Wolf! What can I do to stop him? Let me see. … That's it! (To Wolf) Hey, you! I'll change the story!

9 Wolf: What do you mean by that?

10 Red: (Taking out a pen and writing something) "There lived three big strong piggies in the house."

11 Wolf: You shouldn't do that!

12 (Wolf blows again, but the three big strong piggies come out of the house.)

13 Three Piggies: Hey there! Why did you blow our house?

14 Wolf: Um … I didn't. I just blew my nose.

15 Three Piggies: Don't do that again here. Go away!

16 Wolf: Okay. I'm so sorry.

17 (The piggies go back into the house.)

18 Wolf: I can't believe this happened. I'm so hungry! (Looking at Red's basket) What are those?

19 Red: These are cookies for Grandma.

20 Wolf: Where does she live?

21 Red: She lives at the end of this road.

22 Wolf: (To himself) Grandma is good for lunch, too. (To Red) See you later. (Wolf leaves.)

23 Red: Bye. (Talking to herself) Hmm …. He's going to Grandma's. I think I should change the story again. (Taking out the pen and writing something) Okay. If my story works, Grandma will be safe. I'll follow him. (Red leaves.)

24 Scene2: Grandma's house

25 (Wolf dances around Grandma. She looks very happy and excited.)

26 Red: (Knocking on the door) Grandma, it's me. Are you okay?

27 Grandma: (Laughing happily and opening the door) Sure, Red. Come on in. I was watching Wolf dance for me.

28 Red: Hey, Wolf. Thank you for pleasing my grandmother.

29 Wolf: Well, that's ….

30 Prince: (Opening the door and running in) Hey, you bad Wolf! (Prince jumps over Wolf.)

31 Red: No, no! Stop. He's not dangerous.

32 Grandma: Right. Look. He is dancing for us.

33 Prince: Really? Wolf, I'm sorry. I'm glad you're kind to Grandma.

34 Wolf: Well, … I'm glad, too. By the way, do you have anything to eat?

35 Red: (Taking some cookies out the basket) Would you like some cookies?

36 Wolf: No, thanks. I don't eat cookies. I like chicken.

37 Red: Don't worry. I'll change the story again. Then you will like eating cookies. (Checking the basket) Oh, I lost my pen. What should I do?

38 Wolf: (Dancing and crying) Oh, no! I'm so tired and hungry now.

39 (Andersen comes in.)

40 Andersen: I think you need my help, right?

41 Red: Oh, Mr. Andersen. I'm so glad you're here.

42 Grandma: (To Red) Who's that?

43 Red: He is Mr. Andersen, the famous writer. Have you ever heard of "The Red Shoes"?

44 Grandma: Yes, I have. Is he the one who wrote that story?

45 Red: Right. (To Andersen) I changed the story, and the poor Wolf got tired and hungry.

46 Andersen: You can change the story again.

47 Red: I'm sorry, but I lost the pen you gave to me. Please help me.

48 Andersen: No problem. I'll write a happy ending for everyone. Is that okay?

49 Red: That'll be great!

50 Andersen: All right. I'll use my pen here. "The kind Wolf stops dancing. He can enjoy cakes and cookies."

51 Wolf: (Stopping dancing) I can stop dancing! (Eating cookies) And I can eat cookies! Thank you very much.

52 (Everybody laughs and enjoys cookies together.)

🐺 서술형 실전문제
p.118~119

01 (d)angerous
02 Have
03 Let
04 for
05 (1) himself   (2) under   (3) (g)ets / (l)eave
06 (1) need   (2) check   (3) blew   (4) knocked

07 (1) dance (또는 dancing)   (2) since   (3) to write on
   (4) that
08 (1) I like the pen (which/that) you gave (to) me.
   (2) Mary had dinner with Sam who[that] is her best friend.
   (3) Kate read the book which[that] was about global warming.
09 (A) Scene   (B) delicious   (C) hard
10 for   11 What do you mean by that?
12 ⑤ tiring → tired
13 If I change the story again
14 eating 또는 to eat   15 famous writer

01 주어진 단어는 반의어 관계이다. dangerous: 위험한 safe: 안전한

02 Have you ever heard of ~?: ~에 대해 들어 본 적 있니?

03 대화 중에 질문을 받았을 때, 생각할 시간이 필요하면 'Let me think.'나 'Let me see.'를 말할 수 있다 Let me see.: 어디 보자., 글쎄.

04 be good for: ~에 좋다 thank A for B: B에 대해 A에게 감사하다

05 (1) talk to oneself: 혼잣말하다 (2) under: ~ 아래에 (3) get+형용사: ~해지다 leave: 떠나다

06 (1) need: ~을 필요로 하다 (2) check: 점검하다 (3) blow: (입으로) 불다, (바람이) 불다 (4) knock: 두드리다

07 (1) 지각동사의 목적격보어로 동사원형이나 현재분사가 적절하다. (2) 현재완료의 계속적 용법으로 '~ 이래로'를 뜻하는 since가 적절하다. (3) 종이 위에 쓰는 것이므로 전치사 on을 빠뜨리면 안 된다. (4) believe의 목적어 역할을 하는 절을 이끄는 that이 적절하다.

08 (1) 선행사가 사물이고 gave의 목적어 역할을 해야 하므로 관계대명사 which나 that을 써야 한다. 목적격이므로 생략할 수도 있다. (2) 선행사가 사람이고 is의 주어 역할을 해야 하므로 관계대명사 who나 that을 써야 한다. (3) 선행사가 사물이고 was의 주어 역할을 해야 하므로 관계대명사 which나 that을 써야 한다.

09 (A) '장면 1'이라고 해야 하므로 Scene이 적절하다. scene: (영화·연극·책에 나오는) 장면, (연극·오페라의) 장(場), scenery: 경치, 풍경, (B) 감각동사 look의 보어이므로 형용사 delicious가 적절하다. (C) 집을 '세게' 불었다고 해야 하므로 hard가 적절하다. hardly: 거의 ~ 아니다

10 for lunch: 점심으로

11 by: [수단·방법·원인·작용·매개 따위] …에 의해서, …으로

12 너무 '피곤하다'고 해야 하므로 tired로 고치는 것이 적절하다. tiring: 피곤하게 하는

13 '내가 이야기를 다시 바꾸면'이라는 뜻이다. 조건의 부사절이므로 현재시제로 쓰는 것이 적절하다.

14 like는 목적어로 동명사와 to부정사를 둘 다 취할 수 있다.

15 Andersen은 "빨간 구두"를 쓴 '유명한 작가'이다.

01 ③　　　　02 ⑤　　　　03 ⑤
04 What, mean by
05 (1) By　(2) away　(3) to　(4) of　(5) of
06 (1) if　(2) though　(3) that
07 (1) if → though[although]
　(2) opened → open[opening]
　(3) has met → met　(4) will find → find　(5) it 삭제
08 ④, ⑤　　　　09 to eat
10 practice singing 또는 practicing singing
11 (1) Though　(2) calling　(3) open　(4) been
(5) which　　12 ⑤　　　13 ①　　　14 ②, ⑤
15 blow your nose　　16 (A) happened
(B) himself　(C) safe　　17 ③　　　18 ⑤
19 ④　　　20 (A) happy　(B) excited　(C) happily
21 ①, ②　　　22 I'm glad you're kind to Grandma.
23 ④　　　24 chicken → cookies　　　25 ②
26 ②, ⑤　　　27 have　　　28 ③
29 to dance → dancing　　　30 ④
31 Mr. Andersen did.

01 blow one's nose: 코를 풀다
02 leave: 떠나다
03 ① Shake 병을 열기 전에 흔들어라. ② needs 그것은 새로운 배터리를 필요로 한다. ③ please 그녀는 그를 기쁘게 하기 위해 그것을 했다. ④ follow 나는 이번에는 그의 조언을 따를 것이라고 생각한다. ⑤ stop 너는 언제 일을 그만하니?
04 What do you mean by that?: 그게 무슨 말이야?
05 (1) by the way: 그런데, 그건 그렇고 (2) go away: 가 버리다, 사라지다 (3) talk to oneself: 혼잣말하다 (4) get out of: ~에서 나가다 (5) Have you ever heard of ~?: ~에 대해 들어 본 적 있니?
06 (1) 주절은 미래시제이고 종속절은 현재시제이므로 조건의 접속사 if가 적절하다. (2) 앞과 뒤에 나오는 절의 내용이 상반되므로 양보의 접속사 though가 적절하다. (3) 직접목적어를 이끄는 접속사 that이 적절하다.
07 (1) 앞과 뒤에 나오는 절의 내용이 상반되므로 양보의 접속사가 적절하다. (2) 지각동사의 목적격보어로 동사원형이나 현재분사가 적절하다. (3) 현재완료는 then과 같이 과거를 나타내는 부사와 함께 쓰이지 않는다. (4) 조건의 부사절에서는 현재시제로 미래를 나타낸다. (5) 관계대명사가 접속사와 대명사의 역할을 하므로 it을 삭제해야 한다.
08 목적격 관계대명사가 필요하며 선행사가 사물이므로 which나 that이 적절하다.
09 첫 번째 문장에서는 something을 수식하는 to부정사가 필요하고, 두 번째 문장에서는 부사적 용법의 to부정사가 필요하다. 의미상 to eat이 적절하다.(2) Unless는 접속사로 '~하지 않으면'이라는 의미로 사용된다.
10 지각동사 watch의 목적격보어로 동사원형이나 현재분사가 나와야 하고 practice는 동명사를 목적어로 받으므로 singing이 적절하다.
11 (1) 앞과 뒤에 나오는 절의 내용이 상반되므로 양보의 접속사

가 적절하다. (2) 지각동사 watch의 목적격보어로 동사원형이나 현재분사가 나와야 한다. (3) 조건의 부사절에서는 현재시제로 미래를 나타낸다. (4) have been to: ~에 가 본 적이 있다, have gone to: ~에 가고 없다 (5) 선행사가 사물이고 주어가 필요하므로 관계대명사 which가 적절하다.
12 ⑤는 change the story를 가리킨다.
13 ⓐ for lunch: 점심으로, ⓑ by: (수단·방법·원인·작용·매개 따위) …에 의해서(through), …으로(with)
14 ⓑ와 ①, ③, ④는 부사적 용법, ② 명사적 용법, ⑤ 형용사적 용법
15 '코를 푸는 것'을 가리킨다.
16 (A) happen은 자동사라서 수동태로 만들 수 없으므로 happened가 적절하다. (B) '혼잣말로'라고 해야 하므로 himself가 적절하다. (C) 내 이야기가 제대로 돌아가면 할머니는 '안전하실' 거라고 해야 하므로 safe가 적절하다.
17 ⓑ와 ③번은 (계획 등이) 잘되어 가다, (원하는) 효과가 나다[있다], ① (어떤 직장에서) 일하다, ② 직업, 일자리 ④ (예술 등의) 작품, 저작, 저술, ⑤ 일
18 ⑤ 할머니를 잡아먹으려는 늑대의 속셈을 눈치 채고 Red가 이야기를 다시 바꿔야겠다고 했으므로, '뛰는 놈 위에 나는 놈 있다.'가 적절하다. No matter how good you are, there's always someone better.도 같은 뜻을 나타낸다. ① 남의 떡이 더 커 보인다.(이웃집 잔디가 더 푸르다.) ② 불행한 일은 겹치기 마련이다.(비가 왔다 하면 억수로 퍼붓는다.) ③ 호랑이 굴에 가야 호랑이를 잡는다.(모험하지 않으면 얻는 것도 없다.) ④ 시장이 최고의 반찬이다.
19 ④ 늑대는 너무 배가 고파서 Red의 바구니를 보며 그건 뭐냐고 물었을 뿐이다.
20 (A) 감각동사 looks의 보어이므로 형용사 happy가 적절하다. (B) 감정을 나타내는 동사가 사람을 수식할 때는 과거분사를 쓰므로 excited가 적절하다. (C) Laughing을 수식하므로 부사 happily가 적절하다.
21 ⓐ와 ①, ②번은 동명사, 나머지는 다 현재분사이다.
22 'to'를 보충하면 된다.
23 대화에서 화제를 바꿀 때 쓰는 'By the way'가 적절하다. by the way: 그런데, ① 그러므로, ② 마침내, ③ 그 결과, ⑤ 즉, 다시 말해
24 Red가 이야기를 다시 바꾸면 과자를 먹지 않고 닭고기를 좋아하던 늑대가 '과자' 먹는 걸 좋아하게 될 것이라고 하는 것이 적절하다.
25 ② 당황한, ① 지루한, ③ 만족하는, ④ 우울한, ⑤ 흥분한
26 ⓒ와 ②, ⑤번은 경험 용법, ① 결과 용법, ③ 계속 용법, ④ 완료 용법
27 현재완료로 물었기 때문에 have로 대답하는 것이 적절하다.
28 문맥상 역접의 접속사 but이 알맞다.
29 늑대는 '춤추기를' 멈춘다고 해야 하므로 동명사로 고치는 것이 적절하다. stop+~ing: ~하기를 그만두다, stop+to부정사: ~하기 위해 멈추다
30 ④ Red가 Mr. Andersen이 그녀에게 준 펜을 어디에서 잃어버렸는지는 대답할 수 없다. ① He writes stories. ② Red did. ③ Because she lost the pen he gave to her and couldn't change the story again. ⑤ He wrote a happy ending for everyone.

Shapes Around Us

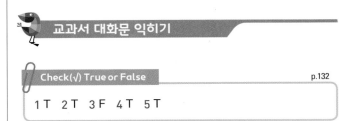

핵심 Check p.130~131

1 ②　　　2 ③　　　3 ④　　　4 ③

시험대비 실력평가 p.128

01 ④　　　02 in charge of　　　03 ⑤
04 took care of　　　05 ②　　　06 ③
07 ④　　　08 ④

01 '이 책꽂이는 혼자 서 있을 수 없어. 이 문제를 어떻게 해결할지 아니?'한

02 Triangle은 옷걸이와 식물들을 담당했다. / 어떤 것 또는 누군가를 책임지는

03 tidy는 형용사로 '단정한, 깔끔한'의 의미다.

04 '~을 돌보다'는 take care of를 사용하고, 돌보았다는 과거시제로 took을 사용한다.

05 마법의 힘을 가진 상상의 생명체

06 당신이 원하는 방식으로 작동하도록 하는 힘을 가지다

07 '세 개의 점으로 어떻게 곡을 그릴 수 있는지 아니?

08 divide A into B: A를 B로 나누다, pick up: ~을 들어 올리다

교과서 대화문 익히기

Check(√) True or False p.132

1 T　2 T　3 F　4 T　5 T

서술형 시험대비 p.129

01 (A) First　(B) Finally
02 (1) There lived, spirits　(2) Take, away, or, roll
(3) try to, tidy　(4) each other　　　03 equal
04 (1) decide　(2) mess　(3) complain　(4) perfect
05 (1) in control　(2) square　(3) pointy

01 물고기를 그리는 순서를 열거하는 표현이다.

02 (1) There lived+주어: ~가 살았다, spirit: 요정, 영혼 (2) take away: ~을 치우다, 명령문 ~, or ...: '~해라, 그렇지 않으면 …할 것이다', roll: 구르다 (3) try to+동사원형: ~하려고 애쓰다. tidy: 단정한, 정돈된 (4) each other: 서로

03 케이크를 똑같은 조각으로 나누는 방법에 대해 이야기하고 있다.

04 (1) 나는 어느 것을 고를지 결정할 수 없어. (2) 아이들이 목욕탕을 엉망으로 만들어 놓았다. (3) 그들은 하고 싶은 일을 할 시간이 없다고 늘 불평한다. (4) 그녀는 완벽한 영어를 말한다.

05 (1) 글의 흐름상 Triangle과 Circle이 나가고 Square가 모든 것을 담당했고(in control) 모든 것을 사각형으로 만들었다가 적절하다. (2) 사람을 다치게 하는 건 '뾰족한' 잎들이므로 형용사 pointy가 적절하다.

교과서 확인학습 p.134~135

Get Ready 2
(1) alone, how to solve / Put, on, bottom
(2) how to divide, into / Let, see, dividing
(3) how to move / Put

Start Off　Listen & Talk A
1 how to make / First
2 how to make / difficult, in half

Start Off　Listen & Talk B
how to divide, into / First, equal, Then, divide, into, Finally

Speak Up Look and talk.
how to draw / First, Then, Finally

Speak Up Mission
how to make / how

Real-life Scene
how to solve / take, at a time / take, to, one by one / without / First, Then / Finally

Express Yourself A
1 how to make / cut off, used
2 how / First, Then, dried, Finally, wrap
3 how to / face, Hold

Learning Diary Check Yourself
to draw / First, Then, Finally / draw, myself

시험대비 기본평가 p.136

01 ③　　　02 ⑤　　　03 how to make it
04 how to divide this cake into four equal pieces

01 '~하는 방법'이란 의미로 '의문사 how+to부정사'를 사용한다.

02 어떤 일을 하는 절차나 방법을 단계적으로 설명할 때 먼저 First 로 시작한다. Finally는 열거할 때 마지막으로 내용을 언급하는 표현이다.

03 '~하는 방법'이란 의미로 'how+to부정사'를 사용한다.

04 '의문사+to부정사'를 이용하고, A를 B로 나눈다는 표현으로 'divide A into B' 구문을 이용하여 문장을 완성한다. 형용사 equal은 명사 pieces를 앞에서 꾸며준다.

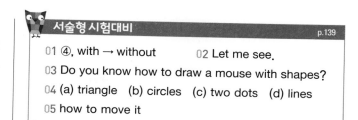

시험대비 실력평가
p.137~138

01 ③	02 (i)n half	03 ④
04 how you should[can] fly this		05 ④
06 ①	07 ②	08 ③	09 ⑤
10 ③	11 shape	12 ①, ④, ⑤

01 대화에서 G가 '연필을 반으로 부러뜨려도 돼?'라고 말하고 있기 때문에 더 많은 삼각형을 만드는 방법을 묻고 있음을 알 수 있다.

02 in half가 '반으로'라는 표현이다.

03 '바람을 마주하면서 이와 같이 들고 있어라'는 G의 대답으로 보아 무언가를 날리는 방법을 묻고 있다는 것을 알 수 있다.

04 '의문사+to부정사'는 '의문사+주어+should[can]+동사원형' 으로 바꾸어 쓸 수 있다.

05 대화의 내용상 '이것을 4개의 같은 조각으로 나누는 방법을 아니?'라고 묻는 것이 가장 적절하다.

06 어떤 일을 하는 절차나 방법을 단계적으로 설명할 때 먼저 First 로 시작한다. 그리고 열거할 때 마지막으로 내용을 언급하는 표현으로 Finally를 사용한다.

07 위 대화에서 A는 동물들을 강 반대편으로 모두 데려갈 수 있는 문제를 푸는 방법을 아는지 묻고 있다.

08 A는 '그 배는 한 번에 너와 셋 중 하나만 옮길 수 있어.'라고 했고, B가 '그건 쉬워.'라고 말한 것으로 보아 하나씩 옮긴다고 말하는 것이 자연스럽다.

09 After that(그 후에)은 '쌀을 가져다 놓고 닭을 데려온 후를 말하므로. 그 다음 개를 데려다 놓고 돌아온다는 내용이 오는 것이 적절하다.

10 ③은 '이것을 어떻게 고치는지 알고 있니?'라는 물음에 '그것은 틀렸어.'라고 말하는 것은 자연스럽지 못하다.

11 '선을 특정 방식으로 결합하거나 바깥쪽 가장자리 주변의 선 또는 선들로 결합하여 형성되는 배열'을 의미하는 '도형(shape)'이 적절하다.

12 도형으로 물고기를 그리는 방법에 대해 단계적으로 설명하는 글이다. 두 번째로 해야 할 일을 말할 때 사용하는 표현으로 Then, Next, Second 등을 사용한다. ③번의 Two는 순서를 나타낼 때 사용하는 표현이 아니다.

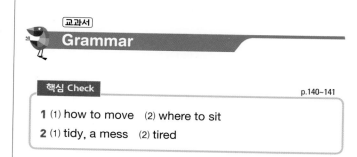

서술형 시험대비
p.139

01 ④, with → without   02 Let me see.

03 Do you know how to draw a mouse with shapes?

04 (a) triangle   (b) circles   (c) two dots   (d) lines

05 how to move it

01 '너와 함께 있으면 개는 닭을 잡아먹고, 닭은 쌀을 먹을 거야.'라는 말은 어색하다. 그래서 with를 without으로 고치면, '하지만 네가 없으면, 개는 닭을 죽일 것이고, 닭은 쌀을 먹을 거야.'라는 뜻이 되어 B가 퍼즐을 푸는 방법을 생각하게 된다.

02 어떤 일에 대해 주의 깊게 생각하고 싶거나 기억하려고 애쓸 때 사용하는 표현

03 일반동사 의문문으로 Do you know로 문장을 시작한다. 그리고 know의 목적어로 'how to+동사원형(draw)'이 오고 마지막으로 draw의 목적어로 a mouse와 부사구 with shapes를 쓴다.

04 그림과 같이 쥐를 그리는 방법은 먼저 큰 삼각형(triangle)을 하나 그리고, 그 다음 두 개의 작은 원(circles)을 그린다. 마지막으로 눈이 되는 두 개의 작은 점(dots)과 수염을 나타내는 6개의 선(lines)을 그린다.

05 '의문사+to부정사'를 이용하여 '어떻게 ~하는지'를 나타낸다. 우리말의 '그것'은 인칭대명사 it을 사용한다.

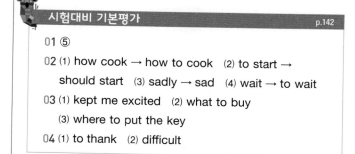

교과서
Grammar

핵심 Check
p.140~141

1 (1) how to move   (2) where to sit

2 (1) tidy, a mess   (2) tired

시험대비 기본평가
p.142

01 ⑤

02 (1) how cook → how to cook   (2) to start → should start   (3) sadly → sad   (4) wait → to wait

03 (1) kept me excited   (2) what to buy
    (3) where to put the key

04 (1) to thank   (2) difficult

01 paper airplanes라는 목적어가 있으므로 how가 적절하다.

02 (1) '의문사+to부정사'가 tell의 직접목적어가 되도록 해야 한다. (2) '의문사+to부정사'는 '의문사+주어+should 동사원형' 과 같다. 두 번째 나오는 I를 생략하고 when to start로 쓸 수도 있다. (3) 목적격 보어로 부사 아닌 형용사가 나와야 한다. (4) ask는 목적격 보어로 to부정사가 나온다.

03 (1) '주어+동사+목적어+목적격 보어'의 형식이 적절하다. (2) '의문사+to부정사'의 어순이 적절하다. (3) '의문사+to부정사'의 어순에서 the key가 put의 목적어이므로 put the key의 어순으로 쓴다.

04 (1) '의문사+to부정사'가 know의 목적어가 되도록 한다. (2) 목적격 보어로 형용사가 나와야 한다.

01 ④　　　　02 I found the book interesting.
03 (1) to start　(2) what　(3) how　(4) healthy
(5) happy　　04 ①　　　05 ②　　　06 ⑤
07 to　　　　08 (1) how you should play
(2) how you can[should] make　(3) what I should do
09 ①　　　10 ②　　　11 ③　　　12 ④, ⑤
13 the book was interesting
14 (1) which dress to buy　(2) made every student
　　nervous
15 (1) going → to go　(2) are → is　(3) what → how
　　(4) should draw → to draw 또는 you should draw
　　(5) smartly → smart　(6) happiness → happy
　　(7) tiring → tired
16 ④　　　17 me sad　　18 Tell me what to buy for
the party tonight. / Tell me what I should buy for the
party tonight.　　　　　　19 ①　　　20 ②

01 ④ 목적어 it이 있으므로 what이 아니라 how 정도가 나와야 한다. leave for the day: 퇴근하다

02 '주어+동사+목적어+목적격 보어'의 형식으로 쓴다.

03 (1) '의문사+to부정사'가 ask의 직접목적어가 되도록 한다. (2) 'why+to부정사'는 쓰지 않는다. (3) the washing machine이 목적어로 나와 있으므로 how가 적절하다. (4), (5) 목적격 보어로 형용사가 나와야 한다.

04 5형식을 만들 수 있는 동사로 형용사를 목적격 보어로 받을 수 있는 동사가 나와야 한다. charge, ask, beg, order 등은 목적격 보어로 to부정사가 나온다.

05 a bookmark가 목적어로 나와 있으므로 how가 적절하며 'why to부정사'는 쓰지 않는다.

06 ⑤번은 4형식 동사로 쓰였고 주어진 문장과 나머지는 5형식 동사로 쓰였다. keep in shape: 건강을 유지하다

07 '의문사+to부정사'가 know의 목적어가 되도록 한다.

08 '의문사+to부정사'는 '의문사+주어+should/can+동사원형'으로 바꾸어 쓸 수 있다.

09 ① make가 사역동사(~시키다)로 쓰인 것이 아니므로 tire를 tired로 바꾸어야 한다.

10 '주어+동사+목적어+목적격 보어'의 형식을 이용하여 나타내며 목적격 보어로 형용사를 쓰는 것에 주의한다.

11 where to put: 어디에 놓아야 할지

12 go는 자동사이므로 목적어가 필요 없으므로 what은 적절하지 않고 'why+to부정사'는 쓰지 않는다.

13 '주어+동사+목적어+목적격 보어'의 5형식 문장을 '주어+동사+목적어'의 3형식 문장으로 바꿀 수 있는 경우이다.

14 (1) '의문형용사+명사+to부정사' 형태로 사용된 경우이다. (2) '주어+동사+목적어+목적격 보어'의 형식을 이용한다.

15 (1) '의문사+to부정사'가 decide의 목적어가 되도록 해야 한다. (2) '의문사+to부정사'가 주어로 쓰이면 단수 취급한다. (3) help의 목적어로 her가 나와 있으므로 how 정도로 바꾸는 것이 적절하다. (4) '의문사+to부정사' 또는 '의문사+주어+should 동사원형'이 적절하다. (5) 형용사가 '~하게'라는 뜻의 부사처럼 해석되더라도 보어 자리에는 형용사를 사용한다는 것에 주의한다. (6) make 동사 다음에 목적격 보어로 명사가 나오면 '목적어를 목적격 보어로 만들다'라는 뜻이 되므로 어색하다. 형용사로 고쳐야 한다. (7) '내가 피곤하게 되는' 것이므로 tiring이 아니라 tired가 적절하다.

16 ④번은 to부정사의 형용사적 용법이지만 나머지는 명사적 용법으로 '의문사+to부정사'로 쓰였다.

17 '영화를 보고 슬펐다'는 것을 make 동사를 이용하여 '주어+동사+목적어+목적격 보어'의 형식으로 쓴다.

18 '의문사+to부정사' = '의문사+주어+should+동사원형', what to buy: 무엇을 사야 할지

19 ① the movie가 우리를 재미있게 해주는 것이므로 interested가 아니라 interesting이 적절하다.

20 ⓑ where to sit, ⓒ what to do, ⓔ keep you warm으로 써야 한다.

01 (1) He showed how to draw a triangle that has three sides of the same length.
(2) When to go there is not decided yet. 또는 When we should go there is not decided yet.
(3) Do you know how to share photos on the Internet?
(4) The bird's song makes him happy.
(5) At first, Sophie thought Nicholas honest.
(6) We found Alita: Battle Angel very interesting.
02 you should(또는 can) solve
03 (1) me full　(2) how to cook
04 (1) Do you know how to grow this flower?
(2) Tell me how many cookies to buy.
(3) They couldn't decide which way to take.
(4) My poor grade made my mom disappointed.
(5) We thought him stupid.
(6) This fan will keep you cool this summer.

05 (1) Do you know how to make triangle gimbap?

   (2) I can't decide what to write about.

   (3) I am not sure where to put the key.

   (4) Tell me which book to read next. 등 어법에 맞게
   쓰면 정답

06 (1) interesting (2) warm (3) kind (4) alone

07 (1) what I should eat

   (2) Which dress she should buy

08 (1) her happy (2) made me excited

01 (1) draw의 목적어로 a triangle이 나와 있으므로 how 정
도로 바꾸는 것이 적절하다. (2) '의문사+to부정사' 또는 '의
문사+주어+should 동사원형'이 적절하다. (3) 'why+to부
정사'는 사용하지 않는다. (4) 형용사 보어가 적절하다. (5) 동
사 thought의 목적격 보어로 형용사가 적절하다. (6) Alita:
Battle Angel이 우리를 재미있게 하는'것이므로 interesting
이 적절하다.

02 '의문사+to부정사' = '의문사+주어+should+동사원형'

03 (1) makes 동사로 '주어+동사+목적어+목적격 보어'의 형식을
이용한다.

   (2) 훌륭한 요리사라는 대답으로 보아 'how to cook
ramyeon(라면을 요리하는 법)'이 적절하다.

04 (1) '의문사+to부정사'가 know의 목적어가 되도록 쓴다. (2)
'의문부사+형용사+명사+to부정사' 형태로 사용되었다. (3) '의
문형용사+명사+to부정사' 형태로 사용되었다. (4) make 동사
를 이용하여 '주어+동사+목적어+목적격 보어'의 형식으로 쓴
다. 엄마가 실망하는 것이므로 disappointed로 써야 한다. (5),
(6) 동사 think와 keep을 이용하여 '주어+동사+목적어+목적
격 보어(형용사)'의 형식으로 쓴다.

05 '의문사+to부정사'는 문장 속에서 주어, 목적어, 보어 역할을 하
는 명사구로 사용되어 '~해야 할지, ~하는 것이 좋을지'라는 뜻
을 나타낸다.

06 목적격 보어로 형용사를 쓰며 부사를 쓰지 않도록 주의해야 한다.

07 '의문사+to부정사'는 '의문사+주어+should/can+동사원형'으
로 바꾸어 쓸 수 있다. 또한 의문사가 의문형용사로 쓰여 to부정
사와의 사이에 명사가 올 수 있다.

08 (1), (2) 소설을 다 읽고 행복을 느꼈고, 소식을 듣고 신나게 됐
으므로 동사 make를 이용하여 행복하게 만들고 신나게 만들었
다고 '주어+동사+목적어+목적격보어'의 형식으로 쓴다.

교과서

Reading

확인문제   p.148

1 T 2 F 3 T 4 F 5 T 6 F

확인문제   p.149

1 T 2 F 3 T 4 F 5 T 6 F

교과서 확인학습 A   p.150~151

01 Spirits   02 There lived
03 controlled   04 was in charge of
05 took care of   06 worked together
07 to make the room better
08 Take, away, pointy   09 waters them
10 Take, away, roll and break
11 exercises with it   12 tidy, make a mess
13 looked at   14 without us
15 all by myself   16 get some rest
17 in control   18 square
19 looked around   20 Much
21 picked up, to hang, on   22 hold my clothes
23 went to water   24 must be
25 picked up, to exercise   26 how to spin
27 to take out   28 have to
29 hurried out of   30 rushed over to
31 what to do
32 all the new square things 33 one another, realized
34 great, the others, once again

교과서 확인학습 B   p.152~153

1 Three Shape Spirits

2 There lived three shape spirits in Mike's room.

3 Square controlled the table, the bookshelf, and
the window.

4 Triangle was in charge of the hangers and the
plants.

5 Circle took care of the round things.

6 They worked together to make a nice room for
Mike.

7 One day Square decided to make the room better
and shouted at the other spirits.

8 "Take these plants away, or their pointy leaves will
hurt someone!" he said to Triangle.

9 "But Mike waters them every day," said Triangle.

10 "Take this hula hoop away, or it will roll and break
something!" he said to Circle.

11 "But Mike exercises with it every day," said Circle.

12 "I try to make this room tidy, but you two always
make a mess," he complained.

13 Triangle and Circle looked at each other.

14 "So you think you can do it without us?" Triangle asked Square.

15 "Sure. I can make this room better all by myself," replied Square.

16 "Great! Then we can get some rest," Circle said to Square.

17 Triangle and Circle went out and Square was now in control.

18 He made the hangers, plants, and all the round things square.

19 Then he looked around and smiled.

20 "Much better!"

21 When Mike came home from school, he picked up a square hanger to hang his jacket on.

22 "What? This will not hold my clothes."

23 He went to water the plants and saw their square leaves.

24 "Poor things. … They must be sick."

25 He picked up the square hula hoop to exercise.

26 "Hmm … I don't know how to spin this."

27 He went to take out his bike and looked at the square wheels.

28 "Well, I can't ride this. I'll just have to walk."

29 Then he hurried out of the house.

30 When the other spirits came back, Square rushed over to them.

31 "Mike doesn't like his room. I don't know what to do," he said.

32 They looked at the hangers, the plants, and all the new square things.

33 Then they looked at one another, and Square realized his problem.

34 "Let's make this room great again," he said to the others, and the three spirits worked together once again.

시험대비 실력평가
p.154~157

01 ③ 02 three shape spirits / Square, Triangle, and Circle 03 ②, ⑤

04 (A) the other (B) tidy (C) without 05 ②, ④

06 ③ 07 He made the hangers, plants, and all the round things square. 08 ②, ⑤ 09 ④

10 I don't know what to do 또는 I don't know what I should do 11 greatly → great 12 ③

13 ② 14 ① 15 Square thought that he could make the room better all by himself without Triangle and Circle. 16 ② 17 ②

18 ③ 19 Triangle and Circle 20 ④

21 I can make this room better all by myself

22 (A) used (B) what (C) happy

23 It made her excited.

01 ⓐ와 ③번은 책임, 담당, be in charge of: ~을 담당하다, ① (상품이나 서비스에 대한) 요금, ② 돌격[공격]하다, ④ 충전하다, ⑤ (요금, 값을) 청구하다

02 '세 도형 요정'을 가리킨다.

03 ① 사공이 많으면 배가 산으로 올라간다(어떤 일에 관여하는 사람이 너무 많으면 일을 망친다는 뜻). ② 백지장도 맞들면 낫다[한 사람이 하는 것보다는 두 사람이 하는 것이 낫다]. ③ 제때의 바늘 한번이 아홉 바느질을 던다(문제를 즉각 처리하면 일이 훨씬 수월해진다). ④ 아무리 안 좋은 상황에서도 한 가지 긍정적인 측면은 있다. ⑤ 백지장도 맞들면 낫다.

04 (A) 세 도형 요정들 중에서 Square가 '나머지' 요정들에게 소리치는 것이므로 the other가 적절하다. another+단수명사, (B) 난 이 방을 '정돈'하려고 애쓴다고 해야 하므로 tidy가 적절하다. tidy: 잘 정돈된, messy: 지저분한, (C) 우리 '없이' 다 할 수 있다고 생각하느냐고 해야 하므로 without이 적절하다.

05 ⓐ와 ①, ③, ⑤는 명사적 용법, ② 형용사적 용법, ④ 부사적 용법

06 'Circle'이 아니라 'Square'가 말했다.

07 square를 목적격보어로 써서, 5형식 문장을 만드는 것이 적절하다.

08 ⓑ와 ②, ⑤번은 '(틀림없이) …일 것이다[…임에 틀림없다]', 나머지는 모두 '…해야 한다(의무)', reception: (호텔 등의) 접수처, 프런트, garage: 차고,

09 사각형 잎사귀들을 가진 식물들이 몇 개 있었는지는 대답할 수 없다. ① Square was. ② He made them in the shape of a square. ③ He went to water the plants. ⑤ As he couldn't ride the bike because of the square wheels.

10 의문사+to부정사 = 의문사+주어+should

11 목적격보어 자리에 부사를 쓸 수 없으므로, 형용사 great으로 고치는 것이 적절하다.

12 위 글은 인격화한 동식물이나 기타 사물을 주인공으로 하여 그들의 행동 속에 풍자와 교훈의 뜻을 나타내는 이야기인 '우화'이다. ① (책·연극·영화 등에 대한) 논평[비평], 감상문, ② (신문·잡지의) 글, 기사, ④ 전설, ⑤ 시

13 ②는 'these plants'를 가리키고, 나머지는 모두 'Triangle and Circle'을 가리킨다.

14 ⓐ shout at: ~에게 소리치다, ⓑ with it: 그것을 가지고, 그 결로

15 Square는 Triangle과 Circle 없이 완전히 혼자서 방을 더 낫게 만들 수 있다고 생각했다.

16 ② 뭘 해야 할지 몰라서 '걱정스러워'하다가 다른 요정들과 다

시 한 번 함께 일하게 되어 '희망에 차고 기대하게' 되었다고 하는 것이 적절하다. worried: 걱정하는, hopeful: 희망에 찬, 기대하는, ① excited: 신이 난, disappointed: 실망한, ③ confident: 확신하는, ④ satisfied: 만족하는, depressed: 우울한, ⑤ upset: 속상한

17 세 요정들 중에서 Square를 제외한 나머지 두 요정을 가리키므로 the others가 적절하다. ① 다른 사람들[것들], ③ 또 하나(의) (셋 이상 중에서 두 번째를 가리킬 때 사용), ④ 몇몇, 몇 개[가지/사람], ⑤ (둘 중의) 다른 하나

18 ③ 방에 새로 사각형이 된 물건들이 몇 개 있는지는 알 수 없다. ① He rushed over to them. ② No, he doesn't. ④ No, he didn't. ⑤ To make the room great again.

19 Triangle과 Circle을 가리킨다.

20 "난 이 방을 정돈하려고 애쓰지만, 너희 둘은 항상 엉망으로 만들어."라고 '불평했다'고 하는 것이 적절하다. ① 칭찬했다, ② 요구했다, ③ 허락했다, ⑤ 방해했다

21 'better'를 보충하면 된다.

22 (A) '낡은' 청바지라고 해야 하므로 used가 적절하다. using: 사용하는, (B) 그걸 들 때 '뭘' 입어야 할지라고 해야 하므로 what이 적절하다. (C) 목적격보어 자리에 부사를 쓸 수 없고 형용사를 써야 하므로 happy가 적절하다.

23 엄마가 '들뜨게 된' 것이므로 excited로 바꾸는 것이 적절하다.

서술형 시험대비　　p.158~159

01 (A) shape　(B) controlled　(C) in
02 He[It] controlled the table, the bookshelf, and the window.
03 for
04 (A) clothes　(B) must　(C) have to
05 자신의 옷을 걸고 있지 못할 것이라고 생각했다. / 불쌍하다고 생각하며, 병든 것이 틀림없다고 생각했다.
06 Square가 훌라후프를 사각형으로 만들었기 때문이다.
07 (1) 옷걸이를 사각형으로 바꾸었다.
　(2) 식물의 잎사귀들을 사각형으로 바꾸었다.
08 I should
09 (1) 사각형 훌라후프를 어떻게 돌리는지 몰라서 운동을 못하게 되었다.
　(2) 자전거의 바퀴가 사각형이 되어서 자전거를 탈 수 없게 되었다.
10 (1) If you don't take this hula hoop away, it will roll and break something!
　(2) Unless you take this hula hoop away, it will roll and break something
11 with → without

01 (A) 명사 뒤에 명사가 나올 경우 앞의 명사는 형용사적 성질을 지니므로 복수형을 만들 수 없고 뒤의 명사에 ~(e)s를 붙

여야 하므로 shape가 적절하다. (B) control–controlled–controlled, (C) in charge of: …를 담당하여

02 Square는 '탁자', '책장', 그리고 '창문'을 담당했다.

03 make는 간접목적어를 직접목적어 뒤로 보낼 때 for를 붙인다.

04 (A) '옷'을 걸고 있지 못할 것이라고 해야 하므로 clothes가 적절하다. cloths: (특정 용도나 어떤 종류의) 천 (조각); 식탁보, 행주, 걸레, clothes: 옷, 의복, (B) 그들은 병든 것이 '틀림없다'고 해야 하므로 must가 적절하다. '추측'을 나타내는 must는 have to로 바꿔 쓸 수 없다. (C) 조동사를 두 개 겹쳐 쓸 수 없으므로 will 다음에 must를 have to로 쓰는 것이 적절하다.

05 Mike가 학교에서 집으로 왔을 때 보인 반응들을 쓰면 된다.

06 Mike는 '사각형 홀라후프'를 집어들고, "흠… 이걸 어떻게 돌리는지 모르겠어."라고 말했다.

08 I don't know how I can spin this.도 가능하다.

09 (1) Mike가 운동을 하기 위해 사각형 홀라후프를 집어 들었지만, "어떻게 돌리는지 모르겠어."라고 했다. (2) 자전거를 꺼내려 가서 사각형 바퀴들을 보고, "난 이걸 탈 수 없어. 그냥 걸어가야 할 것 같아."라고 했다.

10 명령문, or ~= 'If you don't'나 'Unless you'를 앞에 쓰고 or를 생략하면 된다.

11 네가 우리 '없이' 다 할 수 있다고 생각하는 거냐고 하는 것이 적절하므로, with를 without으로 고쳐야 한다.

영역별 핵심문제　　p.161~165

01 finally	02 ⑤	03 ②	04 ②
05 ④	06 ③	07 ④	08 ⑤
09 how to	10 ④	11 ⑤	12 ②
13 ①	14 ⑤	15 ②	

16 which to eat　　17 (1) how　(2) to sit
(3) how　(4) I should　(5) special　(6) found
18 the all round things → all the round things / how to do → what to do

19 ③	20 ②	21 tidy	22 or
23 alone	24 ①	25 ⑤	

26 (A) riding　(B) Square　　27 ④
28 like his room

01 유의어 관계이다. 서두르다 : 마지막으로

02 'how to divide'로 '어떻게 나누는지'를 나타내고, 두 번째 빈칸에는 '~하는 게 어때?'라는 의견을 제안하는 의미로 'How about ~?'을 사용한다.

03 어느 날 Square는 방을 더 낮게 만들기로 결심했고 나머지 요정들에게 소리쳤다. "이 식물들을 치워, 그렇지 않으면 그것들의 끝이 뾰족한 잎사귀들이 누군가를 다치게 할 거야!" 그가 Triangle에게 말했다.

04 '더 작은 부분으로 분리되다'는 의미로 divide(나누다)가 적절

하다. '나는 이 케이크를 네 개의 같은 조각으로 어떻게 나눌 수 있는지 알고 있다.'

05 '전에 알지 못하거나 알아차리지 못한 것을 서서히 이해하기 시작하다'는 의미로 realize가 적절하다

06 ③ by myself는 '혼자서'의 의미다, '저절로'는 of itself를 사용한다.

07 (A)는 첫 번째 그림처럼 3개의 똑같은 사각형으로 나눈다. (B)는 Ben이 '이것을 4개의 똑같은 조각으로 나누는 방법을 아니?'라고 물었기 때문에 나머지 3개의 L 모양을 볼 수 있다는 말이 적절하다.

08 만드는 방법을 열거할 때 'First ~, Then ~, Finally, ~'의 순서로 쓴다.

09 두 대화의 빈칸은 '~하는 방법'을 묻고 있으므로 'how to+동사원형'이 적절하다.

10 'First ~, Then ~, Finally, ~'는 어떤 일을 열거할 때 사용하는 표현이다.

11 B의 대답으로 보아 샌드위치를 만드는 방법을 물어보는 것이 가장 자연스럽다.

12 '종이 비행기를 만드는 방법을 아니?'라는 물음에 어울리는 답은 ②번이다. 나머지 보기는 종이 비행기를 만드는 방법과 무관한 문장이다.

13 첫 문장에서는 형용사를 목적격 보어로 받을 수 있는 동사가 나와야 한다. want, order, ask, force 등은 목적격 보어로 보통 to부정사가 나온다. 두 번째 문장에서는 a square가 divide의 목적어로 나와 있으므로 where나 how가 적절하며 'why+to부정사'는 쓰이지 않는다.

14 ⑤ He wants to know when to begin the project. 또는 He wants to know when he should begin the project. 가 되어야 한다.

15 ① Let's make her happy. ③ The thick clothes keep me warm. ④ Jogging early in the morning makes me healthy. ⑤ Rick painted his house green. ② friendly는 명사 friend에 -ly를 붙여 형용사가 된 단어이다.

16 which to eat: 어느 것을 먹어야 할지

17 (1) the center of the biggest circle in a triangle이 목적어로 나와 있으므로 how가 적절하다. (2) '의문사+to부정사'가 적절하다. (3) why는 '의문사+to부정사'로 쓰이지 않는다. (4) '의문사+to부정사'나 '의문사+주어+should+동사원형'이 적절하다. (5) 목적격 보어로 형용사가 나와야 한다. (6) 목적격 보어로 형용사를 받을 수 있는 동사는 find이다.

18 'all the+형용사+명사'의 어순이 되어야 하며, do의 목적어가 없으므로 how가 아니라 what이 적절하다.

19 ⓐ와 ①, ②, ④는 부사적 용법, ③ 형용사적 용법, ⑤ 명사적 용법

20 ② Square는 탁자, '책장', 그리고 창문을 담당했다.

21 '정돈된 그리고 조직적인 방식으로 배열된', tidy: 깔끔한, 잘 정

돈된

22 명령문 ..., or ~: …해라. 그렇지 않으면 ~할 것이다.

23 by oneself = alone: 혼자

24 ⓐ be in control: ~을 관리[제어]하고 있다, ⓑ 형용사적 용법의 to부정사에 의해 수식을 받는 명사(a square hanger)가 전치사 on의 목적어에 해당한다. hang something on a hanger: 옷걸이에 ~을 걸다

25 ⑤ this는 his bike를 가리킨다. the square wheels는 복수이기 때문에, 'them'으로 받아야 한다.

26 'Square'가 물건들을 사각형으로 만들었기 때문에 Mike는 재킷을 걸기, 훌라후프를 돌리기, 그리고 자전거 '타기'와 같은 일들을 할 수 없었다.

27 ⓐ와 ④번: 시간을 나타내는 접속사(…할 때), 나머지는 다 의문부사(언제)

28 Square가 옷걸이들과 식물들을 사각형으로 만들어서 Mike가 '자신의 방을 좋아하지 않는 것'을 가리킨다.

단원별 예상문제 p.166~169

01 divide 02 (A) First, cut off (B) Finally[Lastly], wrap, up 03 ④ 04 ③
05 The dog will kill the chicken. 06 ④
07 ② 08 ④ 09 ③ 10 ③
11 ④ 12 how to bake 13 ③
14 (1) where I should fish (2) how to get
(3) whom to look (4) which apple I should choose
15 ③, ⑤ 16 Circle did. 17 ⑤
18 ④ 19 ② 20 ①
21 when to put them on 22 ④

---

01 반의어 관계이다. 완전한 : 불완전한 = 결합하다 : 나누다

02 (A) 순서를 나열할 때 '먼저'는 First를 사용한다. cut off: '~을 자르다' (B) 순서의 마지막을 말할 때는 Finally[Lastly]를 사용하고, '~을 싸다'는 말은 wrap up이다.

03 (A) 누군가를 다치게 할 수 있다고 했기 때문에 잎이 뾰족한 pointy가 적절하고, (B) 훌라후프가 굴러가서 무언가를 부순다는 의미로 roll이 적절하다. (C) 너희 둘은 항상 엉망으로 만든다고 말하는 것으로 보아 불평한다는 것을 알 수 있다.

04 '몸의 윗부분을 덮는 짧은 코트'는 재킷이 적절하다.

05 쌀을 가지고 먼저 강을 건너게 되면 개와 닭만 남게 되어 개가 닭을 죽이게 될 것이다.

06 소년이 답을 언제 알고 있었는지는 대화에 언급되어 있지 않다.

07 김 위에 밥을 얹고 싸서 삼각형으로 만드는 것으로 보아 '삼각 김밥'이 적절하다.

08 대화에서 언급된 wrap은 재료인 '포장지'가 아니라 동사로 '싸다'는 뜻으로 사용이 되었다.

09 ③번의 라면을 끓이는 방법을 묻는 말에 대한 답으로 빵을 이용한 샌드위치를 만드는 설명은 적절하지 않다.

10 '~와 마주하다, 직면하다'는 뜻은 face가 적절하다.

11 ④ The boy found the ants very strong. 목적격 보어로 형용사를 쓴다는 것에 유의한다. ⑤ 내 말 오해하지 마.

12 좋아한다는 대답으로 보아 'how to bake cookies'가 적절하다.

13 ③은 4형식으로 쓰였고 주어진 문장과 나머지는 모두 목적어와 목적격 보어가 있는 5형식이다.

14 '의문사+to부정사'는 '의문사+주어+should/can+동사원형'으로 바꿔 쓸 수 있다.

15 ⓐ와 ①, ②, ④: 이야기를 시작할 때 존재를 나타내는 문장에서 뜻이 없이 형식적 주어로 쓰인다. be동사와 주로 쓰이지만, 'come, live, happen' 등과도 쓰인다. ③과 ⑤: 거기에[에서], 그곳에[에서]

16 'Circle'이 둥근 것들을 돌보았다. did는 took care of the round things를 받은 대동사이다.

17 Square는 옷걸이들과 식물들과 모든 둥근 물건들을 '사각형'으로 만들었다.

18 ④는 의문사와 함께 쓰이는 명사적 용법이고, 나머지는 다 부사적 용법(목적)이다.

19 ② 사각형 옷걸이가 자신의 옷을 '걸고 있지 못할' 것이라고 생각했다.

20 ⓐ와 ①번은 [재료를 나타내어] …에서, …으로, ② …의 안에서 밖으로, ③ [원인·동기를 나타내어] …에서, … 때문에, ④ [기원·출처를 나타내어] …에서, …부터, ⑤ …의 범위 밖에, …이 미치지 못하는 곳에

21 대명사 them을 put과 on 사이에 쓰는 것이 적절하다.

22 삼각형 선글라스를 써야 할 때는 알 수 없고, 단지 내 어린 여동생은 언제 그걸 써야 할지 안다고만 되어 있다. ① 글쓴이, ② 종이 박스와 비닐봉지, ③ 글쓴이의 어린 여동생, ⑤ 행복하다.

서술형 실전문제　　　　　p.170~171

01 how to divide this into four equal pieces?

02 First, stand with your back to the wind. Then, hold it up until it catches the wind. Finally, let the line out.

03 (A) Do you know how to divide this cake into four equal pieces?
   (B) How about dividing it this way?

04 (1) Do you know how to make three more triangles with three more pencils?
   (2) Let me know where to grow these flowers.
   (3) Can you tell me when to start?
   (4) The small black circles made it perfect.
   (5) It made me full at lunch time.
   (6) My father believes me honest.

05 or　　　　06 (A) to make　(B) pointy　(C) waters

07 it will roll and break something

08 (1) 훌라후프를 사각형으로 바꾸었다.
   (2) 자전거의 바퀴들을 사각형으로 바꾸었다.

09 hung → couldn't hang / rode → couldn't ride

10 Square가 자전거 바퀴들을 사각형으로 만들었기 때문이다.

01 'how to 동사원형'을 이용하여 문장을 쓴다. 대화의 마지막 B의 말에서 다른 3개의 L 모양을 볼 수 있다고 했으므로 4개의 조각을 만드는 방법을 묻는 말이 적절하다.

02 어떤 일의 절차를 말할 때는 'First …, Then …, Finally, …' 순으로 나열한다. 연을 날리기 위해 먼저 해야 할 일은 바람에 등을 지고 서서, 그 다음 연이 바람을 탈 때까지 잡고 있다가 마지막으로 줄을 놓아 주는 것이 알맞은 순서다.

03 (A) 'how to+동사원형'과 'divide A into B' 구문을 이용하여 문장을 완성한다. (B) '~하는 게 어때?'라는 표현으로 How about 뒤에 동명사(-ing)를 사용하여 문장을 완성한다.

04 (1)~(3) '의문사+to부정사'는 문장 속에서 주어, 목적어, 보어 역할을 하는 명사구로 사용된다. (4)~(6) '주어+동사+목적어+목적격 보어'의 형식을 이용한다. 이때 보어 자리에는 부사가 아니라 형용사를 사용한다는 것에 주의한다.

05 명령문 ~, or … = ~해라, 그렇지 않으면 …

06 (A) decide는 to부정사를 목적어로 취하므로 to make가 적절하다. (B) '끝이 뾰족한' 잎사귀들이라고 해야 하므로 pointy가 적절하다. pointy: 끝이 뾰족한(pointed), pointing: 가리키는, (C) 동사로 쓰였으므로 waters가 적절하다. water: (화초 등에) 물을 주다

07 Circle이 훌라후프를 치우지 않으면 '굴러가서 뭔가를 부술 것이기 때문이다.'

09 Mike가 학교에서 집으로 왔을 때, 그는 옷걸이에 '옷을 걸 수 없었고', 그리고 자전거를 '탈 수 없었다.'

10 Mike는 사각형 자전거 바퀴들을 보고, "음, 난 이걸 탈 수 없어. 그냥 걸어가야 할 것 같아."라고 말했다.

창의사고력 서술형 문제　　　　　p.172

|모범답안|

01 (1) A: Do you know how to share a photo?
   B: Sure. First, press and hold a photo. Then, choose "Share." Finally, choose an SNS.
   (2) A: Do you know how to make potato salad?
   B: Sure. First, boil the potatoes. Then, cut them into pieces. Finally, put some sauce on them.

(3) A: Do you know how to make sandwiches?

B: Sure. First, put an egg on bread. Then, add some vegetables. Finally, put bread on top.

02 (1) Show me how to take care of the cow.

(2) I can't decide what to eat.

(3) Please tell me when to go.

(4) Let's decide where to put it.

(5) Let me know whom to meet.

03 (A) out of　(B) when　(C) excited　(D) happy

단원별 모의고사

p.173~176

01 ③	02 elect	03 ①	04 same
05 ⑤	06 ③	07 how to draw	
08 ②	09 ④	10 ①	11 ③

12 (A) First　(B) into　(C) on　　13 me excited　14 ①, ⑤　15 ⑤　16 ②

17 (1) Do you know how to make triangle sunglasses?

(2) When to finish the works was an important issue.

(3) Tell me whom to meet. 또는 Tell me whom I should meet.

(4) The news made them sad.

(5) We found him honest.

18 Triangle was (in charge of the plants).　19 ②, ⑤

20 ②　　　　　　21 and → or

22 (A) saw　(B) to exercise　(C) how　　23 ③

01 ③번의 excited는 '흥분한'의 뜻으로 feeling relaxed(편안한)는 적절하지 않다. feeling very happy and enthusiastic(매우 행복하고 열광적으로 느끼는)으로 고쳐야 한다.

02 유의어 관계이다. 점 = 고르다, 선택하다

03 '특히 빠르게 계속 돌다'라는 의미로 spin(회전하다)이 적절하다.

04 케이크를 4개의 같은(equal) 조각으로 나누는 법을 묻고 있으므로 B의 대답에는 같은 크기와 모양이 된다는 말이 적절하다. 그래서 same이 와야 한다.

05 (A) in charge of: ~을 담당하여 (B) one another: 서로

06 G가 Let me see.라고 잠깐 생각을 하고 '연필을 반으로 부러뜨려도 돼?'라고 말하는 것으로 보아 답을 찾지 못해 문제가 어렵다는 것을 짐작할 수 있다.

07 B의 대답으로 보아 A는 도형으로 물고기를 그리는 방법을 물어보고 있음을 알 수 있다.

08 at a time: 한 번에, one by one: 하나씩

09 소녀는 개와 쌀과 닭을 함께 배에 태워서 갈 수 없다.

10 이 퍼즐은 4개의 같은 조각으로 나누는 것이다. G의 마지막 말에서 마지막으로, 'L 자 모양의 안쪽 모서리에 있는 3개의 작은

사각형에 색칠해'라고 했기 때문에 ①이 적절하다.

11 ③ '이 퍼즐을 푸는 방법을 아니?'라는 말에 '그것은 언제니?'라고 답하는 것은 어색하다.

12 순서를 열거할 때 (A)에는 First가 적절하다. (B) cut A into B: A를 B로 자르다 (C) put A on B: A를 B에 얹다[놓다]

13 makes 동사로 '주어+동사+목적어+목적격 보어'의 형식을 이용한다. 내가 신이 나게 되는 것이므로 excited로 써야 함에 주의한다.

14 it이라는 목적어가 있으므로 what은 적절하지 않으며 'why+to부정사'는 사용하지 않는다.

15 '동사+목적어+목적격 보어(형용사)'로 쓸 수 있는 동사는 keep이다

16 ② I taught him how he could read English. 또는 I taught him how to read English.

17 (1) '의문사+to부정사'가 적절하며 triangle sunglasses라는 목적어가 있으므로 what은 어울리지 않는다. (2) '의문사+to부정사'가 주어로 쓰이면 단수 취급한다. (3) '의문사+to부정사'나 '의문사+주어+should+동사원형'이 적절하다. (4) 목적격 보어로 형용사가 나와야 한다. (5) 목적어로 목적격 him이 적절하며 목적격 보어로 형용사가 나와야 한다.

18 'Triangle'이 식물들을 담당했다.

19 ⓐ와 ②, ⑤: ~을 돌보다, ① take after: ~을 닮다, ③ look like: ~처럼 보이다, ④ call for: ~을 요구하다

20 ② it은 hula hoop를 가리키고, 나머지는 다 Square를 가리킨다.

21 "이 홀라후프를 치워, 그렇지 않으면 굴러가서 뭔가를 부술 거야!"라고 해야 하므로 or로 고치는 것이 적절하다. 명령문, or ~= ~해라, 그렇지 않으면 / 명령문, and ~= ~해라, 그러면

22 (A) '사각형 잎사귀들을 보았다'고 해야 하므로 went와 병렬 구문을 이루도록 saw라고 하는 것이 적절하다. (B) '운동을 하기 위해' 사각형 홀라후프를 집어 들었다고 해야 하므로 to exercise가 적절하다. (C) 이걸 '어떻게' 돌리는지 모르겠다고 해야 하므로 how가 적절하다.

23 ③ 만족스러워[흡족해] 하는, Square는 물건들을 사각형으로 만든 다음 주위를 둘러보고 미소 지으며 "훨씬 좋군!"이라고 말했다. ① 지루한, ② 실망한, ④ 부끄러운, ⑤ 긴장한, 초조한

30　정답 및 해설

교과서 파헤치기

Lesson 3

1 painter, 화가　2 dangerous, 위험한
3 active, 활동적인, 활발한　4 beach, 해변, 바닷가
5 ride, 타다　6 chat, 담소[이야기]하다　7 princess, 공주
8 street, 길, 도로　9 teenage, 십대의　10 clothes, 옷, 의복
11 rock, 바위, 암석　12 helmet, 헬멧
13 advice, 조언, 충고　14 climb, 오르다, 올라가다
15 push, 밀다　16 mirror, 거울

단어 TEST Step 1
p.02

01 혼자	02 (이빨로) 물다, 베어 물다
03 조심하는, 주의 깊은	04 위험한
05 방향, (주로 복수로) 지시	06 옷, 의복
07 ~에 있다, 존재하다	08 과거, 지난날

09 먼, 멀리　10 인물, 모습　11 등반가
12 실제로, 정말로　13 다음에 나오는, 그 다음의
14 재미; 재미있는　15 안전, 안전성　16 진짜의, 현실적인
17 특별한, 특수한　18 기억하다　19 오르다, 올라가다
20 경치, 풍경　21 조화, 화합　22 ~ 뒤에, 뒤에
23 언젠가, 훗날　24 함께하다, 가입하다
25 종류　26 창조하다, 만들다 27 균형, 평형
28 나중에, 후에　29 아마　30 규칙
31 찾다, 수색하다　32 만지다, 건드리다 33 기술, 기량
34 아직　35 전화를 끊다

| 36 ~을 명심하다, ~을 잊지 않다 | 37 저쪽에, 저기에서 |
| 38 떠들다, 소란 피우다 | 39 ~에 좋다 |

40 ~에 대해 듣다　41 처음으로
42 예를 들면, 예를 들어　43 오르다

단어 TEST Step 2
p.03

01 active	02 sign	03 festival
04 figure	05 push	06 place
07 grass	08 practice	09 advice
10 close	11 safe	12 pose
13 information	14 street	15 rock
16 teenage	17 princess	18 loose
19 mirror	20 helmet	21 museum
22 chat	23 past	24 trick
25 without	26 beach	27 scenery
28 balance	29 harmony	30 clothes
31 careful	32 dangerous	33 safety
34 special	35 for example	
36 for the first time		37 keep ~ in mind
38 be good for	39 in front of	40 hang up
41 make noise	42 hear of	43 over there

대화문 TEST Step 1
p.05~06

Get Ready - 2

1 at, great / riding, know about / What / special, for riding on

2 Don't, into, yet / Why not / shouldn't, without, Put, on

3 Look at, over there, like to take, in front of / shouldn't, over / okay

4 want to watch, in / shouldn't go up, birds / right

Start Off - Listen & Talk A

1 have, ever heard of, climber / seen, on TV / teaching rock climbing, camp, want to join / but, shouldn't climb up / right

2 Have, heard / No, I haven't / favorite, concert, Can I go / shouldn't come home / right

Start Off - Listen & Talk B

Have, heard of / tried, when / doing, for the first time / should bring, something to eat / should, keep in mind / shouldn't make, when / keep that in mind

Step Up - Real-life Scene

It's, Can, see me / hi, up / isn't it, chat, Have, heard of / Yes, I have, want / Guess what, going to go up / great / hang up, scenery / Be, shouldn't use, while you're walking / right. Thank, send, later

Express Yourself A

1 Have you heard of, No, I haven't. Who / famous American singer, actor, figure / Sounds, take pictures / Let's go.

2 shouldn't take, painting, behind / Don't worry, real. So, in front of / Can, selfies, not

대화문 TEST Step 2
p.07~08

Get Ready - 2

1 G: Look at that boy. He's great.
   B: He's riding an MTB. Do you know about it?

G: No. What is it?

B: It's a special bike for riding on a mountain.

2 G: Wait. Don't jump into the water yet.

B: Why not?

G: You shouldn't swim without a life jacket. Put it on.

3 G: Look at the beautiful flowers over there! I'd like to take a selfie in front of them.

B: You shouldn't go over there.

G: Oh, okay.

4 B: I want to watch the birds in the trees.

G: You shouldn't go up too close to the birds.

B: All right, thanks.

Start Off - Listen & Talk A

1 G: Dad, have you ever heard of Kim Soyun, the rock climber?

M: Yes, I've seen her on TV.

G: She's teaching rock climbing at a camp this Saturday. I want to join the camp.

M: Okay, Miso, but you shouldn't climb up too high.

G: All right. Thanks, Dad.

2 G: Have you heard of Rock Boys?

M: No, I haven't.

G: It's my favorite band. There's a concert this Saturday. Can I go?

M: Okay, Minju, but you shouldn't come home too late.

G: All right. Thanks, Dad.

Start Off - Listen & Talk B

B: Have you heard of bird watching?

M: Sure. I tried it when I was a child.

B: That's nice. Actually, I'm doing it for the first time this Saturday.

M: Are you? You should bring warm clothes and something to eat.

B: Okay. What else should I keep in mind?

M: You shouldn't make any noise when you watch the birds.

B: I'll keep that in mind. Thanks, Dad.

Step Up - Real-life Scene

A: Hello, Somin! It's me! Can you see me?

B: Oh, hi, Minjun! What's up?

A: This is so cool, isn't it? We can video chat on the phone! Have you heard of Jeju Olle?

B: Yes, I have. I really want to go there someday.

A: Guess what? I'm on it now. Actually, I'm going to go up Seongsan Ilchulbong now.

B: That's great!

A: Don't hang up. Enjoy the beautiful scenery with me.

B: Be careful! You shouldn't use your cell phone while you're walking.

A: Oh, right. Thank you. I'll send you photos later.

Express Yourself A

1 G: Have you heard of Elvis Presley?

B: No, I haven't. Who is he?

G: He was a famous American singer and actor. We can see a figure of Elvis here.

B: Sounds interesting. I want to take pictures with it.

G: Okay. Let's go.

2 W: You shouldn't take selfies here. Van Gogh's painting is behind you.

B: Don't worry, Mom. It's not his real painting. So I can take selfies in front of it.

W: Really? Sounds interesting. Can I take selfies here, too?

B: Why not?

본문 TEST Step 1   p.09~10

01 Have, ever heard

02 When, take, yourself

03 have, for, about

04 Here, presentations, selfies   05 people, take

06 Though, at, answer   07 Look at, of

08 used, take, herself   09 loos nervous

10 guess why   11 think, first

12 probably, teenage, ever   13 take, at, like

14 take, poses, tricks

15 also, special, fun

16 example, is, famous   17 spots, take

18 touch, even step   19 at, following

20 Though, riding, like

21 holding, brush, painting   22 exist, too

23 visited, before 24 don't, yourself 25 look, but were

26 don't, so   27 look safe

28 should, care, selfies, places

29 bite, time, could   30 are, safety

31 Don't, while, walking

32 Do, pose, near

33 Never, in, places

34 use, make, better

35 can, things, take

36 post, on, website

37 watered, plants, for   38 also, at, times

39 Look at, those 40 about joining, create

01 Have, ever heard, of

02 take, of yourself

03 club, searched for information, for

04 Here, their presentations

05 people, take selfies

06 Though, wasn't, answer   07 Look at

08 used, to take, herself   09 loos nervous

10 Can, guess why

11 think, her first selfie

12 probably, teenage

13 can take selfies, like

14 To take, pictures, poses, use camera tricks

15 also, fun   16 example, famous

17 has special spots, take

18 touch, even step

19 Look at, following

20 Though, riding, looks like

21 just holding, brush, looks like, painting

22 exist, too   23 have visited, before

24 Why don't, yourself   25 look, but

26 don't think so 27 don't look safe

28 should take special care, places like

29 could bite, at any time, could fall

30 Here are, safety tips

31 take, while you're walking

32 not pose, wild 33 Never take selfies, places

34 use, better   35 things, take

36 can post, website

37 watered, school

38 also helped, at many times   39 Look at, those

40 How about, create

1 여러분은 "셀피"에 대해 들어 본 적이 있나요? 여러분 자신의 사진을 찍을 때 그것이 셀피에요.

2 민지의 사진 동아리 학생들은 한 달 동안 셀피에 대한 정보를 찾았습니다.

3 여기 셀피에 대한 그들의 발표 내용이 있습니다.

4 과거의 사람들은 셀피를 찍었나요?

5 그 때는 셀피를 찍는 것이 쉽지는 않았지만. 답은 '그렇다' 입니다.

6 아나스타샤 공주의 이 사진을 보세요. 그녀는 거울을 사용하여 자신의 사진을 찍었습니다.

7 그녀는 긴장되어 보입니다. 왜인지 추측할 수 있나요?

8 글쎄, 나는 그것이 그녀의 첫 번째 셀피였다고 생각해요.

9 그리고 그것은 아마도 세계 최초의 10대 소녀의 셀피였을 거예요.

10 여러분은 빅벤과 피사의 사탑과 같은 세계적으로 유명한 장소에서 셀카를 찍을 수 있습니다.

11 멋진 사진을 찍기 위해서, 단지 재미있는 포즈를 취하고 카메라 기술을 이용하세요.

12 여러분은 또한 재미있는 셀피를 찍기 위해 특별한 박물관을 방문할 수 있습니다.

13 예를 들어, 필리핀에는 유명한 셀프 박물관이 있습니다.

14 그곳은 셀피를 찍기 위한 특별한 장소들이 있습니다.

15 여러분은 그림들을 만질 수 있고 심지어 그림들 안으로 들어갈 수도 있어요.

16 다음 사진들을 보세요.

17 비록 그 소년들은 말을 타고 있는 것은 아니지만, 말을 타고 있는 것처럼 보입니다.

18 비록 그 남자는 단지 커다란 붓을 잡고 있지만, 모나리자를 그리고 있는 것처럼 보입니다.

19 한국에도 셀피 박물관이 있습니다. 나는 전에 춘천에 있는 한 박물관을 방문한 적이 있습니다.

20 여러분도 직접 그곳에 가는 게 어때요? 이 셀피들은 멋져 보이지만,그것들은 좋은 생각이었나요?

21 난 그렇게 생각하지 않아요. 그것들은 안전해 보이지 않습니다.

22 여러분은 야생이나 이와 같이 높은 곳에서 셀피를 찍을 때 특별한 주의를 기울여야 합니다.

23 원숭이가 언제든지 당신을 물거나 또는 당신은 떨어질 수 있습니다.

24 여기 몇 가지 안전 수칙이 있습니다.

25 걸으면서 셀피를 찍지 마세요.

26 야생 동물들과 함께 또는 가까이에서 포즈를 취하지 마세요.

27 위험한 곳에서는 절대 셀피를 찍지 마세요.

28 나는 우리가 더 나은 학교생활을 만들기 위해 셀피를 이용할 수 있다고 생각해요.

29 우리는 학교에서 좋은 일을 할 수 있고 셀피를 찍을 수도 있어요.

30 그리고 나서 우리는 학교 웹사이트에 사진을 올릴 수 있어요.

31 나는 한 달 동안 학교에서 식물과 꽃에 물을 주었습니다.

32 나는 또한 학교 도서관에서 선생님을 여러 번 도왔습니다.

33 그런 것들에 대한 내 셀피를 보세요.

34 저와 함께 더 나은 학교생활을 만들어 보는 건 어떨까요?

1 Have you ever heard of a "selfie"? When you take a photograph of yourself, it's a selfie.

2 The students from Minji's photo club have searched for information about selfies for one month.

3 Here are some of their presentations about selfies.

4 Did people in the past take selfies?

5 Though it wasn't easy at that time, the answer is yes.

6 Look at this photo of Princess Anastasia. She used a mirror to take a picture of herself.

7 She looks nervous. Can you guess why?

8 Well, I think it was her first selfie.

9 And it was probably the world's first teenage selfie ever.

10 You can take selfies at world-famous places like Big Ben and the Leaning Tower of Pisa.

11 To take great pictures, just do fun poses and use camera tricks.

12 You can also visit special museums to take fun selfies.

13 For example, there is a famous selfie museum in the Philippines.

14 It has special spots to take selfies.

15 You can touch the paintings and even step inside them.

16 Look at the following pictures.

17 Though the boys are not really riding horses, it looks like they are.

18 Though the man is just holding a big brush, it looks like he is painting the Mona Lisa.

19 Selfie museums exist in Korea, too. I have visited one in Chuncheon before.

20 Why don't you go there yourself? These selfies look great, but were they a good idea?

21 I don't think so. They don't look safe.

22 You should take special care when you take selfies in the wild or at high places like these.

23 A monkey could bite you at any time, or you could fall.

24 Here are some safety tips:

25 Don't take selfies while you're walking.

26 Do not pose with or near wild animals.

27 Never take selfies in dangerous places.

28 I think we can use selfies to make a better school life.

29 We can do good things at school and take selfies.

30 Then we can post the photos on our school website.

31 I've watered the plants and flowers at school for one month.

32 I've also helped the teacher at the school library many times.

33 Look at my selfies of those things.

34 How about joining me to create a better school life?

Express Yourself-C

1. Have, heard
2. have, seen been to, in front of
3. took, museum

Project-Step 2

1. Safety Rules
2. Have, heard of
3. Though, be safe
4. shouldn't take
5. follow, directions

Link to the World

1. Riding
2. Riding, is, exciting
3. lots of skills
4. turn, freely, even jump
5. Though, easy, exciting
6. can start with
7. When, standing, balancing
8. be careful, should wear
9. shouldn't go, when, riding

Express Yourself-C

1. Have you heard of the pyramids in Egypt?
2. Though I have never seen been to Egypt before, I'm standing in front of a pyramid in this picture.
3. I took it at the selfie museum.

Project-Step 2

1. Fire Safety Rules

2. Have you heard of fire safety rules?

3. Though there's a fire, you can be safe.

4. You shouldn't take the elevator.

5. You should follow the teacher's directions.

Link to the World

1. BMX Bike Riding

2. Riding a BMX bike is very exciting.

3. You can try lots of skills.

4. You can turn the bike freely and even jump with the bike.

5. Though it's not easy, it's very exciting.

6. You can start with standing skills.

7. When you try standing skills, balancing is very important.

8. But be careful. You should wear a helmet and gloves.

9. Also, you shouldn't go too fast when you're riding.

단어 TEST Step 1 · p.21

01 기억하다	02 연습하다	03 학년, 성적
04 매우; 굉장히 좋은	05 옮기다, 이사[이동]하다	
06 2월	07 특별한	08 현장 학습
09 우스운, 웃기는, 재미있는		10 요리하다
11 멀리	12 맛있는	13 기억, 추억
14 메달	15 양로원	16 비밀
17 잃다	18 햇빛	
19 가져다 주다, 가지고 오다		20 웃음
21 암탉	22 속삭이다	23 숙모, 이모
24 ~을 튀기다	25 머리핀	26 전통적인, 전통의
27 두꺼운	28 대회, 시합, 경쟁	29 이웃 (사람)
30 공연하다	31 혼자, 홀로	32 꼭두각시, 인형
33 함께, 같이	34 귀중한	
35 B 때문에 A에게 감사하다		36 ~하는 게 어때?
37 ~와 똑같은, 동종의, 동일한		38 ~으로 들어가다
39 하나씩, 차례차례	40 ~한 것을 기억하다	
41 구멍을 내다	42 ~ 덕분에	43 ~처럼 보이다

단어 TEST Step 2 · p.22

01 together	02 board	03 again
04 wear	05 thick	06 school nurse
07 album	08 fun	09 competition
10 fly	11 alone	12 round
13 puppet	14 science	15 favorite
16 person	17 neighbor	18 cartoon
19 clean	20 precious	21 fresh
22 ago	23 perform	24 tear
25 hairpin	26 grade	27 whisper
28 memory	29 sunlight	30 bounce
31 laughter	32 delicious	33 practice
34 special	35 remember+-ing	
36 look like+명사	37 go into	38 thanks to
39 the same as ~	40 get married	41 thank A for B
42 one by one	43 smile at	

단어 TEST Step 3 · p.23

1 whisper, 속삭이다   2 favorite, 가장 좋아하는

3 tear, 눈물   4 special, 특별한   5 hairpin, 머리핀

6 laughter, 웃음   7 neighbor, 이웃   8 hen, 암탉

9 bounce, 튀기다   10 memory, 기억   11 grade, 학년
12 secret, 비밀   13 hole, 구멍   14 precious, 귀중한
15 perform, 공연하다   16 puppet, 인형, 꼭두각시

대화문 TEST **Step 1**   p.24~25

Get Ready

1 How, watched, last weekend, Do, remember / had, with

2 learned to cut holes, last time, Let's practice / Let's see / remember everything

3 This is, remember me / for calling

Start Off Listen & Talk A

1 remember, our 6th grade / Of course, wore, thick glasses / Guess, moved to, this year / didn't know, Let's visit / Good idea

2 Do, remember / Who, she / our 4th grade / remember, taught a lot of / good dancer, too

Start Off Listen & Talk B

remember, school nurse / nice to everyone / Guess what, getting married / shall, do / Let me see, about making / good idea

Speak Up Look and talk.

last year / Of course / funny pictures, on / great

Speak Up Mission

remember my birthday / Let me see, June / right, not right, June 13

Real-life Scene

who lives alone / Of course, threw, last year / cooked, put, in / delicious, played, together, remember that / won, rounds, good at / are, going to / Let me see / Let's take, this time / Great idea

Express Yourself

1 Do you remember, rode / looked like

2 one in Taiwan / remember, looked like

Learning Diary Check Yourself

singing competition / Of course, practiced, hard / funny pictures, on / great

대화문 TEST **Step 2**   p.26~27

Get Ready

1 G: How are you, Ms. Hwang? We watched TV together last weekend. Do you remember that?

W: Sure, Jieun. I had a great time with you.

2 M: Hi, Minjun. So, you learned to cut holes in the board last time. Let's practice again now.

B: Okay. Let's see. Is this right?

M: Yes. You remember everything.

3 G: Hello, Mr. Yang. This is Minji. Do you remember me?

M: Sure, Minji. Thank you for calling.

Start Off Listen & Talk A

1 G: Do you remember Mr. Kim, our 6th grade teacher?

B: Of course. He wore super thick glasses.

G: Guess what? He moved to a new school in February this year.

B: I didn't know that. Let's visit him together.

G: Okay. Good idea.

2 B: Do you remember Ms. Lee?

G: Ms. Lee? Who is she?

B: She was our 4th grade English teacher.

G: Now I remember. She taught a lot of pop songs in her class.

B: She was a good dancer, too.

Start Off Listen & Talk B

B: Do you remember Ms. Kang, the school nurse?

G: Sure. She was nice to everyone.

B: Guess what? She's getting married next month.

G: Wow! What shall we do for her?

B: Let me see. What about making a special album?

G: That's a good idea.

Speak Up Look and talk.

A: Do you remember the field trip last year?

B: Of course. We played fun games.

A: I have some funny pictures from it on my phone.

B: That's great!

Speak Up Mission

A: Do you remember my birthday?

B: Let me see. It's June 3. Right?

A: That's right. / That's not right. It's June 13.

Real-life Scene

G: Do you remember Ms. Park, the old lady who lives alone?

B: Of course. We threw her a birthday party last year.

G: And she cooked japchae for us. She put some chicken in it.

B: Right. It was delicious. And we played card games together. Do you remember that?

G: Yes. She won all the rounds. She's really good at games.

B: When are we going to see her next, Mina?

G: Let me see. Next Saturday.

B: Let's take some pictures with her this time.

G: Great idea, Junsu.

Express Yourself

1 G: Do you remember the hot air balloon? We rode it in Turkey.

M: Of course. It looked like an elephant.

2 G: Do you remember the rock?

M: Is it the one in Taiwan?

G: Right.

M: I remember it. It looked like a queen's head.

Learning Diary Check Yourself

B: Do you remember the sing'ing competition last year?

G: Of course. We practiced super hard.

B: I have some funny pictures from it on my phone.

G: That's great!

본문 TEST Step 1   p.28~29

01 What's, Memory   02 little, who, next

03 all, who, there 04 favorite, same, his

05 her all, secrets

06 One, talking about   07 Poor, lady, his

08 Why, old, asked

09 Because, lost, memory   10 What's, asked

11 something, remember

12 more, so, neighbors

13 enjoying, sunlight

14 memory, asked

15 Something warm, child

16 reading, cartoon   17 memory, asked

18 Something, brings, laughter

19 was cleaning, medal

20 something, precious as

21 went back, look for

22 went into, took, from

23 Next, looked for

24 always brought, to

25 Finally, found, in

26 as precious, gold   27 went, gave, by

28 What, brought, things

29 to remember, past

30 held, whispered to, ago

31 at, remembered performing, for 32 laughed a lot

33 bounced, to, remembered   34 My friend

35 also remembered, one

36 at each other 37 got, back, with, as

본문 TEST Step 2   p.30~31

01 What's   02 a little boy, lived next to

03 all, who lived

04 favorite person, because, the same as his

05 told her, secrets   06 talking about

07 Poor old lady, said

08 Why, poor, asked

09 Because, lost, said

10 memory, asked

11 something you remember

12 wanted to, went   13 was enjoying

14 he asked   15 Something warm

16 was reading   17 What's a memory

18 brings you laughter   19 was cleaning

20 as precious as

21 went back, to look for

22 went into, from under a hen   23 looked for

24 always brought laughter   25 found, in

26 as, as gold   27 went to, one by one

28 What, thought, brought

29 started to remember

30 held, whispered, found

31 smiled at, remembered performing

32 laughed a lot 33 bounced, to   34 My friend

35 remembered, secrets

36 at each other 37 thanks to, the same, as

본문 TEST Step 3   p.32~33

1 추억이란 무엇일까?

2 Wilfrid Gordon Parker는 요양원 옆에 사는 어린 소년이었다.

3 그는 그곳에 사는 모든 사람들을 좋아했다.

4 하지만 그가 가장 좋아하는 사람은 Nancy Gordon Cooper 할머니였는데, 그 이유는 그녀의 가운데 이름이 그의 것과 같았기 때문이었다.

5 그는 자기의 모든 비밀을 그녀에게 말했다.

6 어느 날, Wilfrid의 부모님은 Cooper 할머니에 관해 이야기를 하고 있었다.

7 "불쌍한 분." 그의 어머니가 말했다.

8 "왜 불쌍한 분이세요?"라고 Wilfrid가 물었다.

9 "왜냐하면 그분은 기억을 잃으셨거든." 그의 아버지가 말했다.

10 "기억이 뭐예요?" Wilfrid가 물었다.

11 "그것은 네가 기억하는 것이란다."라고 그의 아버지가 말했다.

12 Wilfrid는 더 알고 싶어서, 그의 이웃들에게 갔다.

13 Jordan 할머니는 햇볕을 즐기고 있었다.

14 "기억이 뭐예요?" 그가 물었다.

15 "따뜻한 거란다, 아가야." 그녀가 말했다.

16 Mitchell 할머니는 만화책을 읽고 있었다.

17 "기억이 뭐예요?" 그가 물었다.

18 "너에게 웃음을 가져다주는 것이란다." 그녀가 말했다.

19 Hunter 할아버지는 자신의 메달을 닦고 있었다.

20 "그건 금처럼 소중한 거지, 어린 친구."라고 그가 말했다.

21 그래서 Wilfrid는 Cooper 할머니께 드릴 기억들을 찾으러 집으로 돌아갔다.

22 그는 닭장 안으로 들어가서 암탉이 품고 있던 신선하고 따뜻한 달걀을 꺼냈다.

23 다음으로, 그는 자신의 양말 인형을 찾았다.

24 그것은 항상 그의 부모님께 큰 웃음을 안겨 드렸다.

25 마지막으로, 그는 자신의 장난감 상자 속에서 축구공을 찾아냈다.

26 그것은 그에게는 금만큼이나 소중했다.

27 Wilfrid는 Cooper 할머니께 가서 그녀에게 물건들을 하나씩 드렸다.

28 "이상하면서도 귀여운 아이구나! 이 멋진 물건들을 다 가져오다니 말이야."라고 Cooper 할머니는 생각했다.

29 그러다가 그녀는 자신의 과거를 기억해 내기 시작했다.

30 그녀는 따뜻한 달걀을 쥐고 Wilfrid에게, "오래 전에, 나는 나의 이모님 댁 정원에서 작고 푸른 알을 찾았단다."라고 속삭였다.

31 그녀는 양말 인형을 보며 미소를 짓다가 자기 여동생에게 인형극을 공연해 주었던 것을 기억해 냈다.

32 "내 여동생이 엄청나게 웃었지."라고 Cooper 할머니가 말했다.

33 그녀는 축구공을 바닥에 튀게 해서 Wilfrid에게 던져 주다가 그를 기억해 냈다.

34 "Wilfrid? Wilfrid Gordon Parker! 내 친구!"

35 그녀는 또한 그들만의 비밀을 하나씩 기억해 냈다.

36 두 사람은 서로 바라보며 미소 지었다.

37 Cooper 할머니는 가운데 이름이 자신의 것과 같은 어린 소년 덕분에 기억을 다시 찾게 되었다.

1 What's a Memory?

2 Wilfrid Gordon Parker was a little boy who lived next to a nursing home.

3 He liked all the people who lived there.

4 But his favorite person was Ms. Nancy Gordon Cooper because her middle name was the same as his.

5 He told her all his secrets.

6 One day, Wilfrid's parents were talking about Ms. Cooper.

7 "Poor old lady," said his mother.

8 "Why is she a poor old lady?" asked Wilfrid.

9 "Because she's lost her memory," said his father.

10 "What's a memory?" asked Wilfrid.

11 "It is something you remember," said his father.

12 Wilfrid wanted to know more, so he went to his neighbors.

13 Ms. Jordan was enjoying the sunlight.

14 "What's a memory?" he asked.

15 "Something warm, my child," she said.

16 Ms. Mitchell was reading a cartoon.

17 "What's a memory?" he asked.

18 "Something that brings you laughter," she said.

19 Mr. Hunter was cleaning his medal.

20 "It's something as precious as gold, young man," he said.

21 So Wilfrid went back home to look for memories for Ms. Cooper.

22 He went into the hen house and took a fresh, warm egg from under a hen.

23 Next, he looked for his sock puppet.

24 It always brought laughter to his parents.

25 Finally, he found his football in his toy box.

26 It was as precious as gold to him.

27 Wilfrid went to Ms. Cooper and gave her the things one by one.

28 "What a strange, sweet child!" thought Ms. Cooper, "He's brought all these wonderful things."

29 Then she started to remember her past.

30 She held the warm egg and whispered to Wilfrid, "Long ago, I found a small blue egg in my aunt's garden."

31 She smiled at the sock puppet and remembered performing a puppet show for her sister.

32 "My sister laughed a lot," said Ms. Cooper.

33 She bounced the football to Wilfrid and remembered him.

34 "Wilfrid? Wilfrid Gordon Parker! My friend!"

35 She also remembered their secrets one by one.

36 The two smiled at each other.

37 Ms. Cooper got her memory back thanks to the little boy with the same middle name as hers.

Express Yourself

1. On, went to

2. painting that we bought

3. never forget

4. took pictures, traditional dancers

5. saw, town

6. On, arrived in

7. girl who was wearing

8. never forget, experience

9. saw, looked like

Do It Yourself

1. like to tell

2. That person

3. Don't forget that, Just go for it

4. on the last day

5. feel stressed, look at

Link to the World

1. active seniors, share their knowledge

2. teaches, about farming

3. in the past

4. works, to teach

5. cooking class, learn to make

구석구석지문 TEST Step 2　　　　　p.39

Express Yourself

1. On May 29, 2017, we went to India.

2. This is a painting that we bought in the market.

3. I'll never forget the experience.

4. We took pictures of Korean traditional dancers.

5. We saw them at the town festival.

6. On June 7, 2017, we arrived in Laos.

7. We met a girl who was wearing a beautiful dress.

8. I'll never forget the experience.

9. We saw a rock. It looked like a queen's head.

Do It Yourself

1. I'd like to tell you about a student teacher I can't forget.

2. That person is Ms. Jeon.

3. Don't forget that you're great, Miso! Just go for it.

4. This is the bookmark that she gave to me on the last day.

5. When I feel stressed, I always look at this.

Link to the World

1. There are a lot of active seniors who share their knowledge and talents.

2. Mr. Kim in Busan is a smart farmer and teaches people about farming.

3. Ms. Lee was a science teacher in the past.

4. Now she works in a park to teach children about plants and birds.

5. In Ms. Choi's cooking class, young people learn to make gimchi and Korean hot pepper sauce.

Lesson
SP

단어 TEST Step 1　　　　　p.40

01 잃어버리다, 지다　02 ~을 필요로 하다　03 ~을 기쁘게 하다

04 점검하다　　05 따라가다, 뒤따르다

06 (~하는 것을) 막다, 그만두게 하다　07 위험한

08 끝, 마지막　09 장면, 광경　10 신난

11 정면, 앞　12 바구니　13 안전한

14 (외투 등에 달린) 모자　15 두드리다

16 웃다　17 (입으로) 불다, (바람이) 불다

18 떠나다　19 pig의 애칭　20 길, 도로

21 함께　22 ~ 아래에　23 작가

24 유명한　25 흔들리다　26 그런데, 그건 그렇고

27 ~해지다　28 코를 풀다　29 어디 보자., 글쎄.

30 ~에 좋다　31 ~을 꺼내다

32 그럼요, 전혀 문제 되지 않아요.　33 ~의 밖으로

34 ~을 들여다보다　35 혼잣말하다　36 ~해선 안 된다

37 휴식을 취하다　38 ~을 보다

39 가 버리다, 사라지다

40 B에 대해 A에게 감사하다

단어 TEST Step 2　　　　　p.41

01 laugh　02 together　03 under

04 writer　05 blow　06 follow

07 please　08 stop　09 road

10 front　11 famous　12 piggy

13 shake　14 lose　15 check

16 need　17 dangerous　18 basket

19 safe　20 hood　21 end

22 scene　23 knock　24 excited

25 leave　26 look into　27 out of

28 be good for　29 No problem.　30 look at

31 take out　32 go away

33 should not+동사원형　34 Let me see.

35 by the way　36 thank A for B　37 take a break

38 blow one's nose　39 talk to oneself

40 Have you ever heard of ~?

단어 TEST Step 3　　　　　p.42

1 leave, 떠나다　2 blow, (입으로) 불다　3 end, 끝, 마지막

4 famous, 유명한　5 follow, 따라가다, 뒤따르다

6 please, ~을 기쁘게 하다　7 safe, 안전한　8 writer, 작가

9 front, 앞, 정면   10 road, 도로, 길   11 lose, 잃어버리다

12 dangerous, 위험한

13 stop, (~하는 것을) 막다, 그만두게 하다   14 laugh, 웃다

15 hood, (외투 등에 달린) 모자   16 knock, 두드리다

본문 TEST Step 1   p.43~45

01 Red, Hood
02 Scene, front, little
03 in with, basket
04 take, break, under
05 walks, looks into
06 look, for lunch
07 blows, hard, shaking
08 stop, Let, see, change
09 What, mean by
10 Taking, writing, lived
11 shouldn't do
12 blows, but, out of
13 there, Why, blow
14 didn't, blew. nose
15 Don't, Go away
16 so sorry
17 go back into
18 believe, happened, at
19 These, for
20 Where, live
21 lives at, end
22 himself, for, later
23 herself, works, safe, follow
24 Scene, house
25 around, happy, excited
26 Knocking on, it's
27 happily, opening, dance
28 Thank, for pleasing
29 Well, that's
30 running, jumps over
31 not dangerous
32 dancing for
33 glad, kind to
34 too, By, way, anything
35 out, Would, like
36 thanks, don't, like
37 Don't, eating, lost, should
38 crying, tired, hungry
39 comes in
40 think, need, right
41 so glad, here
42 To, that
43 famous, heard of
44 have, one, wrote
45 changed, got tired
46 can change, again
47 lost, gave, help
48 problem, ending, okay
49 That'll be
50 stops dancing, can enjoy
51 stop dancing, can eat
52 laughs, enjoys, together

본문 TEST Step 2   p.46~48

01 Red, Hood
02 Scene, In front of, little
03 comes in with
04 can see, take a break, under
05 walks in, looks into
06 look delicious, for lunch
07 blows, hard, is shaking
08 to stop, Let me see, change the story

---

09 What, mean by
10 Taking out, writing something, There lived
11 shouldn't do
12 blows, come out of
13 there, Why did, blow
14 didn't, just blew. nose
15 Don't do, Go away
16 so sorry
17 go back into
18 can't believe, happened, Looking at
19 These, for
20 Where does, live
21 lives at the end
22 himself, for lunch, too, later
23 herself, going to, works, safe, follow
24 Scene, house
25 dances around, looks, happy, excited
26 Knocking on, it's, okay
27 happily, opening, watching, dance
28 Thank, for pleasing
29 Well, that's
30 running in, jumps over
31 not dangerous
32 is dancing for
33 glad, kind to
34 By the way, have anything to eat
35 Taking, out the basket, Would, like
36 No, thanks, don't, like
37 Don't worry, eating, lost, What should I do
38 crying, so tired, hungry
39 comes in
40 think, need, help, right
41 so glad, here
42 To, Who's that
43 famous, Have, ever heard of
44 have, one, wrote
45 changed, got tired, hungry
46 can change, again
47 lost, gave, help me
48 problem, a happy ending for, okay
49 That'll be great
50 stops dancing, can enjoy
51 stop dancing, can eat
52 laughs, enjoys, together

본문 TEST Step 3   p.49~51

1 빨간 모자

2 장면 1: 아기 돼지 삼 형제의 집 앞에서

3 (Red가 케이크와 과자가 든 바구니를 들고 등장한다.)

4 Red: 이제 아기 돼지 삼 형제의 집이 보인다. 여기 나무 아래에서 좀 쉬어야지.

5 (늑대가 걸어 들어와 집 안을 들여다본다.)

6 늑대: 새끼 돼지들이네! 맛있어 보인다. 점심으로 그들을 먹어야겠어.

7 (늑대가 집을 세게 불자 집이 흔들리고 있다.)

8 Red: 오, 저런 나쁜 늑대 같으니라고! 그를 멈추게 하려면 내가 뭘 할 수 있을까? 어디 보자.··· 바로 그거야! (늑대에게) 이봐! 내가 이야기를 바꾸겠어!

9 늑대: 그게 무슨 말이야?

---

40 정답 및 해설

10 Red: (펜을 꺼내 뭔가를 쓰면서) "크고 힘센 아기 돼지 삼 형제가 그 집에 살고 있었다."

11 늑대: 그렇게 하면 안 돼!

12 (늑대가 다시 집을 분다. 그러나 크고 힘센 돼지 삼 형제가 집에서 나온다.)

13 돼지 삼 형제: 이봐, 거기! 왜 우리 집을 불고 있어?

14 늑대: 음… 그러지 않았어. 나는 그냥 코를 풀었을 뿐이야.

15 돼지 삼 형제: 여기서 다시는 그러지 마. 가 버려!

16 늑대: 알았어. 정말 미안해.

17 (돼지들은 집 안으로 다시 들어간다.)

18 늑대: 이런 일이 일어나다니 믿을 수가 없어. 나는 너무 배가 고파! (Red의 바구니를 보며) 그건 뭐야?

19 Red: 할머니께 드릴 과자들이야.

20 늑대: 어디 사시는데?

21 Red: 이 길의 끝에 사셔.

22 늑대: (혼잣말로) 할머니도 점심으로 좋지. (Red에게) 나중에 보자. (늑대가 떠난다.)

23 Red: 안녕. (혼잣말로) 흠…. 그는 할머니 댁으로 갈 거야. 이야기를 다시 바꿔야겠어. (펜을 꺼내서 뭔가를 쓰며) 좋아. 내 이야기가 제대로 돌아가면 할머니는 안전하실 거야. 그를 따라가 봐야지. (Red가 떠난다.)

24 장면 2: 할머니의 집

25 (늑대가 할머니 주변을 맴돌며 춤을 춘다. 할머니는 아주 행복하고 신나 보인다.)

26 Red: (문을 두드리며) 할머니, 저예요. 괜찮으세요?

27 할머니: (행복하게 웃으며 문을 열면서) 물론이지, Red야. 어서 들어와. 늑대가 나를 위해 춤추는 걸 보고 있었단다.

28 Red: 이봐, 늑대야. 우리 할머니를 기쁘게 해드려서 고마워.

29 늑대: 음, 그게 ….

30 왕자: (문을 열고 뛰어 들어오며) 이봐, 이 나쁜 늑대야! (왕자가 늑대에게 달려든다.)

31 Red: 아니, 아니에요! 멈춰요. 그는 위험하지 않아요.

32 할머니: 맞아. 보세요. 그가 우리를 위해 춤추고 있잖아요.

33 왕자: 정말요? 늑대야, 미안해. 네가 할머니께 잘해 드린다니 기쁘다.

34 늑대: 음 … 나도 기뻐. 그런데, 먹을 것 좀 있어?

35 Red: (바구니에서 과자를 좀 꺼내며) 과자 좀 먹을래?

36 늑대: 고맙지만 됐어. 난 과자를 먹지 않아. 나는 닭고기가 좋아.

37 Red: 걱정하지 마. 내가 이야기를 다시 바꿔야겠네. 그러면 넌 과자 먹는 걸 좋아하게 될 거야. (바구니를 뒤지며) 오, 펜을 잃어버렸어. 어떻게 하지?

38 늑대: (춤을 추며 울부짖으며) 오, 안 돼! 난 지금 너무 피곤하고 배고파.

39 (Andersen이 들어온다.)

40 Andersen: 내 도움이 필요한 것 같은데, 맞지?

41 Red: 오, Andersen 씨. 여기 오셔서 너무 기뻐요.

42 할머니: (Red에게) 저 사람이 누구니?

43 Red: 저분은 유명한 작가 Andersen 씨예요. "빨간 구두"에 대해 들어 보신 적이 있죠?

44 할머니: 그래, 들어 봤지. 그 이야기를 쓴 사람이란 말이지?

45 Red: 맞아요. (Andersen에게) 제가 이야기를 바꿔서 저

불쌍한 늑대가 피곤하고 배고파졌어요.

46 Andersen: 너는 다시 이야기를 바꿀 수 있잖아.

47 Red: 죄송하지만, 제가 작가님이 주신 펜을 잃어버렸어요. 저 좀 도와주세요.

48 Andersen: 문제없지. 내가 모두에게 행복한 결말을 쓸게. 괜찮지?

49 Red: 아주 좋아요!

50 Andersen: 좋아. 여기 내 펜을 써야지. "그 친절한 늑대는 춤추기를 멈춘다. 그는 케이크와 과자를 즐겨 먹을 수 있다."

51 늑대: (춤을 멈추며) 춤을 멈출 수가 있다! (과자를 먹으며) 그리고 과자를 먹을 수 있어! 정말 고마워요.

52 (모두 웃으며 함께 과자를 맛있게 먹는다.)

1 Little Red Writing Hood

2 Scene 1: In front of the three little piggies' house

3 (Red comes in with a basket of cakes and cookies.)

4 Red: Now I can see the three little piggies' house. I'll take a break here under the tree.

5 (Wolf walks in and looks into the house.)

6 Wolf: Baby piggies! They look delicious. I'll eat them for lunch.

7 (Wolf blows the house hard and it is shaking.)

8 Red: Oh, that bad Wolf! What can I do to stop him? Let me see. … That's it! (To Wolf) Hey, you! I'll change the story!

9 Wolf: What do you mean by that?

10 Red: (Taking out a pen and writing something) "There lived three big strong piggies in the house."

11 Wolf: You shouldn't do that!

12 (Wolf blows again, but the three big strong piggies come out of the house.)

13 Three Piggies: Hey there! Why did you blow our house?

14 Wolf: Um … I didn't. I just blew my nose.

15 Three Piggies: Don't do that again here. Go away!

16 Wolf: Okay. I'm so sorry.

17 (The piggies go back into the house.)

18 Wolf: I can't believe this happened. I'm so hungry! (Looking at Red's basket) What are those?

19 Red: These are cookies for Grandma.

20 Wolf: Where does she live?

21 Red: She lives at the end of this road.

22 Wolf: (To himself) Grandma is good for lunch, too. (To Red) See you later. (Wolf leaves.)

23 Red: Bye. (Talking to herself) Hmm …. He's going to Grandma's. I think I should change the story again. (Taking out the pen and writing something) Okay. If my story works, Grandma will be safe. I'll

follow him. (Red leaves.)

24 Scene 2: Grandma's house

25 (Wolf dances around Grandma. She looks very happy and excited.)

26 Red: (Knocking on the door) Grandma, it's me. Are you okay?

27 Grandma: (Laughing happily and opening the door) Sure, Red. Come on in. I was watching Wolf dance for me.

28 Red: Hey, Wolf. Thank you for pleasing my grandmother.

29 Wolf: Well, that's ….

30 Prince: (Opening the door and running in) Hey, you bad Wolf! (Prince jumps over Wolf.)

31 Red: No, no! Stop. He's not dangerous.

32 Grandma: Right. Look. He is dancing for us.

33 Prince: Really? Wolf, I'm sorry. I'm glad you're kind to Grandma.

34 Wolf: Well, … I'm glad, too. By the way, do you have anything to eat?

35 Red: (Taking some cookies out the basket) Would you like some cookies?

36 Wolf: No, thanks. I don't eat cookies. I like chicken.

37 Red: Don't worry. I'll change the story again. Then you will like eating cookies. (Checking the basket) Oh, I lost my pen. What should I do?

38 Wolf: (Dancing and crying) Oh, no! I'm so tired and hungry now.

39 (Andersen comes in.)

40 Andersen: I think you need my help, right?

41 Red: Oh, Mr. Andersen. I'm so glad you're here.

42 Grandma: (To Red) Who's that?

43 Red: He is Mr. Andersen, the famous writer. Have you ever heard of "The Red Shoes"?

44 Grandma: Yes, I have. Is he the one who wrote that story?

45 Red: Right. (To Andersen) I changed the story, and the poor Wolf got tired and hungry.

46 Andersen: You can change the story again.

47 Red: I'm sorry, but I lost the pen you gave to me. Please help me.

48 Andersen: No problem. I'll write a happy ending for everyone. Is that okay?

49 Red: That'll be great!

50 Andersen: All right. I'll use my pen here. "The kind Wolf stops dancing. He can enjoy cakes and cookies."

51 Wolf: (Stopping dancing) I can stop dancing! (Eating cookies) And I can eat cookies! Thank you very much.

52 (Everybody laughs and enjoys cookies together.)

단어 TEST Step 1 p.58

01 원	02 모양, 모습	03 구르다
04 흥분된	05 끓이다	06 끝이 뾰족한
07 공유하다	08 누르다	09 책꽂이
10 완벽한	11 운동하다	12 풀다, 해결하다
13 서두르다	14 비닐봉지	15 나누다
16 고르다, 선택하다	17 막대기, 나뭇가지	18 옷걸이
19 혼잡, 혼란	20 둥근	21 삼각형
22 어려운	23 불평하다	24 사각형
25 통제하다, 조절하다		26 다치게 하다
26 소리치다, 외치다	28 영혼, 요정	29 돌리다, 회전시키다
30 깨닫다, 알아차리다		31 마지막으로
32 물을 주다	33 서두르다, 돌진하다	
34 잘 정돈된, 단정한, 깔끔한		35 서로
36 감싸다, 포장하다	37 ~을 치우다	38 ~을 담당하여
39 자기 혼자서	40 A를 B로 나누다	
41 담당하고 있는, 통제 중인		42 A를 조각으로 자르다
43 반대편		

단어 TEST Step 2 p.59

01 boil	02 control	03 hurt
04 shape	05 face	06 finally
07 choose	08 stick	09 complain
10 hanger	11 triangle	12 solve
13 shout	14 pointy	15 carry
16 share	17 roll	18 bookshelf
19 perfect	20 round	21 tidy
22 divide	23 hurry	24 spin
25 spirit	26 reply	27 mess
28 realize	29 water	30 rush
31 without	32 puzzle	33 square
34 move	35 divide A into B	
36 one by one	37 pick up ~	38 take away
39 put A on B	40 wrap up	41 in charge of ~
42 one another	43 by oneself	

단어 TEST Step 3 p.60

1 pointy, 끝이 뾰족한 2 spirit, 요정 3 roll, 구르다
4 perfect, 완벽한 5 excited, 흥분한 6 decide, 결정하다
7 mess, 혼란, 혼잡 8 complain, 불평하다
9 reply, 대답하다 10 hold, 잡고 있다, 지탱하다

11 ruch, 서두르다, 돌진하다 12 hula hoop, 훌라후프
13 control, 조절하다, 통제하다
14 realize, 깨닫다, 알아차리다 15 hanger, 옷걸이
16 wheel, 바퀴

대화문 TEST Step 1 p.61~62

Get Ready 2

(1) can't stand alone, how to solve / Put, on, bottom
(2) how to divide, into, equal pieces / Let, see, dividing, the same size, shape
(3) doesn't move, how to move / Put wheels

Start Off Listen & Talk A

1 how to make three squares, with three moves / First, move this stick /
2 with, how to make / too difficult for, Can, break, in half / you can't

Start Off Listen & Talk B

how to divide, into, pieces / First, divide, into, equal, Then, divide, into, Finally / other, around

Speak Up Look and talk.

how to draw / First, Then, Finally, in the square

Speak Up Mission

how to make / show you how

Real-life Scene

how to solve / take, across, the river, only carries, at a time / take, to, other side one by one / without, eat the rice / First, Then, come back with / Finally

Express Yourself A

1 how to make / cut off, used jeans
2 looks great / how to make / First, Then, dried, Finally, wrap it up, make a triangle
3 how to fly / has to face, Hold, up

Learning Diary Check Yourself

how to draw, with shapes / First, triangle, Then, dots, Finally, small circles / draw, myself

대화문 TEST Step 2 p.63~64

Get Ready 2

(1) G: This bookshelf can't stand alone. Do you know how to solve this problem?
   B: Put some legs on the bottom.
(2) G: Do you know how to divide this cake into four equal pieces?
   B: Let me see. … How about dividing it this way? Then the pieces will be the same size and shape.

[3] G: This car doesn't move. Do you know how to move it?

B: Sure. Put wheels under the car.

Start Off Listen & Talk A

1 G: These twelve sticks make four squares. Do you know how to make three squares of the same size with three moves?

B: Sure. First, move this stick here.

2 B: Here's a triangle with three pencils. Do you know how to make three more triangles with three more pencils?

G: Let me see. ··· It's too difficult for me. Can I break the pencils in half?

B: No, you can't.

Start Off Listen & Talk B

B: Do you know how to divide this into four equal pieces?

G: Sure. First, divide it into three equal squares. Then, divide each square into four smaller squares. Finally, color three small squares in the inside corner of the L.

B: Oh, I can see three other L shapes around it! You're great!

Speak Up Look and talk.

A: Do you know how to draw a fish with shapes?

B: Sure. First, draw a large square. Then, draw a triangle. Finally, draw a small circle in the square.

Speak Up Mission

A: Do you know how to make paper airplanes?

B: Sure. I'll show you how.

Real-life Scene

B: Do you know how to solve this puzzle?

G: What is it?

B: You must take a dog, a chicken, and a bag of rice across the river. The boat only carries you and one of the things at a time.

G: That's easy. I can take them to the other side one by one.

B: But without you, the dog will kill the chicken, and the chicken will eat the rice.

G: Let me see. … First, take the chicken and come back. Then, take the rice and come back with the chicken.

B: And?

G: After that, take the dog and come back. Finally, take the chicken.

B: You're great!

Express Yourself A

1 B: Do you know how to make this?

G: Sure. First, cut off the leg from used jeans.

2 B: This looks great.

G I think so, too. Do you know how to make it?

B: It's easy. First, put some rice on *gim*. Then, add some dried fish and hot peppers. Finally, wrap it up and make a triangle.

3 B: Do you know how to fly this?

G: Yes. I'll show you how. It has to face the wind. Hold it up like this.

Learning Diary Check Yourself

W: Excuse me. Do you know how to draw a mouse with shapes?

M: Sure. First, draw a large triangle. Then, draw two dots and 6 lines. Finally, draw two small circles.

W: Thanks. I'll draw it myself now.

본문 TEST Step 1   p.65~66

01 Shape, Spirits
02 There lived, spirits
03 controlled, bookshelf, window
04 charge, hangers, plants
05 took care, round
06 worked together, for
07 decided, better, shouted
08 Take, away, pointy
09 waters, every day
10 Take, away, roll, break
11 exercises with, every
12 tidy, mess, complained   13 looked at, other
14 think, without, asked
15 better, by myself   16 get, rest, said
17 went out, in control
18 hangers, round, square
19 looked around, smiled   20 Much better
21 picked up, hang, on   22 hold, clothes
23 went, water, leaves   24 Poor, must be
25 picked up, to exercise   26 how to spin
27 take out, looked at   28 ride, have to
29 hurried out of
30 other, back, over
31 doesn't, what to do
32 hangers, all, square
33 one another, realized
34 great, others, once again

p.67~68

01 Shape, Spirits
02 There lived, shape spirits
03 controlled, bookshelf
04 was in charge of
05 took care of, round things
06 worked together to make
07 to make the room better, shouted at
08 Take, away, pointy leaves
09 waters them every day
10 Take, away, roll and break
11 exercises with it
12 try to, tidy, make a mess, complained
13 looked at each other
14 without us
15 make, better all by myself
16 get some rest
17 went out, in control
18 made, square
19 looked around, smiled
20 Much better
21 came home, picked up, to hang, on
22 hold my clothes
23 went to water
24 must be
25 picked up, to exercise
26 how to spin
27 to take out, looked at
28 can't ride, have to
29 hurried out of
30 other, came back, rushed over to
31 what to do
32 looked at, all the new square things
33 one another, realized
34 great, the others, once again

p.69~70

1 세 도형 요정들
2 Mike의 방에는 세 도형 요정이 살았다.
3 Square는 탁자, 책장, 그리고 창문을 담당했다.
4 Triangle은 옷걸이들과 식물들을 담당했다.
5 Circle은 둥근 것들을 돌보았다.
6 그들은 Mike에게 좋은 방을 만들어 주기 위해서 함께 일했다.
7 어느 날 Square는 방을 더 낫게 만들기로 결심하고 나머지 요정들에게 소리쳤다.
8 "이 식물들을 치워, 그렇지 않으면 그것들의 끝이 뾰족한 잎사귀들이 누군가를 다치게 할 거야!" 그가 Triangle에게 말했다.
9 "하지만 Mike가 매일 그들에게 물을 주는데." Triangle이 말했다.
10 "이 훌라후프를 치워, 그렇지 않으면 굴러가서 뭔가를 부술 거야!" 그가 Circle에게 말했다.
11 "하지만 Mike는 매일 그걸로 운동을 하는데." Circle이 말했다.

12 "난 이 방을 정돈하려고 애쓰지만, 너희 둘은 항상 엉망으로 만들어." 그가 불평했다.
13 Triangle과 Circle이 서로를 쳐다보았다.
14 "그래서 네 생각에는 네가 우리 없이 다 할 수 있다는 거야?" Triangle이 Square에게 물었다.
15 "물론이지. 난 완전히 혼자서 이 방을 더 낫게 만들 수 있어." Square가 대답했다.
16 "잘됐네! 그럼 우린 쉴 수 있겠어." Circle이 Square에게 말했다.
17 Triangle과 Circle이 밖으로 나갔고 이제 Square가 모든 것을 담당했다.
18 그는 옷걸이들과 식물들과 모든 둥근 물건들을 사각형으로 만들었다.
19 그러고 나서 그는 주위를 둘러보고 미소 지었다.
20 "훨씬 좋군!"
21 Mike가 학교에서 집으로 왔을 때, 그는 재킷을 걸기 위해 사각형 옷걸이 하나를 집었다.
22 "뭐야? 이것은 내 옷을 걸고 있지 못할 거야."
23 그는 식물에 물을 주러 가서 그것들의 사각형 잎사귀들을 보았다.
24 "불쌍한 것들.… 그들은 병든 것이 틀림없어."
25 그는 운동을 하기 위해 사각형 훌라후프를 집어 들었다.
26 "흠… 이걸 어떻게 돌리는지 모르겠어."
27 그는 자전거를 꺼내러 가서 사각형 바퀴들을 보았다.
28 "음, 난 이걸 탈 수 없어. 그냥 걸어가야 할 것 같아."
29 그러고 나서 그는 서둘러 집을 나섰다.
30 다른 요정들이 돌아왔을 때, Square는 그들에게 달려갔다.
31 "Mike는 그의 방을 좋아하지 않아. 난 뭘 해야 할지 모르겠어." 그가 말했다.
32 그들은 옷걸이들, 식물들, 그리고 모든 새로 사각형이 된 물건들을 바라보았다.
33 그러고 나서 그들은 서로를 바라보았고, Square는 자신의 문제를 깨달았다.
34 "이 방을 다시 멋지게 만들자." 그가 나머지 요정들에게 말했고, 세 요정들은 다시 한 번 함께 일했다.

p.71~74

1 Three Shape Spirits
2 There lived three shape spirits in Mike's room.
3 Square controlled the table, the bookshelf, and the window.
4 Triangle was in charge of the hangers and the plants.
5 Circle took care of the round things.
6 They worked together to make a nice room for Mike.

7 One day Square decided to make the room better and shouted at the other spirits.

8 "Take these plants away, or their pointy leaves will hurt someone!" he said to Triangle.

9 "But Mike waters them every day," said Triangle.

10 "Take this hula hoop away, or it will roll and break something!" he said to Circle.

11 "But Mike exercises with it every day," said Circle.

12 "I try to make this room tidy, but you two always make a mess," he complained.

13 Triangle and Circle looked at each other.

14 "So you think you can do it without us?" Triangle asked Square.

15 "Sure. I can make this room better all by myself," replied Square.

16 "Great! Then we can get some rest," Circle said to Square.

17 Triangle and Circle went out and Square was now in control.

18 He made the hangers, plants, and all the round things square.

19 Then he looked around and smiled.

20 "Much better!"

21 When Mike came home from school, he picked up a square hanger to hang his jacket on.

22 "What? This will not hold my clothes."

23 He went to water the plants and saw their square leaves.

24 "Poor things. ... They must be sick."

25 He picked up the square hula hoop to exercise.

26 "Hmm ... I don't know how to spin this."

27 He went to take out his bike and looked at the square wheels.

28 "Well, I can't ride this. I'll just have to walk."

29 Then he hurried out of the house.

30 When the other spirits came back, Square rushed over to them.

31 "Mike doesn't like his room. I don't know what to do," he said.

32 They looked at the hangers, the plants, and all the new square things.

33 Then they looked at one another, and Square realized his problem.

34 "Let's make this room great again," he said to the others, and the three spirits worked together once again.

Your Turn

1. how to cook / First, Then, Finally, more minutes
2. how to make / boil, cut, into, put, on
3. how to make sandwiches / put, on bread, add, put, on top

Express Yourself

1. Square
2. out of used jeans
3. what to wear with
4. made, excited, made, happy

Link to the World

1. taught, at, when
2. call, father, math
3. how to draw, three sides, same length
4. how to find, the biggest circle
5. One day, an easier way to study
6. royal road to learning

Your Turn

1. A: Do you know how to cook *ramyeon*?
   B: Sure. First, boil some water. Then, put the *ramyeon* and dried soup mix. Finally, boil for 4 more minutes.

2. A: Do you know how to make potato salad?
   B: Sure. First, boil the potatoes. Then, cut them into pieces. Finally, put some sauce on them.

3. A: Do you know how to make sandwiches?
   B: Sure. First, put an egg on bread. Then, add some vegetables. Finally, put bread on top.

Express Yourself

1. Square for Mom
2. I made a square bag out of used jeans.
3. My mom knew what to wear with it.
4. It made her excited. That made me happy.

Link to the World

1. Euclid taught math at the Library of Alexandria when Ptolemy 1 was the king of Egypt.
2. People call him "the father of math."
3. He showed how to draw a triangle that has three sides of the same length.
4. He also showed how to find the center of the biggest circle in a triangle.
5. One day, Ptolemy 1 asked, "Is there an easier way to study math?"
6. Euclid replied, "There is no royal road to learning."

MEMO

MEMO

적중100

영어 기출 문제집

정답 및 해설

천재 | 정사열